ECCLESIOLOGY
FOR A
GLOBAL CHURCH

THEOLOGY IN GLOBAL PERSPECTIVE SERIES

Peter C. Phan, General Editor
Ignacio Ellacuría Professor of Catholic Social Thought,
Georgetown University

At the beginning of a new millennium, the *Theology in Global Perspective* Series responds to the challenge to re-examine the foundational and doctrinal themes of Christianity in light of the new global reality. While traditional Catholic theology has assumed an essentially European or Western point of view, *Theology in Global Perspective* takes account of insights and experience of churches in Africa, Asia, Latin America, Oceania, as well as from Europe and North America. Noting the pervasiveness of changes brought about by science and technologies, and growing concerns about the sustainability of Earth, it seeks to embody insights from studies in these areas as well.

Though rooted in the Catholic tradition, volumes in the series are written with an eye to the ecumenical implications of Protestant, Orthodox, and Pentecostal theologies for Catholicism, and vice versa. In addition, authors will explore insights from other religious traditions with the potential to enrich Christian theology and self-understanding.

Books in this series will provide reliable introductions to the major theological topics, tracing their roots in Scripture and their development in later tradition, exploring when possible the implications of new thinking on gender and socio-cultural identities. And they will relate these themes to the challenges confronting the peoples of the world in the wake of globalization, particularly the implications of Christian faith for justice, peace, and the integrity of creation.

Other Books Published in the Series

Orders and Ministry: Leadership in a Global Church, Kenan B. Osborne, O.F.M.
Trinity: Nexus of the Mysteries of Christian Faith, Anne Hunt
Eschatology and Hope, Anthony Kelly, C.Ss.R.
Meeting Mystery: Liturgy, Worship, Sacraments, Nathan D. Mitchell
Creation, Grace, and Redemption, Neil Ormerod
Globalization, Spirituality, and Justice, Daniel C. Groody, C.S.C.
Christianity and Science: Toward a Theology of Nature, John F. Haught

THEOLOGY IN GLOBAL PERSPECTIVE SERIES
Peter C. Phan, General Editor

ECCLESIOLOGY FOR A GLOBAL CHURCH

A People Called and Sent

RICHARD R. GAILLARDETZ

ORBIS BOOKS

Maryknoll, New York 10545

Third Printing, December 2010

Founded in 1970, Orbis Books endeavors to publish works that enlighten the mind, nourish the spirit, and challenge the conscience. The publishing arm of the Maryknoll Fathers and Brothers, Orbis seeks to explore the global dimensions of the Christian faith and mission, to invite dialogue with diverse cultures and religious traditions, and to serve the cause of reconciliation and peace. The books published reflect the opinions of their authors and are not meant to represent the official position of the Maryknoll Society. To obtain more information about Maryknoll and Orbis Books, please visit our website at www.maryknoll.org.

Manufactured in the United States of America.

Library of Congress Cataloguing in Publication Data

Gaillardetz, Richard R., 1958-
  Ecclesiology for a global church : a people called and sent / Richard
R. Gaillardetz.
      p. cm. — (Theology in global perspective)
  Includes bibliographical references and index.
  ISBN 978-1-57075-769-3
  1. Church. 2. Catholic Church—Doctrines. I. Title.
  BX1746.G324 2008
  262'.02—dc22
                        2007039092

To Thomas F. O'Meara, O.P.,
teacher, mentor, and friend, who first challenged me
to consider the global horizons of the church

Contents

Foreword

by Peter C. Phan

As Richard Gaillardetz acknowledges in his theological autobiography, the ecclesiology or theology of the church that he inherited from some of the greatest European theologians before and after Vatican II and from the ecumenical council itself, despite their groundbreaking insights, has been woefully parochial. This confession is all the more significant because it comes from one whose abundant writings on the church have made him one of the premier ecclesiologists in the United States. Gaillardetz's acknowledgment of the narrowness of the Western vision of the church does not at all mean that he is going to jettison it. Rather, in this book, he expands and reinterprets it in the light of the experiences of the churches in Africa, Asia, and Latin America, experiences that he himself was fortunate to witness firsthand in writing this book. In other words, this will be an ecclesiology in global perspective.

The subtitle of this work speaks volumes about its basic approach and orientation to the theology of the church. The church is first and foremost a "people called and sent." Called and sent by the Triune God, of course. Called by God as "people," in unbreakable unity and deep solidarity with the people of Israel, the church is a community among all peoples, marked by unity, holiness, universality, and apostolicity, "notes" that are now creatively reinterpreted in light of the global character of the church.

Gaillardetz makes a strong case that in a global ecclesiology mission must be understood as the fundamental dimension of the church's catholicity. But the notion of mission he develops is not the search for conversions but dialogue with cultures and religions, a point repeatedly made by Asian churches and theologians. Similarly, church unity is not uniformity and conformity with an ecclesiastical center but a communion of churches, a view powerfully conveyed by the Latin American "basic ecclesial communities" and the African Synod with its image of church as "family." In the same vein, Gaillardetz reimagines other elements of the church—ministry, discipleship, apostolicity, laity, episcopacy, papacy, magisterium—with a breadth and depth marked by impeccable historical scholarship, deep ecumenical sensitivity, and insightful pastoral perceptiveness.

Gaillardetz is acutely aware that in a book of three hundred pages it is impossible to treat exhaustively every burning issue facing the church today presented by the global South. But it does not take a door-stopper book to convey the range of numerous, at sometimes seemingly overwhelming, challenges facing the contemporary church. This sense of uneasiness and even frustration is caused by the fact that, whereas the West still dominates the world in economic, political, and military terms, and while the Roman Church still retains its juridical power, the center of gravity and vitality has shifted to the global South. In this context, age-old ecclesiological issues and their officially approved answers seem to be quaintly out of joint with reality. Making sense of the contemporary situation of the church in the light of massive changes in the complexion of local churches, the diversity of ministries required to nurture these churches, and the demands of intercultural interreligious dialogue require a different theological framework.

We owe Gaillardetz a heavy debt of gratitude for being a sure-footed guide through this ecclesiological thicket. He is too modest to claim that his book offers a "global ecclesiology." But he has shown us—theologically and pastorally—how we should navigate the troubled waters of postmodernity and globalization while remaining, in hope and courage, a "people called and sent" by the Triune God.

Preface

The Venerable Bede wrote that "every day the church gives birth to the church."[1] Whether you welcome it or lament it, there can be no doubt that over the past four decades a new church is being born. In this volume I will be outlining the basic characteristics of an ecclesiology adequate to this new ecclesial reality. Such a project requires, however, that one understand something of the distinctive shape of this new church. A preliminary indicator is found in the language of demographics. A number of authors have mapped out the demographic shifts that characterize this new church.[2] John Allen summarizes them well:

> In 1900, there were 459 million Catholics in the world, 392 million of whom lived in Europe and North America. Christianity 100 years ago remained an overwhelmingly white, first world phenomenon. By 2000, there were 1.1 billion Catholics, with just 380 million in Europe and North America, and the rest, 720 million, in the global South. Africa alone went from 1.9 million Catholics in 1900 to 130 million in 2000, a growth rate of almost 7,000 percent. This is the most rapid and sweeping demographic transformation of Catholicism in its 2,000 year history. Sao Paolo, Jakarta and Nairobi will become what Leuvein [sic], Milan and Paris were in the Counter Reformation period, meaning major centers of pastoral and intellectual energy. Different experiences and priorities will set the Catholic agenda as leaders from Africa, Asia and Latin America rise through the system, reshaping the texture of church life.[3]

This demographic shift is but one of the many new features of the church of the twenty-first century. Even when it has pretended otherwise, the church has always existed in and not above the world and the forces that shape human events have always exerted their influence on the church as well. We need to consider a few of these forces, if only briefly.

---

[1] *Patrologia cursus completus: Series Latina,* edited by J.-P. Migne, 221 vols. (Paris, 1844-64), 93:166d.

[2] Philip Jenkins, *The Next Christendom: The Coming of Global Christianity* (Oxford: Oxford University Press, 2002); Walbert Bühlmann, *The Coming of the Third Church: An Analysis of the Present and Future of the Church* (Maryknoll, N.Y.: Orbis Books, 1977).

[3] See John Allen, "Ten Mega-Trends Shaping the Catholic Church," *All Things Catholic* (December 22, 2006) http://ncrcafe.org/node/782. For a much more developed portrait of these shifts, see Bryan T. Froehle and Mary L. Gautier, eds., *Global Catholicism: Portrait of a World Church* (Maryknoll, N.Y.: Orbis Books, 2003).

Cultural commentators have referred to our present epoch as postmodern, although some prefer the term "late-modern."[4] Without wishing to deny the obvious gains of modernity associated with the Enlightenment—a greater emphasis on human freedom, technological achievement, the dignity of the human person, the autonomy and integrity of conscience, the authority of human reason—there has been a discernible disenchantment with the price the modern world paid for these gains. Given the pervasiveness of the liberal capitalist ethos, human freedom has too often been reduced to consumer choice with little cultural support for the positive exercise of freedom to become a certain kind of person. The emphasis on personal autonomy has too often led to an atomized individualism limited to purely utilitarian conceptions of community. The promise of technology has often been eclipsed by the ravages it has wreaked on our environment. The triumph of reason has opened the door to a stifling empiricism with little room for mystery and wonder. The Enlightenment's celebration of human progress and universal reason, themes that were oriented toward the liberation of the human spirit, are now seen as unwitting instruments for the suppression of human differences under the specter of totalizing narratives, sometimes referred to as meta-narratives.[5] These are extended theories or systems of thought that offer sweeping interpretations of human history or experience. Examples often given include political or economic systems such as Marxism or capitalism. They are criticized because their totalizing character tends to silence or suppress important elements of human experience that do not fit into the grand narrative. Hence we find in much postmodern thought a preference for "local narratives," specific accounts that focus on the particularities more than the commonalities of history or human experience. The postmodern sensibility is far more attuned to the reality of human diversity and the irreducible plurality of religions, cultures, and ideologies.

Finally, the postmodern epoch is shaped by the complex processes associated with the term "globalization." By globalization I am referring to a tension experienced between conflicting impulses. In the wake of the Second World War, the birth of the United Nations, and the demise of the Soviet Union in 1989, there has been a pronounced impulse toward a more unified view of the world. This sense of global unification has been furthered by advances in modern communications and transportation technologies that have compressed our sense of space and time. Global unification has also been advanced by the

---

[4] Paul Lakeland, *Postmodernity: Christian Identity in a Fragmented Age* (Minneapolis: Fortress, 1997); for a proponent of the language of late modernity, see Charles Taylor, *The Ethics of Authenticity* (Cambridge, Mass.: Harvard University Press, 1991).

[5] The classic definition and discussion of "meta-narratives" is found in Jean-François Lyotard, *The Postmodern Condition—A Report on Knowledge* (Manchester: Manchester University Press, 1984), xxiv.

unfettered expansion of neo-liberal capitalism, which has brought the ethos of the free market and certain icons of Western culture to the world (consider the ubiquity of McDonald's).

At the same time, the phenomenon of globalization has also brought with it a sense of social fragmentation. We have become more aware than ever of persistent cultural and religious differences that resist homogenization and force us to come to terms with a deep pluralism that often seems unbridgeable. This tendency, in its most extreme form, has been expressed in a violent tribalism and the growing appeal of various religious fundamentalisms.

All of these cultural forces have had their impact on the church. Contemporary ecclesiology must take these into account if it is to provide a compelling theological framework for understanding something of the church's nature and mission today. Ecclesiology, the theology of the church, must honor the wisdom of Christianity's great tradition, even as it carefully considers what is actually happening "on the ground" as the church is affected by these new realities. This volume represents a modest effort to sketch out an ecclesiology that is attentive to both.

My own theological autobiography mirrors general trends in Catholic ecclesiology as it has developed in Europe and North America over the last fifty years. I was fortunate to undertake doctoral studies at the University of Notre Dame. Much of my study was dedicated to exploring the groundbreaking ecclesiological contributions of such figures as Yves Congar, Henri de Lubac, Karl Rahner, Marie-Dominique Chenu, Edward Schillebeeckx, Hans Küng, and Gerard Philips. Many of these theologians made seminal contributions to the work of the Second Vatican Council as conciliar *periti*. However, every one of these theologians was from Western Europe and, although their insights opened the door to a more global consideration of the church, it was a door through which they were themselves largely unable to walk. Neither were they able to give full and adequate expression to the perspectives of the many Christian women who constituted the silent majority of the church.

In addition to the groundbreaking work of these theologians, my studies also extended to the greatest testimony to their work, the sixteen documents of the Second Vatican Council. It was virtually impossible to study Catholic ecclesiology in the late 1980s without the work of the council dominating one's reflections. The four decades since the council have seen an unprecedented participation of Catholic theologians in the ecumenical movement. Bilateral and multilateral ecumenical dialogues produced a wealth of formal papers and joint statements that would provide the foundations for the burgeoning field of ecumenical theology.

Much of the Catholic ecclesiology produced in Europe and North America in the last fifty years has been directly influenced by these three sources:

(a) the work of those theologians who paved the way for Vatican II, (b) the council itself along with its postconciliar reception, and (c) the corpus of ecumenical statements that has emerged from decades of formal dialogue among Christians of diverse traditions. My own study has benefited as well from a whole generation of distinguished scholars and ecclesiastical leaders in Europe and North America who have dedicated their careers to a systematic reflection on the three sources mentioned above, figures such as Hermann Pottmeyer, Hervé Legrand, Jean-Marie Tillard, Walter Kasper, Thomas O'Meara, Joseph Komonchak, Francis Sullivan, Avery Dulles, Joseph Ratzinger, Richard McBrien, Patrick Granfield, Giuseppe Alberigo, and others. I am profoundly grateful for all that I have learned from these figures.

Nevertheless, it is difficult to ignore the relatively parochial character of my own background. My education gave me only a limited exposure to a growing body of Christian feminist theological reflection on the church and an even more limited access to the works of theologians and Christian communities from the global South. My dissertation director, Thomas O'Meara (to whom this volume is gratefully dedicated), often reminded me of the broader horizons of a world church that too often went unnoted in the ecclesiology of the West. Long after the completion of my studies, he encouraged me to visit churches in the global South and provided valuable connections that made those field research trips possible.

The invitation from Peter Phan to undertake this volume on ecclesiology represented an opportunity for me to pursue more deliberately than had hitherto been possible the global character of the church. For too long, a story of ecclesial uniformity has been told that failed to do justice to a genuine diversity that has always been present in the church. Recent works in church history have tried to rectify this lacuna.[6]

Considering the church from a global perspective cannot mean attending to all of the different regional and cultural contexts in which the church is flourishing (or sometimes languishing). In short, this cannot be a *report* on the world church in all of its dimensions. In consideration of various ecclesiological themes, it will be important, however, to attend to select developments and representative theological voices drawn from local churches in both the north and the south. During a year-long sabbatical I was able to undertake three focused field research trips to explore local churches on three different continents in the global South (the Philippines, South Africa, and Mexico). All three trips were immensely informative. One of those visits was to the Diocese of San Cristóbal de Las Casas in Chiapas, Mexico. There I was fortunate to

---

[6] As but one example, see Dale T. Irvin and Scott W. Sunquist, *History of the World Christian Movement*, vol. 1 (Maryknoll, N.Y.: Orbis Books, 2001).

discover a local church that embodied many of the most significant ecclesiological developments emerging in the church of the South. Consequently, when
I have occasion in this volume to offer some specific examples of characteristic features of the changing global shape of the church, many of these examples are taken from the church in Chiapas.

Although a full-blown treatment of contemporary methodological issues
confronting ecclesiology today cannot be undertaken here, a few brief considerations and basic presuppositions must be mentioned. First, the ecclesiological vision developed in this volume is intended to be Roman Catholic, not in
an exclusive or polemical sense but in the sense that its central claims are in
keeping with the great and diverse tradition of Roman Catholicism. All Christians, if they are to give an authentic account of their religious identity, must
locate themselves within a particular tradition. To do so is not, in and of itself,
to assert the intrinsic superiority of that tradition but simply to acknowledge
that such a tradition is, in a theological sense, "home." Roman Catholicism has
been my religious home for almost five decades and to try and mask that would
do no service to the cause of genuine ecumenism.

One of the most salient characteristics of our postmodern moment is an
experience of fragmentation and rootlessness. The recovery of a thick sense of
Catholic identity has preoccupied numerous Catholic intellectuals and even our
present pope, Benedict XVI. Unfortunately, this desire to reassert a more robust
Catholic identity has led, in many instances, to a troubling neo-triumphalism.
We see the emergence of new forms of Catholic apologetics that pursue
Catholic identity primarily in a contrastive key, that is, by contrasting the truth
of Catholicism to the errors of other Christian traditions.[7] Yet I am convinced
that it is possible to ground one's religious identity in a distinct religious tradition without falling prey to neo-triumphalism.

Unfortunately, conversation about the church in contemporary Roman
Catholicism has been hampered by the stifling and reductive intellectual
framework of orthodoxy versus dissent. Legitimate concerns regarding the
preservation of Catholic identity have led to a regrettable reduction of the issue
to a preoccupation with what is or is not orthodox. This viewpoint too easily
assumes that what constitutes orthodoxy is self-evident and determined by one
normative account of Catholic Christianity found in papal teaching, the creeds
of the church and the *Catechism of the Catholic Church*. It assumes, in particular, a "standard Catholic ecclesiology." By definition, whatever is not orthodox—that is, any departure from the standard account—is *ipso facto* either
dissent or heresy. This binary view of Catholic identity is far more modern

---

[7] Richard R. Gaillardetz, "Do We Need a New(-er) Apologetics?" *America* 190 (February 2, 2004):
26-33; idem, "Apologetics, Evangelization and Ecumenism Today," *Origins* 35 (May 19, 2005): 9-15.

than many realize. Its reductive perspective is foreign to the great Catholic tradition because it fails to do justice to the diversity of theological perspectives
that have been the lifeblood of the great Catholic heritage. It masks the incon-
trovertible fact that within the great tradition of Catholic Christianity we find
significant disputes—to name but a few: the ancient debates between the theological schools of Antioch and Alexandria regarding the relationship between
the humanity and divinity of Christ, the medieval disputes between Dominicans and Franciscans regarding the nature of the theological enterprise, the
baroque disputes between Dominicans and Jesuits regarding the relationship
between divine grace and human freedom, and the modern disputes between
Thomistic and Augustinian accounts of the church's relationship to the world.
For much of the history of the church, a common rule of faith (*regula fidei*)
was expressed in a diversity of theological, spiritual, canonical, and liturgical
traditions. Normative church pronouncements were few and far between and
were read primarily as boundary markers for legitimate conversation rather
than as reductive encapsulations of the great tradition. The formality and
brevity of these dogmatic pronouncements was never thought to preclude
ongoing theological discussion and significant theological diversity. If Roman
Catholicism is to have a future beyond that of an antiquated curiosity, it must
recover the capacious breadth of its great tradition.

The reflections in this volume will draw from the nascent ecclesiological
vision of the Second Vatican Council, the most significant event in Roman
Catholicism over the last four centuries. Vatican II did not provide a standard
ecclesiology, but it did offer a decisive new orientation for Catholic reflections
on the church. It did so in two ways. The council members recognized the
reductive and atrophied state of theological reflection on the church found in
the dogmatic manuals of the nineteenth and early twentieth centuries. Consequently, the council's reflections on the church took the form not of some normative systematic treatise but of a recovery of the theological breadth and depth
of the Catholic tradition with particular attention to neglected theological perspectives from the Christian heritage of the first thousand years. The council
also recognized the need for a new and positive engagement with the contemporary world. To the extent that the ecclesiological reflections in this volume
are discernibly Roman Catholic, they will be consonant with that conciliar orientation.

Second, the ecclesiological perspectives explored here will be ecumenical. A
genuinely ecumenical ecclesiology will not settle for outlining the bare minimum of ecclesial claims acceptable to all Christians but will seek out fruitful
avenues for moving toward a more formal and visible unity. Yet another characteristic of our postmodern epoch is our increased awareness of cultural and
religious pluralism. It is inevitable that as the dramatic particularity and diver-

sity of the great world religions becomes more evident in our world today, the differences *within* Christianity will have to be seen in a new light. Contemporary reflection on the church axiom "unity in essentials, liberty in doubtful matters, and in all things charity" will acknowledge the not inconsiderable unity among the churches that already exists. It will also highlight the need for far greater discrimination in the determination of what is indeed essential for the unity of the churches and an enhanced willingness to celebrate a life-giving diversity in Christian beliefs and practices.

Third, this ecclesiological account pursues a more global perspective insofar as it acknowledges the unfortunate dominance, throughout much of the history of Christianity, of Western narratives of Christianity's origins. Christian historiography has often imposed an artificial unity on world Christianity. One consequence of this universal Christian narrative was the masking of the character of early Christianity as a diverse global movement. The rediscovery of the global character of the church requires that we reassess many of the presuppositions that provided the theoretical underpinning for four centuries of Catholic missionary work. During that period the Roman Catholic Church often functioned, as Karl Rahner famously put it, as

> an export firm which exported a European religion as a commodity it did not really want to change but sent throughout the world together with the rest of the culture and civilization it considered superior.[8]

This process of cultural exportation accompanying the evangelical mission of the church often naively assumed that the principal identity markers of Western Catholicism were universal and transcultural in character. An ecclesiology attentive to the global character of the church, as we shall see, must recognize that there is no transcultural expression of the Christian gospel and that, too often, what has been presented as transcultural and normative was in fact a very particular Greco-Roman inculturation of the Christian faith. In the same essay in which Rahner made his insightful observation regarding Catholic missionary endeavors, he also noted that the greatest contribution of the Second Vatican Council was its shift from the church as a cultural export firm to a genuinely world church. This study is inspired by that vision and hopes to illuminate, in particular ways, how a Christian vision of the church can be enriched by a greater awareness of the diversity of its inculturated forms flourishing in the world today.

---

[8] Karl Rahner, "A Basic Theological Interpretation of the Second Vatican Council," in *Concern for the Church*, vol. 20 of *Theological Investigations* (New York: Crossroad, 1981), 77-89, at 78.

With these perspectives in mind, let me briefly outline the structure of this book. Chapter 1 will lay out the wide range of biblical conceptions of religious community. Discussions of the biblical foundations of Christianity are too often limited to consideration of the New Testament. This approach ignores the fact that Christianity emerged from the bosom of Israel. If ecclesiology takes the incarnation seriously, then it cannot ignore the Jewishness of Jesus and the ways in which the earliest followers of Jesus drew heavily on the Hebrew Scriptures in developing conceptions of Christian community. Christianity emerged out of Judaism, and it retains to this day a distinctive relationship to Judaism that cannot be ignored in any Christian theological reflection.

One of the first attributes applied to the church in the early centuries was that of "holiness." The church was referred to as the *sancta ecclesia,* on the assumption that the church's holiness was a gift of God made effective in the church not by the effort or merits of the church's members but by the animating presence of the Holy Spirit. In the second century, St. Ignatius of Antioch would refer to the church as "catholic" (a Greek compound of *kata* and *holos,* meaning, literally, "pertaining to the whole") as a means of describing the church as an inclusive and expansive reality. In the third and fourth centuries, the "catholicity" of the church took on a somewhat different meaning; now it denoted the whole church over against various sectarian or dissident groups. Thus, one of the earliest formal creeds, the so-called Apostles' Creed, refers simply to the "holy catholic church." When the Council of Constantinople (381) added an article on the church to the creed that had been approved by the Council of Nicaea (325), four marks were now ascribed to the church, adding the marks of "unity" and "apostolicity."

These four qualifiers have been applied to the church in quite different ways. Since the Protestant Reformation, Roman Catholic theology often referred to them as "notes" or "properties" that were empirically verifiable and allowed one to identify the one, true church.[9] Contemporary theological reflection has largely moved away from such polemical enterprises. Nevertheless, these four qualifiers represent one of the more ancient heuristic devices for reflection on the nature and mission of Christian community. To assert that the church was one, holy, catholic, and apostolic was to make a set of theological claims regarding those qualities of the church which it possessed as a gift made possible by the abiding presence of the Holy Spirit. As gifts of the Spirit given to the church, these four qualities could be distinguished but never separated. Today these ecclesial qualifiers represent not only gifts but also challenges to the extent that the church's oneness, holiness, catholicity, and apostolicity are never

---

[9] See "Notes of the Church," in Christopher O'Donnell, *Ecclesia: A Theological Encyclopedia of the Church* (Collegeville. Minn.: Liturgical Press, 1996), 331-32.

perfectly realized in the life of the church. Fidelity to the Spirit demands that the church continue to grow into these claims.

Chapters 2 through 7 in this volume will be loosely structured around these four marks reread, however, from the perspective of the global shape of the church today. We will not follow theological custom and begin with the unity of the church; chapter 2 will consider instead the church's catholicity in view of the Christian call to dialogical mission in the world. Beginning with catholicity as an invitation to dialogical mission highlights one of the most important ecclesiological insights of the past few decades, namely, the recognition that the church does not so much have a mission as Christian mission has a church.

Reflection on the church's catholicity will then lead, in chapter 3, to a reappraisal of the church's unity, now conceived within the framework of communion, an increasingly influential theological concept that foregrounds church unity as essentially differentiated. The church is not just a spiritual communion; it is an *ordered* communion built up for mission by various forms of public ministry. Chapter 4 will address the ordering of the church's ministries.

Chapter 5 explores the "holiness" of the church read through the lens of the priority of baptism and the call to Christian discipleship that has been so central to the renewed vitality of many of the churches of the global South. Chapter 6 examines traditional claims to the church's apostolicity through the lens of communal memory. Chapter 7 then investigates how questions of apostolic office might be illuminated by seeing that office as a service to the preservation of the church's communal memory.

This project has been in the works for several years, and because of the extensive travel associated with it, a debt of gratitude is owed to many. First, I must thank both the University of Toledo for providing me with a year-long sabbatical to do research for this book and the Louisville Institute for Faith and Culture for offering a grant to help support this research. During my travels I benefited from the generous hospitality of the Dominican Friars in Pietermauritzburg and Johannesburg, South Africa. Without the advanced planning of Kees Keijsper, O.P., my time there would not have been nearly as productive, or as enjoyable. In like manner, I was graciously welcomed into the provincial house of the Franciscan friars in Quezon City, Philippines. There I benefited from the advanced planning of Dan Kroger, O.F.M., who put together a full itinerary of on-site visits and interviews. My appreciation for the riches and diversity of the Asian church was greatly enhanced by conversations with Fr. James H. Kroeger, a Maryknoll missioner who teaches on the faculty of the Loyola School of Theology in Manila and who has dedicated his life to the Asian church; Prof. Jose de Mesa, one of the most accomplished lay theologians in the Filipino church; and Catalino Arévalo, S.J., a Filipino theologian who was for decades at the center of the work of the Federation of Asian Bishops Conferences and was the first Asian to serve on the International Theological Commission.

My travel to Chiapas, Mexico, was facilitated by my friend and New Testament scholar Barbara Reid, O.P., who also accompanied me to Chiapas. Her expert facility in Spanish was of invaluable assistance to me when my own halting Spanish failed me during several interviews. While in Chiapas we joined company with a small delegation from the Catholic Theological Union in Chicago led by Prof. Michel Andraos. It was Michel's many connections in the region that gained us entrance into Zapatista-controlled territory in the Highlands of Chiapas. I wish to also offer my gratitude to Fr. Miguel Alvarez, a Scalabrini priest residing in Mexico City, who arranged for my interviews with the now retired bishop of San Cristóbal, Bishop Samuel Ruiz.

Although it at times appears otherwise, theology is not a solitary profession. All theologians rely on the generous contributions of our peers, both through studying their work and by inviting them to respond to our own efforts. For all its failings, this volume has been improved by the careful reading of early versions of this manuscript by James Bacik, Stephen Bevans, and Peter Phan.

As most married scholars will attest, a book-length project can put a strain on one's family life. When such a project also requires extended travel, the strain increases exponentially. Yet I have benefited from the Job-like patience of my wife, Diana, who with good cheer kept our household running well when this project took me away from home. My sons, David, Andrew, Brian, and Gregory, have also provided their support and, on many an occasion, a much-needed distraction from the demands of this project. Finally, I want to thank Peter Phan and Bill Burrows of Orbis for their insightful editorial leadership and support.

Abbreviations

Quotations of Vatican II documents are from Austin Flannery, ed., *Vatican Council II: Constitutions, Decrees, Declarations* (Northport, N.Y.: Costello, 1996). Unless otherwise indicated, all other church documents are taken from the Vatican Web site.

AA	*Apostolicam Actuositatem,* Vatican II Decree on the Apostolate of the Laity (1965)
AG	*Ad Gentes,* Vatican II Decree on the Missionary Activity of the Church
AMECEA	Association of Member Episcopal Conferences of Eastern Africa
ARCIC	Anglican-Roman Catholic International Commission
BEC	basic ecclesial communities
BEM	World Council of Churches' Lima document, *Baptism, Eucharist and Ministry* (1982)
CA	*Centesimus Annus,* Pope John Paul II, Encyclical on the hundredth anniversary of *Rerum Novarum* (1991)
CCC	*Catechism of the Catholic Church* (1997)
CD	*Christus Dominus,* Vatican II Decree on the Bishops' Pastoral Office in the Church
CDF	Congregation for the Doctrine of the Faith
CELAM	Consejo Episcopal Latinoamericano
CN	*Communionis Notio,* Congregation for the Doctrine of the Faith, "Letter on Some Aspects of the Church Understood as Communion" (1992)
CT	*Catechesi Tradendae,* Pope John Paul II, Apostolic Exhortation on Catechesis in Our Time (1979)
DI	*Dominus Iesus,* Declaration of the Congregation for the Doctrine of the Faith on the Unicity and Salvific Universality of Jesus Christ and the Church (2000)
DS	Denzinger-Schönmetzer, *Enchiridion Symbolorum*
DV	*Dei Verbum,* Vatican II Dogmatic Constitution on Divine Revelation (1965)
EN	*Evangelii Nuntiandi,* Pope Paul VI, Apostolic Exhortation on Evangelization in the Modern World (1976)
ES	*Ecclesiam Suam,* Pope Paul VI, Encyclical on the Church (1964)

EV	*Evangelium Vitae*, Pope John Paul II, Encyclical on the Value and Inviolability of Human Life (1995)
FABC	Federation of Asian Bishops' Conferences
FC	*Familiaris Consortio*, Pope John Paul II, Apostolic Exhortation on the Role of the Christian Family in the Modern World (1981)
LG	*Lumen Gentium*, Vatican II Dogmatic Constitution on the Church (1964)
LWF	Lutheran World Federation
MC	*Mystici Corporis*, Pope Pius XII, Encyclical on the Body of Christ (1943)
PL	*Patrologiae cursus completus, Series Latina*, edited by J.-P. Migne. 221 vols. Paris, 1844-91.
PO	*Presbyterorum Ordinis*, Vatican II Decree on Priestly Ministry and Life (1965)
PP	*Populorum Progressio*, Pope Paul VI, Encyclical on the Development of Peoples (1967)
RM	*Redemptoris Missio*, Pope John Paul II, Encyclical on the Permanent Validity of the Church's Missionary Mandate (1990)
SA	*Slavorum Apostoli*, Pope John Paul II, Encyclical Commemorating the Eleventh Centenary of the Evangelizing Work of Saints Cyril and Methodius (1985)
SC	*Sacrosanctum Concilium*, Vatican II Constitution on the Sacred Liturgy (1963)
SECAM	Symposium of the Episcopal Conferences of Africa and Madagascar
SRS	*Sollicitudo Rei Socialis*, Pope John Paul II, Encyclical on the Twentieth Anniversary of *Populorum Progressio* (1987)
UR	*Unitatis Redintegratio*, Vatican II Decree on Ecumenism (1964)
USCCB	United States Conference of Catholic Bishops
UUS	*Ut Unum Sint*, Pope John Paul II, Encyclical on Ecumenism (1995)
WCC	World Council of Churches

1

A People Called to Community

Much of Christianity's developing communitarian consciousness was inherited from ancient Israel. Indeed, many of the tensions and conflicts that would mark the history of Christianity had already emerged in the history of Israel. Ancient Judaism began as a small religious movement inspired by a remarkable vision of God and the unique communal life their God called them to. It is here, in the story of Israel, that Christian ecclesiology really begins.

EARLY YAHWISM'S UNDERSTANDING OF COMMUNITY

We look to what contemporary Jews refer to as the Tanakh and Christians as the Old Testament for insight into ancient Israel's sense of itself as community. This task is not as straightforward as it might seem, for in fact the Tanakh is not one book but many books written over a period of almost ten centuries. It includes multiple written traditions that are themselves dependent on more ancient oral traditions. Often these traditions, separated by centuries, were subsequently interwoven. We must also make a distinction between concrete experiences of community in ancient Israel and theological conceptions of community. The former is a much more complex and differentiated reality and can only with great difficulty be reconstructed using various historical methods. The latter, theological understandings of community, is somewhat more accessible through careful biblical scholarship. What I will be exploring here is the biblical testimony to certain theological conceptions of community, while leaving aside the question of who in fact would have adhered to these theological understandings at any given point in history.

When we consider the earliest stage of the faith of Israel, what might be referred to as "early Yahwism," we discover a sense of community thoroughly shaped by one event: the exodus. The narrative of a small nomadic people, enslaved by Egypt, liberated from their captivity by a God who refused to be named, would be decisive for early Hebrew identity. Their identity as a people was forged by this tale of emancipation. Virtually all of the earliest oral and

1

written traditions belonging to ancient Israel revolve around the exodus. "The starting point of the Yahwistic community, therefore, was neither a cosmic vision, nor a timeless code of law. It was an experience of God entering the concreteness and particularity of human life to save humans from their bondage."[1]

In a world and a time in which most ancient religions appealed to gods who supported rigidly stratified social structures, the ancient Hebrew people professed belief in a God who initiated a covenant relationship with slaves, the marginal, and the powerless. The originary event of early Hebrew identity was interpreted as a repudiation of divinely sanctioned caste systems in favor of a rough communal equality grounded in an event that established their shared dependence on their Liberator God. As Michael Walzer has observed, the liberation accomplished in the exodus was not merely a freedom *from* oppression but it was a freedom *for* the formation of a covenantal community.[2]

One of the earliest strands of the Yahwist tradition envisions Israel as a priestly people: "Now therefore, if you obey my voice and keep my covenant, you shall be my treasured possession out of all the peoples. Indeed, the whole earth is mine, but you shall be for me a priestly kingdom and a holy nation" (Ex. 19:5-6). From the very beginning we can see a tension between Israel's idealized image of itself as a consecrated or priestly people and the historical record that suggests that Israel shared the practice of most other ancient peoples in having a priestly caste responsible for religious sacrifice.

The origins of ancient Israel's sense of itself as a community, at least in its own telling, begins not with any human act of organization but with divine initiative. The Hebrews believed it was God's action, not their own, that forged them as a people. Moreover, for ancient Israel, the exodus represented not merely a solitary divine action; it was followed by an ongoing redemptive presence and activity in their history. God's relationship to Israel was described as *hesed*, "steadfast love," and referred to an experience of God's fidelity to the covenant relationship established with the people. God's activity in history was interpreted as the in-breaking of a divinely constituted order, a cosmic harmony, *shalom*. This *shalom*, in turn, could be realized in Israel only to the extent that it imitated God's own acts of justice and compassion.

Two words, *ṣedeq*, often translated as "righteousness," and *mishpaṭ*, often translated as "justice" or "judgment," actually have overlapping fields of meaning. The translation of *ṣedeq* as "righteousness" is particularly problematic, John

---

[1] Paul D. Hanson, *The People Called: The Growth of Community in the Bible* (Louisville: Westminster John Knox, 1986), 56. Much of my treatment of ancient Hebrew conceptions of community is drawn from Hanson's magisterial study.

[2] Michael Walzer, *Exodus and Revolution* (New York: Basic Books, 1985), 53, 73-90.

Donahue claims, because the English term suggests a sense of personal virtue, whereas the biblical term is more concerned with right relationship in the legal and communal sense. Donahue contends that the biblical sense of justice, both referring to the justice of God and the justice demanded of God's people, is "fidelity to the demands of relationship."[3] Israel's developing sense of its communal identity was shaped by its understanding of its God. Walter Brueggemann sees in this early Yahwism the construction of an "alternative community." In early Yahwism we find

> [t]he emergence of a new social community in history, a community that has historical body, that had to devise laws, patterns of governance and order, norms of right and wrong, and sanctions of accountability. The participants in the Exodus found themselves, undoubtedly surprisingly to them, involved in the intentional formation of a *new social community* to match the vision of *God's freedom.* That new social reality, which is utterly discontinuous with Egypt, lasted in its alternative way for 250 years.[4]

It is in the light of this alternative vision of community that we can appreciate the social significance of Torah.

Torah emerged in ancient Israel as a response to God's initiative in establishing a covenant community. Christians have suffered from a skewed and often reductive understanding of Torah as "law" and have opposed it to the freedom of the gospel. This view, based on a limited and noncontextual reading of the Gospels and St. Paul, does not do justice to the ancient Hebrew sense of Torah. Torah was before anything else a grateful response to God's initiative. It was manifested in communal structures and ordinances, to be sure, but above all, it was manifested in ancient Hebrew worship. The importance of worship for understanding Torah and Israel's own self-understanding as a community cannot be exaggerated. The response of Israel to God's covenantal love in the form of worship served as a perpetual reminder that all social and organizational structures were relativized in the face of their fidelity to Yahweh, their one true king. It was also, at least implicitly, a repudiation of imperialism. As Brueggemann notes, the stirring doxological statement "The Lord will reign for ever and ever" (Ex. 15:18) implied a whispered countertheme, "and not the pharaoh."[5] Thus, Torah can be understood as ancient Israel's understanding of

---

[3] John R. Donahue, "The Bible and Catholic Social Teaching: Will This Engagement Lead to Marriage?" in *Modern Catholic Social Teaching: Commentaries and Interpretations*, edited by Kenneth R. Himes (Washington, D.C.: Georgetown University Press, 2005), 9-40, at 14.

[4] Walter Brueggemann, *The Prophetic Imagination*, 2nd ed. (Minneapolis: Fortress, 2001), 7.

[5] Ibid., 18.

the concrete demands of right relationship with one another and with God. Both communal structures and worship were responses to God's redemptive activity in the exodus.[6]

As important as this insight is, Torah must not be overly romanticized. Biblical scholarship makes it abundantly clear that the earliest Hebrew traditions freely borrowed from other ancient religions and cultures as they sought to give form to their communal identity. There is an irreducible tension in early Hebrew traditions between often conservative social and legal structures borrowed from other ancient societies that appeared to preserve a stratified and thoroughly patriarchal social structure, and elements that clearly challenged that stratification. This tension can be found in the Book of the Covenant (Ex. 20:21-23:19). Here we find two sets of laws, case laws largely borrowed from other ancient cultures, and Yahwistic laws that reveal a much more distinctive sense of Hebrew identity. The latter laws reflected a conviction that their communal identity was to mirror the actions and concerns of the God who saved them and called them into being as a people. Consequently, these laws call for a special concern for the stranger ("for you were strangers in the land of Egypt" [Ex. 23:9]), the widow, the orphan—in short, ancient Israel was to be especially sensitive to the needs of the vulnerable in their society. Paul Hanson points out that, while other ancient religions affirmed an obligation for the poor and powerless (the Code of Hammurabi demanded that the king show concern for the poor), Israel was unique in its conviction that the responsibility for the well-being of the powerless fell upon the whole community, not just the king.[7] Torah was to mirror the justice and compassion of Israel's God.

This ancient Yahwistic vision of community is never abandoned by Israel, but it does go through a series of modifications and developments over the course of Israel's history. One of the most significant of these occurs with the introduction of the monarchy. Prior to the monarchy there was only an attenuated sense of Israel as a coherent nation. Israel existed after the exodus as a loose confederation or league of tribes that functioned more or less independently and shared a primitive form of early Yahwistic belief. Indeed, at this early stage, the most dominant sense of community was rooted in the extended family and was based on kinship.

These tribes were led by charismatic leaders or "judges," who, in response to some external threat, could rally all the tribes together to engage in battle against a common enemy. Yet these leaders generally returned to their local tribes after having led the confederation in a common cause. A decisive break

---

[6] Hanson, 42.
[7] Ibid., 47.

with this practice is reported in 1 Samuel, a complex text that underwent considerable redaction by the Deuteronomist.

AMBIVALENCE ABOUT MONARCHY

Discerning the historical core underlying this heavily worked narrative on the rise of the monarchy is a complex task. Most scholars see a tension in the narrative's assessment of the rise of Saul as the first king of Israel. As with the judges, the narrative tells of Saul's emergence as king, chosen by God and acclaimed by the people. The central difference is that Saul is apparently called to a permanent office (1 Sam. 10:27b-11:15). There are obvious political reasons for this new development, foremost of which would have been the need for greater centralization of leadership in the face of hostile forces. Yet 1 Samuel reveals simmering political and theological tensions regarding this new development. Those in favor of the emerging monarchy sought to characterize it as a kind of "limited kingship."[8] This new institution could be reconciled with early Yahwistic conceptions of community only insofar as the king served by the will of Yahweh and the assent of the people. Strictly excluded, however, was an absolute dynastic kingship of the kind that would emerge later under Solomon. Both of these elements are dominant in the story of Saul's anointing by Samuel. Yet also embedded in the narratives of 1 Samuel is another tradition that sees any form of monarchy as fundamentally at odds with a conception of a community that submits exclusively to the kingship of God. In any event, as the monarchy emerged under first Saul and then David, we see a related compensatory development in the form of the prophet, a charismatic figure who emerged as a kind of check against the monarchy. The prophet echoed the ancient Yahwistic traditions of unconditional fidelity to covenant relationship. The role of the prophet to ensure the king's fidelity to the ideals of Yahwism is reflected in the distinctive relationship between King David and Nathan, and nowhere more so than where Nathan challenges David for having placed himself beyond the demands of covenant community by having Uriah the Hittite killed that he might make his wife, Bathsheba, his own (2 Sam. 11-12).[9]

A second stage in the emergence of the monarchy occurs under Solomon. Almost all vestiges of a limited kingship still bound by a Yahwistic vision of community disappear with Solomon. Underlying significant legendary material celebrating the glory of Solomon is a more troubling historical record.

---

[8] Ibid., 89-100.
[9] Ibid., 103.

Solomon takes the throne by dynastic succession. Under his rule authority is centralized, a standing army is created, alliances with other kings are engaged, and the court is patterned on the more hierarchical models found in Egypt and elsewhere. The construction of the temple cannot be separated from the construction of a royal palace. "The Solomonic temple was constructed completely in the style of Canaanite models. An authentic imperial shrine had come to replace David's rustic tent as the new home of Yahweh."[10]

The shift in worship effected by the building of Solomon's temple was momentous. The once central theme of Israel's deliverance by Yahweh from slavery is supplanted by a royal ideology that distracts from God's redemptive deeds to celebrate Yahweh's choice of David as king and the temple as God's dwelling place. This shift is captured in the mythic poetry of the royal psalms: "I have set my king on Zion, my holy hill" (Ps. 2:6).

George Mendenhall has harshly judged the reign of Solomon as "the paganization of Israel."[11] Brueggemann sees in the reign of Solomon the antithesis of the alternative community envisioned by Moses and early Yahwism. According to Brueggemann, the reign of Solomon possessed three characteristics: (1) conspicuous affluence, (2) oppressive social policy, and (3) the endorsement of state-controlled religion. Here we have the foundations of what Brueggemann calls a "royal consciousness," espoused by a religious community that sees its religious convictions as a means of supporting the status quo.[12] For him what we have at work is a type of religious community that has reappeared at various points in human history. It is a communal vision numb to the gap between what is and what ought to be. It is a community bereft of a "prophetic imagination," incapable of mourning its failure to live up to the demands of the covenant and incapable as well of hoping for a new and different future.

What can be said about the conflicts regarding a monarchy in ancient Israel? The earliest strands of Yahwistic belief struggled with a tension between the need for a stable ordering of the community that led the ancient Hebrew peoples to borrow freely from other cultures and the demands of covenant relationship, which called for the creation of a community determined to mirror the justice and compassion of their God. With the rise of the monarchy an analogous tension emerged, now between the need to preserve absolute fidelity to God as the one true ruler of the people and to live according to the radical demands of the covenant and the practical need for institutional structures that could provide unity and protection for the people.

---

[10] Ibid., 106.

[11] George E. Mendenhall, "The Monarchy," *Interpretation* 29 (1975): 155-70, at 160.

[12] Brueggemann, 25-37.

PROPHETIC CALLS TO RETURN TO COVENANT COMMUNITY

With the split between the northern and southern kingdoms after Solomon, the monarchy continued in rather different forms. The north sought to recover the ancient model of the limited kingship and protested against a centralization of worship in the temple. The south continued the Davidic dynasty. In a real sense, neither preserved well the conceptions of community honored in early Yahwism. This is a point that will be made continually by prophets in the north such as Elijah and by the Deuteronomic reforms in the south. Later Amos would exemplify the prophetic tradition in his searing indictment of Israel for its failure to live up to the most ancient Hebrew convictions regarding right relationship with the community:

> Thus says the LORD: For three transgressions of Judah, and for four, I will not revoke the punishment; because they have rejected the law of the LORD, and have not kept his statutes, but they have been led astray by the same lies after which their ancestors walked. So I will send a fire on Judah, and it shall devour the strongholds of Jerusalem. Thus says the LORD: For three transgressions of Israel, and for four, I will not revoke the punishment; because they sell the righteous for silver, and the needy for a pair of sandals—they who trample the head of the poor into the dust of the earth, and push the afflicted out of the way; father and son go in to the same girl, so that my holy name is profaned; they lay themselves down beside every altar on garments taken in pledge; and in the house of their God they drink wine bought with fines they imposed. (Amos 2:4-8)

Amos's message is clear; Israel had departed from the very essence of Yahwistic community, that is, a commitment "to protect the poor and vulnerable as an expression of divine righteousness and compassion."[13] The only recourse, Amos contended, was through conversion. Israel must forsake empty sacrifices and "let justice roll down like waters, and righteousness like an ever-flowing stream" (Amos 5:24).

The message of northern prophets like Amos and Hosea was amplified during the Deuteronomic reform in the south. It was a reform that offered a renewed vision of community that emanated from pure worship of the one true God and a recommitment to the centrality of the sacred narrative of God's liberating activity in the exodus. The life of the community was to be sustained by fidelity to the demands of covenant relationship. The Deuteronomic

---

[13] Hanson, 154.

rearticulation of the Torah was comprehensive in its attempt to apply the demands of covenant relationship in every aspect of one's daily life and, in particular, with one's communal relationships. If anything, the demands of covenant community preserved in the ancient Yahwistic traditions are further radicalized. This is apparent in the ways in which earlier discrimination against women is, if not eliminated, at least softened.

A discernible shift in conceptions of community is evident in the seventh century B.C.E. in the writings of Jeremiah. Here we see for the first time a distinction between the spiritual status of the community and that of the individual. The covenant is now a pact not only between God and the people but between God and the individual. This concern for the individual in the community is further developed in the following centuries in the wisdom literature, perhaps nowhere more poignantly than in the Book of Job. In Job the righteous sufferer speaks out in dissent against a received tradition that saw calamity as a punishment for sin. Job's refusal to capitulate introduces a new tension, the claims of the individual against the received wisdom of the community. Somewhat surprisingly, we find an argument for the value of theological dissent within the community embedded in the structure of the biblical canon itself!

Finally, if the exodus remained the seminal event in Israel's core narrative of its identity before God, the Babylonian exile, following upon the fall of the southern kingdom and the destruction of Jerusalem in 587 B.C.E., would be seared in the subsequent self-understanding of Israel. During the exile, Israelites would find themselves severed from two crucial features that shaped their identity—the temple of Jerusalem and the land itself. This is given poignant expression in Ps. 137:1-4.

> By the rivers of Babylon—
>   there we sat down and there we wept
>   when we remembered Zion.
> On the willows there
>   we hung up our harps.
> For there our captors
>   asked us for songs,
> and our tormentors asked for mirth, saying,
>   "Sing us one of the songs of Zion!"
> How could we sing the LORD's song
>   in a foreign land?

Some of the most profound literature of the Tanakh attempts to respond to the crisis of faith posed by the exile.

ISRAEL'S RESPONSE TO THE EXILE

Coming out of a priestly tradition, Ezekiel contended that because of Israel's grotesque impurity and the punishment that this impurity incurred (the exile), the future of the people depended entirely on a new creative act of God. This promise of a new creation, God's replacement of a "stony heart" with a "heart of flesh" (Ezek. 36:26), was contingent on Israel's willingness to reestablish the right worship of God and obedience to divine decrees as central to their identity. The priestly source (P) that gave the Pentateuch its final form in the sixth century shared company with Ezekiel in calling for purification of Israelite worship. The restoration of God's favor after the exile required that Israel recenter its life on worship and temple sacrifice. The consequence was a heightened consciousness of the distinction between the pure and the impure, the sacred and the profane. An elaborate sacrificial system emerged that had as its goal the sanctification of all of Israel's life and gave a dramatically enhanced role to the priests. Although this emphasis on sacral priests would create new difficulties in the centuries ahead, "Ezekiel and the Priestly Writing serve as important reminders that the vision of God's saving action must be translated into the forms of worship and the structures of community that shape the life of faith in this world."[14]

One of the more eloquent responses to the tragedy of the exile is found in what biblical scholars call Second Isaiah, Isaiah 40-55. The author shares with the Priestly Writing and Ezekiel a conviction that the exile is a consequence of Israel's infidelity to God. The exile induced a "pedagogy of brokenness" intended to draw Israel back to God.[15] The hope that God might draw forth from the exile a new community rededicated to God was seen on the analogy of the original exodus. Second Isaiah in effect promised a new exodus in which God might create a new community. Yet the new community promised in Second Isaiah broke with that to emerge out of the first exodus by its more universal scope:

> And now the LORD says, who formed me in the womb to be his servant, to bring Jacob back to him, and that Israel might be gathered to him, for I am honored in the sight of the LORD, and my God has become my strength— he says, "It is too light a thing that you should be my servant to raise up the tribes of Jacob and to restore the survivors of Israel; I will give you as a light to the nations, that my salvation may reach to the end of the earth." (Isa. 49:5-6)

[14] Ibid., 250.
[15] Ibid., 236.

A restored Israel was now to be a servant community fulfilling God's saving intention for the world. A number of scholars have seen in this text a basis for exploring an Old Testament theology of mission.[16]

It is unfortunate that we find few if any attempts to enact the sweeping cosmic vision of Second Isaiah. Too idealistic in its conception, it soon gave way to a more pragmatic program for restoring Israel led by the Zadokite priesthood (a caste of priests who exercised leadership during the exile and were given exclusive responsibility for the temple cult under the reforms of King Josiah). This restoration was built on two planks: (1) a careful accommodation with the Persians, who had permitted the return of the Israelites from exile, and (2) a program for rebuilding the temple and reestablishing the temple cult based on a developed clerical system with the Zadokite priests at the pinnacle of the hierarchy. This restoration was informed by the priestly vision of Ezekiel and the Priestly Writing, which made the authentic restoration of Israel dependent on the recovery of Israel's ritual sanctity. Only through a renewed fidelity to the temple cult and strict obedience to God's ordinances could Israel again become a suitable habitation for God.[17] Yet this program was not without its difficulties. In the sixth and fifth centuries, rival priestly groups, particularly the Zadokite priests and the now increasingly marginalized Levitical priests, fought for power. In place of Second Isaiah's bracing vision of a community called to embody God's *shalom* before the world, we find an ever more restrictive view of communal holiness limited to competing groups of priestly elites. "The people of Judah accordingly entered the fifth century as a hierocratic community dominated by a priestly class dedicated to the pragmatic concerns of consolidating and maintaining control over the land and its cult, and not hesitating to use the political power at its disposal to accomplish its purposes."[18]

The restorationist impulse of the Zadokite priests was given a new energy in the effective leadership of two fifth-century figures, the priest Ezra and the royal official Nehemiah. Their program to reestablish the distinctive identity of Israel around the temple cult was remarkably successful. Under Ezra, Torah, which had hitherto referred to that broad complex of communal structures, legal ordinances, and spiritual imperatives concretizing the demands of covenant relationship, had become equated with a written text, the five books of Moses. Torah now came to be understood as a quasi-constitutional document.[19] Fidelity to Torah, particularly as regards worship of God, and ethnic

---

[16] See especially James Chukwuma Okoye, *Israel and the Nations: A Mission Theology of the Old Testament*, American Society of Missiology Series 39 (Maryknoll, N.Y.: Orbis Books, 2006), 129-43.

[17] Hanson, 260.

[18] Ibid., 278.

[19] Ibid., 293.

purity, preserving the "holy seed," became the defining features of Israel. During this period we witness an unprecedented preoccupation with Israel's separation of itself from its neighbors. Strikingly absent is the ancient Yahwistic commitment to compassion toward the foreigner.

Israel's exclusionary policy, defining itself over against all other nations and strictly prohibiting any mixture with other peoples, must be seen, at least in part, as an understandable response to a difficult political situation characterized by external threats to its continued existence. It also reflects the widespread assumption that the exile was God's punishment for having failed to maintain purity before God. Yet this exclusionary vision was not without its dissenters. Two particularly noteworthy examples of a "dissenting" view are found in the Books of Ruth and Jonah.

Ruth is a non-Jew, a Moabite woman whose marriage to Boaz, a Jew, brings her under the mantle of God's care. In a surprising reversal of expectations, as the story proceeds the now-widowed Ruth refuses to abandon her Jewish mother-in-law, Naomi. Ruth's fidelity to her mother-in-law becomes an ironic exemplar of the compassion for the vulnerable that is supposed to be reflective of Israel's own actions and commitments. The Book of Ruth may plausibly be read as a protest against the exclusionary Zadokite vision of an ethnically pure Israel.

The second dissenting voice is found in the Book of Jonah. Fundamentalist preoccupations with the historicity of Jonah being swallowed by a "great fish" have distracted from the provocative message of this ancient parable. It is a story of a reluctant Jewish prophet, Jonah, called to offer a message of judgment to a sinful, pagan people, the Ninevites. Interestingly, the Book of Jonah and Isaiah 66 offer the only two texts in the Hebrew Bible that recount a prophet being sent to pagan peoples.[20] To Jonah's dismay, the Ninevites respond to this divine judgment by dramatic, communal repentance. Accepting the repentance of this pagan people, the God of Israel relents and shows compassion to this pagan people. The message of this story is that God's compassion is not limited to Israel; it extends to all who are open to the call to repentance. In both Ruth and Jonah we hear minority voices protesting against the rigidly exclusionary vision of postexilic Israel and harking back to the more universal communal vision of Second Isaiah.

ISRAEL UNDER HELLENISTIC AND ROMAN DOMINATION

Finally we must consider the shifts in communal consciousness that occurred in the final three centuries prior to the Common Era. This was a period begun

---

[20] Okoye, 80.

by Alexander the Great's conquest of the region and constituted by the gradual hellenization of Israel. Responses to Hellenistic rule during these centuries
were remarkably varied. On the one hand, there is evidence of an extreme
assimilationist program on the part of some Jews who enthusiastically and
uncritically embraced Hellenistic culture. On the other hand, we have the
Maccabean revolt instigated by the Seleucid leader Antiochus IV Epiphanes'
desecration of the temple in Jerusalem. The revolt was undertaken by Jewish
parties committed to keeping alive a distinctive Jewish identity centered on
fidelity to Torah and a determination to purge the land of Israel of all foreign
influences. Ironically, the success of the revolt led the Maccabean leaders, having established a marginal independence for Israel, to embark on programs of
political accommodations with foreign powers such as Rome. The priestly tradition of holy separation reflected in the vision of Ezra and Nehemiah gave
birth to two quite different responses to the presence of foreign elements in
Israel.

One response was undertaken by a group known as the Essenes. This
priestly group denounced the defilements of the priestly caste responsible for
the temple cult in Jerusalem. They were convinced that fidelity to the sacral
demands of Torah required their geographic separation from all sources of
defilement. Consequently, they formed quasi-monastic communities in the
desert. A second response emerged in the rise of Pharisaism. Equally committed to a rigorous fidelity to Torah, the Pharisees were distinguished by their
belief that they could maintain ritual purity amidst external defilements (e.g.,
the presence of Gentiles in their midst) through a creative and comprehensive
application of Torah to every circumstance of ordinary life. What emerged in
the Pharisaic tradition was, in effect, two forms of the Torah—the written
Torah and an oral Torah consisting in creative applications to daily life.
Another distinguishing feature of early Pharisaism was its shift of the locus of
Jewish worship from the Temple to the household and the sphere of ordinary
existence.[21]

This brief review of the varying conceptions of community in ancient Israel
brings to light a number of fundamental tensions. First, in the emergence of the
ancient monarchy we saw a tension between an egalitarianism based on common subservience before the sole sovereignty of Yahweh and the practical need
for leadership structures that could provide a visible center of unity and effectively regulate the life of the community. Without the monarchy, ancient Israel
may not have survived. With the monarchy Israel had to struggle between a

---

[21] See Jacob Neusner, *The Rabbinic Traditions about the Pharisees before 70*, 3 vols. (Leiden: Brill,
1971); idem, *From Politics to Piety: The Emergence of Pharisaic Judaism* (Englewood Cliffs, N.J.: Prentice-
Hall, 1973).

limited monarchy committed to the service of Yahweh and an absolutist and hereditary monarchy prone to dilute the demands of authentic Yahwist faith. As Brueggemann has so compellingly put the matter, the emergence of the monarchy also raised a question regarding the community's relationship to the larger culture: will it be an alternative community striving to embody God's compassion and steadfast love, or will it succumb to a royal consciousness prone to accept social stratification and the status quo?

Yet another community tension was revisited in the postexilic period, as an essentially hierocratic vision of Israel structured around the priesthood came to dominance, threatening the possibility that individuals might achieve holiness apart from the temple cult. This was accompanied by the tension between the need for Israel to preserve its distinctive identity and a more universal vision that related the mission of Israel to the universal scope of God's saving will. A rigorous program of what can only be called "ethnic purity" espoused by Ezra and Nehemiah was held in check by the universalist vision of Second Isaiah, Ruth, and Jonah.

Third, during the period of the monarchy we find the conviction that God's kingdom could be encountered in Israel under the leadership of a king faithful to God. After the exile, as Israel dealt with the realities of first Persian and then Greek and Roman domination, reflections on God's kingdom were increasingly projected into the future. Only following upon some future day of judgment would the *shalom* of Yahweh be fully realized in a new kingdom of God. Hence, we find here a tension between God's kingdom encountered as a present reality and God's kingdom realized in some future fulfillment.

Finally, we encounter the struggle shared by all great religious traditions regarding the dangers and possibilities associated with engaging surrounding cultures without diluting or distorting the distinctiveness of one's own heritage. The wisdom tradition brought distinctive meditations on Torah into conversation with certain Hellenistic concepts, and the Pharisaic tradition insisted on ritual purity but did so through a creative application of Torah to every aspect of daily life that allowed the Pharisees to avoid fleeing all foreign engagements. As we shall see, many of these tensions will emerge in a new key in early Christianity.

THE BEGINNINGS OF THE JESUS MOVEMENT

The first part of this chapter surveyed developing understandings of community evident in the history of ancient Israel. We concluded with a consideration of a variety of Jewish movements that responded in different ways to the question of preserving their covenant identity as God's people in the last two

centuries prior to the Common Era. However, there is one final Jewish movement that demands our consideration. Early in the first century of the Common Era, a man of obscure origins, Jesus of Nazareth, came into contact with
yet another figure, John the Baptist. The Baptist bore certain similarities to the
Essenes. He came "from the desert" where the Essenes had established their
communities; he lived an ascetic existence, wearing a hair shirt and living on
"locusts and wild honey." Like the Essenes, he administered a water baptism,
but unlike the ritual of the Essenes, John's baptism was offered only one time,
was not self-administered and was expressly associated with a commitment to
conversion.

Both Matthew and Luke offer accounts of John's central message. It is difficult to know the extent to which these accounts draw from the substance of
John's actual message and the extent to which they are retrojections of the
Christian message back to the time of John. However, since virtually all scholars agree on the historicity of Jesus' baptism by John, it is not unreasonable to
speculate that Jesus may have been genuinely impressed with key elements of
John's message and may have embraced that message even as he subjected it to
fuller development. If we can accept Matthew's account of John's teaching as
having some historical core, then it would seem that for all of John's superficial similarities to the Essenes, he was in fact departing from both their
extreme form of Jewish particularism and that of the Pharisees.

> But when he saw many Pharisees and Sadducees coming for baptism, he
> said to them, "You brood of vipers! Who warned you to flee from the wrath
> to come? Bear fruit worthy of repentance. Do not presume to say to your-
> selves, 'We have Abraham as our ancestor'; for I tell you, God is able from
> these stones to raise up children to Abraham. Even now the ax is lying at the
> root of the trees; every tree therefore that does not bear good fruit is cut
> down and thrown into the fire.
>
> "I baptize you with water for repentance, but one who is more powerful
> than I is coming after me; I am not worthy to carry his sandals. He will bap-
> tize you with the Holy Spirit and fire. His winnowing fork is in his hand,
> and he will clear his threshing floor and will gather his wheat into the gran-
> ary; but the chaff he will burn with unquenchable fire." (Matt. 3:7-12)

John's message rejects the Jewish particularism that had dominated the postexilic period in favor of a vision of God's kingdom open to all who accept the
way of repentance and commitment to a life of justice and compassion.[22] John
stood, it would seem, much more in the tradition of the Book of Jonah.

---

[22] John Riches, *Jesus and the Transformation of Judaism* (London: Darton, Longman & Todd, 1980),
97.

It is quite possible that the Baptist's ministry and message had an impact on Jesus, triggering his own public ministry with a striking new message about God's kingdom. The first words of Jesus reported to us by the author of the Gospel of Mark aptly summarize the core of Jesus' message and mission: "The time is fulfilled and the kingdom of God has come near; repent and believe in the good news" (Mark 1:15). Jesus takes the message of God's kingdom as he would have received it from his own immersion in the Hebrew Scriptures and through the ministry of John and reinterprets it in significant ways. First, Jesus combines two distinct traditions, the emphasis on the kingdom of God as a present reality, stressed during the monarchical period, and the postexilic view of the kingdom as a future eschatological reality.[23] As a present reality, Jesus daringly suggested that the kingdom of God was breaking into history *now*, in his own life and ministry. The signs he performed, exorcisms and healings, were not the deeds of a wonder-worker, but signs of God's reign already making itself present in his person through manifestations of dominion over the forces of evil. Yet in many of his parables on the kingdom, for example, that which compares the kingdom to a mustard seed, God's reign is presented as a future reality whose full dimensions cannot be imagined. Other parables suggest Jesus' subversive vision of the kingdom, as when he responds to the question "Who is my neighbor?" by telling the parable of a Good Samaritan, in which a member of the despised Samaritans is offered as a more exemplary neighbor than either a priest or a Levite.[24]

Perhaps the most radical departure from received understandings of the kingdom is reflected in Jesus' challenge of accepted notions of cultic purity. His teaching represented a fundamental challenge to the purity regulations concerning the Jews' conduct with one another and with outsiders. According to Jesus, it is not the forces from without but those which arise from within that are destructive because they militate against forgiveness and mercy.[25] Consider Mark 7:14-15: "Then he called the crowd again and said to them, 'Listen to me, all of you, and understand: there is nothing outside a person that by going in can defile, but the things that come out are what defile.'"

Jesus employed the language of the *basileia*, or "kingdom," while carefully discarding its associations with either military revolution or ritual purity. Nevertheless, Jesus was able to use the language by appealing to its core meaning: that of God's establishment of divine rule over men and women. This was a meaning that allowed for God's dealings with Jews and Gentiles, and it entailed

---

[23] Daniel J. Harrington, *The Church According to the New Testament: What the Wisdom and Witness of Early Christianity Teach Us Today* (Franklin, Wis.: Sheed & Ward, 2001), 3-4.

[24] See William R. Herzog II, *Parables as Subversive Speech: Jesus as Pedagogue of the Oppressed* (Louisville: Westminster John Knox, 1994).

[25] Riches, 139.

the rejection of any notion of purity as separation from the impure. Jesus' embrace of the marginalized represented one of the more distinctive elements of his ministry. Although the Synoptic Gospels record his explicitly calling forth twelve men, they also report the inclusion of many women among his followers in an unprecedented break with the rabbinic custom prohibiting women from publicly associating themselves with a rabbi. The Gospels further suggest that Jesus counted women not only as disciples but as friends with whom he shared intimate table fellowship, as with Mary and Martha. Two thousand years removed, it is almost impossible for us to appreciate the revolutionary character of Jesus' easy acceptance of the dignity and value of women.

Jesus was able to refocus the notion of the reign of God by recontextualizing it. The new context was his own life and ministry: his ministry to the sick, the possessed, the poor, the outcast, and the oppressed. This context allowed for a proclamation of the kingdom as not just a future reality but as something that was in some way present in the person of Jesus and his work. This represents a distinct modification of the notion of the kingdom, which in the Tanakh was often associated with the destruction of enemies. Thus, Jesus' exorcisms represented a divine power over Satan established by prayer (not by military might).

Jesus' message of the kingdom also occurred in the context of his fellowship meals with tax collectors and other sinners. The table fellowship was a cultic meal, encouraged by the Pharisees, which celebrated divine communion with God's people. By celebrating such a meal with outcasts Jesus offered a complete revision of the conventional understanding of holiness and purity that broke down the exclusivism of both the Pharisees and the Essenes.

Elisabeth Schüssler Fiorenza's bold attempt at a feminist reconstruction of Christian origins suggests that Jesus' vision of the *basileia* of God was marked by a commitment to "inclusive wholeness." "The central symbolic actualization of the *basileia* vision of Jesus is not the cultic meal but the festive table of a royal banquet or wedding feast."[26] As a faithful Jew, Jesus did not repudiate the binding character of Torah. Yet he offered an unusually free and liberating attitude toward Torah by reminding his listeners that the Torah was offered to bring one into God's *shalom* by directing a life of holiness. Torah did not exist for its own sake but as a means for making Israel into a people of justice and compassion. Consequently, it is justice and compassion that must determine the proper interpretation and application of Torah. Jesus would emphasize that in the faithful application of the 613 ordinances of the Torah, the twofold love command, that is, the inseparability of love of God and love of neighbor, must

---

[26] Elisabeth Schüssler Fiorenza, *In Memory of Her: A Feminist Theological Reconstruction of Christian Origins* (New York: Crossroad, 1983), 119.

guide the fulfillment of all other laws.[27] Schüssler Fiorenza contends that the locus for holiness in Jesus' teaching and ministry is not the temple but the people:

> The Jesus movement in Palestine does not totally reject the validity of Temple and Torah as symbols of Israel's election but offers an alternative interpretation of them by focusing on the people itself as the locus of God's power and presence. . . . Human holiness must express human wholeness, cultic practice must not be set over and against humanizing praxis. . . . Everyday life must not be measured by the sacred holiness of the Temple and Torah, but Temple and Torah praxis must be measured and evaluated by whether or not they are inclusive of every person in Israel and whether they engender the wholeness of every human being. Everydayness, therefore, can become revelatory, and the presence and power of God's sacred wholeness can be experienced in every human being.[28]

It is Jesus' radical vision of the *basileia* of God that motivates his outreach and embrace of all who were marginalized in first-century Palestine, especially women.

Jesus' distinctive view of the kingdom is further evident in his own relationship with God. He addressed God with a familiarity, using the Aramaic "Abba," that was a source of scandal to many. Moreover, when teaching his disciples to pray, he invited them into that same relationship of intimacy with God. In conclusion, Jesus of Nazareth was a faithful Jew who creatively reworked his own Jewish heritage by offering a quite distinctive account of God's action. It was an action typified not by judgment of God's enemies but by forgiveness, mercy, love, and generosity.

May we conclude from this focus on the proclamation of the kingdom of God that Jesus did not desire to establish a church? This has certainly been the claim of many scholars. Alfred Loisy, the late-nineteenth- and early-twentieth-century modernist put it provocatively: "Christ preached the Kingdom of God, and the Church appeared instead."[29] Such scholars point to Jesus' belief in an imminent coming of God's eschatological reign. Jesus would not have instituted a church because he believed that his coming signaled the imminent end of history. They further note that Jesus' teaching finds its intelligibility within the Jewish thought world. Even his choice of the Twelve seems almost certainly motivated by its eschatological symbolism as a reconstitution

---

[27] Harrington, 5.
[28] Schüssler Fiorenza, 120.
[29] Alfred Loisy, *The Gospel and the Church* (Philadelphia: Fortress, 1976), 166.

of the Twelve Tribes. Jesus was a Jew, one might well argue. He understood himself to be a Jew, and if he saw himself as leading the Jewish faith in a new direction, there is no evidence that he intended to be the founder of a new religion.

However, the assumption that the apocalyptic character of Jesus' teaching argues against his intention to found a community ignores the example of the Essene community. This community clearly assumed the imminent realization of the day of judgment, yet this expectation did not prevent them from establishing a community replete with structural elements. In any event, this approach to the question unfairly stacks the deck by considering the foundation of the church strictly in terms of institutional structure. Obviously, we will have a hard time demonstrating how the historical Jesus explained the nature and practice of the seven sacraments, dictated the Niceno-Constantinopolitan Creed, and outlined the rubrics for the eucharistic sacrifice!

Is it not enough, however, to recognize that Jesus gathered around him a community of followers? There is ample evidence that he assumed the role of a rabbi who desired to school his disciples in the ways of God's reign. If he did not explicitly intend to found a new religion, it is, nevertheless, not an understatement to speak of him as a religious revolutionary within Judaism, challenging fundamental Jewish structures (e.g., as evident in the "cleansing of the temple"). He invited his followers to share in his work and sent them out in mission. We can assume from the general tenor of his message that he intended that the work for the kingdom would continue after his death.

In one of his early works Hans Küng put it this way:

> As soon as men gathered together in faith in the resurrection of the crucified Jesus of Nazareth and in expectation of the coming consummation of the reign of God and the return of the risen Christ in glory, the Church came into existence.[30]

In other words, the church, properly understood, is a post-Easter phenomenon, and any understanding of the church being founded by Christ must look not primarily to his pre-Easter, historical ministry but rather to the post-Easter encounter with the risen Lord that animated the disciples and constituted them, empowered by the Spirit, as a community. The church can be understood as instituted by Christ not in the sense that the historical Jesus was interested in the establishment of a church; rather, it was as a response to their encounters with the risen Lord and the coming of the Spirit that the early

---

[30] Hans Küng, *The Church* (New York: Sheed & Ward, 1967), 75.

Christians felt the need for the establishment of a community of believers. Hence, the foundation of the church should be understood both christologically and pneumatologically. The institutional and the charismatic must go hand in hand. Nevertheless, biblical scholars have done the church a great service by stressing that Jesus' emphasis was not on the church but on the kingdom of God.

FROM JESUS MOVEMENT TO CHURCH

Jesus' mission and message were continued in the work of his followers, many of whom were zealous in finding converts and creating small communities of faith throughout the Jewish Diaspora. With Paul's mission we encounter a decisive new development in early Christianity. The Christian message was now offered to Gentiles as well. The work of reconstructing the makeup of these early Christian communities is fraught with difficulties, as the documentary evidence, apart from the New Testament, is sketchy. All the communities were centered on Jesus, but many shifted away from a focus on his life and teaching, typical of the Jesus movement while he lived, to the saving significance of his death and resurrection. This is reflected in the writings of Paul, in which scant mention is made of Jesus' historical ministry or the substance of his teaching. Paul preached Christ crucified and risen, the source of our salvation.

Christianity first grew in urban rather than rural areas, and its appeal seemed to span all classes.[31] Most early gatherings of Christians met in the homes of some of the wealthier members, constituting "house churches" that might have comprised as many as forty or fifty members.[32]

Paul's Ecclesiological Vision

It is from the writings of Paul that we get the most fully developed reflection on the theological significance of Christian communal life. Paul's theology of the church was grounded in two insights: first, that salvation came through contact with the saving power of the death and resurrection of Christ, and, second, that this saving contact came through baptism into Christ's "body" the church. Indeed, the early church's theology of baptism might be thought of as

---

[31] See Wayne A. Meeks, *The First Urban Christians: The Social World of the Apostle Paul* (New Haven: Yale University Press, 1983).
[32] Harrington, 50.

the first Christian ecclesiology.[33] To be baptized a Christian meant being baptized into a mystical participation in Christ's death and resurrection as one was
simultaneously initiated into Christ's body the church. Paul's theological reflections on the Christian community centered on the metaphor of the body. By
speaking of the church as a body, Paul privileged the communal nature of
Christian life, a spiritual coexistence, and the interdependence of all the
members.

If for Paul baptism initiated the believer into the life of the community, the
bonds of this community with one another and with God were further nourished through the celebration of the eucharist. The eucharist was a sacred meal
that celebrated the twofold communion, or *koinōnia,* that Christians had with
God in Christ and with one another.

Paul's theological understanding of the celebration of the "breaking of the
bread," gives us further insight into his understanding of Christian community. Here is Paul's account of the practice of this sacred meal:

> For I received from the Lord what I also handed on to you, that the Lord
> Jesus on the night when he was betrayed took a loaf of bread, and when he
> had given thanks, he broke it and said, "This is my body (*sōma*) that is for
> you. Do this in remembrance (*anamnēsis*) of me." In the same way he took
> the cup also, after supper, saying, "This cup is the new covenant in my blood.
> Do this, as often as you drink it, in remembrance of me." For as often as you
> eat this bread and drink the cup, you proclaim the Lord's death until he
> comes.
>
> Whoever, therefore, eats the bread or drinks the cup of the Lord in an
> unworthy manner will be answerable for the body and blood of the Lord.
> Examine yourselves, and only then eat of the bread and drink of the cup. For
> all who eat and drink without discerning the body, eat and drink judgment
> against themselves. (1 Cor. 11:23-29)

Careful reflection on Paul's description of this ancient meal helps us appreciate the ways in which it contributed to the community's memory.[34]

First, Paul connects this ritual action with the redemptive work of Christ.
The death of Jesus constitutes a "new Passover" sacrifice. To celebrate this meal,
as with baptism, is for Paul a ritual participation in the dying and rising of

---

[33] Gerard Austin, "Restoring Equilibrium after the Struggle with Heresy," in *Source and Summit: Commemorating Josef A. Jungmann, S.J.,* ed. Joanne M. Pierce and Michael Downey (Collegeville, Minn.: Liturgical Press, 1999), 35-47 at 37.

[34] Eugene LaVerdiere, *The Eucharist in the New Testament and the Early Church* (Collegeville, Minn.: Liturgical Press, 1996), 31-43.

Christ. Second, Paul's use of the Greek term *sōma*, or "body," is worth exploring in more detail. The word *sōma* in this context does not mean "flesh," nor
does it refer to a physical or corporeal reality. Rather, *sōma* refers to the whole
person as the subject of a relationship. This is emphasized in Paul's addition of
the "... that is for you" to "this is my body." The implication here is that Christ
engages the believer with his whole being in a personal relationship or
encounter through the eucharistic action.

Third, the reference to eating the bread and drinking the cup in an "unwor-
thy manner" is alluding to the passage immediately preceding the account of
the eucharist's institution by Jesus. It would appear that Paul had heard of a
scandal in the behavior of the church at Corinth occasioned by the gathering
together for their common worship.

> Now in the following instructions I do not commend you, because when
> you come together it is not for the better but for the worse. For, to begin
> with, when you come together as a church, I hear that there are divisions
> among you; and to some extent I believe it. Indeed, there have to be fac-
> tions among you, for only so will it become clear who among you are gen-
> uine. When you come together, it is not really to eat the Lord's supper. For
> when the time comes to eat, each of you goes ahead with your own supper,
> and one goes hungry and another becomes drunk. What! Do you not have
> homes to eat and drink in? Or do you show contempt for the church of God
> and humiliate those who have nothing? What should I say to you? Should
> I commend you? In this matter I do not commend you! (1 Cor. 11:17-22)

Paul believed that the celebration of the Lord's Supper placed certain ethical
obligations on the community. His admonishments suggest that some social
stratification within the Corinthian community may have endured wherein the
poor did not have equal access. It may well be that the wealthy were either
meeting earlier to eat a more sumptuous meal on their own, before the poorer
members of the community arrived, or that they were eating in a separate room.
Paul sternly admonished the community that this action was not appropriate
for those who had entered into the covenant of Christ. They were eating the
bread and drinking the cup "unworthily." For Paul, the question was not one of
irreverence in the reception of the eucharistic elements (a common concern
with some Catholics today); the Corinthian community was irreverent because
of its divisions and, perhaps, because of its insensitivity to the poor in its
midst.[35]

---

[35] For further consideration of the ethical dimensions of the eucharist in Paul, see Gerd Theissen,
The Social Setting of Pauline Christianity: Essays on Corinth (Philadelphia: Fortress, 1982), esp. chap. 4.

Fourth, Paul believed that the eucharist effected a fellowship or commun-ion (*koinōnia*) with Christ and with one another by the power of the Spirit:

> The cup of blessing that we bless, is it not a sharing (*koinōnia*) in the blood of Christ? The bread that we break, is it not a sharing (*koinōnia*) in the body of Christ? Because there is one bread, we who are many are one body, for we all partake of the one bread. (1 Cor. 10:16-17)

Here, as with baptism, the eucharist is seen as a ritual that draws believers into relationship, one referred to as *koinōnia,* in which believers are drawn simultaneously into communion with God and communion with fellow believers.

Finally, Paul's theology of church presupposed a primary role for the Holy Spirit, who constituted the *koinōnia* or communion of all believers. The church is not an aggregate of individuals; it is a new relational reality that confers iden-tity upon those who enter into its life. By baptism into the Christian commu-nity one participates in a new reality; one is a new creation. Yet this communion among believers is not the fruit of mere human effort. The *koinōnia* among believers is the consequence of a *koinōnia* in Christ and in the Spirit.

Paul's theology of community is dynamic and organic. It conceives of Chris-tian community as constituted by a shared life in Christ begun in baptism and nurtured in the eucharist. Paul, like others, referred to the church as an *ekklēsia.* The term was taken over from Greek civic life, where it referred to parti-cipation in a public assembly. Individuals were "called out" to deliberate on common matters. As applied to Christian community, the *ekklēsia* was the com-munity of believers called by God by the power of the Spirit into common life in Christ.[36]

Other Pauline Ecclesiological Trajectories

Aside from the authentic Pauline literature—1 and 2 Corinthians, 1 Thessa-lonians, Romans, Galatians, Philippians, Philemon—there are a number of New Testament texts that lay claim to the Pauline tradition even though many are in fact written a good generation or so after Paul's death. These Deutero-Pauline texts reveal churches at a significantly different state of development than what we encounter, for example, in the church of Corinth reflected in Paul's correspondence. All borrow, in varying degrees, from Paul's theology, yet their distinctive ecclesiological contexts produce interesting variations on a Pauline ecclesiology.

---

[36] Harrington, 49.

The first post-Pauline development we might consider is found in the Deutero-Pauline letters to the Colossians and the Ephesians. These letters, written approximately twenty years after Paul's death, reveal an innovation in Pauline ecclesiology. When Paul used the term "church," he did so primarily with respect to the local community. That is, he wrote of "the church at Corinth" or "the church in Jerusalem" (1 Cor. 1:2; see also 2 Cor. 1:1; Gal. 1:1; Rom. 16:16). As we shall see in a later chapter, Paul certainly had a sense of the spiritual connectedness of all the churches, but his writings attended almost exclusively to the pastoral questions and concerns of local communities.

In Colossians and Ephesians we find Paul's vision of church expanded. Now the *ekklēsia* can also refer to the whole church. The one church encountered in each and every local church is the one body of Christ with Christ as its head. It should not surprise us that in letters that push Christology in a more universal direction, with their vision of the cosmic Christ recapitulating or summing up all creation into himself, we would also find a more universal vision of the church.

A second Deutero-Pauline trajectory of church development is found in the Pastoral Letters, 1 and 2 Timothy and Titus, texts likely written near the end of the first century. These letters depict a community that is much more developed and has learned to accommodate itself to its surrounding culture. This is reflected in several passages that encourage women to conform to the social expectations of the larger Greco-Roman culture. These are communities that have not forgotten Paul's expansive vision of a church animated by many charisms, but they are more aware than even Paul was of the problem of divisions in the church. Consequently, without precluding a place for charisms, the church of the Pastoral Letters is more concerned with stable leadership structures that can help preserve the unity of the church and ensure its authentic teaching. It is in these letters that we find in-depth discussions of stable church offices and a concern for a careful discernment of suitable candidates for these offices.

Other New Testament Visions of Christian Community

The universality of the church is evident in another biblical trajectory found in Luke-Acts. This two-volume work offers us first in the Gospel of Luke a compelling narrative of Jesus' inexorable journey toward Jerusalem, where his destiny as savior of the world would be publicly manifested. Part 2, the Acts of the Apostles, follows with a theologically rich account of the early church discovering its missionary imperative to bring the gospel of Jesus to the ends of the earth. We shall return to consider the Acts of the Apostles in more detail in the next chapter. Undergirding this two-part journey, first toward Jerusalem and then out to the whole known world, is a theology of the Holy Spirit. The Spirit's presence permeates the Jesus narrative. It is the Spirit who overshadows Mary, fills her sister Elizabeth and later Zechariah, rests upon Simeon and finally anoints Jesus at his baptism by John. Prior to Jesus' ascension he commissions the disciples: "But you will receive power when the Holy Spirit has come upon you; and you will be my witnesses in Jerusalem, in all Judea and Samaria, and to the ends of the earth" (Acts 1:8). It is that same Spirit who falls upon the believers at Pentecost and who empowers them in their ministry to bring the gospel of Jesus to the whole world. When Paul and Barnabas come to Jerusalem to make a case for their mission to the Gentiles, the decision is announced in the following form: "For it has seemed good to the Holy Spirit and to us to impose on you no further burden than these essentials" (Acts 15:28). Luke's appreciation for the pneumatological conditioning of the church is central to his theological vision. It is the Spirit that transforms a collective of individuals into a living communion of believers. Without this pneumatological dimension, there is a danger of the concept of communion degenerating to secular conceptions that ignore the way the believer is reconfigured in communion with other believers and with God. Luke's pneumatological perspective provides him with a more universal scope in his presentation of Jesus' mission. It is the power of the Spirit that allows the message of Jesus to transcend its Jewish context, and it is the Spirit that impels the church outward to bring the gospel to the whole world.

Another distinguishing feature of Luke's work is his relatively positive treatment of women. Although some scholars have argued that certain passages may be functioning to keep women in their place (e.g., the story of Mary and Martha in Luke 10:38-42), the dominant treatment of women in this Gospel stands in striking contrast to the patriarchal presuppositions of the time.[37] In the infancy narratives, Elizabeth, Mary, and Anna embody the best features of the Israelite tradition. We find women in the public company of Jesus, and women appear much more frequently as positive characters in Jesus' parables.[38]

Another very influential image of the church hinted at in other places but explicit in Acts of the Apostles is the image of the church as a "community of brothers and sisters." Some form of the Greek term *adelphos*, or "brother/sister," appears fifty-seven times in Acts of the Apostles. It is commonly, though not exclusively, used to designate all the followers of Christ, particularly those in

---

[37] Barbara Reid, *Choosing the Better Part?: Women in the Gospel of Luke* (Collegeville, Minn.: Liturgical Press, 1996).
[38] Harrington, 111.

Jerusalem.[39] The term stresses the establishment of new bonds of community like those established by kinship but now on the basis of a kinship of faith rather than blood.

Earlier we recalled Israel's sense of itself as a holy people called into covenant relationship with God, not by virtue of its own merit but as the result of God's free election. Some early Christians returned to this vision in their reflection on their own identity before God. It is now commonly accepted that 1 Peter was not written by the apostle Peter but may have come from a Petrine tradition with its origins in the preaching of Peter. It was probably written between 70 and 90 C.E. The text draws on images found in the Hebrew Scriptures in the Book of Exodus of Israel as a priestly people:

> Come to him, a living stone, though rejected by mortals yet chosen and precious in God's sight, and like living stones, let yourselves be built into a spiritual house, to be a holy priesthood, to offer spiritual sacrifices acceptable to God through Jesus Christ. For it stands in scripture:
> "'See, I am laying in Zion a stone,
>   a cornerstone chosen and precious;
>   and whoever believes in him will not be put to shame."
> To you then who believe, he is precious; but for those who do not believe,
>   "The stone that the builders rejected
>   has become the very head of the corner,"
> and
>   "A stone that makes them stumble,
>   and a rock that makes them fall."
> They stumble because they disobey the word, as they were destined to do.
>   But you are a chosen race, a royal priesthood, a holy nation, God's own people, in order that you may proclaim the mighty acts of him who called you out of darkness into his marvelous light.
>   Once you were not a people,
>   but now you are God's people;
>   once you had not received mercy,
>   but now you have received mercy. (1 Pet. 2:4-10)

The hope of Israel has now been fulfilled in Jesus such that those who believe in Jesus are now part of God's people. The people of God is no longer to be defined by race but by faith in Christ. Membership into God's people is

---

[39] Jean Rigal, *L'ecclésiologie de communion: Son évolution historique et ses fondements* (Paris: Cerf, 1996), 19.

brought about by baptism. A central theme in the Tanakh returns here: just as membership in the covenant with Yahweh was the consequence not of human effort or merit but of God's election, so too the Christian community is constituted by election at God's initiative.

1 Peter also explores the image of the church as a brotherhood or sisterhood captured in the use of the term *adelphos,* as we saw in the Acts of the Apostles. In 1 Peter the Greek *adelphotēs* (fraternity) is used as a technical term to refer to the church in which believers have become brothers and sisters by Christian initiation—it is the church itself that now is called a fraternity.[40] While "fraternity" is not a dominant term for the church in the New Testament, it will be a favorite image of the later church writers.

Discerning a nascent ecclesiology in the Synoptic Gospels is no easy task. One must draw a number of inferences from each Gospel's presentation of Jesus' life and ministry in order to posit a distinctive vision of the Christian community. Regarding Mark's Gospel, for example, the spare narrative does not provide a wealth of clues about the evangelist's understanding of community. Mark's Gospel is from first to last a story of Jesus, the suffering Messiah whose true identity is disclosed only on the cross. Yet we do find in this Gospel a theme that plays itself out in all three Synoptic Gospels, and that is the theme of discipleship. When we consider the significant role that blood relations played in ancient Jewish identity the following pericope is particularly illuminating:

> Then his mother and his brothers came; and standing outside, they sent to him and called him. A crowd was sitting around him; and they said to him, "Your mother and your brothers and sisters are outside, asking for you." And he replied, "Who are my mother and my brothers?" And looking at those who sat around him, he said, "Here are my mother and my brothers! Whoever does the will of God is my brother and sister and mother."(Mark 3:31-35)

Communal identity is no longer to be attached to kinship or ethnicity but to a more profound spiritual bond established through common discipleship. Moreover, the shape of Christian discipleship is determined by the model of the suffering Messiah. Christian discipleship, that is, will be marked by the cross.[41]

---

[40] Michel Dujarier, *L'Église fraternité: les origines de l'expression adelphotès-fraternitas aux trois premiers siècles du christianisme* (Paris: Cerf, 1991), 33.

[41] Harrington, 104.

It is commonly accepted today that the authors of both Matthew and Luke had Mark's Gospel in front of them and adapted it freely in order to present the Christian message most effectively to their particular audiences. The predominantly Jewish-Christian character of the community associated with the Gospel of Matthew provides a distinctive ecclesiological perspective. Matthew's Gospel is the only Gospel actually to use the word *ekklēsia*. Struggling with the extent to which Judaism would continue to lay claim to Christian identity, the community of Matthew seemed much more interested in structural continuities with Judaism. Jesus' own teaching is resituated within first-century rabbinic debates, such as the question of working on the Sabbath. The teaching responsibilities of the synagogue are transferred to the early Christian communities, and the apostles are portrayed as the new rabbis (with Peter offered as the chief rabbi possessing the power to "bind and loose," an expression imported from synagogal authoritative structures) who will be called to teach the new law of Jesus Christ.

The ecclesiology of the Johannine community stands in sharp contrast to that of Paul. Where Paul's principal ecclesial metaphor, the body, stressed ecclesial interdependence among its members, the Johannine model focuses on the vertical relationship between Christ and believer. This is reflected in the two images of the church found in John's Gospel, the vine and branches (John 15:5) and the sheep and shepherd (John 10:1-16). In both sets of images it is the vertical relationship with Christ rather than the horizontal relationships among church members that is stressed. This suggests a vision of the Christian community that is much more egalitarian. The primary category within the community of followers of Jesus is not that of the apostle but that of the disciple. In fact, the Greek word *apostolos* never appears in the Johannine literature. After Christ's resurrection it is the Paraclete-Spirit who continues Christ's presence in the Christian community, and it is this Spirit that preserves the community in truth.

The Johannine literature is well known for its so-called love mysticism. It is a theme not without its implications for Christian community. The followers of Jesus ought to be distinguished by their life of love: "I give you a new commandment, that you love one another. Just as I have loved you, you also should love one another. By this everyone will know that you are my disciples, if you have love for one another" (John 13:34-35). This teaching had already been enacted in a story, unique to John and placed at the Last Supper, namely, the washing of feet. In this story Jesus offers his own actions as an example of that loving service that should characterize the actions of the Christian community. In the First Letter of John, love defines the spiritual bonds of community. Here we see a distinctive appropriation of the notion of *koinōnia* that already appeared in Paul's writing and in the Acts of the Apostles. "We declare to you what we have seen and heard so that you also may have fellowship with us; and truly our fellowship is with the Father and with his Son Jesus Christ" (1 John 1:3). For the author of the first Johannine epistle, there is a mystical unity between love of God and love for one another:

> God is love, and those who abide in love abide in God, and God abides in them.... Those who say, "I love God," and hate their brothers or sisters, are liars; for those who do not love a brother or sister whom they have seen, cannot love God whom they have not seen. The commandment we have from him is this: those who love God must love their brothers and sisters also. (1 John 4:16b, 20-21)

By recognizing the inseparability of the life of love and communion with God, the Johannine tradition, in its own way, affirms the unity of the so-called vertical and horizontal dimensions of communion.

Ironically, the egalitarian nature of the Johannine community, with its emphasis on the equality of discipleship and its claim that each believer possesses the Spirit, may have ultimately contributed to its demise. In this epistle we find evidence of a fierce polemic between competing Christian factions. We, of course, get to hear only one side of the polemic as the Johannine community claims the Spirit for itself and dismisses the other factions as "Antichrists."

STRUCTURING OF MINISTRY IN THE CHURCHES OF THE NEW TESTAMENT

We cannot speak with any real historical exactitude about the nature of ecclesial ministry in the first few decades of the church's existence. Because of the initial Christian expectations for the imminent second coming of Christ, there was very little concern for lasting ministerial structures. Only as the church began to realize that the *parousia* was not necessarily imminent did stable ministerial forms receive more attention.

The first Christian communities were predominantly Jewish-Christian, and so it was natural that certain leadership structures borrowed from the Jewish synagogue would be adapted to the demands of the Christian community. Some communities were apparently led by a group of elders (*presbyteroi*) modeled after the leadership of the elders in the synagogue. Other early Christian communities included a leadership role for itinerant prophets who would move from community to community proclaiming God's message to the Christian people. There is some evidence to suggest that these prophets may even have presided at the eucharist. This less institutional style of leadership, however, soon became associated with certain heretical sects such as Montanism and Gnosticism and would be opposed by a greater emphasis on a stable church office. Even among those communities who were not led by the prophets, these itinerants held a very important role in the early communities.

Our best sources for learning about the nature of ministry in the early church are the writings of Paul. In his letters Paul describes largely urban communities which met in households and were sustained by a plurality of gifts, or charisms. Much has been made of the place of charisms in the early church, with the result that some scholars have assumed a more technical and precise understanding of charism in the early church than may be warranted by the evidence. Paul uses the term to refer to any among a variety of spiritual gifts. In general, however, it can be said that Paul did not view charisms as gifts given to an individual; rather they manifested themselves in an individual believer for the sake of the church: "since you are eager for spiritual gifts, strive to excel in them for building up the church" (1 Cor. 14:12). What we think of as formal ministries would appear to have been simply one form of the more general category of charisms. Paul assumed that all believers would participate in the building up of the life of the community and its mission in the world. At the same time, Paul did acknowledge more stable forms of service in the life of the community that he referred to as *diakonia*.[42] The term *diakonia*, often translated as "service," did not refer to some menial activity but to one's having been sent or commissioned to fulfill the work or mandate of another. Paul recognized a rudimentary ordering of these ministries:

> Now you are the body of Christ and individually members of it. And God has appointed in the church first apostles, second prophets, third teachers; then deeds of power, then gifts of healing, forms of assistance, forms of leadership, various kinds of tongues. Are all apostles? Are all prophets? Are all teachers? Do all work miracles? Do all possess gifts of healing? Do all speak in tongues? Do all interpret? But strive for the greater gifts. And I will show you a still more excellent way. (1 Cor. 12: 27-31)

According to Paul, although there might be an ordering of charisms or ministries, no one ministry was superior to the others.

---

[42] At the forefront of this scholarship is the work of John N. Collins. See his *Diakonia: Re-interpreting the Ancient Sources* (New York: Oxford University Press, 1990); idem, *Are All Christians Ministers?* (Collegeville, Minn.: Liturgical Press, 1992); idem, *Deacons and the Church: Making Connections between Old and New* (Harrisburg, Pa.: Morehouse, 2002).

For as in one body we have many members, and not all the members have the same function, so we, who are many, are one body in Christ, and individually we are members one of another. We have gifts that differ according to the grace given to us: prophecy, in proportion to faith; ministry, in ministering; the teacher, in teaching; the exhorter, in exhortation; the giver, in generosity; the leader, in diligence; the compassionate, in cheerfulness. (Rom. 12: 4-8)

These various gifts and ministries both enriched and, on occasion, divided the communities. There appeared to be a gradation in the stability of these many gifts with some being relatively occasional and others manifesting a certain degree of permanence. Lists such as this reveal less about the specific character of any of these ministries than about their diversity and fluidity.[43]

At various points Paul refers to "apostles," "rulers" of local communities (1 Thess. 5:12) and "hosts" of house churches (1 Cor. 16:19; Rom. 16:5). His letter to the Philippians mentions "bishops and deacons" (*episkopois* and *diakonois* [Phil. 1:1]), titles that, however, were not yet anything like the developed offices those terms would designate a century later. At this point it is probably better to stay with a more literal rendering of those terms as simply "overseers" and "helpers." Whatever the precise meaning of these terms, they do suggest some degree of formal ministerial responsibilities differentiated from the charisms exercised by each baptized member of the community.

The scholarly appraisal of the ministerial structures of the Pauline communities has been hampered for centuries by Protestant–Catholic polemics. Many Protestant scholars in the late nineteenth and early twentieth centuries emphasized the charismatic structure of the Pauline communities.[44] Catholic, Anglican, and Reformed scholarship, on the other hand, stressed the priority of institutional apostolic office.[45] This tension between office and charism is hardly a new development. Indeed, we should recall that even ancient Israel

---

[43] Thomas F. O'Meara, *Theology of Ministry*, rev. ed. (New York: Paulist Press, 1999), 67.

[44] The classic articulation was by Rudolph Sohm, *Kirchenrecht I: Die geschichtlichen Grundlagen* (Leipzig: Duncker & Humblot, 1892). Twentieth-century figures influenced by this approach include Hans von Campenhausen, *Ecclesiastical Authority and Spiritual Power in the Church of the First Three Centuries* (Stanford, Calif.: Stanford University Press, 1969), and Ernst Käsemann, "Ministry and Communion in the New Testament," in idem, *Essays on New Testament Themes* (London: SCM, 1964), 63-94.

[45] For the Reformed perspective, see Philippe-H. Menoud, *L'Eglise et les ministères selon le Nouveau Testament* (Neuchâtel: Delachaux & Niestlé, 1949). From the Anglican perspective, see Gregory Dix, "The Ministry in the Early Church," in *The Apostolic Ministry*, ed. K. E. Kirk (London: Hodder & Stoughton, 1946), 183-303. Finally, for a mid-twentieth-century Catholic viewpoint that contrasts the necessary role of church office with the strictly optional role of charisms, see Joseph Brosch, *Charismen und Ämter in der Urkirche* (Bonn: P. Hanstein, 1951).

struggled with a similar tension in its ambiguous assessment of the monarchy begun with Saul. A thousand years before Jesus of Nazareth, Israel sought to hold in tension the need for stability in leadership with the conviction that, for Israel, God alone was king. This tension simply continued in Christianity, albeit in a new key.

In the last fifty years, however, a more balanced perspective seems to be emerging. This perspective recognizes the anachronistic character of both the "charism-versus-office" framework when applied to first-century Christianity and the assumption that a technical understanding of charism was already present in Paul's thought.[46] Contemporary scholars are more inclined to assert a more fluid continuum of gifts in the Pauline churches that were exercised in more or less stable forms.[47]

When we turn to the communities out of which the Pastoral Letters emerged, perhaps a full generation after Paul, evidence of more structured church leadership abounds. Daniel Harrington contends that what we may be seeing here are two distinct models of leadership structures: the first coming from predominantly Jewish-Christian communities and offering a presbyteral structure, and the second coming from Pauline communities that were largely Gentile in makeup and employed the bishop-deacon structure drawn from leadership models found in the Greco-Roman world. If this is the case, the Pastoral Letters may reflect a later stage in which these two models are beginning to come together.[48] Titles such as *diakonos, presbyteros,* and *episkopos* (deacon, presbyter, bishop) emerge, but with unclear distinctions; the latter two titles may at times have been used interchangeably.

Given the importance of the question in the contemporary church, we know surprisingly little about who actually held these early church leadership positions. Regarding the role of women, for example, contemporary biblical scholars have highlighted evidence suggesting the role that women may well have played as church leaders and ministers. These studies draw attention to Pauline references to Phoebe (Rom. 16:9), whom Paul refers to as a *diakonos,* and Prisca and her husband, Aquila, who are referred to by Paul as "co-workers" (Rom.

---

[46] Albert Vanhoye, "The Biblical Question of 'Charisms' after Vatican II," in *Vatican II: Assessments and Perspectives,* volume 1, ed. René Latourelle (New York: Paulist Press, 1988), 439-68.

[47] Enrique Nardoni, "Charism in the Early Church since Rudolph Sohm: An Ecumenical Challenge," *Theological Studies* 53 (1992): 646-62.

[48] Harrington, 162. For more on the influence of synagogal structures on the emergence of Christian leadership structures, see James T. Burtchaell, *From Synagogue to Church: Public Services and Offices in the Earliest Christian Communities* (Cambridge: Cambridge University Press, 1992). For more on the influence of the Greco-Roman social world, see Meeks; and Margaret Y. MacDonald, *The Pauline Churches: A Socio-historical Study of Institutionalization in the Pauline and Deutero-Pauline Writings,* Society for New Testament Studies Monograph Series 60 (Cambridge: Cambridge University Press, 1988).

16:3-5).[49] However, by the time of the Pastoral Letters (1 and 2 Timothy, Titus), likely written a full generation after the authentic Pauline letters, we see the influence of household codes that discouraged the leadership of women.[50] If a form of gender egalitarianism ever existed—and there is some evidence that it did at least as an ideal—it was unable to survive against forces both internal and external to the community.

As we assess the broad range of ecclesiological trajectories evident in the biblical literature, a number of points need to be made.[51] We must resist trying to identify some *ur*-ecclesiology underlying the diverse traditions. For the first generations of Christians, their communal consciousness was marked by a startling diversity of theological starting points. Yet it is possible to recognize some central and frequently recurring themes. First, when we begin with a consideration of Jesus' own teaching and ministry, we recognize the priority of the kingdom of God. Although it is difficult to assert that Jesus established anything like an institutional church, it is undeniable that he called forth a community of disciples in order to share in and continue his mission to proclaim and realize the coming reign of God. The call to mission is grounded in Jesus' own ministry and teaching. This theme receives dramatic development in Acts of the Apostles.

Second, whether or not the term *koinōnia* was explicitly employed, the relational underpinnings of Christian community can be recognized in virtually every biblical trajectory. There is little extended consideration of the spirituality of the individual Christian; the Christian life is conceived always as a life of shared belonging and discipleship. Third, this shared belonging was articulated in a rich diversity of metaphors each of which suggested a spiritually grounded solidarity among believers (e.g., "the body of Christ," "a priestly people," "a flock" a "fraternity"). Fourth, relative to our contemporary ecclesial setting, it is striking to realize that, with the possible exception of the communities associated with the Pastoral Letters, specific church structures received relatively little attention. Where formal structures of ministry were considered at all, they were conceived relationally as a call to public communal service rather than as an opportunity for the discrete exercise of power. We can see in numerous passages concerns regarding the Christian analogue to the "royal con-

---

[49] Schüssler Fiorenza, 160-84; Carolyn Osiek and Kevin Madigan, eds., *Ordained Women in the Early Church: A Documentary History* (Baltimore: Johns Hopkins University Press, 2005).

[50] Hervé Legrand, "*Traditio perpetuo servata?* The Non-ordination of Women: Tradition or Simply an Historical Fact?" *Worship* 65 (1991): 482-508.

[51] For an excellent survey of these trajectories, particularly as they relate to the rise of leadership structures, see Raymond E. Brown, *The Churches the Apostles Left Behind* (New York: Paulist Press, 1984).

sciousness" associated with the ancient Israelite monarchy. In the Synoptic Gospels there are injunctions against exercising ecclesial authority in the manner of Gentile rulers (Mark 10:42-45; Matt. 20:25-28) or the scribes and Pharisees (Matt. 23:1-7). Paul defended his authority as a service of the gospel (cf. Gal 1:1-9) directed toward the building up rather than the tearing down of the church of Jesus Christ (cf. 2 Cor. 13:10).

This chapter's brief survey of ecclesiological themes and perspectives in the Scriptures cannot do justice to the richness of the many biblical treatments of community. It is hoped, however, that this sketch demonstrates that there was no single theology of community from which all later views were derived. From the very beginning, conversion to the life of discipleship, the way of Jesus Christ, gave rise to divergent yet complementary accounts of Christian community. This ecclesiological diversity will continue throughout the history of the church, often in spite of sporadic attempts to impose one ecclesiological vision upon the church. It is beyond the scope of this work to trace the history of ecclesiology over two millennia. For that one might well turn to Yves Congar's magisterial *L'Église de Saint Augustin à l'époque moderne* or the more recent two-volume work of Roger Haight, *Christian Community in History.*[52] In the chapters that follow, we will explore some fundamental perspectives on the church based on a reconsideration of the four marks of the church in global perspective.

QUESTIONS FOR REFLECTION

1. What was gained and what was lost with ancient Israel's adoption of the monarchy? How has Christianity had to struggle with the same temptations?
2. What are some ways in which a Christian theology of mission can be informed and enriched by the Hebrew Scriptures?
3. What are some of the benefits of considering the origins of Christianity as an emerging Jesus movement rather than as a fully developed religious institution?
4. Christian politicians today often speak of "family values." How does Jesus' teachings about discipleship and the reign of God turn conventional understandings of family values on their head?
5. How do two distinct metaphors—Paul's metaphor of the body and John's metaphor of the vine and branches—complement each other and illuminate important aspects of Christian community?

---

[52] Yves Congar, *L'Église de Saint Augustin à l'époque moderne* (Paris: Cerf, 1970); Roger Haight, *Christian Community in History*, 2 vols. (New York: Continuum, 2004-5).

SUGGESTIONS FOR FURTHER READING AND STUDY

Brown, Raymond E. *The Churches the Apostles Left Behind*. New York: Paulist Press, 1984.

Brueggemann, Walter. *The Prophetic Imagination*. 2nd ed. Minneapolis: Fortress, 2001.

Dunn, James D. G. *Unity and Diversity in the New Testament: An Inquiry into the Character of Earliest Christianity*. 3rd ed. London: SCM, 2006.

Gager, John C. *Kingdom and Community: The Social World of Early Christianity*. Englewood Cliffs, N.J.: Prentice-Hall, 1975.

Hanson, Paul D. *The People Called: The Growth of Community in the Bible*. Louisville: Westminster John Knox, 1986.

Harrington, Daniel J. *The Church According to the New Testament: What the Wisdom and Witness of Early Christianity Teach Us Today*. Franklin, Wis.: Sheed & Ward, 2001.

Lohfink, Gerhard. *Jesus and Community: The Social Dimension of Christian Faith*. New York: Paulist Press, 1984.

Meeks, Wayne A. *The First Urban Christians: The Social World of the Apostle Paul*. New Haven: Yale University Press, 1983.

Okoye, James Chukwuma. *Israel and the Nations: A Mission Theology of the Old Testament*. American Society of Missiology Series 39. Maryknoll, N.Y.: Orbis Books, 2006.

Schüssler Fiorenza, Elisabeth. *In Memory of Her: A Feminist Theological Reconstruction of Christian Origins*. New York: Crossroad, 1983.

Theissen, Gerd. *The Gospels in Context: Social and Political History in the Synoptic Tradition*. New York: T&T Clark, 2004.

———. *The Social Setting of Pauline Christianity: Essays on Corinth*. Philadelphia: Fortress, 1982.

2

A People Sent in Mission

In ecclesiological reflections guided by the four marks of the church, the unity of the church is the customary starting point. However, if we consider the beginnings of the Christian movement, I believe a case can be made that early Christian communal consciousness was as much oriented toward the church's catholicity and sense of mission as it was toward its unity. The church's catholicity reminds us that ecclesial unity is always a *differentiated* unity, a unity-in-diversity. The oneness of the faith is often discovered only by first courageously attending to what manifests itself as foreign or different.

The goodness of difference finds its first religious warrant, for Christians, in the doctrine of creation. If creation has been created good, then much that appears different and threatening in the world must be open, in principle, to a unity that celebrates rather than recoils from the reality of created difference. The ancient doctrine of *creatio ex nihilo* means, as Peter Phan has put it, that creation

> is not a mere prolongation of the same divine substance into time and space, as emanationists suggest. Rather, it consists in bringing into existence a genuine other, ontologically different from the divine, which reflects and embodies divine plurality in the variety and multiplicity of creation.[1]

The incarnation itself further warrants the goodness of difference in its conviction that God has truly become other than God's self in Jesus of Nazareth. Finally, Christians celebrate difference as grounded in the triune being of God, who is a tri-unity of distinct subsistent relations. Consequently, created distance need not be opposed to unity but may in fact be a condition for its possibility. Catholicity is a theological expression of this reality that the reach of God's love is neither divisive nor oppressive but gathers up genuine difference in an inclusive wholeness.

---

[1] Peter C. Phan, *Being Religious Interreligiously: Asian Perspectives on Interfaith Dialogue* (Maryknoll, N.Y.: Orbis Books, 2004), xxi.

Katholikos is derived from the two Greek words, *kath' holou*, which might be translated as "pertaining to or oriented toward the whole." Although it is the perpetual temptation of the church to rebuff difference in favor of a stifling uniformity, such a view cannot be reconciled with an authentic appreciation for the church's catholicity. The catholicity of the church also presupposes an understanding of Christian mission. It is the conviction that no aspect of creation is inhospitable to the good news of Jesus Christ that has led Christians from the very beginning to preach the gospel to all nations. All cultures are potentially receptive to the gospel, and all cultures have gifts to offer for the enrichment of the gospel.

In this chapter we will reflect on the church's catholicity from the perspective of what we might call dialogical mission, a belief that the church's catholicity is enriched by a courageous and respectful engagement with the diversity of created reality out of the conviction that God's Spirit will create something new and wonderful out of this engagement for the benefit of both church and creation.

CATHOLICITY IN THE BIBLICAL TRADITION

The catholicity of the church was anticipated in the Hebrew Scriptures. Texts in the Hebrew Scriptures that stressed the ethnic purity of God's people were often challenged by other passages that contained the seeds of a more universal vision. One of the seminal events for the history of Israel was the Babylonian captivity. That event instigated two quite different responses. One was to see the Babylonian captivity as a punishment for mingling with other nations. This response led to the emphasis in Second Temple Judaism on Jewish exclusivism. A second response saw the return from captivity as an opportunity for a new beginning. In Second Isaiah, the author interprets the return from exile as a new exodus with the hope that a reconstituted Israel might become a servant community offering God's salvation to the world: "I will give you as a light to the nations, that my salvation may reach to the end of the earth" (Isa. 49:6). The covenant was not only for Israel but was a promise offered to all peoples. The Books of Ruth and Jonah offered two distinct voices dissenting from the exclusivism that preoccupied much of Second Temple Judaism. These texts suggest that there were ancient Jewish voices already articulating the "catholicity," if you will, of God's covenant.

Although the term *katholikos* does not appear in the New Testament, there is no more profound exposition of its meaning and ecclesial logic than that found in the Acts of the Apostles. The central theme of Acts is the coming to be of the church as a missionary community confident that the gospel is hospitable to all peoples and cultures. Consider Jesus' final words to his disciples prior to his ascension: "But you will receive power when the Holy Spirit has come upon you; and you will be my witnesses in Jerusalem, in all Judea and Samaria, and to the ends of the earth" (Acts 1:8). The catholicity of the church is revealed in and through the church's missionary mandate.

Stephen Bevans and Roger Schroeder write: "One of the most important things Christians need to know about the church is that the *church* is not of ultimate importance."[2] According to Acts, the church was constituted by the Spirit in the upper room, but only as a community sent forth in mission. Luke recounts this mission unfolding in progressive stages. In the story of Pentecost human language becomes itself a metaphor for how the catholicity of the church unfolds in the church's mission:

> When the day of Pentecost had come, they were all together in one place. And suddenly from heaven there came a sound like the rush of a violent wind, and it filled the entire house where they were sitting. Divided tongues, as of fire, appeared among them, and a tongue rested on each of them. All of them were filled with the Holy Spirit and began to speak in other languages, as the Spirit gave them ability.
>
> Now there were devout Jews from every nation under heaven living in Jerusalem. And at this sound the crowd gathered and was bewildered, because each one heard them speaking in the native language of each. Amazed and astonished, they asked, "Are not all these who are speaking Galileans? And how is it that we hear, each of us, in our own native language? Parthians, Medes, Elamites, and residents of Mesopotamia, Judea and Cappadocia, Pontus and Asia, Phrygia and Pamphylia, Egypt and the parts of Libya belonging to Cyrene, and visitors from Rome, both Jews and proselytes, Cretans and Arabs—in our own languages we hear them speaking about God's deeds of power." (Acts 2:1-11)

After Christ's death and resurrection, the Holy Spirit came down upon the believers gathered in Jerusalem. As those who received the Holy Spirit gave testimony to God's deeds, Jewish foreigners from throughout the known world all heard and comprehended their testimonies. The differences of language were transcended by the Spirit, allowing each to understand the other. Yet note that those from other lands heard those giving witness *in their own languages*. Cultural difference was not destroyed but became the very instrument for a realization of a more profound spiritual unity.

---

[2] Stephen B. Bevans and Roger P. Schroeder, *Constants in Context: A Theology of Mission for Today* (Maryknoll, N.Y.: Orbis Books, 2004), 7.

This biblical narrative of the origins of the church suggests an essential ecclesiological principle: the Holy Spirit does not erase difference but renders difference nondivisive. The account suggests that the church, born of the Spirit, is from its beginning open to diverse languages and cultures. Those gathered in Jerusalem were still Jews, even if from the culturally diverse Jewish Diaspora. Acts tells the story of a new religious movement that began in Jerusalem and then moved outward, becoming progressively more inclusive in its reach.[3] Chapter 8 recounts the ministry of Philip, who first preaches, quite successfully, to the despised Samaritans and then to the Ethiopian eunuch. The former were considered, at best, half Jews, and the eunuch was likely a member of a group of people known as "Godfearers," who were uncircumcised yet sympathetic to Judaism.

The next stage is reflected in the narrative of "the conversion of Peter" in Acts 10-11.[4] After receiving a disturbing vision in which he was instructed by God to eat unclean food, Peter was invited to the house of the Gentile centurion Cornelius. There Peter perceived more fully the universal scope of the Christian mission: "I truly understand that God shows no partiality, but in every nation anyone who fears him and does what is right is acceptable to him" (Acts 10:34-35). This insight was confirmed when he witnessed the Holy Spirit descending on all who heard him preach, Jew and Gentile (Acts 10:44-48), in an echo of Pentecost.

This expanding catholicity achieved a new phase in the momentous "council of Jerusalem." It is difficult to exaggerate the significance of this meeting of early Christian leadership. Paul and Barnabas had already been successfully preaching the gospel to both Jews and Gentiles. Apparently this outreach to the Gentiles was not welcomed by all the followers in Antioch. Consequently, Paul and Barnabas were sent to Jerusalem to obtain the approval of the leadership there. After critical debate, the missionaries received the approval of the Jerusalem leadership, and with that Christianity underwent a shift that would have ramifications for centuries to come. There could no longer be a question of limiting the mission to share the gospel of Jesus Christ: the good news of Christ was to be offered to all peoples.

We spoke earlier of catholicity's foundation in the doctrine of creation. In the "Captivity Letters" attributed to Paul, this budding vision of the church's catholicity is further grounded in the incarnation. In the Letter to the Colossians we encounter another biblical term, *plērōma*, generally translated as "fullness," describing the incarnation: "For in him the whole fullness of deity dwells bodily, and you have come to fullness in him who is the head of every ruler

---

[3] What follows draws considerably from Bevans and Schroeder's reading, 14-30.

[4] James D. G. Dunn, *Acts of the Apostles* (Peterborough, U.K.: Epworth, 1996), 10.

and authority" (Col. 2:9-10). This passage articulates an essential, vertical dimension of the church's catholicity—the fullness of God's self-disclosure in Christ.[5] Here we see a central paradox of the Christian faith, namely, that the fullness of God, God's own catholicity if you will, comes into human history in a particular form as a Galilean Jew. Wolfgang Beinert writes:

> Jesus is the entire salvation of God for the entire world. From the perspective of salvation history, the property of catholicity belongs to him in an original and primary way. He and he alone is already "catholicity" in its fullness.[6]

The catholicity of the Christian faith lies in the tension between the universal and the particular. The relationship between the particular and the universal is a topic to which we shall return later.

CATHOLICITY AND THE EARLY MISSIONARY ORIENTATION OF THE CHURCH

Christianity is commonly viewed as a Western religion. This is doubtless because throughout much of the past thousand years, Christianity flourished in Europe. Moreover, it was largely from Europe that Christianity eventually spread, first to the Americas and later to Africa and Asia. This Christian expansion followed closely the European nations' pretensions to global empire, and it has long been tainted by that association. The conviction that Christianity is essentially a Western religion has also informed Christian historiography.

Standard accounts of the origins and initial spread of Christianity have highlighted Christianity's inexorable march westward throughout the Mediterranean then up into Gaul and on to England. Many are also familiar with the parallel development of Christianity in the eastern half of the Roman empire, in what would become Byzantium. There, particularly under the leadership of the sixth-century emperor Justinian, the Byzantine church was effectively integrated into the imperial state in a way that would have long-standing consequences for the shape of Byzantine Christianity. Byzantine Christianity and Western Christianity continued for much of the first millennium down a rocky road of increasingly tense relations over political, liturgical, and doctrinal disputes, culminating in the formalization of schism in the early eleventh century.

---

[5] Avery Dulles, *The Catholicity of the Church* (Oxford: Clarendon Press, 1985), 31.
[6] Wolfgang Beinert, "Catholicity as a Property of the Church," *The Jurist* 52 (1992): 455-83, at 469.

However, the story of the origins of Christianity goes far beyond these two orbits.

More recent historiography has drawn our attention to the fact that Christianity grew as fast or faster both east of Jerusalem and along the Nile southward toward Ethiopia.[7] Christianity's expansion in Ethiopia would take it beyond the direct influence of either Rome or Persia, leading to the first genuinely African form of Christian life. There the Scriptures would be translated into the native language of Ge'ez. The Ethiopian Christians were heirs to a Palestinian form of Christianity, and even today certain Ethiopian churches retain such Jewish elements as the observance of dietary laws and a Saturday as well as a Sunday Sabbath.[8]

Some of the most ancient Christian communities were established northeast of Palestine, with the gospel finding expression in the language of Syriac, a dialect closely related to Aramaic. Syriac Christianity retained a strongly Semitic character, particularly in its liturgy and theology. This presented a striking contrast to the more hellenized forms of Christianity that would eventually flourish in Byzantium and the Western church. It is primarily in the language of Syriac that the gospel would spread eastward through Mesopotamia and Persia, on to India, Tibet, Mongolia, and China.[9]

In the third century Christian merchants and, eventually, a missionary known as St. Gregory the Illuminator, brought the Christian faith to Armenia, creating an Armenian church that represented yet another distinctive form of Christianity, one still preserved today in the Armenian Apostolic and the Armenian Catholic churches. Christianity would extend as well into the boundaries of the Persian empire, where Christians often faced persecution because of suspicions that they were sympathetic to the rival Roman empire. Christianity in Persia also retained certain Jewish elements even as it interacted with the dominant Zoroastrian religion of the region. The unique form of Persian Christianity is reflected in the originality of two of its most distinguished early theologians, Aphraates and Ephraem, whose thought was largely free of Hellenistic philosophical influences. As but one indication of the originality of their thought, both employed feminine images of the Holy Spirit in their theological reflections.[10] Christianity in this region struggled to survive as it would face oppression at the hands of the Zoroastrian majority. By the sev-

---

[7] Bevans and Schroeder, 75-98.

[8] Ronald Roberson, *The Eastern Christian Churches: A Brief Survey*, 6th ed. (Rome: Edizioni Orientalia Christiania, 1999), 31.

[9] Dale T. Irvin and Scott W. Sunquist, *History of the World Christian Movement*, volume 1 (Maryknoll, N.Y.: Orbis Books, 2001), 57.

[10] Ibid., 197-98.

enth century, Persian Christians would be overwhelmed by the rapid growth of Islam. From that point on, Persian Christianity would survive only as a beleaguered minority religion in the region. In spite of these obstacles, some Persian missionaries apparently reached India, although legend has it that they were preceded in India by the first-century missionary endeavor of the apostle Thomas. The small Christian enclaves established in India would maintain a tenuous relationship with the communities of Persia while creating their own Christian forms of life. Whatever the origins of this Indian form of Christianity, they maintained a theological and liturgical tradition with affinities to the Assyrian church. One such group, sometimes known as the "Southists," or "Knanaya," claims to have developed from seventy-two Jewish-Christian families who came to India in the fourth century. Today descendants of this eastern missionary imperative are found in the Assyrian church of the East, the Syrian Orthodox church, the Malankara Orthodox Syrian church, the Syro-Malabar Catholic church and the Syro-Malankara Catholic church.[11]

In the seventh century an east Syrian missionary named Alopen reached China during the reign of the T'ang dynasty.[12] He arrived during a period of religious tolerance, so much so that the Chinese emperor encouraged him to translate the Christian Scriptures into Chinese. He and his associates inaugurated a remarkable interaction with Chinese Buddhism. We have discovered a number of provocative treatises authored by either Alopen or a colleague, one of which is titled the *Jesus-Messiah Sutra*; it incorporates a number of Buddhist terms and concepts in its account of the Christian faith. Indeed, this may be the first Christian text authored in Chinese.[13] For almost three centuries a small Christian community with several monasteries survived there, making, however, few Christian converts. As the political tides turned and foreign religions came under suspicion, this community eventually died out.

Finally, as we mark the expansion of Christianity into diverse global contexts, we must note the remarkable missionary endeavors of two brothers, Constantine (later known by his monastic name, Cyril) and Methodius, who in the ninth century undertook a dramatic missionary endeavor to the Slavic nations that had begun to populate the Danube River basin. Traveling together to Moravia, the brothers created a Slavonic alphabet and translated the Scriptures and certain liturgical texts into the Slavic language. This endeavor was opposed by the neighboring Frankish bishops, who were scandalized that the liturgy was being translated into a vernacular tongue.[14] At that time it was

---

[11] For a history of these churches, see Roberson.
[12] Irvin and Sunquist, 314-22.
[13] Ibid., 317.
[14] Ibid., 368.

commonly held that only Hebrew, Greek, and Latin were suitable languages for Christian worship.

This brief sketch of the early expansion of Christianity, far from comprehensive, demonstrates the extent to which, over the course of the first millennium, Christianity was from the beginning global in its impulse, embracing a catholicity quite open to cultural difference. Philip Jenkins captures the import of this development: "Founded in the Near East, Christianity for its first thousand years was stronger in Asia and North Africa than in Europe, and only after about 1400 did Europe (and Europeanized North America) decisively become the Christian heartland."[15] Christianity spread rapidly in part because it was free to communicate not only the Scriptures but the Christian message itself into the language and culture of various peoples. By the end of the first millennium Christianity had long been transposed from its original Hebrew cultural context into a surprising diversity of cultures: Hellenist, Coptic, Armenian, Persian, Syrian, Indian, Slavic, and even Chinese.

Unfortunately, it is also the case that by the end of the millennium many of the Eastern Christian communities outside of Byzantium eventually dissolved into minority Christian enclaves in the face of the spread of the Islamic cultural revolution. The Western church, in turn, increasingly aligned itself with Western political powers and lost all contact with the diverse Christian forms that emerged out of quite different cultural contexts.

CATHOLICITY REDUCED

Our understanding of catholicity is a function of our conception of the church.[16] If the manifestation of the church's catholicity during the first millennium flowed from both the church's missionary impulse and a sense of the universal church as a communion of local churches (a concept we shall explore in a later chapter), the church's ecclesiological foundations shifted dramatically over the course of the second millennium. The theological significance of the local church gradually atrophied, and the universal church achieved a more hierarchical form. Within a fundamentally pyramidal view of the universal church there was little place for a genuine diversity of local churches. The theological and sacramental underpinnings of the church were replaced by canon law, and the church's relationship to the world at large was determined by the

---

[15] Philip Jenkins, *The Next Christendom: The Coming of Global Christianity* (New York: Oxford University Press, 2002), 15.

[16] Beinert, 456.

emergence of Christendom, the complex symbiotic relationship between church and empire that was sustained by a relatively common medieval culture.

A renewed sense of mission emerged in the sixteenth through nineteenth centuries during the so-called Age of Discovery. Christian missionary work often rode the wave of European colonialism. Missionary endeavors to the Americas were shaped by the *padroado* (or *patronatus*) system, in which the pope granted to the royalty of Spain and Portugal principal responsibility for the evangelization of the peoples they encountered in their conquests. Regrettably this often led to the church's complicity in many abuses and the enslavement of indigenous peoples conquered by the explorers and conquistadores. Some studies suggest that as many as sixty million indigenous peoples died either directly or indirectly as a result of these conquests in the Americas.[17]

In Asia the church's missionary endeavors were not so directly tied to military conquest, but they nevertheless depended on the colonial impulse. Missionary work was primarily concerned with the quantitative expansion of the church by way of the *plantatio ecclesiae,* the creation of new churches in mission territories. The conquest paradigm for church mission was still operative inasmuch as missionaries generally disparaged local cultures and sought to purge indigenous peoples of their cultural heritage as a precondition to receiving the gospel. However, the tendency toward the disparagement of local cultures was not universal. Figures like Bartolemé de Las Casas, Matteo Ricci, Roberto de Nobili, and Alexandre de Rhodes all challenged the dominant missionary paradigm of their time.

Early Challenges to the Conquest Paradigm
of Church Mission

Bartolemé de Las Casas (1474-1566) initially traveled to Latin America in 1502.[18] In 1514, having witnessed the enormous cruelty visited upon the indigenous peoples there, Las Casas underwent a profound conversion. He joined the Dominican Order and spent the rest of his life speaking out on behalf of the indigenous populations in the Americas. He vigorously opposed the enslavement of the local peoples, insisting that the human rights of the indigenous be honored and that they be introduced to Christ by way of gentle persuasion.[19] He was later made bishop of Chiapas, Mexico, where he

---

[17] Bevans and Schroeder, 175.

[18] Gustavo Gutiérrez, *Las Casas: In Search of the Poor of Jesus Christ* (Maryknoll, N.Y.: Orbis Books, 1993).

[19] Bevans and Schroeder, 176-77.

continued to speak out on behalf of the Mayan peoples there and against abuses of the Spanish *encomienda*. This was a pernicious economic system in which the conquistadores were encouraged by the church to serve as trustees over the indigenous peoples they conquered, purportedly in order to ensure their evangelization in the Catholic faith.

Las Casas's more prophetic stance toward common missionary practices paralleled the innovative approaches of Jesuit missionaries in South America, who introduced novel missionary strategies based on the creation of "reductions," communities of indigenous peoples placed under Jesuit protection against the slave traders. The Jesuits lived simply among the tribal peoples and went to great lengths to learn their languages while encouraging them to take responsibility for making their communities economically self-sustaining. The egalitarian structure of these communities was somewhat romanticized in the popular film *The Mission*. For all of their legitimate advances, it must be said that the Jesuits were also strict disciplinarians within these communities and did little to encourage indigenous leadership. Nevertheless, their vigorous opposition to the *encomienda* system represented an important protest against a manifestly unjust system.

In Asia, an alternative to the dominant conquest model of missionary outreach appeared, as a few Jesuit missionaries explored a new model that sought to accommodate itself more openly to the local cultures. At the forefront of this new approach was Matteo Ricci's groundbreaking work in China.[20] Ricci and his colleague Michele Ruggieri arrived in 1583 and immediately set about mastering Mandarin and learning all they could from Chinese classical literature. They initially adopted the dress of Buddhist monks, but as their studies continued they eventually took on the role of respected Chinese scholars. Ricci studied Confucianism and was convinced that Confucian terminology could be adapted to Christianity, including the Confucian term for God. He carefully assessed the practice of ancestor veneration and concluded that it had a more cultural than religious function and therefore was not in opposition to the Christian faith. Although he never personally met the emperor, Ricci and his companions were eventually received into the Chinese imperial court and after his death the emperor willingly provided a burial site for him. Ricci's innovative practices were motivated by his conviction that Christianity could thrive in Asia only if it were not perceived as a foreign religion. Unfortunately, Ricci's approach, known as the "Chinese Rites," did not meet with Roman approval.

---

[20] Ibid., 187-89. For more on the innovative Jesuit practices in the East see Andrew Ross, *A Vision Betrayed: The Jesuits in Japan and China, 1542-1742* (Maryknoll, N.Y.: Orbis Books, 1994).

The Jesuits were accused of compromising the faith, and in 1645 they received an injunction from Rome against Ricci's cultural accommodations. This ruling was rescinded upon appeal, but in 1715 Pope Clement XI issued the papal bull *Ex Illa Die*, which formally condemned most of Ricci's views. The condemnation was reiterated in even stronger terms by Pope Benedict XIV in 1742. It was not until 1939 that Pope Pius XII finally rescinded the condemnations.

Another innovative Jesuit missionary, Roberto de Nobili, also challenged the conquest missionary paradigm during his extended stay in India. Upon arriving there, de Nobili set about mastering the languages of Tamil, Telugu, and Sanskrit and generally held local customs and practices in high regard. He studied sacred Hindu texts and envisioned one day creating a seminary that would wed Christian beliefs with Hindu philosophy.[21] One negative consequence of this respect for local culture was his relatively uncritical accommodation to the Indian caste system. This led him to limit his work of evangelization to the upper castes. Only centuries later would Christianity spread to the *dalits*, or "untouchables."

Yet a third Jesuit to work against the dominant missionary paradigm was Alexandre de Rhodes.[22] The Jesuits had sent a few missionaries to Cochinchina (modern-day Vietnam) in 1615. But it was the arrival of de Rhodes that would constitute the real beginning of Vietnamese Christianity. Much like de Nobili and Ricci, de Rhodes immediately adapted himself to local custom and dress. In imitation of Cyril and Methodius, he helped create an entirely new alphabet to facilitate the translation of Christian texts and the creation of a new Vietnamese catechism. He was more suspicious of Confucianism and ancestor veneration than was Ricci, but he did empower indigenous religious leadership, developing many local Vietnamese catechists.

As a final testimony to the fact that Catholic missionary work did not always follow the dominant conquest pattern, we must consider a remarkable document from the Congregation for the Propagation of the Faith. This particular document, published in 1659, was addressed to two bishops of dioceses in Vietnam and offered instructions on dealing with indigenous customs:

> Do not attempt in any way, and do not on any pretext persuade these people to change their rites, habits and customs, unless they are openly opposed to religion and good morals. For what could be more absurd than to bring France, Spain, Italy or any other European country to China? It is not your

---

[21] Bevans and Schroeder, 189-90.

[22] Peter Phan, *Mission and Catechesis: Alexandre de Rhodes and Inculturation in Seventeenth Century Vietnam* (Maryknoll, N.Y.: Orbis Books, 1998).

country but the faith you must bring, that faith which does not reject or belittle the rites or customs of any nation as long as these rites are not evil, but rather desires that they be preserved in their integrity and fostered.[23]

This document demonstrates that in the seventeenth century there were voices heard even in the Vatican advocating greater cultural sensitivity in mission practice.

These noteworthy voices represented an important beginning in the eventual recovery of a theology of mission that respected the integrity of local peoples and their cultures. Each vigorously affirmed the rights of indigenous peoples and each sought to understand local culture on its own terms. Their efforts to accommodate the gospel to local culture had real limits, however. They presumed an artificial distinction between indigenous cultural and religious practices, affirming the former while condemning the latter.[24] Moreover, there was little sense that these cultures were themselves mediations of God's grace.

The Development of the Church's Siege Mentality

The Reformation, and later the Enlightenment, precipitated the gradual demise of Christendom, that uneasy partnership of church and empire that could be traced back to the fourth century. The Reformation rent asunder the precious unity of the Western church of the Middle Ages, and when the seventeenth and eighteenth centuries saw the rise of modern science, the emergence of nationalism and the age of reason, the medieval synthesis of church and culture was lost, replaced by suspicion and festering animosities. The Catholic Church's stance toward the world moved from a confident, if often combative, engagement with society to a defensive siege mentality.

Ecclesiastical pronouncements on "worldly affairs," condemnations of unwarranted state interference in church matters, denunciations of anti-clericalism, and a repeated assertion of the state's obligation to preserve the right of Catholics to practice their faith, all reflected the church's negative judgment on the demise of Christendom and the rise of liberalism.[25] This siege mentality

---

[23] Joseph Neuner and Jacques Dupuis, eds., *The Christian Faith in the Doctrinal Documents of the Catholic Church* (New York: Alba House, 1982), 309-10.

[24] Bevans and Schroeder, 202.

[25] "Liberalism" itself is a contested term, but as used here it refers to what, from Catholicism's perspective, was a cultural perspective shaped by "the Lutheran revolt against the church's authority and on behalf of free examination, in the naturalism of the Renaissance, in the Enlightenment's repudiation of tradition, authority and community, in the secularization of the political sphere, in the posses-

would only be strengthened by the French Revolution. As T. Howland Sanks observed, "if the Age of Reason had threatened the authority of the church in various intellectual spheres, the Age of Revolution threatened its very existence."[26] A certain ecclesial paternalism predominated in Catholicism's engagement with the larger society.

With the pontificate of Leo XIII in the late nineteenth century, the church embarked on a more positive, if still quite cautious, engagement with the issues of the larger world. Yet this stance was short-lived. The violent reaction to Modernism early in the pontificate of Pope Pius X reinforced key elements of the siege mentality preponderant since the Reformation. A largely critical stance toward society continued in the first half of the twentieth century with the papacy issuing sharp rebukes of significant elements of modern capitalism, socialism, industrialism and continuous state encroachment in church matters. Strikingly absent from all of these ecclesial engagements is any sense that the church had anything to learn from the world. In such an ecclesial climate, there could be little place for a sense of the church's catholicity as an embrace of diversity in the church through its engagement with diverse peoples and cultures. When under siege the only appropriate response is a drive for rigorously enforced uniformity in all matters. Such a church could find no place for respectful dialogue with the world and no place for dialogue within the confines of the church itself. It would be left for the pontificate of John XXIII and the Second Vatican Council to reimagine a more dialogical, and therefore a more catholic, church.

THE GRADUAL RECOVERY OF THE CHURCH'S CATHOLICITY

At the heart of the renewal of Vatican II was a reaffirmation of the church's catholicity as something more than geographic expansion. One key component of this reaffirmation was the growing recognition of the theological significance of diverse human cultures, a recognition that began, however haltingly, in the first half of the twentieth century.

---

sive individualism of capitalist economics, and in the cultural anarchy produced by an unrestrained freedom of opinion, speech, and the press. Common to all these developments were an exaltation of the individual and a definition of freedom as exemption from external constraint." Joseph Komonchak, "Vatican II and the Encounter between Catholicism and Liberalism," in *Catholicism and Liberalism: Contributions to American Public Philosophy*, ed. Bruce Douglass and David Hollenbach (Cambridge: Cambridge University Press, 1994), 76-99, at 76.

[26] T. Howland Sanks, *Salt, Leaven and Light: The Community Called Church* (New York: Crossroad, 1992), 99.

Early-Twentieth-Century Developments regarding the Relationship
between Church and Culture

In the early decades of the twentieth century we find several magisterial statements that suggest a new openness to the value of local cultures in the missionary work of the church. In 1919 Pope Benedict XV issued an encyclical
on the missions entitled *Maximum Illud*. In it he emphasized the value of
encouraging indigenous vocations with the idea that eventually indigenous
priests and not foreign missionaries would have primary pastoral responsibility in the new churches. He explicitly warned missionaries to be wary of allowing nationalist loyalties to color their missionary endeavors. He noted how
history reminds us that many unchurched peoples have been repelled from the
faith by missionaries more concerned with nationalistic and cultural conquest
than with preaching the gospel. Missionaries must not be content with a cur-
sory knowledge of local language and custom; rather, they must immerse themselves in the language and cultures of the peoples they would serve.

In 1926, Pope Pius XI wrote his encyclical on the missions entitled *Rerum
Ecclesiae*. He too acknowledged the need for indigenous vocations while also
condemning cultural condescension on the part of missionary clergy. Pope Pius
XII, in 1944, gave an important address to the Pontifical Mission Aid Societies,
which, according to Aylward Shorter, may have included the first ecclesiastical
affirmation of a genuine plurality of cultures.[27] In 1951, Pius XII promulgated
his own encyclical on missions, *Evangelii Praecones*. In that document he
quoted extensively from his 1944 address and offered the following remarkable
statement:

> The herald of the gospel and messenger of Christ is an apostle. His office
> does not demand that he transplant European civilization and culture, and
> no other, to foreign soil, there to take root and propagate itself. His task in
> dealing with these peoples, who sometimes boast a very old and highly
> developed culture of their own, is to teach and form them so that they are
> ready to accept willingly and in a practical manner the principles of Chris-
> tian life and morality; principles, I might add, that fit into any culture, pro-
> vided it be good and sound, and which give that culture greater force in
> safeguarding human dignity and in gaining human happiness.[28]

---

[27] Aylward Shorter, *Toward a Theology of Inculturation* (Maryknoll, N.Y.: Orbis Books, 1988),
183.

[28] *Evangelii Praecones*, in *Modern Missionary Documents and Africa*, ed. Raymond Hickey (Dublin:
Dominican Publications, 1982), 99.

This distinction between the gospel and the cultural forms that mediate the gospel was further developed by Pope John XXIII in his 1959 encyclical *Princeps Pastorum:*

> Whenever authentic values of art and thought can enrich the culture of the human family, the Church is ready to encourage and give her patronage to these products of the spirit. As you know, she does not identify herself with any one culture to the exclusion of the rest—not even with European and Western culture, with which her history is so closely linked.[29]

Statements such as these by twentieth-century popes marked an important advance in church thinking on the diversity of cultures. These statements often clashed, however, with countervailing views that believed that Catholicism possessed its own integral and universal culture. Within the latter framework it might be appropriate for the church to adapt itself to local cultures to a limited extent, but in these instances cultures were viewed more as costumes, external trappings that could be draped interchangeably over a body (the church) without truly affecting the body itself in any substantive way. This limited affirmation of the goodness of diverse cultures was the point of departure for Vatican II's exploration of the nature and scope of the church's catholicity.

Vatican II's Shift to a More Dialogical Conception of Church

John O'Malley, noted church historian, recently observed that the notion of dialogue is found on virtually every page of the conciliar documents.[30] This dialogical vision of the church is grounded in the trinitarian shape of both creation and divine revelation. As the Genesis accounts remind us, God spoke the world into existence by the power of the Spirit. This communicative event of creation is then perfected in the realm of salvation history as the divine Word has continued to be spoken into human history and made effective in the Spirit. Divine self-communication, Vatican II reminded us, achieved its unsurpassable form in the incarnation. The church itself is born out of this dynamism as it receives the one and unsurpassable revelation of God in Christ. The council further elucidates the trinitarian theology of dialogue in *Dei Verbum*, teaching

---

[29] *Princeps Pastorum,* in *Modern Missionary Documents and Africa,* 143.
[30] John W. O'Malley, "Vatican II: Did Anything Happen?" *Theological Studies* 67 (March 2006): 3-33, at 28.

that it is the Holy Spirit who allows the church to receive God's Word. It is the Holy Spirit who

> moves the heart and converts it to God, and opens the eyes of the mind and makes it easy for all to accept and believe the truth. The same Holy Spirit constantly perfects faith by his gifts, so that revelation may be more and more deeply understood. (DV 5)

In this manner, the church is conceived out of the divine dialogue effected at every step by the missions of Word and Spirit. This dialogue is the engine driving a theology of tradition that sees the apostolic faith advancing through an ecclesial engagement between the intimate experience of God's Word available to all believers and the teaching office of the church (DV 8). The necessity of ecclesial dialogue is presupposed in the council's teaching on the sense of the faithful (LG 12) and the need for bishops to consult the faithful (LG 37). It is fundamental to the council's teaching on episcopal collegiality (LG 23).

Written while the council was still in session, Pope Paul VI's underappreciated encyclical *Ecclesiam Suam* offered a theology of dialogue that explicitly influenced the council and found its way into *Gaudium et Spes*:

> In virtue of its mission to enlighten the whole world with the message of the Gospel and to gather together in one spirit all women and men of every nation, race and culture, the church shows itself as a sign of that amity which renders possible sincere dialogue and strengthens it. Such a mission requires us first of all to create in the church itself mutual esteem, reverence and harmony, and to acknowledge all legitimate diversity; in this way all who constitute the one people of God will be able to engage in ever more fruitful dialogue, whether they are pastors or other members of the faithful. For the ties which unite the faithful together are stronger than those which separate them: let there be unity in what is necessary, freedom in what is doubtful, and charity in everything. (GS 92)

This remarkable passage establishes the essential link between the church's catholicity and its dialogical nature. Dialogue with the world, moreover, presupposes that the church preserves its dialogical character in its internal life. A church that cannot embrace new perspectives and even disagreement within the church will never be able to accept new perspectives and disagreement in its relationship with the world.[31]

---

[31] Two seminal works that have pursued a more thoroughgoing, dialogical ecclesiology are Bradford Hinze, *Practices of Dialogue in the Roman Catholic Church: Aims and Obstacles, Lessons and Laments*

Vatican II's Teaching on the Catholicity of the Church

In *Lumen Gentium* the council expressed the church's catholicity as a unity-in-diversity:

> In virtue of this catholicity, each part contributes its own gifts to other parts and to the entire church, so that the whole and each of the parts are strengthened by the common sharing of all things and by the common effort to achieve fullness in unity. (LG 13)

The council's treatment of the church's catholicity was extended much further, however.

As we shall see in the next chapter, the church's catholicity was extended to include all Christian peoples (LG 15). Moreover, the council suggested that all peoples—Jews, Muslims, practitioners of other great religious traditions, spiritual seekers, and men and women of good will—are in some way related to the church (LG 16-17). This theological appreciation for the church's catholicity was further enriched by the following themes: the church's missiological orientation toward the world, reflections on the biblical metaphor of the reign of God, and a new consideration of the relationship between church and culture.

Catholicity and the Mission of the Church in the World

For much of the first millennium, Christian missionary endeavors were motivated by a desire to spread the gospel and a willingness to see this gospel incarnated in diverse cultural contexts. For much of the second millennium, however, Christian mission was oriented toward the salvation of souls and the quantitative expansion of the church into new territories by way of the *plantatio ecclesiae*. Christian mission served the expansion of the church.

The encyclicals of Pope John XXIII and Vatican II's *Gaudium et Spes* inaugurated a different stage in the church's mission by linking it to a new form of ecclesial engagement with the world. This new form of engagement with the world was reflected in Pope John's two social encyclicals, *Mater et Magistra* and *Pacem in Terris*. The spirit of these documents, along with Pope John's stirring speech at the opening of the council, encouraged the bishops to establish a fresh period of interaction with the world. If a broad agreement had existed among the members of the council that a new stance toward the larger world was required, significant disagreements emerged when they attempted to flesh out the specific shape of this new orientation.

(New York: Continuum, 2006), and Gerard Mannion, *Ecclesiology and Postmodernity: Questions for the Church in Our Time* (Collegeville, Minn.: Liturgical Press, 2007).

Many depictions of the fault lines of debates at the council focus on disagreements between "progressive" bishops open to church reform and "traditionalists" who resisted reform. However, the lines of debate regarding the document that would become *Gaudium et Spes* were quite different. Bishops and *periti* belonging to the "progressive" camp disagreed with one another when it came to articulating an adequate exposition of the church's relationship to the world. On the one hand, there were influential figures who adopted a more Thomistic anthropology that granted a genuine, if limited, autonomy to the natural order and viewed grace not so much as a divine force sent to "fix" what was broken as a divine principle that transcendentally elevated the natural order, bringing it to its perfection.[32] Without wishing to deny the reality of human sinfulness, those who promoted this perspective were more willing to grant the limited, but still positive, natural potentialities of the human person and human society, even as they acknowledged the need for these potentialities to find their fulfillment in the life of grace.

On the other hand, there were also many bishops and *periti* who advocated a more Augustinian anthropological perspective, one that would draw a sharp line between sin and grace. Grace was a divine force oriented toward the healing of a fundamentally broken human nature. For these council members and theologians, the natural order possessed no autonomous status, serving primarily as the arena for the working out of the drama between sin and grace in human history. These figures were quite concerned that early versions of the text seemed influenced by the neoscholastic tendency merely to juxtapose the natural and supernatural orders rather than configuring them in their constitutive relation to one another.[33] They simply did not believe that events transpiring in the natural order could serve in any significant way as a preparation for the working of God's grace in the world.

Forty years after the promulgation of the pastoral constitution, these disputes are seen in a different light. *Gaudium et Spes* has been accused of excessive optimism as regards its stance toward the world. Yet the document certainly affirmed the reality of human sin:

> Often refusing to acknowledge God as their source, men and women have also upset the relationship which should link them to their final destiny; and at the same time they have broken the right order that should exist

---

[32] See Komonchak, 86-88.

[33] See Joseph Ratzinger, "The Church and Man's Calling: Introductory Article and Chapter I," in *Commentary on the Documents of Vatican II*, ed. Herbert Vorgrimler, 5 vols. (New York: Herder, 1969), 5:119-20.

within themselves as well as between them and other people and all creatures. (GS 13)

Later the constitution presented human history as a tale of humanity's "com-
bat with the powers of evil" (GS 37). Nevertheless, on balance, the constitution's
dominant tone is better reflected in the council's confident assertion that "the
achievements of the human race are a sign of God's greatness and the fulfillment of his mysterious design" (GS 34).

Clearly emboldened by the theology of dialogue that Pope Paul VI outlined
in his first encyclical, *Ecclesiam Suam*, the council itself acknowledged the fruitfulness of a respectful dialogue with the world. The council insisted that the
church had much to offer the world in the gospel of Jesus Christ. At the same
time, the council recognized that "it has profited from the history and development of humankind" (GS 44). The crucial change in the title of the document in which the conjunction "and" was replaced by the preposition "in" (from
"Church *and* the Modern World" to "Church *in* the Modern World") suggests
an understanding of the church's task to transform the world without negat-
ing the positive features of contemporary society. More importantly, the title
presupposed a vital but hitherto neglected category for configuring the church's
relationship to the world, namely, the role of mission.

The missiological orientation of the church toward the world was announced
in the council's Decree on the Church's Missionary Activity, *Ad Gentes*: "The
church on earth is by its very nature missionary since, according to the plan of
the Father, it has its origin in the mission of the Son and the holy Spirit" (AG
2). Just as God's being is fundamentally oriented toward the world that God created, so too the church exists in mission as a sacramental sign of salvation to the
world. Both *Ad Gentes* and *Gaudium et Spes* proposed a theology of mission far
removed from the late medieval and Counter-Reformation view of church mission as a quantitative and geographic expansion of the boundaries of the church
and which "manifested itself supremely within the context of the European colonization of the non-western world."[34] With the new orientation of the council, church mission became a theological imperative.

Thus the church, at once a visible organization and a spiritual community,
travels the same journey as all of humanity and shares the same earthly lot
with the world: it is to be a leaven and, as it were, the soul of human society in its renewal by Christ and transformation into the family of God . . .

---

[34] David Bosch, *Transforming Mission: Paradigm Shifts in Theology of Mission* (Maryknoll, N.Y.:
Orbis Books, 1991), 237.

the church then believes that through each of its members and its community as a whole it can help to make the human family and its history still
more human. (GS 40)

The council's treatment of the church's relationship to the world sought to preserve an uneasy tension between affirming legitimate human endeavors and
insisting on the world's need for transformation. The council's admission that
it could learn from the world offered a new insight into the church's catholicity; it suggested that some of the church's experience of ecclesial diversity may
come by way of its engagement with the world, and this engagement, in turn,
depended on the church's capacity for authentic dialogue.

The Church's Mission in Service to the Reign of God

At a relatively late stage in the history of *Lumen Gentium,* a proposal was made
by several Latin American bishops to incorporate into the document the biblical metaphor of the reign or kingdom of God. Although this proposal came
too late to allow the theme to be integrated into the whole of the document,
it does appear in several passages. For example, in article 5 of *Lumen Gentium*
the council asserted boldly that the church does not exist for its own sake but
in service of the coming reign of God:

> Henceforward the church, equipped with the gifts of its founder and faith-
> fully observing his precepts of charity, humility and self-denial, receives the
> mission of proclaiming and establishing among all peoples the kingdom of
> Christ and of God, and is, on earth, *the seed and the beginning of that king-
> dom.* (LG 5; emphasis mine)

Later in that same document the council refers to the church as a "messianic
people" and asserts that, as such, the church's destiny is realized in that

> kingdom of God which has been begun by God himself on earth and which
> must be further extended until it is brought to perfection by him at the end
> of time when Christ our life, will appear and "creation itself also will be
> delivered from its slavery to corruption into the freedom of the glory of the
> sons and daughters of God." (LG 9)

Here again the power of the biblical image of the kingdom of God, an image
that so dominated Jesus' own preaching, is evoked. In the teaching of the council, the kingdom of God, which was manifested in human history as Jesus
Christ, continues as a force in history and will find its consummation only in
the eschaton. The church is not to be equated with the kingdom of God but
rather exists in human history as "the seed" and beginning of this kingdom.

Vatican II on Church and Culture

A third way in which the council was able further to develop our understanding of the catholicity of the church was first introduced in the Constitution on the Liturgy, *Sacrosanctum Concilium*. That document echoed earlier papal statements affirming the inherent goodness of diverse human cultures:

> Even in the liturgy, the church does not wish to impose a rigid uniformity in matters which do not affect the faith or the well-being of the entire community. Rather does it cultivate and foster the qualities and talents she respects and fosters the spiritual adornments and gifts of the various races and nations. Anything in people's way of life which is not indissolubly bound up with superstition and error the church studies with sympathy and, if possible, preserves intact. It sometimes even admits such things into the liturgy itself, provided they harmonize with its true and authentic spirit. (SC 37)

In spite of its positive tone, this passage still suggests something of the "culture as costume" perspective. The liturgy constitution presents the church's engagement with local cultures as a form of cultural "adaptation" and "accommodation." There remains an underlying assumption that the structure of the Roman liturgical rite would remain intact and normative. The council did not envision the creation of any new rites but merely the possibility of "grafting" onto the Roman rite certain local cultural customs.

The bishops' sense of the theological significance of human cultures matured over the course of the council. In *Gaudium et Spes,* the bishops wrote:

> It is a feature of the human person that it can achieve true and full humanity only by means of culture, that is, through the cultivation of the goods and values of nature. Whenever, therefore, there is a question of human life, nature and culture are intimately linked together. (GS 53)

The council went on to define that which constitutes culture.

> The word "culture" in the general sense refers to all those things which go to the refining and developing of humanity's diverse mental and physical endowments. We strive to subdue the earth by our knowledge and labor; we humanize social life both in the family and in the whole civic community through the improvement of customs and institutions; we express through our works the great spiritual experiences and aspirations of humanity through the ages; we communicate and preserve them to be an inspiration for the progress of many people, even of all humanity. Hence it follows that culture necessarily has historical and social overtones, and the word

"culture" often carries with it sociological and ethnological connotations; in this sense one can speak about a plurality of cultures. (GS 53)

In this passage we see a much fuller recognition that cultures are indeed much more than mere costumes that one chooses to put on or take off at will; they pertain to the very substance of our lives. It follows then that, far from being a matter indifferent to the life of faith, the diverse human cultures enrich the Christian life. As the church fulfills its mission in the proclamation of the good news of Jesus Christ to all nations, it recognizes that this saving gospel, the foundation of our Christian unity, must find expression in and through human culture.

> Since the kingdom of Christ is not of this world, in establishing this kingdom the church or people of God does not detract from anyone's temporal well-being. Rather it fosters and takes to itself, insofar as they are good, people's abilities, resources, and customs. In so taking them to itself it purifies, strengthens, and elevates them. . . . The universality which adorns the People of God is a gift from the Lord himself whereby the Catholic church ceaselessly and effectively strives to recapitulate the whole of humanity and all its riches under Christ the Head in the unity of his Spirit. (LG 13)

Finally, we see the relationship of faith and culture developed along the analogy of the incarnation in the council's Decree on the Church's Missionary Activity, which was one of the final documents to be approved by the council:

> The seed which is the word of God grows out of good soil watered by the divine dew, it absorbs moisture, transforms it and makes it part of itself, so that eventually it bears much fruit. So too indeed, just as happened in the economy of the incarnation, the young churches, which are rooted in Christ and built on the foundations of the apostles, take over all the riches which have been given to Christ as an inheritance. They borrow from the customs, traditions, wisdom, teaching, arts and sciences of their people everything which could be used to praise the glory of the Creator, manifest the grace of the saviour, or contribute to the right ordering of christian life. (AG 22)

These three themes—the church's positive yet critical engagement with the world, the missiological significance of the metaphor of the kingdom of God, and the maturation of the relationship of faith and culture—had the potential to enrich the council's reflections on the catholicity of the church. Unfortunately, it was not possible for the council to integrate these themes into one coherent theology of the catholicity of the church. That task would remain the work of the postconciliar church.

Postconciliar Developments

Many of the central conciliar themes touched on above would receive much greater attention in the influential pontificates of Pope Paul VI and Pope John Paul II.

The Pontificate of Paul VI

It is Pope Paul VI who offered the most developed reflections on the dialogical nature of the church in his first encyclical, *Ecclesiam Suam*. For the pope, dialogue has its origins in the triune being of God, who engages humanity in a supernatural act of self-communication (ES 70). The pope conceived of Christian dialogue according to a series of concentric circles: the outermost circle represented that sphere in which the church engaged in dialogue with the entire human community. The next circle, moving inward, attended to the need for dialogue with the great religions of the world. The next circle attended to an ecumenical dialogue among Christians, and the innermost circle was devoted to the need for dialogue within Roman Catholicism. Insufficient attention has been given to the ecclesiological orientation offered by this encyclical. Paul VI saw dialogue as lying at the very heart of the church's nature and mission.

The dialogical nature of the church and its mission was further explored in *Populorum Progressio,* which applied the principle of dialogue to the question of suffering and poverty in the third world. The pope called for a new dialogue between civilizations and cultures based on the dignity of the human person and not on "commodities or technical skills" (PP 73). Such dialogue must pursue not merely economic development but integral human development.

Pope Paul was convinced that the church's catholicity could only be enriched by the dialogue between faith and culture. In 1969 the pope addressed this topic in a major speech given while visiting Uganda. There he put forward with remarkable bluntness the question of the church's catholicity in a pluralistic world:

> A burning and much discussed question arises concerning your evangelizing work, and it is the adaptation of the gospel and of the Church to African culture. Must the Church be European, Latin, Oriental . . . or must she be African? This seems a difficult problem, and in practice may be so, indeed.[35]

On the one hand, he went on to insist that the church's catholicity could be preserved only by an unswerving adherence to the teaching of Christ as it was preserved in the church's own doctrine. On the other hand, this one faith could

---

[35] *Modern Missionary Documents and Africa,* 203.

and must find a plurality of expressions. In this sense, the pope insisted, there must be a unique and authentic "African Christianity." The catholicity of the church virtually *demanded* a spirit of dialogue with local cultures.

Finally, we must remark on what was perhaps Paul VI's most theologically mature document, his apostolic exhortation on evangelization, *Evangelii Nuntiandi*. In this exhortation the pope reframed the task of evangelization within the necessary engagement of the gospel with diverse cultures. The pope writes, "In the mind of the Lord the Church is universal by vocation and mission, but when she puts down her roots in a variety of cultural, social and human terrains, she takes on different external expressions and appearances in each part of the world" (EN 62). For Paul VI, the modern dichotomy that had emerged between faith and culture was "the drama of our time" (EN 20). Although the pope resisted the politicization of Christian salvation, he acknowledged that Christian understandings of salvation did possess social and political dimensions.

In spite of the pope's positive recognition that the church actually existed in the world in a diversity of cultural forms, he often wrote as if the gospel was able to take root in these diverse forms because the gospel itself was transcultural and only took on certain "external expressions." Of course there is a sense in which this is correct, if by that what we mean is that the gospel is capable of finding resonances in all cultures. However, this way of putting the matter gives the impression that we have some access to the "pure gospel" untouched by cultural forms. Such an assertion would deny the reality of the incarnation. From the moment the Word was made flesh as a Galilean Jew the gospel has been inculturated. In spite of this shortcoming, Pope Paul VI took insights that were developed only abstractly and inconsistently at the council and applied them to the actual life of the church in such complex pastoral contexts as the newly emerging churches of Africa and Asia.

The Pontificate of John Paul II

A theology of the catholicity of the church received further development in the voluminous writings of Pope John Paul II as he explored from multiple perspectives both the interplay of faith and culture and a theology of mission. This Polish pope was by far the most traveled pope in church history. His many visits to diverse local churches throughout the world doubtless gave him a unique perspective on the cultural pluralism present in the church. Indeed, one might argue that the relationship between faith and culture was one of the leitmotifs of his entire pontificate. The theme appeared in one of his earliest papal documents, the apostolic exhortation *Catechesi Tradendae*. This text marks the first time the word "inculturation" appeared in a papal document:

As I said recently to the members of the Biblical Commission: "The term 'acculturation' or 'inculturation' may be a neologism, but it expresses very well one factor of the great mystery of the Incarnation." We can say of catechesis, as well as of evangelization in general, that it is called to bring the power of the Gospel into the very heart of culture and cultures. For this purpose, catechesis will seek to know these cultures and their essential components; it will learn their most significant expressions; it will respect their particular values and riches. In this manner it will be able to offer these cultures the knowledge of the hidden mystery and help them to bring forth from their own living tradition original expressions of Christian life, celebration and thought. Two things must however be kept in mind. On the one hand the Gospel message cannot be purely and simply isolated from the culture in which it was first inserted (the biblical world or, more concretely, the cultural milieu in which Jesus of Nazareth lived), nor, without serious loss, from the cultures in which it has already been expressed down the centuries; it does not spring spontaneously from any cultural soil; it has always been transmitted by means of an apostolic dialogue which inevitably becomes part of a certain dialogue of cultures. (CT 53)

Key elements of this passage would reappear in his many addresses delivered on his travels. Particularly significant is his acknowledgment that the gospel has itself always been encountered in some inculturated form. This follows from the analogy of the incarnation. It is this insight that requires catechesis and evangelization to take the form of a dialogue of cultures.

Perhaps the pope's most dramatic statement on the relationship between faith and culture came on the occasion of the creation of the Pontifical Council for Culture in 1982:

The synthesis between culture and faith is not just a demand of culture, but also of faith.... A faith which does not become culture is a faith which has not been fully received, not thoroughly thought through, not faithfully lived out.[36]

Although his sense of the mutually informing character of faith and culture was profound, it was doubtless filtered through his own Polish heritage. It is not surprising that he would offer the apostles to the Slavs, Cyril and Methodius, as the prime examplars of the work of inculturation, describing their evangelizing efforts as "the incarnation of the gospel in native cultures" (SA 21). For

---

[36] *L'Osservatore Romano* [English edition] (June 28, 1982), 7.

all of John Paul II's positive rhetoric regarding inculturation, he continued to see his native Poland as the paradigm for understanding the relationship between faith and culture. Polish culture was to be revered because it had been so thoroughly infused, in his view, with basic Christian values. The pope seemed considerably less confident of the spiritual value of those cultures untouched by the gospel.

John Paul II asserted that inculturation was an ecclesial activity carried out by the people themselves within their local churches. In *Redemptoris Missio*, his encyclical on Christian mission, he wrote:

> In effect, inculturation must involve the whole people of God, and not just a few experts, since the people reflect the authentic *sensus fidei* which must never be lost sight of. Inculturation needs to be guided and encouraged, but not forced, lest it give rise to negative reactions among Christians. It must be an expression of the community's life, one which must mature within the community itself, and not be exclusively the result of erudite research. The safeguarding of traditional values is the work of a mature faith. (RM 54)

This statement suggests that it is the local church that is, in effect, the agent of the process of inculturating the Christian gospel.

John Paul II's positive rhetoric regarding the work of inculturation often stood at odds with Vatican policies that reflected a deep-seated suspicion of theologies of inculturation. Moreover, in the midst of his many positive statements regarding the necessary inculturation of the gospel one can also find a number of more cautious passages. At times this caution even gave way to a kind of apocalypticism reflected in his concerns regarding a "culture of death" at work in the world.[37] Frequently, when the pope chose to interpret the "signs of the times" in his encyclicals, the analysis highlighted the negative features of the world today.

As regards the ecclesial process of inculturation itself, John Paul II shared with Pope Paul VI two principal concerns: first, a concern for the dangers of "culturalism," the unacceptable compromise of vital gospel values in favor of local cultural values[38] and, second, a concern for the need to maintain doctrinal fidelity through adherence to the magisterium. There is little evidence that the pope was able to reconcile this second concern with the claim, cited earlier, that it is the people of the local church who are to be the agents of the process of inculturation.

---

[37] See SRS 24; CA 39; EV, 12, 19, 21, 24, 26, 28, 50, 64, 87, 95, 100.
[38] Shorter, *Toward a Theology of Inculturation*, 218.

A further lens for grasping John Paul II's understanding of the church's catholicity is his theology of Christian mission. In *Redemptoris Missio*, the pope carefully correlated the mission of the church to the reign or kingdom of God. He insisted on the inseparability of Jesus and the kingdom of God, noting that the "proclamation and establishment of God's kingdom" constituted the essential purpose of Jesus' mission (RM 13). Jesus revealed the kingdom not just in his teaching but "in his actions and his own person" (RM 14). Central to the manifestation of the kingdom of God are Jesus' ministries of healing and forgiving, ministries that result in transformed human relationships. The kingdom thereby grows

> as people slowly learn to love, forgive and serve one another. . . . The kingdom's nature, therefore, is one of communion among all human beings—with one another and with God. The kingdom is the concern of everyone: individuals, society, and the world. Working for the kingdom means acknowledging and promoting God's activity, which is present in human history and transforms it. Building the kingdom means working for liberation from evil in all its forms. In a word, the kingdom of God is the manifestation and the realization of God's plan of salvation in all its fullness. (RM 15)

The pope warned against overly reductive interpretations of the kingdom of God that focus exclusively on the socioeconomic and political spheres of human existence without reference to their transcendent horizon. This last point is crucial; he did not deny the social and political dimensions of the kingdom of God, challenging only attempts to remove any transcendent reference (RM 17). In this encyclical the pope explicitly connected two themes from the council: the church as a sacrament of salvation and the reign of God. According to the pope, insofar as the church is a sacrament of God's saving offer, it will always be linked to the kingdom of God as its sacramental sign:

> The Church is the sacrament of salvation for all humankind, and her activity is not limited only to those who accept her message. She is a dynamic force in mankind's journey toward the eschatological kingdom, and is the sign and promoter of gospel values. (RM 20)

The church serves the kingdom in a special way by its proclamation of the good news of Christ and by its effort to spread gospel values.

Perhaps John Paul II's most profound contribution to a contemporary understanding of church mission came by way of an extended meditation on the Spirit as the transcendent agent of that mission. According to the pope, the mission of the church involves the proclamation of Jesus, to be sure, but it also entails the recognition that the Spirit of God is already at work among all peoples and cultures even prior to the proclamation of Christ.

> The Spirit manifests himself in a special way in the Church and in her members. Nevertheless, his presence and activity are universal, limited neither by space nor time. . . . The Spirit's presence and activity affect not only the individuals but also society and history, peoples, cultures and religions. Indeed, the Spirit is at the origin of the noble ideals and undertakings which benefit humanity on its journey through history: "The Spirit of God with marvelous foresight directs the course of the ages and renews the face of the earth." The risen Christ "is now at work in human hearts through the strength of his Spirit, not only instilling a desire for the world to come but also thereby animating, purifying and reinforcing the noble aspirations which drive the human family to make its life one that is more human and to direct the whole earth to this end." (RM 28)

Peter Phan has perceptively teased out the implications of this passage for a theology of mission:

> If this statement is true, then Christian mission can no longer be what it was, a one-way proclamation of a message of salvation to a world of "pagans" totally bereft of God's self revelation and grace. Rather, it is first of all a search for and recognition of the presence and activities of the Holy Spirit among the peoples to be evangelized, and in this humble and attentive process of listening, the evangelizers become the evangelized, and the evangelized becomes the evangelizers.[39]

The exercise of the church's evangelizing mission must be dialogical in character.

We have seen in the pontificates of Paul VI and John Paul II a maturation of several conciliar themes that have advanced our understanding of the breadth and depth of the church's catholicity. Pope Paul VI, in particular, grasped the necessary relationship between the church's own dialogical nature, grounded in the dialogical character of divine revelation—a reality that ought to be reflected in its own ecclesial relationships—and its dialogical mission to the world. Both popes affirmed the necessity of the church's dialogue with the world, and both

---

[39] Peter C. Phan, *In Our Own Tongues: Perspectives from Asia on Mission and Inculturation* (Maryknoll, N.Y.: Orbis Books, 2003), 43.

recognized the need for a theology of mission that affirmed the positive value of local cultures. John Paul II further developed the council's brief reflections on the kingdom of God, recognizing that the kingdom of God, while linked to the church, is not identical with it and may be encountered in the world beyond the visible boundaries of the church. The presence of the kingdom in the world is a sign of the Holy Spirit, whose activity is recognizable beyond the boundaries of the church.

These two pontificates spanned a period of over four decades (bridged, of course, by the brief pontificate of Pope John Paul I). Their reflections would offer theological grist for contemporary theologians intent on developing a theology of the church's catholicity appropriate to a postmodern church grappling with its increasingly global character.

CATHOLICITY IN A POSTMODERN CHURCH

More than forty years after the council one hears with greater frequency of the limits of Vatican II. The claim is sometimes made that Vatican II brought the Roman Catholic Church into an honest engagement with modernity at the precise historical moment in which the world was shifting from modernity to what can only be called a postmodern epoch. Certainly there are aspects of the church today that the council's teaching could not have fully anticipated (e.g., the flourishing of lay ministry in the church), just as there is a global consciousness that was just beginning to make itself felt at the council. This does not mean that the council's teaching is without any relevance for the church today. As Gerard Mannion observed, "the enduring legacy of Vatican II . . . is its unswerving commitment to *dialogue* among the human family."[40] Hermann Pottmeyer contrasts this dialogical understanding of ecclesial life with a more juridical preconciliar conception of the church.[41] If there is a common characteristic of the many ecclesiological trajectories that have emerged since the council under the rubric of communion ecclesiology, it is the dominance of relational and dialogical understandings of the church.

This conciliar commitment to dialogue has been accompanied by another insight that was given real although incomplete expression in the council documents, the importance of honoring the growing sense of the particular in the face of the modern penchant for universal accounts of human experience.

---

[40] Mannion, 110.

[41] Hermann Pottmeyer, "Dialogue as a Model for Communication in the Church," in *The Church and Communication*, ed. Patrick Granfield (Kansas City: Sheed & Ward, 1994), 97-103, at 97.

As was noted in the introduction, one of the most commonly discussed features of postmodern thought lies in the suspicion of what are often called meta-narratives. Critics have claimed that the Christian gospel, particularly as it is articulated in official doctrinal pronouncements, has too often functioned as a grand narrative that masks its own particularity and dependence on a distinct cultural and historical context. At the same time, this narrative is imposed on other peoples and cultures in a way that suppresses the unique wisdom and insight of that local context. This criticism cannot be simply dismissed out of hand. For extended periods in the history of the church, doctrine has been presented as if it were a collection of absolute, transcultural, and transhistorical truths. Indeed, variations on this perspective are evident among church leaders today. Some today hold that the church possesses its own distinctive and autonomous culture of faith, one that can fruitfully interact with other local cultures but which must always be seen as superior to those cultures and which, therefore, can only adapt to those local cultures at a relatively surface level. Pope Benedict XVI has, both as an influential theologian and now as pope, articulated something of this viewpoint. We need to consider his argument, and the responses it has engendered, in more detail.

Whose Religion Is Christianity?

About a year ago, Pope Benedict XVI gave a controversial lecture at the university where he once taught in Regensburg, Germany. The address received a good deal of attention because of his quotation of a fourteenth-century Byzantine emperor who offered an exceedingly unflattering assessment of Islam. Largely overlooked, however, was an even more provocative section of the pope's address, namely, his description of the link between Christianity and Hellenistic thought.[42] Benedict made a rather bold claim regarding Christianity's relationship to Greek thought:

> This inner rapprochement between biblical faith and Greek philosophical inquiry was an event of decisive importance not only from the standpoint of the history of religions, but also from that of world history—it is an event that concerns us even today. Given this convergence, it is not surprising that Christianity, despite its origins and some significant developments in the East, *finally took on its historically decisive character in Europe*.[43]

---

[42] For another analysis of the Regensburg address that comes to similar conclusions, see Peter Phan, "Speaking in Many Tongues: Why the Church Must Be More Catholic," *Commonweal* (January 12, 2007): 16-19.

[43] Pope Benedict XVI, "The Regensburg Academic Lecture," *Origins* 36 (September 28, 2006): 250 (emphasis mine).

If one considers not only this most recent lecture but his pre-papal writings, it becomes evident that although Pope Benedict is not opposed to the process of cultural engagement per se, he has vigorously insisted that in Europe the church achieved its own unique cultural form, a form that drew heavily, though not without modification, from Greek philosophical thought. Although the pope believes that the European Christian form may engage other cultural contexts, it can never lose its priority.[44] In an address he first delivered in 1993, then Cardinal Ratzinger argued for the notion of "interculturality" in which the proper form of such dialogue is between the church's own universal culture of the faith and other local cultures. Aylward Shorter has referred to this as the "two culture theory."[45] Presupposed in this cultural exchange is a fundamental asymmetry as the universal culture is always to be given priority.

At Regensburg, Pope Benedict also challenged contemporary theological interest in cultural pluralism, which he equated with cultural relativism, seeing it as the latest stage in a troubling attempt to de-hellenize the church. The pope believes it was providential that the Christian faith was so decisively influenced by Hellenistic culture, first by way of the Greek Septuagint and then by the authorship of the New Testament texts in the Greek language.

There is another way of reading our Christian origins, however, one that acknowledges the distinctive and even prominent role played by Hellenistic culture but which does not tie Christianity decisively to its Western forms. This alternative reading also gives prominence to the Greek New Testament but to a much different purpose. Where Pope Benedict sees this as evidence that Greek thought has a permanent and decisive place in Christianity, the African Christian scholar Lamin Sanneh, in his book *Whose Religion Is Christianity?* takes a strikingly different view. For him, what is most noteworthy about the Greek New Testament is that it was *not* written in Aramaic, the language of Jesus. Sanneh sees the Greek New Testament as evidence that Christianity has always been fundamentally a "translated religion."[46]

In interreligious dialogue, particularly among the Abrahamic religions of Christianity, Judaism, and Islam, many have embraced the Islamic characterization of all three Abrahamic traditions as "religions of the book." Yet, as attributed to Christianity, this is true only in a secondary sense. Christians assert that the fullness of divine revelation came not in a text but in a person.

---

[44] Joseph Cardinal Ratzinger with Vittorio Messori, *The Ratzinger Report* (San Francisco: Ignatius Press, 1985), 103; Ratzinger, "In the Encounter of Christianity and Religions, Syncretism Is Not the Goal," *L'Osservatore Romano* [English edition] (April 26, 1995), 5-8.

[45] Aylward Shorter, "Faith, Culture and the Global Village," *South Pacific Journal of Mission Studies* (March 1996): 31-38.

[46] Lamin Sanneh, *Whose Religion Is Christianity? The Gospel beyond the West* (Grand Rapids: Eerdmans, 2003).

Although Christians commonly refer to Scripture as the Word of God, properly speaking it is Jesus of Nazareth who is the Word of God incarnate; Scripture represents the inspired and authoritative testimony to that divine Word. Jesus did not leave us a text. He did not write any memoirs or leave behind a manual of instruction. Christianity was born out of the communal encounter with Jesus of Nazareth. The first Christian texts that would eventually become Scripture were written decades after Jesus' death and resurrection. Jesus left behind not a sacred text but a community of believers who kept alive his story through communal worship, storytelling, and distinctive moral conduct.

The Scriptures are not sacred texts because of some miraculous origin; they are, at their very core, human accounts of the Christ-event. They are sacred, for Christians, because they are held to be Spirit-inspired communal accounts of the work God accomplished in and through Jesus of Nazareth. At the same time, they are also our first witness to that process of religious intercultural dialogue that lies at the heart of Christianity. The Christian Scriptures recount the first moment in Christian intercultural dialogue, namely, that between the Aramaic preaching of Jesus conducted in a Hebraic cultural world, and a Greek-speaking Hellenistic cultural milieu enshrined in the texts of the New Testament. In short, the Christian Scriptures are the product of the process of human translation. Sanneh provocatively draws out the significance of this:

> Being the original Scripture of the Christian movement, the New Testament Gospels are a translated version of the message of Jesus, and that means Christianity is a translated religion without a revealed language. The issue is not whether Christians translated their Scripture well or willingly, but that without translation there would be no Christianity or Christians. Translation is the church's birthmark as well as its missionary benchmark: the church would be unrecognizable or unsustainable without it.[47]

Translation becomes an apt metaphor for the church's catholicity.

> The fact of Christianity being a translated, and translating, religion places God at the center of the universe of cultures, implying free coequality among cultures and a necessary relativizing of languages vis-à-vis the truth of God. No culture is so advanced and so superior that it can claim exclusive access or advantage to the truth of God, and none so marginal or inferior that it can be excluded.[48]

---

[47] Ibid., 97.
[48] Ibid., 105-6.

As we have seen, both Vatican II and Pope John Paul II employed the analogy of the incarnation to elucidate the process of inculturation or intercultural dialogue. However, this African scholar has provocatively teased out the full implications of this approach The Word became flesh in a historical, culturally situated person, Jesus of Nazareth. The fullness of divine revelation was encountered in a first-century Palestinian Jew who preached in Aramaic. This commitment to the incarnation as the heart of the catholicity of the faith means that the growth of Christianity was predicated on its capacity to sustain religious, intercultural communication (a phrase I take to be roughly synonymous with inculturation or contextualization).

This emphasis on vernacular translation has led Sanneh and other scholars[49] to reread the history of Christian missions. Many works of Western historiography and cultural anthropology have taken an openly critical view of Christian missionary endeavors from the sixteenth to the nineteenth centuries, considering it "imperialism at prayer."[50] History has long judged these endeavors by the cultural condescension of the missionaries rather than by the unique forms of Christianity that actually emerged as a result of their endeavors. The need for Christian missionaries to engage in the process of vernacular translation in the production of Bibles and catechisms of use to indigenous peoples meant that these missionaries were, whether they liked it or not, dependent on the local populations. In other words, the need for vernacular translations put the receptor communities in the driver's seat in the process of Christian mission. Sanneh writes:

> Consequently, however much mission tried to suppress local populations, the issue of the vernacular helped to undermine its foreign character. . . . Vernacular agency became the preponderant medium for the assimilation of Christianity, and although missionaries did not consciously intend to occupy a secondary position, their commitment to translation made that necessary and inevitable.[51]

There is a deep irony in this situation. It is largely the ethnographic studies of contemporary anthropology that have decried Western colonialism and, indirectly, the Western Christian missionary impulse, for its destruction of indigenous cultures. Yet early Christian missionaries were, by virtue of the demands

---

[49] See esp. Andrew F. Walls, *The Cross-Cultural Process in Christian History: Studies in the Transmission and Appropriation of Faith* (Maryknoll, N.Y.: Orbis Books, 2002).

[50] Lamin Sanneh, *Translating the Message: The Missionary Impact on Culture* (Maryknoll, N.Y.: Orbis Books, 1989), 88.

[51] Ibid., 159, 161-62.

of vernacular translation, the first pioneers in ethnographic field research, who had no choice but to seek to understand local indigenous cultures on their own terms.[52] Thus, even those missionaries whose evangelical zeal was tainted by colonialist assumptions often achieved results quite at cross-purposes with their intentions. That is, they set in motion the indigenous appropriation of the Christian gospel that gave rise to Christian forms quite different from those championed by the missionaries themselves. Conversely, those missionary endeavors that were resistant to vernacular translation and insisted on bearing the Christian faith in the custom and language of the West were rarely successful in their endeavors.

The process of intercultural communication has always been present in the church even when it was not acknowledged as such. This intercultural process is not simply an accidental accommodation of a religion that possesses its own autonomous faith culture; rather, it is the essential process behind Christianity's capacity to be a genuine global religion. As Stephen Bevans has eloquently put it:

> Through us God must become Asian or African, black or brown, poor or sophisticated. Christians must be able to speak to inhabitants of twenty-first century secular suburban Lima, Peru, or to the Tondo slum dweller in Manila, or to the ill-gotten affluence of a Brazilian rancher. Christianity, if it is to be faithful to its deepest roots and to its most basic insight, must continue God's incarnation in Jesus by becoming contextual.[53]

The catholicity of the church can only be sustained, particularly in our postmodern context, by careful, attentive intercultural dialogue.

Catholicity as Intercultural Dialogue

Stephen Bevans has considered the perils and possibilities of sharing the Christian gospel by way of intercultural dialogue in his work in contextual theology. He notes that, in a sense, any attempt to share the gospel by way of intercultural dialogue, or what he refers to as contextualization, is a form of translation.[54] Yet Bevans identifies six particular models of contextual theology, each of which operates from a distinct set of premises. The most common approach

---

[52] Ibid., 193.

[53] Stephen B. Bevans, *Models of Contextual Theology* (rev. and exp. ed., Maryknoll, N.Y.: Orbis Books, 2002), 12.

[54] Ibid., 37.

adheres closely to common presuppositions regarding linguistic translation understood as a ready, one-to-one correspondence of meanings across linguistic traditions. It is the model that seems to dominate the contemporary magisterial treatments of the topic that we surveyed above. This model of intercultural dialogue assumes, to begin with, that divine revelation can be articulated in propositional form.[55] Practitioners of this approach to intercultural dialogue admit that the Christian faith may be expressed in various culturally conditioned forms, but they are confident that these can be identified and stripped away, revealing a pure, transcultural message. This pure message can then be translated into modes of expression particular to the receiving culture. This assumes a "kernel-and-husk" view of divine revelation in which there is a universally accessible kernel of divine truth overlaid with the husk of cultural expressions. This model can admit, for example, that certain doctrinal formulations contain cultural influences, but it assumes that these can be readily identified and excised from the timeless, inner meaning of that doctrinal formulation. Emphasis is placed on preserving the universal identity of the Christian faith at all costs. Bevans contends that this approach may be the best available in a situation in which the gospel is first being shared with a particular people at a time when they are not yet able actively to appropriate the faith in their own categories.[56] However, the model also has significant shortcomings.

Robert Schreiter identifies two weaknesses with this model.[57] First, its understanding of culture assumes that there are readily identifiable cultural patterns that can be decoded, rendering them immediately intelligible to someone foreign to that culture. This cultural analysis is often superficial and does not recognize that some cultural patterns may be unique to a given culture, significantly complicating the task of translation. In these instances another culture may not possess a cultural pattern or meaning which is "dynamically equivalent." The second weakness concerns the "kernel-and-husk" conception of divine revelation, which has been challenged by contemporary hermeneutics. To follow the metaphor, we never have the kernel without the husk.

The kernel-and-husk theory reflects an inadequate understanding of the incarnation. The view that the Word incarnate simply took on the appearance of humanity was condemned as heretical in the early church. The doctrine of the incarnation insists that the Word incarnate was "enfleshed" in humanity and that it assumed the human condition in its entirety. God's self-communication in the person of Jesus of Nazareth cannot be abstracted from

---

55 Ibid., 40.
56 Ibid., 140.
57 Robert Schreiter, *Constructing Local Theologies* (Maryknoll, N.Y.: Orbis Books, 1985) 6-21.

Jesus of Nazareth's historical existence. It is in the life, preaching, death, and resurrection of this one Palestinian Jew that we have received the unsurpassable self-communication of God. It is not in spite of but *through* Christ's life and ministry, in all its cultural and historical particularity, that we encounter God's saving Word. In the end, the translation model fails to do justice to the mystery of the incarnation.

A second approach to sharing the gospel by way of intercultural dialogue is, to some extent, a reaction to this translation model. Bevans refers to it as the anthropological model.[58] Where the translation model takes the preservation of the distinctive identity of the Christian gospel as its starting point, the anthropological approach focuses on preserving the cultural identity of the peoples who receive the gospel message. There is a confidence in the goodness of creation that leads the practitioner of this approach boldly to assume that God is always already present among all peoples. Consequently, this form of intercultural dialogue first wishes to understand the distinctive patterns and values of a given culture, open to the signals of God's presence already found in that culture. "The theologian must start where the faith actually lives, and that is in the midst of peoples' lives."[59] In this model the local community must be the agent of inculturation, the active reception and appropriation of the gospel into their own cultural context.

The overriding assumption regarding the goodness of local cultures may constitute one of the weaknesses of this model. There is a danger of cultural romanticism that assumes that all things indigenous are necessarily good and to be affirmed. We find little allowance for the possibility that the gospel may need to challenge significant elements of the local culture as simply at odds with fundamental gospel values. Sensitive Christian missionaries eager to learn from the local African cultures have, nevertheless, felt compelled by the gospel to condemn such indigenous African practices as genital mutilation performed on African adolescent girls as a rite of passage. Even those Christian missionaries most committed to the anthropological model of intercultural dialogue tend to balk at the injustice and latent sexism that appear to underlie practices such as this.

The cultural romanticism of the anthropological model has led to a trenchant critique by theologians who draw inspiration from the biblical prophetic tradition and contend that all human cultural forms must stand before the judgment of the gospel. This countercultural approach has had its greatest appeal in instances where cultural forms have seemed particularly toxic. Bevans

---

[58] Bevans, 54-69.
[59] Ibid., 61.

mentions the 1985 South African *Kairos* document, which harshly criticized apartheid, and Pope John Paul II's condemnations of the "culture of death" that he believed had become so prevalent in Western culture.[60] This approach calls the Christian community to adopt a distinct cultural form shaped by the gospel, one that functions as what Gerhard Lohfink calls a "contrast community."[61]

Although there is undeniable value in each of these models, I am going to focus on a fourth model that tries to balance the concerns raised in each of these three previous models, what Bevans refers to as the synthetic or dialogical model.[62] This model holds together the concerns for preserving the integrity of the gospel with a commitment to be attentive to the local culture. The dialogical model recognizes that although every cultural context is distinct, there are common elements that can be discovered among various cultures. Yet we can discover these shared understandings across cultures only to the extent that we engage in a careful, respectful and reciprocal dialogue. Sharing the Christian message is a special instance of this kind of intercultural dialogue. Michael Amaladoss has emphasized this point in his writing.[63] We are talking not about inserting the gospel into a culture, Amaladoss insists, but about a dialogue between a particular cultural formulation of the Christian faith and a particular local culture. The dialogical model recognizes that the Christian message is always presented in a particular cultural form; there is no transcultural kernel. So any sharing of the gospel is, by definition, an act of intercultural dialogue.

This model neither romanticizes nor demonizes culture. In some situations there will be cultural elements to be celebrated and in other situations there will be elements that will have to be criticized. Moreover, the criticism and celebration can move in both directions. In other words, it is not only the case that Western Christianity may criticize some elements of African culture; it may also be the case that African culture will have valid criticisms to level against the Western formulations of the Christian gospel.

In the careful work of intercultural communication, what happens in a sense is the emergence of a new cultural zone of shared meaning.[64] When two cultural worlds contact one another, the success of that contact inevitably creates a new cultural reality. This is because, as Aylward Shorter writes:

---

[60] Ibid., 118.

[61] Gerhard Lohfink, *Jesus and Community: The Social Dimension of Christian Faith* (New York: Paulist Press, 1984).

[62] Bevans, 88-102. I cannot develop here two further models offered by Bevans, the praxis model and the transcendental model.

[63] Michael Amaladoss, *Beyond Inculturation: Can the Many Be One?* (Delhi: Indian Society for Promoting Christian Knowledge, 1998), 14-17.

[64] Funitaka Matsuoka, "A Reflection on 'Teaching Theology from an Intercultural Perspective,'" *Theological Education* 36 (1989): 35-42.

Inculturation is not merely a dialogue between Gospel and culture, it is the Gospel bringing into existence a new cultural creation. It is essentially an instance of creativity. . . . Inculturation at the grassroots means, among other things, stimulating liturgical and catechetical creativity in the community.[65]

This is why languages and cultures are dynamic and not static realities. As peoples of different languages and cultures interact, the languages and cultures undergo inevitable change.

Whenever we proclaim the gospel, whether to those who are hearing it for the first time or to established Christian communities, we must abandon any hope of presenting that gospel in some pristine transcultural, transhistorical mode. As the World Council of Churches statement on intercultural hermeneutics clearly asserts: "There is no 'pure' gospel that can be understood apart from the various forms in which it is embodied in culture and language."[66]

This admission of the culture-laden character of our presentation of the faith need not resign us to the twin extremes of ecclesial sectarianism on the one hand and cultural imperialism on the other. It means simply that we must accept that there is no other way to profess our faith. What is demanded is a style of dialogue that recognizes that we cannot anticipate in advance the outcome of such conversation. In a true engagement between the Christian gospel and a particular culture something new is likely to be born.

Clearly this was the result of St. Paul's proclamation of the faith of a Jewish sect to a Gentile audience. Paul did not simply translate the one gospel; there was a new transformation of that one gospel message as it was proclaimed to a Hellenistic world. The concrete outcome of Paul's mission to the Gentiles could not possibly have been anticipated.

This understanding of the dynamics of intercultural dialogue would appear to challenge, however, the universality of the Christian faith. If, as many theologians who work in the field of contextual theology suggest, all theology is fundamentally local,[67] is Christianity doomed to be nothing more than a loose collection of local theologies with little shared meaning? Put differently, how do we move from the particular to the universal? The answer is, we don't. What we do is allow one particular cultural context to engage another and allow for the creation of emerging, contextualized shared understandings. As these mul-

---

[65] Shorter, *Toward a Theology of Inculturation*, 263.

[66] World Council of Churches, "On Intercultural Hermeneutics," in *New Directions in Mission and Evangelization*, ed. James A. Scherer and Stephen B. Bevans, 3 vols. (Maryknoll, N.Y.: Orbis Books, 1999), 3:187.

[67] See Schreiter, *Constructing Local Theologies*; Clemens Sedmak, *Doing Local Theology: A Guide for Artisans of a New Humanity* (Maryknoll, N.Y.: Orbis Books, 2002).

tiple intercultural exchanges take place, it becomes possible to recognize certain overlapping insights and rough correspondences. The universal is not so much imposed as it is discovered in the processes of the overlapping intercultural communications that transpire. Schreiter has helped elucidate this by distinguishing between two forms of cultural hermeneutics. The first is an intercultural hermeneutics that attends to the specific dialogue between cultures and is concerned with preserving the cultural distinctiveness of both parties in the exchange. The second is a cross-cultural hermeneutics that "seeks those forms of sameness that will allow easier communication in a world with so many cultures. Consequently, it seeks commonalities or at least common categories that will promote communication and understanding."[68] This emphasis on cultural dialogue suggests that the universal faith of the church abides not as some transcultural reality that is imposed on other cultures but as a reality always emerging *out of* careful intercultural exchange. Intercultural dialogue sees the catholicity of the church as a dynamic reality. The church is constantly being reborn in a rich global network of intercultural exchanges. We need to be precise in our understanding of this process. The intent is not to deny the transcendence of the gospel itself, but merely to recognize that no one cultural form itself captures that transcendence. There is a universal dimension that, paradoxically, is encountered only in the overlapping particularities of cultural expressions. Christopher Duraisingh, an Anglican theologian, offers particular insight into this dynamic:

> The gospel story is for all places and times, but it is never available to us apart from its embodiment in particular cultures. The story of God's love in Christ becomes the good news only as it is enfleshed in a particular culture; yet this gospel can never be identified with any one of its particular expressions, for it transcends them all. While all cultures are worthy expressions of the gospel story, no cultural expression of it, even the classical, can become the exclusive norm or exhaustive means for drawing out the richness of God's love in Christ. It is only as the multiplicity of traditions that mark the global church are recognized and brought into dialogue with each other that the church can discern and witness to the "multi-colored wisdom of God" that the author of the letter to the Ephesians speaks of.[69]

This new appreciation for the church's catholicity combines two themes that have come to prominence in much postmodern literature, the priority of

---

[68] Robert J. Schreiter, *The New Catholicity: Theology between the Global and the Local,* Faith and Culture Series (Maryknoll, N.Y.: Orbis Books, 1997), 42.

[69] Christopher Duraisingh, "Contextual and Catholic: Conditions for Cross-Cultural Hermeneutics," *Anglican Theological Review* 82 (Fall 2000): 687.

dialogue and the emphasis on particularity. A proper grasp of this new catholicity requires, however, that we remain mindful of some important insights regarding intercultural dialogue.

First, culture is a dynamic rather than a static concept. There is no such thing as a pure culture of any kind. We must be wary of any approach to church and culture that essentializes a culture or succumbs to a romanticization of a culture. This sometimes happens, particularly in dealing with certain indigenous cultures, when cultural outsiders appeal to a "fossil culture," that is, the indigenous culture as it may have existed prior to colonization and the inevitable modern engagement with other cultures.[70] Cultures are always shifting and adapting to new contexts and ongoing engagements and exchanges with other cultures.

Second, culture can be understood both as an integrated reality, a set of shared meanings and values that bind a people together, and as a contested reality constituted by inequities in power and participation in the social life of a community. The first view of culture is based on classic ethnographic studies that have researched relatively self-contained societies. These studies presented culture as an integrated system of meanings and values that allowed members to feel "at home" within a given society. For example, theologians have long drawn from the insights into culture provided by the distinguished anthropologist Clifford Geertz.[71] Geertz saw cultures as complex and largely inherited symbol systems that helped the participants in that culture derive meaning from their experience. Schreiter describes this as an *integrated* conception of culture.[72] The difficulty with this approach is the tendency of integrated conceptions of culture to treat distinct cultures as organic and self-contained wholes. These conceptions stress the fixed and invariant elements of a particular culture and often reveal more about the cultural observer than about the culture being observed. This view of culture has been increasingly challenged in postmodern thought, particularly by those who draw on the work of figures such as Michel Foucault and consequently view culture in terms of contested power relations.[73] This Foucaultian critique has been particularly attractive to missiologists sensitive to ways in which the conquest model of mission often took advantage of huge power inequities in Western colonialism. Not surpris-

---

[70] The term "fossil culture" is taken from John Pobee, *Toward an African Theology* (Nashville: Abingdon, 1979), 44.

[71] Clifford Geertz, *The Interpretation of Cultures* (New York: Basic Books, 1973).

[72] Schreiter, *New Catholicity*, 46-61. Schreiter, in turn, is borrowing the term from the work of Margaret S. Archer, *Culture and Agency: The Place of Culture in Social Theory* (Cambridge: Cambridge University Press, 1989), 1-21.

[73] Kathryn Tanner, *Theories of Culture: A New Agenda for Theology* (Minneapolis: Fortress, 1997).

ingly, many contemporary theologies of mission are particularly sensitive to postcolonial thought, that is, an emerging theological perspective attuned to the ways in which colonialism systematically disrupted and often destroyed local indigenous cultures.

Further disrupting the formation of a coherent cultural identity is the growing impact of globalization, which has tremendously complicated the terms of cultural engagement. Cultural boundaries that were once preserved by geography are now blurred by modern communications and transportation that make instantaneous interactions with people across the globe an everyday reality. The pervasive extension and influence of neo-liberal capitalism with its consumerist ethos and the fantasized account of human reality spread by way of the Western entertainment industry have created a hyperculture based more on image and fantasy than on reality.[74] These more postmodern approaches are wary of any account of the engagement of cultures that sees intercultural engagement solely as an opportunity for mutual enrichment and is naïve to the dangers of cultural disruption.

The Asian Church as a Laboratory for the Becoming of a Dialogical Church

Dialogical mission as a way of comprehending the catholicity of the church today has been explored over the past few decades in the laboratory of the Asian church, in general, and in the many documents of the Federation of Asian Bishops' Conferences, in particular. Asian Christianity has always had to deal with its minority status. Because of the unique status of the Asian churches, they have had to attend in a special way to the meaning and character of the church's mission. One finds throughout the documents of the FABC an emerging understanding that the church fulfills its mission to proclaim the good new of Jesus Christ through dialogue. In their understanding, dialogue is not one event to be placed alongside the work of evangelization; it is how evangelization and the mission of the church are properly pursued. Indeed, what is most impressive about the FABC's work is the way in which it has taken the emphasis on dialogue found in the documents of Vatican II and in Pope Paul VI's first encyclical, *Ecclesiam Suam*, and made it central to their theology of mission.[75]

---

[74] Schreiter, *New Catholicity*, 55.

[75] Yet another important resource for a theology of dialogue is the 1990 Vatican document *Dialogue and Proclamation*, promulgated by the Secretariat for Non-Christians and the Congregation for the Evangelization of Peoples. For the text and commentary, see William R. Burrows, ed., *Redemption and*

The reasons for this Asian emphasis on dialogue are many. One possibility, however, starts from the fact that Christianity has historically been a foreign religion in Asia. Indian theologian Felix Wilfred insists that this is not due to the fact that Christianity came to Asia from the outside. Buddhism, he points out, came to China, Japan, and Thailand from the outside and yet it is not considered an alien religion in those regions.

> The main reason why Christianity has been viewed as alien is because the local Churches in the countries of Asia have, by and large, kept themselves aloof from the mainstream of the life of the people, their history, struggles and dreams. They have failed to identify themselves with the people, even though in terms of charity many praiseworthy services have been rendered.[76]

According to Edmund Chia, the work of the FABC has focused on dialogue as a way of acknowledging the Asian church's previous failure to really engage its sociocultural context.[77]

The Asian bishops insisted that in their particular context, the fulfillment of the church's mission entailed a threefold dialogue with the people and especially the poor, with the religious traditions of the region and with the local cultures. This threefold dialogue, in turn, is realized in the respective tasks of liberation, interreligious dialogue, and inculturation. The church's dialogue with the poor and the consequent work of liberation follow from an understanding of the church's mission to be a sacrament of salvation before the world and a sign of God's reign. The Asian bishops have been at the forefront, in the decades since the council, in exploring the metaphorical power of the reign of God as a way of focusing the church's mission. To serve the reign of God means concretely serving the cause of peace and justice through the enunciation of God's solidarity with the poor and suffering and the denunciation of all structures of injustice and oppression.

For Aloysius Pieris, the dialogue with local cultures and the work of inculturation is not a matter of undertaking some formal program; it is a direct consequence of simple involvement with the life of the people.[78] Given Christianity's minority status, involvement in the lives of the people, in turn, will entail a dialogue with the deep religiosity of Asia.

Dialogue: Reading Redemptoris Missio and Dialogue and Proclamation (Maryknoll, N.Y.: Orbis Books, 1993).

[76] Felix Wilfred, "The Federation of Asian Bishops' Conferences (FABC): Orientations, Challenges and Impact," in *For All the Peoples of Asia, Federation of Asian Bishops' Conferences Documents from 1970 to 1991*, vol. 1, ed. Gaudencio Rosales and C. G. Arévalo (Quezon City, Philippines: Claretian Publications, 1997), xxiv.

[77] Edmund Chia, *Towards a Theology of Dialogue* (Bangkok: Edmund Chia, 2003), 231.

[78] Aloysius Pieris, *An Asian Theology of Liberation* (Maryknoll, N.Y.: Orbis Books, 1988), 38.

Foundational to FABC's theology of dialogue is a pneumatology that readily acknowledges, echoing John Paul II, that the Spirit is actively at work beyond the boundaries of the church.[79] This has led Asian Christianity to adopt a posture of humble listening to the insight and wisdom of the great religious traditions and popular religious practices of the region. The imperative for dialogue is rooted also in the Asian notion of harmony, which one FABC document describes as "the intellectual and affective, religious and artistic, personal and societal soul of both persons and institutions in Asia."[80]

The dialogical imperative has multiple dimensions. For example, it would be a great mistake to imagine that what the Asian church leadership has in mind is primarily the kind of formal dialogue among religious leaders and thinkers exemplified in the many bilateral ecumenical dialogues found within Christianity or in papal meetings with great religious leaders of other traditions. Chia insists that the "idea of interreligious dialogue as a specific activity is a western concept."[81] No, the Asian bishops have been insistent on the priority of the *dialogue of life*.[82] This dialogue is rooted in the everyday encounters with peoples of very different religious traditions. Again, the minority status of Asian Christians guarantees that this will be an occurrence far more ordinary and common than most Westerners could imagine. This dialogue of life helps one gain a more sympathetic understanding of one's dialogue partner as everyday interactions breed a sense of trust.

The dialogue of life, sown from the seeds of many daily encounters, leads to a *dialogue of action*, a willingness to work together for justice based on common values.[83] This is not a matter of simply working side by side for common goals. What we are talking about here is what liberation theologians have referred to as *praxis*, committed action accompanied by theological reflection.[84] Common action for the sake of justice presupposes solidarity with those who suffer as well as common reflection both on the causes of their suffering and on the appropriate means for redressing that suffering. This shared *praxis* provides the foundation for the creation of "basic human communities," communal relationships constructed around a sense of common humanity.[85]

The testimony of Asian church leaders suggests that only after having established a dialogue of life and action is it possible to enter into that more formal

---

[79] "First Bishops' Institute for Interreligious Affairs on the Theology of Dialogue," in *For All the Peoples of Asia*, 1:249; see also 3:237-328.

[80] *For All the Peoples of Asia*, 1:249.

[81] Chia, 248n.159. This account of the praxis of dialogue in Asian Christianity draws considerably from Chia's systematic analysis, 248-59.

[82] *For All the Peoples of Asia*, 1:300.

[83] Ibid., 1:15. For further reflection on this theme, see Michael Amaladoss, *Walking Together: The Practice of Inter-Religious Dialogue* (Anand, Gujarat, India: Gujarat Sahitya Prakash, 1992).

[84] For a lucid account of *praxis* as it relates to intercultural dialogue, see Bevans, 70-87.

[85] *For All the Peoples of Asia*, 3:3.

mode of dialogue, a *dialogue of discourse*. It is at this level that we see the specific participation of religious leaders and theologians in formal conversations around set themes. The goal here is not one of conversion, nor one of apologetics, but rather one of deeper understanding. The dialogue of discourse recognizes that there is an insight into another tradition that simply cannot be obtained by learning *about* that tradition; one must engage the tradition itself.

The many reactions to Pope Benedict's treatment of Islam in his Regensburg address included an open letter written to the pope by thirty-eight Islamic scholars.[86] These scholars gently upbraided the pope for basing his reflections on a characterization of Islam drawn from studies by non-Muslim scholars. Their point was not that it was impossible for a non-Muslim to understand Islam, but that there was a crucial perspective that was to be gained by seeking to understand Islam by actually engaging Muslims directly.

Finally, these three modes of dialogue lead to a *dialogue of spirituality* or of religious experience. At this level the dialogue partners move to the most intimate dimension of interreligious dialogue, namely, the sharing of one's religious experience. It may even lead to a cautious sharing of forms of prayer and worship.[87] The most famous example of this was the 1986 World Day of Prayer convened by Pope John Paul II. Twenty years later, in 2006, Pope Benedict XVI visited Istanbul, in part to heal the rifts with Islam caused by his Regensburg lecture, and silently prayed, facing Mecca, alongside a Muslim cleric at the Blue Mosque.

Now we come to a crucial and much-controverted question about the nature of such dialogue. From a Christian perspective, is the dialogue with other religions and cultures limited to seeking deeper understanding or does it have an evangelical component? Does it also seek conversion? Asian bishops and theologians have often fielded these questions, and many have objected to the way the question is formulated. Against periodic accusations that the Asian church has seen interreligious dialogue as an alternative to Christian mission, the Asians bishops have consistently responded that they understand dialogue as a vital modality of Christian mission.[88]

---

[86] "Open Letter to the Pope," *Origins* 36 (November 2, 2006): 333-36.

[87] These four dimensions of interreligious dialogue were nicely summarized in *Dialogue and Proclamation:* "a. The *dialogue of life*, where people strive to live in an open and neighborly spirit, sharing their joys and sorrows, their human problems and preoccupations. b) The *dialogue of action*, in which Christians and others collaborate for the integral development and liberation of people. c) The *dialogue of theological exchange*, where specialists seek to deepen their understanding of their respective religious heritages, and to appreciate each other's spiritual values. d) The *dialogue of religious experience*, where persons, rooted in their own religious traditions, share their spiritual riches, for instance, with regard to prayer and contemplation, faith and ways of searching for God or the Absolute" (# 42).

[88] Phan, *In Our Own Tongues*, 18-25.

Several convictions lead to this position. First, the Asian bishops have furthered an insight briefly articulated at Vatican II and then haltingly explored by Pope John Paul II, namely, the conviction that the mission of the church is not oriented, in the first instance, to the salvation of souls but rather to the furthering of God's reign. Thus, for example, when Christians engage in a dialogue of action with peoples of other religions, working for justice and the liberation of peoples, this work is integral to Christian mission. Second, authentic dialogue, particularly the dialogue of discourse and the dialogue of spirituality, must include a moment when the Christian conversation partner is free to share his or her most profound convictions regarding the gracious love of God that has come to our world in Jesus of Nazareth by the power of the Holy Spirit. Proclamation of the good news of Jesus Christ will often be an element of genuine interreligious dialogue. As the Vatican document *Dialogue and Proclamation* puts it:

> Interreligious dialogue does not merely aim at mutual understanding and friendly relations. It reaches a much deeper level, that of the spirit, where exchange and sharing consist in a mutual witness to one's beliefs and a common exploration of one's respective religious convictions. (DP 40)

Such honest sharing of faith may in fact lead to the conversion of one's dialogue partner. The goal, however, is for an honest communication of one's own faith convictions, leaving in God's hands how one's partner chooses to hear and respond to that which is shared.

If such dialogue is to be sincere, it will include as well the opportunity to listen to the religious testimony of one's partner. Honest dialogue requires that Christian partners exhibit the same openness and receptivity to the sharing of their partners that they expect their partners to offer them. But could such dialogue bring about a change on the part of the Christian? Yes. Would such a change necessarily lead them away from their own Christian convictions? No. *Dialogue and Proclamation* attends very perceptively to the possibility that the Christian might be changed by interreligious dialogue:

> Moreover, the fullness of truth received in Jesus Christ does not give individual Christians the guarantee that they have grasped that truth fully. In the last analysis, truth is not a thing we possess, but a person by whom we must allow ourselves to be possessed. This is an unending process. While keeping their identity intact, Christians must be prepared to learn and to receive from and through others the positive values of their traditions. Through dialogue, they may be moved to give up ingrained prejudices, to revise preconceived ideas, and even sometimes to allow the understanding of their faith to be purified. (DP 49)

This statement explains why interreligious dialogue can never be considered optional for the Christian community. The encounter with other religions can become a means for the transformation of Christianity itself.

Feminist Perspectives on the Catholicity of the Church

In this consideration of catholicity from a postmodern perspective, we cannot overlook the contributions and insights of contemporary Christian feminism. Women have, of course, always been a part of the church and have often borne the lion's share of the work involved in the church's mission, as any history of Christian education, for example, would demonstrate. However, where it has not been outright invisible, the role of women in the life of the church has often been hidden, in the sacred texts and official narratives of the Christian tradition. Consequently, contemporary feminist thought has demanded that Scripture and tradition be subjected to a twofold hermeneutical strategy.[89] On the one hand, contemporary feminist studies have developed a hermeneutic of suspicion intent on developing the skills necessary to interpret Scripture and tradition with an eye for evidence of patriarchal bias. Anne Clifford offers examples of this bias:[90] (1) the value of women is often determined by their capacity to bear sons (see Genesis 30); (2) numerous biblical passages treat women as the property of men (Deuteronomy 22); (3) women are presented as the victims of misogynistic violence (Judges 11; 19);[91] (4) women are often explicitly ordered to keep silent in the church or are explicitly subordinated to men (1 Cor. 14:33-35; 1 Tim. 2:8-15). The patriarchal passages from the church tradition are simply too numerous to mention. In many instances, a hermeneutic of suspicion will involve not only identifying patriarchal and misogynistic narratives but also noting the silences, the places where a woman's perspective is simply absent.

Most Christian feminists believe, however, that in spite of the patriarchal bias of Scripture and tradition, there are also powerful liberative elements that need to be critically retrieved and given more attention than is customary. This is sometimes referred to as a hermeneutics of retrieval and remembrance. Clif-

---

[89] For introductions to feminist hermeneutics, see Elisabeth Schüssler Fiorenza, *Bread Not Stone: The Challenge of Feminist Biblical Interpretation* (Boston: Beacon, 1984); Letty Russell, *Feminist Interpretation of the Bible* (Philadelphia: Westminster, 1985); Sandra M. Schneiders, *The Revelatory Text: Interpreting the New Testament as Sacred Scripture* (New York: HarperCollins, 1991). For a helpful summary, see Anne Clifford, *Introducing Feminist Theology* (Maryknoll, N.Y.: Orbis Books, 2001), 46-91.

[90] Clifford, 66-72.

[91] See Phyllis Trible, *Texts of Terror: Literary Feminist Readings of Biblical Narratives* (Philadelphia: Fortress, 1984).

ford uses the parable of the woman who sweeps her entire house in search of the "lost coin" to describe the work of feminist hermeneutics, which seeks out biblical passages that are liberative.[92] The Song of Songs celebrates the erotically driven love between a man and a woman. The Book of Ruth offers the wonderful partnership between Ruth and Naomi. In the New Testament, feminist scholars will note the shocking way in which Jesus allowed women into his company. They will bring into the foreground the fact that the biblical testimony consistently posits the women disciples as the first to encounter the risen lord. This hermeneutics of retrieval is not limited to Scripture. Feminist retrievals have brought to our attention important contributions women have made in the Christian tradition, whether it is the mystical wisdom of Hildegard of Bingen and St. Teresa of Avila, or the persistence of St. Catherine of Siena, who challenged a pope and shamed him into returning the papacy from Avignon to Rome.

The story of the place of women in the church is a story filled with pain. Yet many insist that this is not the whole story. Natalie Watson writes:

> The church, though excluding women from some of its most meaningful moments, has also been the space in which women have been able to develop their own discourses of faith, often against or in spite of patriarchy. The religious life provided women with a unique space in which to develop a "women's world" in which men were often simply accepted as visitors. . . . More generally, women account for the majority of those who attend church services.[93]

Watson acknowledges that for many women, belonging to the church has meant living with the contradictions that are so evident in Christianity's attitude toward women in the past and present.

Obviously, to address the place of women in the church is to consider questions of profound injustice, past and present. But it is also a question of catholicity. When the church is deprived of the full participation of over 50 percent of its membership, the fullness of the Christian faith, as testified to in the lives of believers, is inevitably compromised. Earlier we considered the importance of acknowledging the particularity of local cultures. Here I am suggesting that this concern for honoring the particularity of human experience extends to the experience of women in the church. There is no one generic female perspective on human life any more than there is a generic African

---

[92] Clifford, 72.

[93] Natalie K. Watson, *Introducing Feminist Ecclesiology* (London: Sheffield Academic Press, 2002), 3.

perspective. There are, however, many particular narratives of women's suffering and flourishing, and the catholicity of the church depends on the embrace of those stories as part of the Christian tradition.

A distinct but related postmodern theological tradition has been associated with the complex ways in which many women experience the church as people of color. African American and Latina women, for example, often bear the burden of a double prejudice, the testimony to which has something quite important to teach the larger Christian community. This has led to fertile theological explorations of the experience of African American Christian women, often referred to as "womanist theology,"[94] and Latina Christian women, often referred to as "mujerista theology."[95] The catholicity of the church demands that these perspectives be given their due.

We must be clear about the fact that this is not a matter of *bringing women into the church*; they have always been there and have most frequently comprised the church's most dedicated membership. No, what the church's catholicity demands is a full acknowledgment of their presence, a rightful celebration of their gifts, a ready hearing of their legitimate grievances and, most important, a commitment to the ecclesial reform necessary to grant them the full recognition and rightful privileges due the baptized people of God.

Karl Barth once remarked that "the church is catholic or it is not the church."[96] In this chapter we have tried to spell out the full implications of Barth's observation. The church has its origins in the incarnation, God's irrevocable pledge to humankind in Jesus of Nazareth. Just as the universal significance of Christ for all humankind was disclosed in the particularities of time and place, so too the church derives its catholicity from its capacity for realization in diverse peoples and cultures. Because the church has no one sacred language or culture, it is capable of flourishing in all languages and cultures. This catholicity is enriched wherever the church fulfills its mission in a respectful, dialogical engagement with the world.

If the church is essentially catholic in its nature and mission, its catholicity is also eschatological in character. Catholicity is not just an attribute of the church; it is a demand and a goal. Wherever the need for control leads church leadership to be suspicious of new forms of Christian life emerging daily throughout the world, there the church's catholicity suffers. Wherever there is

---

[94] Delores Williams, *Sisters in the Wilderness: The Challenge of Womanist God-talk* (Maryknoll, N.Y.: Orbis Books, 1993).

[95] Ada María Isasi-Díaz, *En la Lucha=In the Struggle: Elaborating a Mujerista Theology* (Minneapolis: Fortress, 2004).

[96] Karl Barth, *Kirchliche Dogmatik* 4/2 (Zurich: Theologischer Verlag, 1953), 784.

an unwillingness to learn from other religions and cultures, there the church's catholicity suffers. Wherever the church remains aloof to the in-breaking of God's reign in the world—even beyond the boundaries of the church—there the church's catholicity suffers. The church is a pilgrim people, a people on a journey between Pentecost and the culmination of all history in Christ. As we travel on that pilgrimage may we keep ever before us the vision of Pentecost as a community that has learned to hear and celebrate the one Christian faith, each in their own language.

QUESTIONS FOR REFLECTION

1. What is the significance of Bevans and Schroeder's statement: "One of the most important things Christians need to know about the church is that the *church* is not of ultimate importance"?
2. What do you think is most threatening to Christians today regarding the possibility of the full and diverse inculturation of the Christian faith?
3. Is it possible for a Christian to be committed to genuine interreligious dialogue without abandoning her own Christian convictions and her desire to share her faith with non-Christians? How would you reconcile the two?
4. Can Christianity be universal in its scope if its core message is not "transcultural"?

SUGGESTIONS FOR FURTHER READING AND STUDY

Amaladoss, Michael. *Beyond Inculturation: Can the Many Be One?* Delhi: Indian Society for Promoting Christian Knowledge, 1998.

Bevans, Stephen B. *Models of Contextual Theology.* Revised and expanded ed. Maryknoll, N.Y.: Orbis Books, 2002.

Bevans, Stephen B., and Roger P. Schroeder. *Constants in Context: A Theology of Mission for Today.* Maryknoll, N.Y.: Orbis Books, 2004.

Bosch, David. *Transforming Mission: Paradigm Shifts in Theology of Mission.* Maryknoll, N.Y.: Orbis Books, 1991.

Dulles, Avery. *The Catholicity of the Church.* Oxford: Clarendon Press, 1985.

Irvin, Dale T., and Scott W. Sunquist. *History of the World Christian Movement.* Volume 1. Maryknoll, N.Y.: Orbis Books, 2001.

Jenkins, Philip. *The Next Christendom: The Coming of Global Christianity.* New York: Oxford University Press, 2002.

Mannion, Gerard. *Ecclesiology and Postmodenrity: Questions for the Church in Our Time.* Collegeville, Minn.: Liturgical Press, 2007.

Phan, Peter C. *In Our Own Tongues: Perspectives from Asia on Mission and Inculturation.* Maryknoll, N.Y.: Orbis Books, 2003.

Roberson, Ronald. *The Eastern Christian Churches: A Brief Survey.* 6th ed. Rome: Edizioni Orientalia Christiania, 1999.

Sanneh, Lamin. *Translating the Message: The Missionary Impact on Culture.* Maryknoll, N.Y.: Orbis Books, 1989.

———. *Whose Religion Is Christianity? The Gospel beyond the West.* Grand Rapids: Eerdmans, 2003.

Schreiter, Robert J. *Constructing Local Theologies.* Maryknoll, N.Y.: Orbis Books, 1985.

———. *The New Catholicity: Theology between the Global and the Local.* Faith and Culture Series. Maryknoll, N.Y.: Orbis Books, 1997.

Shorter, Aylward. *Toward a Theology of Inculturation.* Maryknoll, N.Y.: Orbis Books, 1988.

Walls, Andrew F. *The Cross-Cultural Process in Christian History: Studies in the Transmission and Appropriation of Faith.* Maryknoll, N.Y.: Orbis Books, 2002.

———. *The Missionary Movement in Christian History.* Maryknoll, N.Y.: Orbis Books, 1996.

Watson, Natalie K. *Introducing Feminist Ecclesiology.* London: Sheffield Academic Press, 2002.

Wostyn, Lode L. *Doing Ecclesiology: Church and Mission Today.* Quezon City, Philippines: Claretian Publications, 1990.

3

A People Called to Communion

In chapter 2 we considered the catholicity of the church as it related to dialogical mission. The church's catholicity reminds us that the unity of the church is, following the analogy of the triune life of God, a differentiated and relational unity. The relationship between the church's catholicity and its unity follows upon the relationship between the unity of God and God's tripersonal being. The doctrine of the Trinity does not articulate a distinct attribute of God overlaid on God's one divine nature like one color transparency being laid over another. This misconception was fueled by the tendency of scholastic theologians like St. Thomas Aquinas to treat God's one divine nature (*De Deo Uno*) prior to treating God's tripersonal being (*De Deo Trino*). This schema would mistakenly suggest (against Thomas's intention) that these were two completely separate aspects of God's being that could be considered apart from their relationship to each other.[1] In fact, however, the doctrine of the Trinity describes *how* God is one. It teaches us that God's unity is a relational, differentiated, and fecund unity. By analogy, so it is with the church. If the oneness of the church accentuates the church's deep spiritual unity as the one people of God and body of Christ, the catholicity of the church highlights the relational, differentiated, and fecund character of the church's unity.

An early Christian sense of the unity of the church was conditioned by the limits of ancient travel and communication. Contact with other Christians was, for the most part, limited to one's own local community of believers. At least in the early decades, Christianity remained a minority movement subject to periodic persecutions. These conditions made it only natural to develop strong bonds with other local believers within a given community. At the same time, there is little evidence for any incipient congregationalism in early Christianity, that is, the view that each local community was strictly autonomous and self-contained. Early Christian communities tended to view themselves as spiritually bound together with other Christian communities, even if the nature of those bonds were not always clearly articulated.

---

[1] Karl Rahner, *The Trinity* (New York: Herder & Herder, 1970), 16-17; Catherine Mowry LaCugna, *God for Us: The Trinity and Christian Life* (New York: HarperCollins, 1991), 145-52.

Early Christianity's consciousness of its unity was sustained within a historical situation in which there was, by contemporary standards, a striking pluralism of beliefs and practices.[2] One should recall that for the first two centuries of Christianity, there was no universally agreed upon canon of Scripture, no developed creed (beyond brief interrogatory baptismal formulae), no universally accepted organizational structures, no standard liturgical books. Yet in the midst of this widespread diversity, Christians still believed themselves to be united in faith. When gathered together in local community, they were God's holy people, the body of Christ in that place. As such they were also spiritually united with other such communities.

CHURCH LOCAL AND UNIVERSAL

The relationship between each local church's sense of itself as authentically "church," and these churches' convictions regarding their relationship to the whole Christian movement was complex.[3] The default assumption of early Christianity was that most church issues were to be dealt with at the local level, and only when issues clearly had consequences for the broader community (e.g., what to do with Christians who betrayed the faith during persecution only subsequently to request reentry into the community) were decisions to be made by representative gatherings of regional churches (synods).[4] Early in the postbiblical period, the biblical concept of *koinōnia* would be extended to the spiritual relationship that existed among the churches. There was a common conviction that all eucharistic communities abided together in shared ecclesial *koinōnia* or communion.[5] For the early church, the sacrament of the eucharist brought about not only the communion of those gathered at each altar but the communion of all local churches.

---

[2] James D. G. Dunn, *Unity and Diversity in the New Testament: An Inquiry into the Character of Earliest Christianity*, 3rd ed. (London: SCM, 2006).

[3] In ecclesiology, the term "local church" is a highly analogous concept. This is, I believe, its principal strength. There is some debate in Roman Catholic ecclesiology and canon law regarding the use of the term "particular church" rather than "local church" when referring to a Roman Catholic diocese, often regarded as the fundamental ecclesiological unit within Catholicism. This was certainly the practice of the 1984 Code of Canon Law. However, there are good reasons for preferring the semantic flexibility of the term "local church," which, in various contexts, might refer to a basic ecclesial community—a parish, a diocese, or the church of a particular geographic region. In each of these instances, what is shared is a sense of defining particularity over against the universality implicit in references to the whole church.

[4] Roger Haight, *Christian Community in History*, 2 vols. (New York: Continuum, 2004-5), 1:133.

[5] Ludwig Hertling, *Communio: Church and Papacy in Early Christianity* (Chicago: Loyola University Press, 1972; German original, 1943).

As Christianity developed in the early centuries, theological reflections on the church gave prominence to what today we would speak of as a relational view of the church, that is, a church constituted by the ecclesial relationships established in baptism and nurtured in the eucharist. Indeed, the eucharist would, throughout most of the first millennium, play a central role in ecclesiology. When Christians gathered at the table of the Lord to partake in the Lord's banquet, they believed that this action not only drew them into saving communion with God in Christ but also constituted them as Christ's body the church. From the time of the first centuries of the church's life, the metaphor of the "body of Christ" was evocative, with a rich breadth of meaning. The "body of Christ" could refer to (a) the Word made flesh, (b) the eucharistic body, or (c) the body of Christ the church. Henri de Lubac, in his classic study *Corpus Mysticum,* observed that, although it was true that the church constituted the eucharist, it was equally true that the eucharist established the church: *eucharistia facit ecclesiam.* The fluidity in the meaning of the metaphor of the body of Christ helped preserve the important connections between sacramental theology and ecclesiology.[6]

In virtually all of the ancient Christian writers, the eucharist and the church were intimately related. The eucharist was related to the church as cause to effect, as means to end, and as sign to reality. Of course at this point there were as yet no great battles over the conditions for the efficacy of the sacrament aside from unity with the church. It is difficult to exaggerate these early church presuppositions regarding the ecclesiality of the eucharistic celebration. Consider the following passage from a famous sermon of St. Augustine:

> Since you are the body of Christ and his members, it is your mystery that is placed on the Lord's table, it is your mystery that you receive. . . . Be what you see, and receive what you are. (*Sermon* 272)

Reflecting the Eastern Christian tradition, St. John Chrysostom writes:

> For what is the bread? It is the body of Christ. And what do those who receive it become? The Body of Christ—not many bodies but one body. For as bread is completely one, though made of up many grains of wheat, and these, albeit unseen, remain nonetheless present, in such a way that their difference is not apparent since they have been made a perfect whole, so too are we mutually joined to one another and together united with Christ. (*In Epistolam I ad Corinthios Homiliae* 24.2)

---

[6] Henri de Lubac, *Corpus mysticum: l'eucharistie et l'Eglise au Moyen âge: Etude historique* (Paris: Aubier, 1949).

It was this eucharistic unity, this sense that each and all churches were the body of Christ in that place, that created the space for a high level of diversity in belief and practice.[7]

The principal eucharistic liturgical texts had become fixed during the fourth through the seventh centuries. The resulting stability greatly enhanced the influence of liturgy on the church's operative ecclesiology. The deep eucharistic roots of early Christian reflection on the church helped secure a strong theological appreciation for the integrity of each local church. Each community in which the Word was proclaimed and the bread broken was the body of Christ "in that place." This provided a sound sacramental foundation for the unity of the churches, at least in principle. Patrick Burns succinctly captures the eucharistic foundations of ecclesial communion, which had fully developed by the third century:

> The basic unity of the church in the third century was the local eucharistic congregation, united under one bishop and the college of presbyters and college of deacons who assisted him in his pastoral ministry. Such local churches were not substations of the church universal or branch offices of a world-wide organization. Rather the local Christian community, united in faith in the saving word and in eucharistic fellowship in the body of the Lord, was the church of God for its locality, the effective presence of the whole Christ in its concrete life and worship. Yet precisely the principle of unity of this local church, the saving presence of Christ in word and sacrament, made it aware of its essential relationship to the other local Christian communities throughout the world (where the same Lord and the same Spirit brought about the same ecclesial reality). The local church, without ceasing to be fully church, existed only in a world-wide communion of churches which constituted the church universal.[8]

This eucharistic framework preserved a balance between the theological integrity of each local church and the communion of all the churches. An ecclesiology attuned to ancient trinitarian convictions had to affirm that church unity, if grounded in the triune life of God, could not be based in a stifling uniformity but rather had to affirm unity as communion, that is, a unity-in-diversity in keeping with the trinitarian differentiated unity of God.

---

[7] See Jean-Marie R. Tillard, *Flesh of the Church, Flesh of Christ: At the Source of the Ecclesiology of Communion* (Collegeville, Minn.: Liturgical Press, 2001).

[8] Patrick Burns, "Communion, Councils, and Collegiality: Some Catholic Reflections," in *Papal Primacy and the Universal Church,* ed. Paul C. Empie and T. Austin Murphy (Minneapolis: Augsburg, 1974), 152.

The trinitarian and sacramental foundations of the church led to an understanding of church unity as communion. Unity conceived from the perspective of biblical *koinōnia* reflected a concern for shared life more than uniformity in belief and practice. These convictions provided deep and compelling theological checks against the ever-present ecclesial dangers of congregationalism and a monolithic and dominating ecclesial universalism.

CHRISTIAN UNITY AT RISK IN THE FIRST MILLENNIUM

If the sacramental and trinitarian foundations of the church of the first millennium created the theological space necessary for affirming unity in the midst of diversity, it is also true that in the concrete life of the church, where theological ideals confronted numerous historically and sociologically contingent circumstances, this unity was always at risk. Paul Avis has sagely observed that

> [e]cclesiology ... is commonly stated in the ideal mode. It airily evokes what the Church is in the purposes of God, but disdains the messy human reality. So often ecclesiology offers a "God's eye view" but turns a blind eye to the human aspect.[9]

Sweeping schematizations of church history often assume a fundamental church unity continuing throughout the first millennium. This generalization masks a far more contentious reality.

The diversity of Christian communities reflected in the Scriptures would only increase in the following centuries. The history of many of these divisions has been written by the victors, and so we tend to look back on early Christianity from the perspective of an orthodoxy challenged by various heretical and schismatic movements. But such an approach is anachronistic and fails to take account of the ways in which many of these movements that were later viewed as heretical or schismatic (e.g., Montanists, Valentinians, Marcionites, Ebionites, Novationists) assumed that they were in fact authentically Christian.[10]

Early Christianity would develop in diverse cultural, social, and political contexts that had, at times, only minimal contact with one another. In the mid-second century the Christian faith was established among the Assyrian peoples

---

[9] Paul Avis, *Beyond the Reformation? Authority, Primacy and Unity in the Conciliar Tradition* (London: T&T Clark, 2006), 204.

[10] See Bart Ehrman, *Lost Christianities: The Battles for Scripture and the Faiths We Never Knew* (New York: Oxford University Press, 2003).

in upper Mesopotamia, a region that would be conquered by the Persians in the third century. Persian Christianity was heavily influenced by the christological perspectives associated with the school at Antioch. They were, in part, the targets of the condemnations issued at the Council of Ephesus, which was aimed at resolving disputes regarding the relationship between the humanity and divinity of Christ. The Persian church rejected the teaching of Ephesus, partly for theological reasons and partly to distance itself from the Roman empire, with which Persia was often at war.[11]

In the fifth century, Christianity roiled under a series of doctrinal disputes regarding the person of Jesus Christ. The Council of Chalcedon, held in 451, sought to resolve this dispute, teaching that Christ was one person with two natures, divine and human. A number of Christian communities rejected the theology they felt was implicit in this teaching, although in some cases, political disputes with the Byzantine empire may also have entered in.

As Christianity took root in the Mediterranean, it was inevitable that it would be influenced by larger cultural contexts. Beyond the distinctions in Christian traditions that we have already discussed, a more sweeping division in Christianity began to develop in the third and fourth centuries corresponding to the two dominant cultures of the time, Roman/Latin and Byzantine/Greek. The eventual schism between the Christian churches associated with these two cultures is often dated in 1054, but their drift apart began much earlier. This progressive drift was the result of a volatile confluence of political, social, economic, and theological factors.

As early as the third century we can detect subtle but growing theological differences between the Eastern and Western traditions. The Western theological trajectory was more practical, the East more speculative. The West was influenced by Roman legal categories, the East by the dynamics of corporate worship. These incipient theological differences would be accompanied in the fourth century by the division of the Roman empire into two relatively autonomous sectors, East and West. The dominant role of the Eastern emperor as a spiritual and ecclesiastical leader obviated the need for a single church figure to serve as a minister of unity. This created the conditions for a more synodal form of church government in which patriarchs and metropolitans would govern their churches in communion with standing synods of bishops. The West saw the authority of the bishop of Rome increase without competition from any significant imperial figure.

By the end of the seventh century the Eastern empire, now known as Byzantium, had lost virtually all political control and influence over Italy, as it found

---

[11] Ronald Roberson, *The Eastern Christian Churches*, 6th ed. (Rome: Edizioni Orientalia Christiana, 1999), 15.

itself increasingly preoccupied with the Islamic threat to the East. In 726, the Byzantine emperor Leo III further exacerbated relations with the West when he condemned the use of icons as a form of idolatry. Pope Gregory II interpreted this as yet another example of Byzantium espousing heresy, and he denounced Leo bitterly. Leo struck back against Gregory's successor, Gregory III, by confiscating papal lands in southern Italy, thus robbing the papacy of its principal source of income. This dispute paved the way for the Western church's fateful turn away from Byzantium and toward the political powers of the north for support.

The creation of the papal states (they would not actually be referred to as "papal states" until the late Middle Ages) constituted the decisive and permanent political break between Rome and the Byzantine empire centuries before the formalization of this schism in the mutual excommunications of 1054. Even after these excommunications, however, significant bonds of unity would continue to endure between the Eastern and Western churches until the brutal sacking of Constantinople as part of the Fourth Crusade in 1204.

Conceptions of ecclesial unity in the Eastern church would continue to be shaped by that church's close relationship to dominant political empires, first Byzantium, at least nominally until 1453, and then the Ottoman empire (with the exception of the Eastern churches in Poland, Lithuania, and parts of Russia) until 1923. Even today, the unity of the various Orthodox churches is both mediated and sometimes impeded by distinct ethnic/linguistic traditions. The problem of unity in the West was a bit more complicated.

DEVELOPING CHURCH STRUCTURES IN SERVICE OF THE COMMUNION OF THE CHURCHES

For much of the first millennium Christian unity was interpreted theologically as a spiritual communion with deep sacramental and trinitarian roots. The delicate balance between the autonomy of the local churches and the unity of all the churches in one spiritual communion would be maintained through the communion manifested among the bishops within and between various regions. This communion among the churches was realized in many ways. When Christians traveled, they often took with them a letter of commendation from their bishop and offered it to the bishop of the church in the geographic locale they were visiting. If the local bishop accepted the letter, the visitor would be allowed to participate at the eucharist.[12] The acceptance of

---

[12] See Werner Elert, *Eucharist and Church Fellowship in the First Four Centuries*, trans. N. E. Nagel (St. Louis: Concordia, 1966); Kenneth Hein, *Eucharist and Excommunication: A Study in Early Christian Doctrine and Discipline* (Frankfurt: Lang, 1975).

the letter of commendation was a tacit acknowledgment of the communion between the two churches.

A second expression of the communion among the churches was found in the early practice of the bishops of a given region gathering in a synod. In the second and third centuries local bishops began meeting on a regional basis in gatherings that would become known as "synods" to address questions of common concern. (The term "synod" stems from the Greek prefix, *syn*, which means "together," and *hodos*, which means "way"—a synod is then a medium for local churches to "come together," or "walk together.") Often the matters demanding attention were disciplinary, but occasionally these synods would pronounce on matters of doctrine. In the late second century we have evidence of an episcopal synod called to respond to the Montanist threat, and we know that in 190 Bishop Victor of Rome called for a series of regional synods to address the discrepancies in the dating of Easter. This practice of gathering in regional synods suggests that very early in the history of Christianity it was recognized that bishops who were pastors of local churches bore responsibility for the larger church as well.

The early "ecumenical councils" were in fact little more than regional synods, generally convened at the instigation of the emperor, which dealt with matters of import for the universal church. As their solutions were accepted by the church universal, their "ecumenical status" (from the Greek word *oikoumene*, meaning "the whole inhabited world") would be acknowledged in subsequent centuries. The first seven became ecumenical only after they were received by all of the churches. Only much later would concerns over the juridical validity of councils come to the fore.

For the first three centuries of Christianity, the emerging biblical canon, the office of the bishop, and the practice of convening regional synods all played growing roles in preserving the unity of the churches. By the fourth century, however, the authority of the church of Rome and its bishop had grown in the West. In part this was due to the political and commercial significance of the city of Rome. In part it was due to the unique prestige associated with the church of Rome in virtue of the tradition that Rome had witnessed the martyrdom of not one but two apostles, Peter and Paul (we shall discuss the papacy in relationship to the church's apostolicity in a later chapter). The church's organizational structure had developed along regional lines; certain churches with particularly strong claims to an apostolic heritage gained a greater measure of prestige and authority. Some of these churches would be viewed as "patriarchal" sees and would exercise a certain authority over other churches in their geographic region (Rome, Antioch, Alexandria, and later Constantinople). When the Roman empire split in two, Rome was the only patriarchal see in the West, giving it an unparalleled authority. Moreover, by the end of the third

century, the authority of Rome as the church of Sts. Peter and Paul would converge with the tradition that the *bishop* of Rome was the successor to St. Peter,
the head of the apostles. Finally Rome's prestige was enhanced by its having
"backed the right horse" regarding a number of early church disputes, including the dating of Easter and the understanding of the relationship between the
humanity and divinity of Christ.

From the fourth century on we see a series of popes, from Damasus to Gregory, making claims to a unique papal authority over the whole church. Toward
the end of the first millennium, allegiance to the papacy in the West appeared
to enhance papal authority. Not surprisingly, this authority was far more widely
accepted in the West than in the East. In the East the church's complex relationship to the emerging Byzantine empire led it to see the emperor rather
than the pope as the principal guarantor of the church's unity. According to
Eamon Duffy,

> The bishops of the East saw no cause to challenge any of this. They accepted
> the Christian vocation of the Emperor as God-given, and they saw their
> role as that of obedient collaborators with the Lord's anointed. . . . Between
> the imperial vision of Byzantium . . . and the theological ethos of Rome,
> there was a great and growing gap. The experience of the popes as they set
> themselves to meet the needs of Italy and the West in the years after impe-
> rial reconquest would see that gap widen to a gulf.[13]

Even as regards the West, it is perhaps best not to exaggerate the impact of
papal authority. At the end of the first millennium, in spite of the grand claims
to papal authority, the effective authority of these popes was much less
significant.

The vast majority of Christians in the first millennium would never have
seen the pope, never have read anything that he had said or written, and indeed,
probably could not have identified him by name. Even bishops, the more direct
objects of papal initiatives, in the midst of theoretical disputes regarding the
extent and limits of their own authority, experienced a remarkable degree of *de
facto* autonomy. Up to this point in time, popes did not appoint bishops (except
in dioceses that were sub-urbicarian sees surrounding Rome); they did not con-
vene, preside over, or set the agenda for ecumenical councils; they did not can-
onize saints; they did not write encyclicals; they did not call bishops to Rome
for regular *ad limina* visits; they were never referred to as "sovereign pontiff,"

---

[13] Eamon Duffy, *Saints and Sinners: A History of the Popes* (New Haven: Yale University Press, 1997),
45.

and the titles "pope" and "vicar of Christ" were used in reference not only to them but to other bishops and even emperors. In short, throughout this first millennium of the church, it would simply have been false to say that popes "ran the church." Church historian John O'Malley writes:

> In the early Middle Ages, (and well beyond) the popes' principal duty, many believed, was to guard the tombs of the Apostles and officiate at the solemn liturgies of the great basilicas. In that period, although some of the popes of course had a broad vision of their responsibilities and dealt about weighty matters with the leaders of society, for the most part they behaved as essentially local figures, intent on local issues.[14]

All of this would change in the eleventh century.

THE MEDIEVAL TRANSITION
IN ECCLESIOLOGICAL FOUNDATIONS

The sacramental and relational foundations that allowed for a fruitful tension between the diverse experiences of local churches and a conviction regarding their universal bond as one body of Christ began to erode between the ninth and thirteenth centuries. We shall consider six factors in this gradual erosion of the dominant ecclesiological vision of the first millennium: (1) the devolution of a eucharistic ecclesiology, (2) the Gregorian reforms elicited by the lay investiture controversy, (3) Gratian's compilation of church law, (4) the rise of a hierocratic ecclesiology grounded in the Neoplatonic vision of Pseudo-Dionysius, (5) the Western schism and the rise of conciliarism, and (6) failed efforts at reunion between East and West.

The Devolution of a Eucharistic Ecclesiology

The controversy began in the ninth century, when Paschasius Radbertus, a monk from the monastery of Corbie, wrote the first full systematic treatise on the eucharist, *On the Body and Blood of the Lord*. In that treatise he described Christ's presence in the bread and wine in excessively physicalist language. In the early centuries of Christianity, there is ample evidence that most Christians believed in what we might generically refer to as a doctrine of eucharis-

---

[14] John W. O'Malley, "The Millennium and the Papalization of Catholicism," *America* (April 8, 2000): 14.

tic real presence. However, the focus of that doctrine was on the eucharist's ultimate *purpose*, mainly bringing the believer into contact with the saving work of Christ crucified and risen. Paschasius affirmed that Christ was present in the elements of bread and wine, *in veritate*, 'in truth." But "in truth," for Paschasius, meant physically present. His focus was on the *contents* of the sacrament, not the *purpose*.[15] For example, Paschasius insisted that the body of Christ in the eucharist was the same as the earthly body of Christ born of Mary, albeit received in a different way. Indeed, he suggested that the appearances of bread and wine have no reality but are mere veils to save us from the revulsion one would feel at eating natural flesh and blood.

In response, another ninth-century monk from Corbie, Ratramnus, at the invitation of the emperor, wrote a critique of Paschasius's account of the eucharistic presence, sharing the same title as that of his opponent. His approach reacted to Paschasius's physicalism by offering a more spiritual approach to eucharistic presence. Ratramnus held that Christ was present in the eucharistic elements, *in figura*.[16] By this Ratramnus was apparently referring to a more symbolic, nonphysicalist mode of presence. Yet his understanding of the symbolic was also defective as he appeared to suggest two distinct realities—the physical and the spiritual—uneasily joined together. Ultimately (long after his death) Ratramnus's view was condemned as inadequate to the insights of the tradition, and Christian thinkers came to rely on Paschasius's far more physicalist approach. In the end, neither Paschasius nor Ratramnus was able to overcome the problematic opposition of the symbolic and the real.

Part of the answer would begin to be explored in the eleventh century. Lanfranc, the Archbishop of Canterbury, had begun to consider the idea of an essential or substantial change in the eucharistic elements that occurred even as the outward appearance remained unchanged. The Latin verb that would eventually be used to describe this change was *transubstantiare*, and it would be used in a decree of the Fourth Lateran Council in 1215. However, it would be left to St. Thomas to master the language of Aristotelianism and sketch out the basic structure of a scholastic understanding of eucharistic real presence that would dominate Catholic thought for over seven hundred years.

As these debates raged on, we must note an important unintended consequence, namely, the gradual reduction of eucharistic theology to questions of eucharistic presence: how and in what manner is Christ encountered in the eucharistic elements? Strikingly absent from these debates is the more ancient consciousness of the relationship between the eucharist and the becoming of

---

[15] John H. McKenna, "Eucharistic Presence: An Invitation to Dialogue," *Theological Studies* 60 (1999): 302.

[16] Ibid.

the church. A sharp distinction would develop between the eucharist as the "true" body of Christ (a shift owing much to an Aristotelian emphasis on substantial reality) and the church as the "mystical" body of Christ. In fact, the first place where the phrase *corpus mysticum* appears in reference to the church is in Boniface VIII's *Unam Sanctam* (1302).

The Lay Investiture Controversy

The gradual fall of the Roman empire in the West created a political and social vacuum in which basic civic services were no longer being provided to the people. Bishops soon filled this vacuum and began functioning as both spiritual and civic leaders in local communities. While they were responding to a real societal need, the increasing exercise of civic authority risked obscuring their responsibilities for pastoral leadership. As bishops' civic authority grew, their spiritual authority was often transferred to the local parish priests, who soon became, rather than the bishops, the main sacramental ministers in the church.

The growing civic responsibilities of church leadership drew bishops into a feudal system in which they were often subject to the influence of feudal nobility. Feudal lords set aside lands that would be given to those who held ecclesiastical office, guaranteeing the officeholder the revenues that accrued from those lands. The gift of these lands was called a *benefice*. Consequently, to be given an episcopal office was not just to be given spiritual authority; it was to be given a lifelong source of income. Not surprisingly, the granting of these benefices, done at the discretion of the medieval lords and princes, frequently led to abuse. Many were given benefices as a reward for loyalty, with no interest in spiritual service. Because of this increasingly common practice, the spiritual needs of the faithful were often unmet and the autonomy of the church was compromised by the inordinate influence of the nobility.

This situation led to the famous reforms in the eleventh century of a monk named Hildebrand, better known as Pope Gregory VII (1073-85). Pope Gregory challenged the abuse of benefices and the practice of *simony* (the exchange of ecclesiastical services for money) and reasserted the authority of the pope in all clerical appointments. Gregory's reforms were not intended to gain papal control over the appointment of bishops but merely to preserve their proper autonomy. In other words, he sought to use the sovereignty of the papacy to restore the free elections of the bishops. He did not claim for himself the authority to appoint bishops but only to depose, reinstate, and transfer them. However, the upshot of these reforms was the incremental solidification of all ecclesiastical authority in the papacy. Gregory did not think the bishops were mere representatives of the pope. Yet his overall vision of the church suggested one universal diocese with the pope as its bishop and the other bishops as vicars of the pope.

Gregory began measures to standardize canon law for the whole church. He required that all archbishops receive the *pallium* (a woolen vestment worn around the neck as a sign of pastoral authority) from the pope within three months of their election, and he widened the use of papal legates in other countries, the authority of whom was held as superior to that of local bishops and metropolitans. Gregory's view of the papacy is succinctly presented in his *Dictatus Papae*, in which he lays sweeping claim to sovereign power over all matters spiritual and secular. As Gregory reshaped the tradition, the pope became a virtual replacement for Christ on earth. It was during this period in church history that the title *vicarius Christi* ("vicar of Christ," a title previously shared by all bishops and even kings and emperors) took on a different meaning. No longer did it have the sense of one who is transparent to God's will and purposes, as it did during the first millennium. The title now suggested an earthly surrogate for Christ and was to be applied exclusively to the pope.

Gregory sought to preserve the freedom of the local churches in selecting their bishops, however, as William Henn has observed,

> one may wonder whether the juridical means used to achieve this end may not have overshadowed the desired effect. The desired freedom was won, but the fundamental "sacramentality" of the church was somewhat forgotten in the face of the overriding insistence that the church is a juridically structured society.[17]

From this point on, as we shall see later, the papacy would be "no longer merely the center and bond of unity, but the very source and origin of all churches."[18]

Gratian and the Rise of Canon Law

In 1140 Gratian compiled his famous *Decretals*, a collection of various papal decrees, conciliar canons, decisions of church fathers, and so on, which he systematized. Included in this collection were the so-called *False Decretals of Isidore*. These famous forgeries, which sought to root an expansive view of papal authority in the distant past (e.g., the *Donation of Constantine*), were probably

---

[17] William Henn, *The Honor of My Brothers: A Brief History of the Relationship between the Pope and the Bishops* (New York: Crossroad, 2000), 107-8.

[18] Klaus Schatz, *Papal Primacy: From Its Origins to the Present* (Collegeville, Minn.: Liturgical Press, 1996), 86.

authored in the mid-ninth century and had as their principal goal not so much the desire to expand papal authority as the determination to undermine the abusive exercise of authority on the part of the provincial metropolitans, who were often appointed by the princes and whose proximate influence was far more threatening than the geographically remote authority of the pope. The relative distance and presumed objectivity of Rome were preferred over the corruption of the local metropolitan.

What resulted was a comprehensive systematization of ecclesiastical law, patterned after Roman law, which, once universally promulgated, facilitated an unprecedented growth in the administrative unity of the church. In particular, Gratian stressed the role of the pope as supreme judge and legislator. This unification of administrative authority also made it much easier for the papacy to collect ecclesiastical revenues. This administrative systematization brought with it a new factor in the life of the church, the emergence of the Roman curia as the administrative arm of the papacy patterned after the imperial court. It is not insignificant that the great popes of the twelfth and thirteenth centuries would all be canon lawyers.

The Emergence of a "Hierocratic" Ecclesiology

One of the most influential theological sources of the sixth through the tenth centuries was the writing of Pseudo-Dionysius, a late-fifth- or early-sixth-century Christian writer who took the name of Denis (Latinized as Dionysius) the Areopagite, the disciple of Paul. This work was tremendously influential, in no small part due to its purported apostolic origins, origins that were not seriously disputed until the fifteenth century. His work, particularly influenced by the late Neoplatonist Proclus, was essentially a Christianization of Neoplatonism in which, in two works, *The Celestial Hierarchy* and *The Ecclesiastical Hierarchy,* he posited a divine ordering of the whole cosmos according to a set of descending levels of being. It was assumed that the church mirrored the celestial hierarchies of the angels with a corresponding ontological ordering of levels of ecclesial being within the church. The ordering of the church in this work drew from a fundamentally liturgical conception of the church; hence in its patterning it did not always focus on offices but sacramental rites as well. Moreover, Pseudo-Dionysius did not conceive of this ecclesiastical hierarchy as a ladder as if one could move from one order to the next—it simply depicted the divinely ordered structured of the cosmos.[19]

---

[19] Andrew Louth, *The Origins of the Christian Mystical Tradition* (Oxford: Clarendon Press, 1981), 171.

Nevertheless, in the late Middle Ages Pseudo-Dionysius would be tremendously influential in encouraging the transposition of a plurality of *ordines* that existed in the church into a descending hierarchy that understood these *ordines* as participating in varying degrees of the fullness of being and power. This would be the case particularly among Franciscan theologians like St. Bonaventure who were particularly taken with this cosmic schema. Yves Congar has attributed to them the development of a truly "hierocratic" ecclesiology.[20]

The combination of the demise of a eucharistic ecclesiology, the Gregorian reforms, the systematization of canon law, and the emergence of this hierocratic conception of the church cumulatively pushed the Western church further away from the predominantly sacramental and trinitarian foundations of the first millennium and toward an increasingly juridical and bureaucratic ecclesiology. This legal and bureaucratic framework would make it increasingly difficult to preserve a sense of church unity as a *communio*, a unity in diversity, favoring instead a more monarchical and imperialist view.

Conciliarism

If the high Middle Ages saw more and more sweeping assertions of papal authority, reactions against this centralization of authority also appeared. A number of medieval canonists developed a corporatist conception of the church as the *congregatio fidelium*, a community whose unity was founded not on any one ecclesiastical structure but on Christ. One should note, however, that we are now far removed from the early view of the church's unity as a communion of local churches. The church is now conceived as a universal corporation of believers. From this corporatist perspective, ecclesial power originated from Christ and was distributed throughout the church.[21] Medieval political theorists such as John of Paris and Marsilius of Padua challenged the view that monarchy was the highest form of government. Their call for the rights of all the people to participate in government would inevitably be applied to the church as a social body. Some of these ideas came to the fore in the aftermath of the Western schism.

One can trace the beginnings of this schism all the way back to the second half of the thirteenth century. The gradual emergence of French and English

---

[20] Yves Congar, *L'Église de Saint Augustin à l'époque moderne* (Paris: Cerf, 1970), 226ff.

[21] See Brian Tierney, *Foundations of the Conciliar Theory: The Contribution of the Medieval Canonists from Gratian to the Great Schism*, Cambridge Studies in Medieval Life and Thought 4 (Cambridge: Cambridge University Press, 1955); Francis Oakley, *Council over Pope? Towards a Provisional Ecclesiology* (New York: Herder, 1969); idem, *The Conciliarist Tradition: Constitutionalism in the Catholic Church, 1300-1870* (Oxford: Oxford University Press, 2003); Avis.

monarchies out of medieval feudalism led to a similar deployment of monarchical and imperial structures in the papacy.[22] By this time the burdens of papal
centralization in the form of onerous papal taxation were beginning to take
their toll on many church members. Support for the papacy began to waver.
Innocent IV's crusade against Frederick II drew little support and raised serious questions regarding the papacy's responsiveness to truly spiritual needs.

In the early fourteenth century the papacy moved to Avignon, and by the
end of the century there were first two and then three different claimants to
the Holy See, further eroding the credibility of the papacy. This situation led
to the summoning of the Council of Constance in 1413. This council agreed
that the only viable solution was the resignation of all three claimants and the
election of a new pope. In order to prevent further papal abuses, Constance
issued an early decree on church reforms, entitled *Frequens*, that required the
regular convocation of ecumenical councils for addressing the needs of the
church. In 1415 the council also promulgated the now famous decree *Haec
Sancta*, which appeared to claim, among other things, the ultimate supremacy
of the council regarding matters of faith. However, the precise interpretation
of this decree is a matter of some dispute. Some read the decree as affirming
an important ecclesial principle, namely, that under certain conditions a council might be able to assert its authority over a pope who had abused or
exceeded his authority. Others read it as a more enduring claim regarding the
superiority of council over papacy.

At the next council, held first at Basle, then Ferrara, and finally Florence,
the more radical conciliarists became marginalized and lost most of their support. With the decree *Laetentur Coeli*, the council dramatically reaffirmed the
primacy of the pope over any council. Scholars are still struggling to reconcile
the claims of *Haec Sancta*, an apparently valid conciliar decree, with those of
Laetentur Coeli. Sadly, after the conciliarist controversy, the papacy would fall
prey to a persistent paranoia regarding any claims to the legitimate authority
of the bishops over against that of the papacy. This fear of resurging conciliarism would haunt the papacy and render much more difficult the task of
papal reform.

Failed Attempts at Reunion between East and West

In 1274 the Second Council of Lyons was called largely to facilitate a reunion
between East and West. An agreement was worked out, one that seemed to

---

[22] O'Malley, 14.

demand far more concessions from the East than from the West. Not surprisingly, the agreement was not accepted by Eastern Christians. Another attempt was undertaken in 1439 at the Council of Florence. Again the East was forced to make significant theological and doctrinal concessions, and, again, the agreement was not accepted by the Eastern church. The growing cultural divides and political sequestering of East and West impeded further attempts at reunion. One significant factor was the tendency toward centralization of authority under the papacy and the need for ecclesiastical uniformity in the West. This led to a gradual shift in the Western rhetoric regarding the resolution of the division between West and East from that of "reunion" to that of "return." The Western church did not help matters with its dubious strategy of *uniatism*, that is, a program of missionary endeavors to the Christian East with the intention of inviting Eastern Christians into union with Rome while allowing for the continuation of their own Eastern traditions through the creation of various Eastern Catholic churches. The continued existence of the Eastern Catholic churches remains today a bone of contention in ecumenical conversations between Roman Catholicism and Eastern Orthodoxy.

As the church stood on the eve of the Reformation, it is difficult to exaggerate how far it had traveled from the dominant theological assumptions of much of the first millennium. Each shift, taken in isolation, is perfectly defensible. Cumulatively, however, what would emerge in the fifteenth century is a vision of the church shaped much more by historical exigencies than by any compelling theological vision.

THE REFORMATION AND NEW CHALLENGES
TO THE UNITY OF THE CHURCH

The common periodization of the history of Christianity that refers to the sixteenth-century "Reformation" is potentially misleading. One could make the case that the history of Christianity is a history of a church constantly challenged, threatened, and reinvigorated by church reform.[23] Certainly the great reformers of the sixteenth century were preceded by such earlier reformers as John Wycliffe (1329-1384), Jan Hus (1369-1415), and Girolamo Savonarola (1452-1498). Nevertheless, the reformation movements of the sixteenth century had an unparalleled impact on Christianity's consciousness of itself as a united Christian church. Although Luther did not initially seek separation

---

[23] Christopher M. Bellitto, *Renewing Christianity: A History of Church Reform from Day One to Vatican II* (New York: Paulist Press, 2001).

from the church of Rome, the deep and comprehensive attacks on the Christian church of the time, combined with the ill-fated intransigence of the popes, led to a fracturing of Christianity so profound that, four centuries later, Christianity is still trying to recover.

The Reformation and the Re-Imagination of Christian Unity

It is safe to say that most of the sixteenth-century reformers were no longer persuaded by the ability of any set of ecclesiastical structures, in and of themselves, to preserve the unity of the church. The unity of the church must be sought not in any one institutional structure but in the one faith in Jesus Christ offered in response to the Word of God.

Among the many contributions of the Reformation, we must note its recovery of a theology of the local church, which had been largely lost for the previous six centuries. Luther began his ecclesiological reflections with the local congregation where the Word of God was preached and the sacraments were administered. In Roger Haight's reading of Luther, "the congregational focus means that the local community constitutes the primary organizational point of reference for the church."[24] At the same time, Luther certainly affirmed the reality of the universal church. He described this universal ecclesial reality not in structural terms but as the *communio sanctorum*, the body of the saints bound by a common baptism and a common faith in Christ. He was not, in principle, opposed to bishops, though he did not view them as a necessary feature of the church. For him, church offices, councils, princes, and other nobility were all instruments put to the service of preserving the unity of the church.

Calvin shared with Luther both a determination to recover the theological integrity of the local church and an emphasis on the universal church as the communion of saints. Much more than Luther, however, Calvin would emphasize the need for institutional forms of governance *within* the local church (e.g., the office of pastor, the local consistory). He would also stress more than Luther the universality of the church realized as a communion of churches. However, this communion would be preserved not by way of the papacy or a universal episcopate but through the sharing of word and sacrament among the churches and perhaps the convening of some new form of church council.[25]

The English Reformation brought with it ecclesiological reforms that were more subtle than those of Luther or Calvin. This should not surprise us, since

---

[24] Haight, 2:74.
[25] Ibid., 2:135; see also Avis, 118-20.

the Church of England emerged as the consequence of a set of contingent historical events rather than from the religious genius of any one individual. One distinctive feature of the emergent Anglican tradition was its attempt to articulate a theory of continuity with the historical church. Where Luther and Calvin presume a sharp caesura in connection with the late medieval church, Anglican thinkers sought ways to articulate a continuity with the medieval church. In this regard, the liturgy, as enshrined in the Book of Common Prayer, served as a privileged form of connection with the church of earlier epochs. Haight has offered the unique contributions of the sixteenth-century theologian Richard Hooker as reflective of the Anglican temper. Hooker saw the emergence of the Church of England as one national church abiding within a larger universal church admitting of many different ecclesial forms.[26] Paul Avis sees in Hooker's ecclesiology a remarkably sophisticated retrieval of the ecclesiological insights of the medieval conciliarists.[27]

Finally, we might note the perspective of those churches that emerged out of the Radical Reformation, that is, the churches related to the Anabaptist and Baptist movements. These churches recovered much of the more rigorist mentality of some forms of early Christianity. The church comprised all the elect but was experienced within the local congregation, which possessed almost complete autonomy. Most of these "free church" traditions acknowledged a spiritual unity among all Christians but recognized no institutional mechanism for manifesting this unity.

Beyond the theological vision of any one Reformation tradition we discover the larger issue of the fundamental breach in church unity brought about by these several sixteenth-century reformations. Most of the churches of the Reformation, save for Anglicanism, largely solved the question of church unity by each claiming a unity with the early church and eventually accepting a *de facto* denominationalism.

Roman Catholic Unity from Trent to Vatican I

The Council of Trent was largely a council of reaction, the agenda of which was determined by the Reformation. Yet it was also a council of reform that at least implicitly recognized numerous abuses in the discipline of the church that were in need of correction. In the century after Trent, Roman Catholic ecclesiology would be dominated by an apologetic impulse. For many of the baroque

---

[26] Haight, 2:215-16.
[27] Avis, 142-48.

Catholic apologists bent on defending Catholicism against the attacks of the reformers, the institutional integrity of the church was essential for the preservation of the church's unity. For example, St. Robert Bellarmine reacted to Luther's denigration of the visible church by insisting that ecclesial institutions were integral to the very definition of the church: "The church is a gathering of persons which is as visible and palpable as the gathering of the people of Rome, the kingdom of Gaul or the Republic of Venice."[28] It is during the late sixteenth and early seventeenth centuries that the medieval understanding of the church as a *societas perfecta*, a "perfect society," came to dominate Catholic ecclesiology. The idea was not that the church was morally perfect but rather that it was completely self-sufficient, possessing all the institutional resources necessary for the fulfillment of its mission.

Unity would increasingly be understood as uniformity. During this period we see a major extension of Rome's influence over the praxis of local churches. For example, the Roman curia was reorganized and strengthened in the second half of the sixteenth century. In response to many of the liturgical and sacramental abuses that helped instigate the Reformation, the Council of Trent undertook serious sacramental and liturgical reforms. What emerged was a condemnation of many abuses but at the same time a vast standardization of virtually every aspect of liturgical and sacramental practice. Prior to Trent, the West had seen a gradual standardization of certain central aspects of the liturgy, most notably regarding the Western use of the Roman canon. But aside from that there was a great deal of diversity in liturgical custom. This would be largely brought to a halt with Trent. After the council, Pope Sixtus V established the Congregation of Sacred Rites in 1588, which sought to standardize liturgical practice. This congregation undertook the reform of the Roman liturgical books, which would become the norm for the whole church. This rigid liturgical and sacramental uniformity would remain largely intact until Vatican II.

In the nineteenth century the Catholic Church saw itself further threatened by the rise of the nation state, political liberalism, and the Enlightenment. The relinquishment of the papal states, long considered essential for preserving the sovereignty and rightful autonomy of the church in the fulfillment of its mission, was being demanded by an increasingly militant Italian unification movement. In the eyes of many church leaders, the unity of the church depended on a free and sovereign papacy. National churches were seen as particularly subject to political manipulation and therefore were viewed by the papacy as a

---

[28] Robert Bellarmine, *De Conciliis, et Ecclesia, De Controversiis: Christianae Fidei Adversus Haereticos* (Rome: Giunchi et Menicanti, 1836), II: book 3, chap 2, 90.

threat to the church's unity. Pope Pius IX was eager to facilitate a shift in the locus of ecclesiastical powers away from the local churches and toward Rome. During the reign of Pius IX, the authority of local bishops decreased and that of the curia was expanded. Nuncios, originally only diplomatic liaisons to governments, became increasingly involved in the internal affairs of the churches in the countries in which they served. The *ad limina* visit of bishops to Rome, a practice that had fallen into disuse, was revived. Appeals to the curia by the lower clergy against their bishops were heard and encouraged. This strong shift toward the centralization of papal authority is often referred to as Ultramontanism (literally "beyond the mountains," referring to the tendency of northern European churches to look beyond the Alps to Rome for leadership in all ecclesiastical matters great and small). This Ultramontanist viewpoint dominated the deliberations of Vatican I and led to the promulgation of *Pastor Aeternus,* a document that strongly affirmed the authority of the pope and indirectly encouraged a century of Catholic papo-centrism.

THE MODERN IMPETUS TOWARD CHRISTIAN UNITY

It was within twentieth-century Protestantism that the ecumenical movement was born out of a shared vision to restore visible unity among all Christians.[29] In 1910 various Protestant church leaders met in Edinburgh, Scotland, for the World Missionary Conference in order to resolve disputes in their various missionary endeavors. The first meeting of the World Conference on Faith and Order in Lausanne, Switzerland, was held in 1927. In 1948 we see the creation of the World Council of Churches out of several other ecumenical entities. Today the WCC includes over three hundred member churches. Although Roman Catholicism is not officially a member, it is a member of the WCC's Faith and Order Commission, and it collaborates regularly with the WCC.

For most of the second millennium, Roman Catholicism had understood itself to be in complete historical continuity with the church of the New Testament. As divisions emerged within the Christian tradition, the Roman Catholic perspective was generally to interpret these splits from within the framework of either heresy (e.g., Cathari/Albigensians, Waldensians, the sixteenth-century reformers, the Jansenists) or schism (e.g., the Orthodox churches of the East and the Old Catholic Church, which emerged in the late

---

[29] For a concise history of the ecumenical movement, see Jeffrey Gros, Eamon McManus, and Ann Riggs, *Introduction to Ecumenism* (New York: Paulist Press, 1998), 9-34.

nineteenth century). Catholic thought, at least as officially articulated in ecclesiastical statements, was not open to any acknowledgment of shared membership in the body of Christ on the part of non-Catholic Christians. The so-called branch theory, first articulated within Anglicanism in the nineteenth century, was officially condemned in a letter of the holy office to Anglican bishops in 1864.[30] This view helps explain initial Catholic suspicion of the ecumenical movement as it emerged in the early twentieth century. In 1928, Pope Pius XI, in his encyclical *Mortalium Animos*, condemned indifferentism, which for him meant "indifference" to the unique claim of the Roman Catholic Church to be the one, true church of Jesus Christ here on earth. Pius XI gave expression to what has been called a Catholic "ecumenism of return" when he wrote:

> The union of Christians cannot be fostered otherwise than by promoting the return of the dissidents to the one true Church of Christ, which in the past they so unfortunately abandoned; return, we say, to the one true Church of Christ which is plainly visible to all and which by the will of her Founder forever remains what he himself destined her to be for the common salvation of human beings.[31]

Fifteen years later, Pope Pius XII issued an important encyclical, *Mystici Corporis*, which reasserted Pius XI's absolute identification of the Mystical Body of Christ with the Roman Catholic Church. Pius XII admitted that non-Catholic Christians are in "a certain relationship with the Mystical Body of the Redeemer" by an "unconscious desire and longing" (MC 103), but he insisted that they still could not be considered truly members of Christ's church.

The Second Vatican Council on the Unity of the Church

Alternative conceptions of church unity were already being explored in Catholic theology in the nineteenth century by members of the German Tübingen school and the English theologian John Henry Newman. These contributions were drawn into larger theological conversation, however, only in the decades immediately preceding the Second Vatican Council. As the con-

---

[30] Latin text is found in H. Denzinger, rev. A. Schönmetzer, *Enchiridion symbolorum definitionum et declarationum de rebus fidei et morum* (Freiburg: Herder, 1976) [DS] ## 2885-88.

[31] Translation is taken from Joseph Neuner and Jacques Dupuis, eds., *The Christian Faith in the Doctrinal Documents of the Catholic Church* (New York: Alba House, 1982), 376.

ciliar documents moved from preparatory drafts, which were often little more than summary presentations of the dominant neoscholastic theology of the church, to their final form, there was a consistent effort to recover many of the ecclesiological motifs and emphases that had been dominant in the first millennium. The church was considered the new people of God, the new temple, the body of Christ, a sacrament of salvation, a messianic people, and a pilgrim church.

Underlying many of these appropriations of biblical and patristic concepts and images was a recovery of the church as *communio*. Following the subtlety of its biblical usage, the council employed the concept to articulate a twofold fellowship: vertically with God in Christ by the power of the Holy Spirit, and horizontally as effecting a spiritual fellowship among believers. Attending to the vertical dimension, the council affirmed that God the Father

> gives life to human beings dead in sin. . . . The Spirit dwells in the church and in the hearts of the faithful, as in a temple, prays and bears witness in them that they are his adopted children. He guides the church in the way of all truth and, uniting it in fellowship and ministry, bestows upon it different hierarchic and charismatic gifts, and in this way directs it and adorns it with his fruits. By the power of the gospel he [the Spirit] rejuvenates the church, constantly renewing it and leading it to perfect union with its spouse. (LG 4)

In that same article we find attention to the horizontal dimension. The Spirit "guides the church in the way of all truth" and unites it "in fellowship and ministry (*in communione et ministratione unificat*)." The *communio* experienced in the church is also a reality to be offered to the world. Hence the council presented the church as a sacrament, a sign and instrument "of communion with God and of the unity of the entire human race" (LG 1). In the church believers experience, most profoundly, the life of communion into which all humanity is invited. The council's nascent theology of communion, a theology of the church that highlights the relational character of all forms of ecclesial life, is reflected in the council's teaching on the universal church as a communion of local churches.

The Church Local and Universal

For almost four hundred years, the unity of the church had been conceived in terms of a uniformity in doctrine, worship, law, and theology. Such a conception of unity left little room for a theology of the local church as a place where the Christian faith might take a distinctive form. The Protestant Reformation's recovery of the theological significance of each local church simply furthered the Catholic determination to assert ecclesial uniformity.

It was the liturgical renewal of the nineteenth and twentieth centuries, with its renewed emphasis on the ecclesial celebration of the liturgy, that paved the way for the council's recovery of a theology of the local church. The first step was taken in the council's deliberations on the draft document on the liturgy. In that document we find the first step toward a recovery of a eucharistic ecclesiology affirming that in each local church where the gospel was proclaimed and the eucharist celebrated under the presidency of the bishop or priest, the body of Christ was there made present. This theme would be taken up anew in later council documents.

According to *Lumen Gentium*, the celebration of the eucharist effects a communion among those believers gathered at each eucharistic celebration as all are united in the breaking of the bread. Echoing St. Paul (1 Cor. 10:16-17), the council writes that "in the sacrament of the eucharistic bread, the unity of believers, who form one body of Christ, is both expressed and achieved" (LG 3). This is reaffirmed in article 11: "strengthened by the body of Christ in the eucharistic communion, they manifest in a concrete way that unity of the people of God which this most holy sacrament aptly signifies and admirably realizes." Finally, the centrality of the eucharist in the life of the local church is evident in article 26, which states that the faithful gathered together in the eucharist under the ministry of the bishop are,

> the new people called by God, in the holy Spirit and with full conviction. In them the faithful are gathered together by the preaching of the gospel of Christ, and the mystery of the Lord's Supper is celebrated "so that by means of the flesh and blood of the Lord the whole brotherhood and sisterhood of the body may be welded together." In any community of the altar, under the sacred ministry of the bishop, a manifest symbol is to be seen of that charity and "unity of the mystical body, without which there can be no salvation." In these communities, though they may often be small and poor, or dispersed, Christ is present through whose power and influence the one, holy, catholic and apostolic church is constituted. For "the sharing in the body and blood of Christ has no other effect than to accomplish our transformation into that which we receive."

In the eucharistic *synaxis*, the Christian community proclaims in word and celebrates in ritual and symbol its most profound reality, its truest identity as a people whose lives are being conformed to that of Christ by the celebration of the paschal mystery.

This theology of the local church, in turn, had an impact on the council's theology of the universal church. No longer does the council treat the local church exclusively as if it were merely a subdivision of the universal church.

The council taught that "it is in and from these [local churches] that the one and unique catholic church exists" (LG 23). Here we find the beginnings of a retrieval of the ancient conviction that the universal church was, in fact, a communion of churches.

Unfortunately, the emerging theology of the local church was not maintained consistently in the conciliar documents. The exploration of a eucharistic theology of the local church did not sufficiently inform a second topic, namely, the college of bishops' relationship to the pope, sharing in pastoral authority over the universal church. The teaching on episcopal collegiality emerged as a reaction to the papo-centrism of the last century. This teaching was not developed, however, in tandem with the theology of the local church, which saw the universal church as a communion of local churches.[32] Consequently, we can discern in the conciliar documents two ecclesiological approaches that stand in some tension: one begins with the local church and sees the universal church as a communion of local churches, and the other maintains a preconciliar universalist ecclesiology that privileges the universal church. This ambiguity would fuel, as we shall see, a significant postconciliar debate.

The Council's Treatment of Ecumenism

The council's deliberations on the unity of the church were not limited to questions of the relationship between the local and universal church. The bishops were convinced that they could no longer ignore the developments that had occurred in the budding ecumenical movement. Although Catholics had generally not been allowed, prior to the council, to participate in ecumenical meetings, many bishops who attended the council had developed cordial relationships with leaders of non-Catholic churches even before the council. Theologians such as the Dominican Yves Congar, who had already authored several groundbreaking ecumenical studies, were invited to the council as theological advisers and played a key role in the drafting of council documents. Pope John XXIII himself had said from the beginning of his pontificate that he wished the council to address the sad divisions that existed in Christianity. In his famous allocution on January 25, 1959, announcing the council, he mentioned two general aims for the council, the edification of the whole Christian faithful and a "renewed cordial invitation to the faithful of the separated Churches

---

[32] This point was made quite cogently some years ago by Hervé Legrand in an important essay, "Collégialité des évêques et communion des églises dans la réception de Vatican II," *Revue des Sciences philosophiques et théologiques* 75 (1991): 545-68. Interestingly, a similar point was also made by the early Joseph Ratzinger; see *Das neue Volk Gottes: Entwürfe zur Ekklesiologie* (Düsseldorf: Patmos-Verlag, 1969), 184-87.

to participate with us in this feast of grace and brotherhood [the upcoming council], for which so many souls long in all parts of the world."[33] The Secretariat for Christian Unity, created by Pope John in 1960, was responsible for inviting non-Catholic observers to the council. It did a remarkable job of giving those observers access to draft documents being considered by the council. The secretariat also funneled the responses of the observers to the appropriate conciliar drafting committees.

Most of the discussion of ecumenical issues occurred in debates regarding two documents, the Decree on Ecumenism (*Unitatis Redintegratio*) and the Dogmatic Constitution on the Church (*Lumen Gentium*). In order to appreciate the final position of the council, it is necessary to know something of the history of several key texts in these documents.

The early draft on the church (which would eventually become *Lumen Gentium*) reflected the views of Popes Pius XI and XII discussed above. However, debates during the first session of the council demonstrated that this position was no longer acceptable to many bishops and theologians. The council reevaluated how it understood the Catholic Church's relationship to other Christian communities. For example, in an early draft of this document it was said that only those who acknowledge the whole structure of the visible Roman Catholic Church (profession of faith, sacraments, and church governance) are incorporated in the fellowship of the church "in the true and absolute sense of the term" (*incorporantur . . . reapse et simpliciter loquendo*). This passage was amended to read that those who accept the Roman Catholic Church and its entire structure and all the means of salvation "are fully incorporated" (*plene . . . incorporantur*) into the church of Christ. This modest change in language suggested that there were degrees of incorporation into the body of Christ, such that even if one were not a member of the Roman Catholic Church one could, in some sense, belong to the body of Christ. The council explicitly affirmed that all baptized Christians were "linked with" (*coniunctum esse*) the church (LG 15).

One theological development that facilitated this shift in thinking was a recovery of the ancient insight regarding the sacramentality of the church. The long-standing restriction of the term "sacrament" to the seven sacraments of the church gave way to the view that the church itself was inherently "sacramental." As we saw earlier, the council wrote that "the church, in Christ, is a sacrament—a sign and instrument, that is, of communion with God and of the unity of the entire human race" (LG 1).

---

[33] Quoted in Giuseppe Alberigo, "The Announcement of the Council," in *History of Vatican II*, ed. Giuseppe Alberigo and Joseph A. Komonchak, 5 vols. (Maryknoll, N.Y.: Orbis Books, 1995), 1:15. Alberigo notes that the official Latin version sanitized this text in typical fashion, substituting the word "communities" for "churches," "follow" for "participate," and "search" for "feast."

It is the visible, human dimension of the church that becomes, by the work of the Holy Spirit, the efficacious sign of God's saving presence in human history.[34] The attribution of sacramentality to the church itself highlighted the proper relationship between the church's outer, historical reality—the realm of human activity, institution, structure, office, law, and doctrine—and the inner reality of the church as a participation in the mystery of the triune life of God. The visible dimensions of the church were not functionalized, yet neither were they seen as ultimate realities in themselves.

For Catholicism, the visible dimension of the church is evident in the proclamation of the Word, in the profession of a baptismal faith, in the celebration of the sacraments, in the ordained ministry of the church, in the Petrine ministry, but also in the work for justice and liberation, in peacemaking, in the life of holiness and Christian discipleship. Yet these visible signs are not "free-floating" signs; as Christian signs they make sense only within the life of the church itself.

This consciousness of the sacramentality of the church informed the council's thinking on the relationship between Roman Catholicism and other Christian churches. *Lumen Gentium* stated clearly that these ecclesial elements, these signs, were also present outside of the Roman Catholic Church (LG 8). The council noted that non-Catholic Christian communities also shared the Scriptures, celebrated the sacraments (though perhaps not all were acknowledged as such in the Roman Catholic communion), worked for justice and peace, and aspired to the life of holiness through discipleship to Christ. But if these elements are present outside the Roman Catholic Church, they nevertheless cannot cease being *ecclesial* signs that share in the sacramentality of the church of Christ. Hence LG 15 refers to the non-Catholic Christian communities in which these signs are present as "churches or ecclesiastical communities." The Decree on Ecumenism, *Unitatis Redintegratio,* in article 3d, asserts that these "churches and communities" (*ecclesiae et communitates ecclesiales*) outside of the Roman Catholic Church are themselves means of salvation.

The advance beyond the preconciliar view is noteworthy. Though Pius XII had acknowledged that individual non-Catholic Christians were in "a certain relationship with the Mystical Body of the Redeemer," the council was now acknowledging not just individual Christians but their churches as well. Where Pius XII saw the Roman Catholic Church as the one, true church, the council was saying that wherever these ecclesial signs are present—wherever the

---

[34] The council members were influenced by the work of Karl Rahner and Otto Semmelroth. Both theologians had written of the church as a "primordial sacrament." See Karl Rahner, *The Church and the Sacraments* (New York: Crossroad, 1963); Otto Semmelroth, *Church and Sacrament* (Notre Dame, Ind.: Fides, 1965).

Scriptures are being proclaimed, the sacraments celebrated and Christians striving to follow Christ, there, at least to a limited extent, is the church of Jesus Christ.

It is this line of ecclesiological development that ultimately led to the important change in the text of LG 8. The initial version of this text followed Pope Pius XII, insisting, "*The Roman Catholic church is the mystical body of Christ . . . and only the one that is Roman Catholic has the right to be called church.*"[35] Given the developments mentioned above, this assertion was no longer theologically tenable. Even as the council members sensed this, they did not yet have a theological schema adequate to this new realization. Consequently, they were content to make a single word change that reflected their rejection of the strict identification of the Catholic Church and the church of Christ. The final text now reads, "this . . . church, constituted and organized as a society in the present world, *subsists in* the Catholic Church. . . . Nevertheless, many elements of sanctification and of truth are found outside its visible confines" (LG 8). The use of the verb "subsists" was crucial. The council wished to affirm, in this revised text, that while the church of Christ has always existed in history, and continues to do so in the Roman Catholic Church, the church of Christ also goes beyond the boundaries of Roman Catholicism.

I do not wish to overstate the shift in the council's thinking. It must be admitted that, in the view of the council members, the ecclesiality of non-Catholic Christian churches could not be put on the same level as that of the Roman Catholic Church in every regard. These same council documents frankly asserted certain "defects" that, from the Catholic perspective, were present in other Christian traditions. The significance that the council gave to these "defects" and their implications for understanding the ecclesiality of non-Catholic traditions has been a matter of dispute.

Since the council, the Congregation for the Doctrine of the Faith (CDF) has issued several statements that assert either explicitly or implicitly that the body of Christ *only* subsists in the Catholic Church, outside of which can be found merely "elements of the church" but not the church itself. In 1985, the CDF proposed this view in a document criticizing Leonardo Boff's controversial book *Church, Charism and Power.*[36] In 2000, the CDF issued its controversial document *Dominus Iesus,* in which it stated that "the Church of

---

[35] *Acta Synodalia sacrosancti Concilii oecumenici Vaticani 2* (Vatican City: Typis Vaticanis, 1970–), I/4, 15.

[36] "Doctrinal Congregation Criticizes Brazilian Theologian's Book," *Origins* 14 (April 4, 1985): 683-87. Leonardo Boff, *Church, Charism and Power: Liberation Theology and the Institutional Church* (New York: Crossroad, 1985).

Christ, despite the divisions which exist among Christians, continues to *exist fully* only in the Catholic Church" (#16).[37]

The teaching of the 1985 and 2000 CDF documents must be balanced against the teaching of the council itself. Nowhere did the council itself say that the church of Christ "exists fully only in the Catholic church."[38] The council *did* assert that the church of Christ continued to exist in the Catholic Church in a unique way (I take this to be the basic meaning of the Latin verb *subsistit*).[39] It also held that "it is through Christ's Catholic church alone, which is the universal help toward salvation, that *the fullness of the means of salvation* can be obtained" (UR 3). The distinction, easily missed, is significant.

The council taught that in Roman Catholicism there existed "the fullness of the means of salvation." In other words, it was saying that at a strictly formal level, the Catholic Church lacked nothing vital to manifesting God's grace and God's saving truth in the world. The Catholic Church possessed the Scriptures, the sacraments, the apostolic office of bishops (entrusted with the responsibility for authenticating the apostolic faith proclaimed in the churches), the Petrine office (entrusted with securing the unity of the churches), and so on. The council readily acknowledged that many other Christian churches and ecclesial communities possessed at least some of these "elements of sanctification and truth" and that, consequently, these other Christian churches were also means of salvation. The bishops could not ignore, however, that other Christian churches had, from their point of view, abandoned certain means of salvation (e.g., some of the sacraments or the apostolic office of the bishop) or celebrated them in a fashion that was, from the Catholic perspective, "defective."

No conciliar document, nor any postconciliar document that I am aware of, addresses an altogether different question, namely, whether these "means of salvation" are being appropriated in the life of the Catholic Church in a manner that truly brings church members into a full spiritual communion in the life of Christ. Francis Sullivan puts the matter well:

---

[37] English translation is found in *Origins* 30 (September 14, 2000): 209-19.

[38] Cardinal Walter Kasper has admitted that this formulation went beyond the teaching of the council. He, however, gives the passage in *Dominus Iesus* a more irenic reading. The observation is made in his *prolusio* given to the Pontifical Council for Promoting Christian Unity during its plenary meeting, November 12-17, 2001. Cardinal Walter Kasper, "Present Situation and Future of the Ecumenical Movement," *Information Service* 109 (2002): I-II.

[39] See Francis A. Sullivan, *The Church We Believe In: One, Holy, Catholic and Apostolic* (Mahwah, N.J.: Paulist Press, 1988), 23-33. For a more recent discussion, see Karl Becker's article insisting on a restrictive reading of the *subsistit* passage, "The Church and Vatican II's *Subsistit* Terminology," *Origins* 35 (January 19, 2006): 514-22; and Francis Sullivan's rebuttal in "Response to Karl Becker, S.J., on the Meaning of *Subsistit In*," *Theological Studies* 67 (June 2006): 395-409.

Of course it must be kept in mind that this is a question of *institutional integrity*: of fullness of the *means* of salvation. There is no question of denying that a non-Catholic community, perhaps lacking much in the order of means, can achieve a higher degree of communion in the life of Christ in faith, hope and love than many a Catholic community.[40]

This insight, absent from *Dominus Iesus,* is fully consonant with the vision of the council. Cardinal Walter Kasper, current president of the Pontifical Council for Christian Unity, himself admitted that this language of a "fullness" abiding in the Roman Catholic Church

> does not refer to subjective holiness but to the sacramental and institutional means of salvation, the sacraments and the ministries. Only in this sacramental and institutional respect can the Council find a lack (*defectus*) in the churches and ecclesial communities of the Reformation. Both Catholic fullness and the *defectus* of the others are therefore sacramental and institutional, and not existential or even moral in nature; they are on the level of the signs and instruments of grace not on the level of the *res*, the grace of salvation itself.[41]

While the distinction did not receive explicit development, I believe the council's determination to limit its comparison of churches to the question of institutional means of salvation introduced a crucial distinction between the *institutional integrity* of a church and its *ecclesial vitality.*

The concern the council raised about defects in the institutional integrity of a given Christian church must be interpreted, however, in the context of the council's teaching that the church of Jesus Christ is itself a mystery because it participates in the mystery of God. Although it may be possible to make claims about the presence or absence of institutional elements in a given Christian tradition, it is not theologically justifiable, in my view, to move to assertions of where, when and how the church of Jesus Christ "fully exists," as *Dominus Iesus* put it.

A second source of controversy in the decades after the council concerned the bishops' use of the phrase "churches and ecclesiastical communities," with reference to non-Catholic Christian communities. It has been commonly assumed that this phrase was coined in order to distinguish between those non-

---

[40] Sullivan, *Church We Believe In,* 28.

[41] Kasper, "Present Situation and Future of the Ecumenical Movement." The English translation is not my own, and I question the accuracy of the translation of "*defectus*" here as "lack." It does not carry that strong a sense in Latin.

Catholic communions that had a valid eucharist and, therefore, valid orders, from those that did not. In this reading, only the former communions merited the title "church" in the true and proper sense. Such a restrictive reading of the council is found, once again, in *Dominus Iesus*.[42] A careful reading of the council *acta* does not support this interpretation. Jerome Hamer's study of this topic in 1971 demonstrated that it was the intention of the bishops at the council to affirm in a positive way the genuine ecclesiality of non-Catholic Christian communities rather than to insist on a restrictive use of the term "church."[43] In part, the conjoining of the two terms "churches" and "ecclesiastical communities" was proposed in sensitivity to the fact that most Protestant traditions in the West did not refer to their worldwide membership as if it were a single "church," preferring terms like "communion," "federation," or "alliance."[44] Although the council certainly assumed the importance of valid orders and eucharistic communion for church life, it wished to leave open the particular question of the status of orders and the eucharist in individual non-Catholic Christian communions.

Other Ecumenical Contributions

In the late 1950s and the 1960s, as the Roman Catholic Church concerned itself with the council, the ecumenical movement was making its own contributions to renewed reflections on the unity of the church. Many ecumenical documents began to employ the biblical concept of *koinōnia/communio* in their treatment of the unity of the church.

The World Council of Churches began to conceive of Christian unity as a "conciliar fellowship."[45] The WCC assembly held in Nairobi in 1975 explicated this vision:

> The one Church is to be envisioned as a conciliar fellowship of local churches which are themselves truly united. In this conciliar fellowship, each local church possesses, in communion with the others, the fullness of catholicity, witnesses to the same apostolic faith, and therefore, recognizes

---

[42] "On the other hand, the ecclesial communities which have not preserved the valid episcopate and the genuine and integral substance of the Eucharistic mystery, (61) are not Churches in the proper sense" (*Dominus Iesus* #17).

[43] Jerome Hamer, "La terminologie ecclesiologique de Vatican II et les Ministeres Protestants," *Documentation Catholique* (July 4, 1971): 625-28.

[44] John Hotchkin, "Canon Law and Ecumenism: Giving Shape to the Future," *Origins* 30 (October 19, 2000): 289-98, at 294.

[45] This development is traced in Gros et al., 145-50.

the others as belonging to the same Church of Christ and guided by the same Spirit . . . they are bound together because they have received the same baptism and share in the same eucharist; they recognize each other's members and ministries. They are one in their common commitment to confess the gospel of Christ by proclamation and service to the world. To this end, each church aims at maintaining sustained and sustaining relationships with her sister churches, expressed in conciliar gatherings whenever required for the fulfillment of their common calling.[46]

Note the extent to which the WCC echoed Vatican II in its theology of the universal church as a communion or *koinōnia* of local churches. At the 1991 WCC assembly in Canberra, this vision was further explored, again using conceptual frameworks quite similar to those employed at Vatican II:

> The unity of the church to which we are called is a *koinōnia* given and expressed in the common confession of the apostolic faith; a common sacramental life entered by the one baptism and celebrated together in one Eucharistic fellowship; a common life in which members and ministries are mutually recognized and reconciled; and a common mission witnessing to the gospel of God's grace to all people and serving the whole of creation. The goal of the search for full communion is realized when all the churches are able to recognize in one another the one, holy, catholic and apostolic church in its fullness. . . . In such communion churches are bound in all aspects of life together at all levels in confessing the one faith and engaging in worship and witness, deliberation and action.[47]

This promising trajectory of thought in ecumenical dialogue saw *koinōnia* as articulating a deep spiritual bond among individual believers, local churches, and diverse Christian traditions. As was articulated at Nairobi, the goal of a church bound together in *koinōnia* would be not a monolithic unity but a unity in plurality.

Over the last three decades the Lutheran World Federation (LWF) has developed an alternative formulation of Christian unity as a "reconciled diversity." This concept was first accepted by the LWF at its 1977 assembly in Dar-es-Salaam, applied to the churches *within* the LWF, and then extended to ecumenical relations with other Christian traditions. It has the advantage of

---

[46] Michael Kinnamon and Brian E. Cope, eds., *The Ecumenical Movement: An Anthology of Key Texts and Voices* (Grand Rapids: Eerdmans, 1997), 110.

[47] Quoted in Gros et al., 66.

making explicit the value of an enduring diversity among the churches. However, it has been criticized by some Catholic ecumenists, most notably, Yves Congar, for accepting the continued distinct confessional identities of the various churches and for not seeking as the goal of ecumenism a full visible unity preserved by shared institutional structures such as a Petrine ministry.[48]

The struggle in all of these dialogues is to find a way to articulate the goal of Christian unity that affirms a genuine spiritual and organic communion but does not require every Christian tradition to suppress all the gifts of its own confessional identity.

One much-discussed proposal came from the late Cardinal Jan Willebrands, who, in an address in Cambridge, England, in 1970, spoke of a future church that would be not only a communion of communions but a communion of different kinds of communions. Willebrands referred to ecclesial *typoi*, contending that over the course of two thousand years various ecclesial "types" have emerged that were characterized by a distinctive theological perspective, canonical discipline, spirituality, piety, and liturgical expression. He then made the bold declaration: "The life of the church has need of a great variety of *typoi* which show the plenitude of the catholic and apostolic character of the one holy church."[49] Though Willebrands's proposal has been sympathetically received by some Catholic theologians and other ecumenical dialogue partners, it has received little further development since his address in Cambridge.

THE CHURCH AS A GLOBAL COMMUNION OF LOCAL CHURCHES: POSTCONCILIAR DEVELOPMENTS

In one of the most famous assessments of the enduring significance of Vatican II in all the postconciliar literature, Karl Rahner contended that Vatican II marked the beginning of the church's "discovery and official realization of itself as *world-Church*."[50] This was the case not only because of the large number of native-born bishops from outside Western Europe and North America who participated in the council, not only because of the council's positive appreciation of the role of culture in the expression of the Christian faith, but because the council had begun to appreciate the local church as the place where the universal church was concretely realized. The council rejected any notion of

---

[48] Yves Congar, *Diversity and Communion* (Mystic, Conn.: Twenty-third Publications, 1982), 149-52.

[49] Secretariat for Christian Unity, *Information Bulletin* (11, III, 1970), 14.

[50] Karl Rahner, "A Basic Theological Interpretation of the Second Vatican Council," in *Concern for the Church*, vol. 20 of *Theological Investigations* (New York: Crossroad, 1981), 78.

the local church as a mere branch office of the universal church; the local church was the historical "eventing," if you will, of the church universal.

This theology suggested that each local church not only receives from the universal church but also offers to the church universal its own particular gifts and insights as the geographical and cultural site in which the gospel is always being proclaimed, received, and lived out. This line of development, however, was not universally embraced.

An Important Debate on the Theology of the Local Church

In 1992 the Congregation for the Doctrine of the Faith issued its instruction on the church as communion, *Communionis Notio.* That document rejected any ecclesiology that sought to give priority to the local church over the universal church or that viewed the universal church as a federation of autonomous local churches. Indeed, the CDF insisted on the chronological and ontological priority of the universal church over the local church. According to the CDF, the story of Pentecost affirms the priority of the universal church, and the CDF goes on to cite early church sources that write of the church existing before creation itself (CN 9).

This document soon occasioned a remarkable public debate between two esteemed curial figures, Cardinal Walter Kasper, who began the debate as bishop of Rottenburg-Stuttgart and continued it as a highly visible curial official, and Cardinal Joseph Ratzinger, then the prefect for the CDF and a likely participant in the drafting of *Communionis Notio.*[51] Kasper expressed concerns regarding the document's assertion of the ontological and chronological priority of the universal church over the local church. In particular, he called into question the CDF's reading of the Pentecost event. Kasper insisted that what Acts 2 asserted was that the universal church was no mere abstraction but was realized concretely in the local church of Jerusalem. At Pentecost, the universal and the local appeared as a single reality. Kasper feared that the insistence on the priority of the universal over the local represented a veiled attempt to justify an excessive centralization of church authority in the papacy and the Roman curia.

Ratzinger soon responded to Kasper. He admitted the dangers of an over-centralization of church authority but insisted that this was a problem of jurisdiction and competency and must be kept separate from the theological

---

[51] This debate is summarized by Kilian McDonnell in "The Ratzinger/Kasper Debate: The Universal Church and Local Churches," *Theological Studies* 63 (2002): 227-50.

assertion of the priority of the universal church. The debate ended in a kind of grudging rapprochement in which Kasper acknowledged the preexistent mystery of the church. He insisted, however, that this did not warrant any priority for the universal church, since the preexistent mystery of the church must in some sense include both the universal and local dimensions of the church's eventual historical reality. For Ratzinger's part, he still held to the priority of the universal church but did not see this as contradicting the simultaneity of the universal and local church in history.

Although the debate might appear rather technical and remote from concrete pastoral concerns, it is a debate with quite practical consequences. An emphasis on the priority of the universal church will almost inevitably downplay the local church as a kind of incarnation of the church, if you will, in a very particular social and cultural setting. *Pace* Cardinal Ratzinger/Pope Benedict, only a theology of the church that asserts the simultaneity of the local and universal dimensions of the church can avoid the centralization of authority that has haunted Catholicism for most of the second millennium. And only an affirmation of the simultaneity of the local and universal church can provide an adequate foundation for considering the full catholicity of the church.

Rediscovering a Theology of Local Church in the Global South

Nowhere was the council's renewed emphasis on the local church received more quickly than in the church of Latin America. The CELAM (Consejo Episcopal Latinoamericano) meeting at Medellín in 1968 was a landmark attempt to combine the council's commitment to "read the signs of the times" with its renewed emphasis on the local church. This constituted a crucial step in the implementation of conciliar teaching as regional church leaders began to address their own geopolitical situation in the light of the gospel.

If the 1968 Medellín conference marked the turning point for the Latin American church, in Asia it was Pope Paul VI's pastoral visit to Manila in 1970 that gave encouragement to the pursuit of an authentically Asian vision of the church. That meeting with 180 Asian bishops led, two years later, to the creation of the Federation of Asian Bishops' Conferences (FABC). This ecclesiastical entity would produce, over the next three decades, a remarkable body of theologically profound reflections on the Asian church.[52]

In its 1974 meeting in Taipei, the FABC produced a document on evangelization in Asia in which they asserted that "the primary focus of our task of

---

[52] James H. Kroeger, *Becoming Local Church: Historical, Theological, and Missiological Essays* (Quezon City, Philippines: Claretian Publications, 2003), esp. 31-54.

evangelization . . . is the building up of a truly local church."[53] Each local church is to draw on the gifts of the local culture. The Asian bishops write: "For the local church is the realization and the enfleshment of the Body of Christ in a given people, a given place and time. . . . The local church is a church incarnate in a people, a church indigenous and inculturated."[54] This emphasis on inculturation marks one of the distinctive features of the Asian ecclesial renewal. Peter Phan observes that

> whereas the Catholic church in Latin America has been more concerned with the socio-economic oppression of the poor and marginalized, and hence more focused on liberation, Asian Christians, while also concerned with the issues of justice, have been more engaged the *inculturation* [*sic*] of the Christian faith.[55]

Phan goes on to insist, however, that in the Asian experience, liberation and inculturation are inseparable dimensions of the church's mission.[56]

The Asian church's minority status (Catholics constitute less than 3 percent of Asia's population of 3.5 billion, and over half of that number are found in the Philippines!) has led it to stress the need for the local church to engage in a threefold dialogue with the poor, indigenous cultures and other religious traditions. For them the principle of subsidiarity, which holds that pastoral decisions concerning the life of the local church are best made at the local level, is not an abstract sociological axiom but a concrete principle of ecclesial action that flows from the very nature of the local church. Because of this pastoral insight, the Asian bishops have been at the forefront of those calling for a greater autonomy on the part of local churches, particularly in the areas of liturgy and catechesis. The bishops insisted that this affirmation of the importance of the local church in the task of evangelization was not an alternative to traditional Catholic belief in the universal church but a new way of considering the universal church. The local church, they wrote,

> is not a community in isolation from other communities of the Church one and catholic. Rather it seeks communion with all of them. With them it professes the one faith, shares the one Spirit and the one sacramental life. In

---

[53] "Evangelization in Modern Day Asia," in *For All the Peoples of Asia: Federation of Asian Bishops' Conferences Documents from 1970 to 1991*, vol. 1, ed. Gaudencio Rosales and C. G. Arévalo (Quezon City, Philippines: Claretian Publications, 1997), 14 (# 9).

[54] Ibid., ## 10, 12.

[55] Peter C. Phan, *In Our Own Tongues: Perspectives from Asia on Mission and Inculturation* (Maryknoll, N.Y.: Orbis Books, 2003), 207.

[56] See also Aloysius Pieris, *An Asian Theology of Liberation*, Faith Meets Faith (Maryknoll, N.Y.: Orbis Books, 1988).

a special way it rejoices in its communion and filial oneness with the See of Peter, which presides over the universal Church in love.[57]

The Asian bishops recognized that if the church's universality is to be more than a stifling uniformity, then a genuinely indigenous local church must be a precondition for the church's universality. James Kroeger, reflecting on the theology of the local church emerging in Asia, notes that "in the Catholic experience, the more that each local Church becomes truly inculturated, indigenized and localized, the more this same Church through the power of the Holy Spirit becomes universal."[58]

Not surprisingly, this reaffirmation of the local church led many of the bishops to suggest the need for a reconsideration of the exercise of the Petrine ministry, particularly through the Roman curia, as a service to the unity of the church. In the events leading up to the 1998 Asian synod, one saw a tension between Roman leadership accustomed to heavy involvement in the planning of such events and Asian bishops, who felt the need for greater Asian participation in synodal planning. A number of Asian bishops complained that the *lineamenta,* that is, the outline document proposed as a starting point for synodal preparation, seemed totally unaware of the real contributions that had been made by the FABC over several decades in developing an authentically Asian reflection on the church. The Japanese bishops opined that "from the way the questions are proposed, one feels that the holding of the synod is like an occasion for the central office to evaluate the performance of the branch offices."[59] Because of these complaints, there were significant improvements in the *instrumentum laboris,* or working draft document to be discussed at the synod itself. In Pope John Paul II's postsynodal exhortation, *Ecclesia in Asia,* the pope acknowledged the Asian appropriation and development of the church as a communion of local churches. The pope writes:

> Each particular church must be grounded in the witness of ecclesial communion which constitutes its very nature as Church. The Synod Fathers chose to describe the Diocese as a *communion of communities* gathered around the Shepherd where the clergy, consecrated persons and the laity are engaged in a "dialogue of life and heart" sustained by the grace of the Holy Spirit. (*Ecclesia in Asia* #25b)[60]

---

[57] "Evangelization in Modern Day Asia," #11.

[58] Kroeger, 47.

[59] "Asia's Bishops Respond to Rome," in *The Future of the Asian Churches: The Asian Synod & Ecclesia in Asia,* ed. James H. Kroeger and Peter C. Phan (Quezon City, Philippines: Claretian Publications, 2002), 11-19, at 11.

[60] In Kroeger and Phan, 125-96 at 160.

In Asia, there is a "new way of being church" and it begins with the rebirth of a theology of the local church characterized by dialogue and the participation of all believers.[61]

The Global Significance of Basic Ecclesial Communities

Basic ecclesial communities (BECs) first made their appearance in Brazil in the 1950s, largely as a pastoral necessity. BECs flourished sometimes within and sometimes in tandem with traditional parochial church structures.[62] Only infrequently were priests present at these gatherings, and, consequently, the celebration of the sacraments was not always a part of their meetings. The base communities comprised Christians who gathered together for prayer and reflection on Scripture. This communal reading of Scripture by a small number of Christians was something of a novelty. Carlos Mesters writes of his early experience of small Christian communities in Brazil:

> We who always had the Bible in hand find it difficult to imagine and comprehend the sense of novelty the gratitude, the joy and the commitment that goes with their reading of the Bible. But that is why these people generally read the Bible in the context of some liturgical celebration. Their reading is a prayer exercise. Rarely will you find a group that reads the Bible simply for better understanding. Almost always their reading is associated with reflection on God present here and now, and hence with prayer. They live in a spirit of gratefulness for God's gift.[63]

This sensitivity to discovering God's presence in their midst also led these communities to recognize God's absence and an awareness of their social situations, so often characterized by gross injustice and oppression, as counter to God's will for them.

Liberation theologians have insisted on the real ecclesiological significance of these communities, affirming that they merit the title "local churches." Leonardo Boff, in his book *Ecclesiogenesis*, wrote:

> We must face the new experiences of church in our midst. We in Brazil and Latin America are confronted with a new concretization of church, without

---

[61] "Journeying Together Toward the Third Millennium," in *For All the Peoples of Asia*, 1:287.

[62] Marcello de Carvalho Azevedo, *Basic Ecclesial Communities in Brazil: The Challenge of a New Way of Being Church* (Washington, D.C.: Georgetown University Press, 1987).

[63] Carlos Mesters, "The Use of the Bible in Christian Communities of the Common People," in *Liberation Theology: A Documentary History*, ed. A. T. Hennelly (Maryknoll, N.Y.: Orbis Books, 1990), 14–28, at 23.

the presence of consecrated ministers and without the eucharistic celebration. It is not that this absence is not felt, is not painful. It is, rather, that these ministers do not exist in sufficient numbers. This historical situation does not cause the church to disappear. The church abides in the people of God as they continue to come together, convoked by the word and discipleship of Jesus Christ. Something *is* new under the sun: a new church of Christ.[64]

Boff contended that for all of the real advances of the council in its renewed ecclesiology of the local church, the council's treatment was inadequate insofar as it still defined the church in terms of the ministry of the bishop and the celebration of the eucharist.

In many ways, these BECs resembled certain preconciliar lay movements constituted by small faith-sharing communities (e.g., Catholic Action, the Christian Family Movement) influenced by the Cardijn Method: "observe—judge—act."[65] What was distinctive in these communities was the way in which they read the Scriptures through the interpretive lens of their own experiences of suffering and injustice. Scripture was appealed to not for abstract truths but for a vital faith response to the concrete experience of these believers. These base communities would spread throughout much of Latin America in the 1970s and 1980s.

The emergence of basic ecclesial communities was by no means limited to Latin America. They have also played an important role in the startling growth of the church of Africa. The pastoral development of BECs first began in Eastern Africa with the encouragement of AMECEA (Association of Member Episcopal Conferences of Eastern Africa) and then spread throughout the continent.[66] The bishops saw these communities not as simply a response to a shortage of priests but as an opportunity to bring the church closer to "where the ordinary life of the people takes place."[67] They also saw the work of BECs as essential to the development of a genuine autonomy for the church of Africa. According to George Kwame Kumi, "they [the Eastern African bishops] viewed the BECs as a means to *localize* and *incarnate* the Church and to make it *self-ministering, self-supporting and self-propagating.*"[68]

---

[64] Leonardo Boff, *Ecclesiogenesis: The Base Communities Reinvent the Church* (Maryknoll, N.Y.: Orbis Books, 1977), 13.

[65] Fr. Joseph Cardijn was a Belgian priest who in the early twentieth century played an important role in the lay apostolate movement.

[66] George Kwame Kumi, "Basic Ecclesial Communities as Communion," *African Ecclesial Review* (*AFER*) 37 (June 1995): 160-79.

[67] As quoted in Kumi, 164.

[68] Ibid.

One of the most important contributions made by the African church to the development of basic ecclesial communities has been initiated by the Lumko Institute. This pastoral institute was originally founded by then Fr. Fritz Lobinger, a German-born priest who served almost his entire life as a *Fidei Donum* missionary in Africa. In 1986 he was named bishop of the Diocese of Aliwal North in South Africa.[69] Lumko has since developed an effective pastoral theology of the local church. Built on clusters of basic ecclesial communities, the vision of Lumko is grounded in the conviction that too many African Christian communities had become "provided-for churches" in which the laity saw themselves as little more than recipients of the pastoral ministrations of the priest.[70] Lumko has developed an impressive set of training materials designed to help local communities make the transition from the "provided-for model" to the "communion of communities" model in which larger parishes are made up of clusters of BECs, each of which is led by a team of lay ministers. These communities meet in homes to study the gospel and then gather with other BECs at the Sunday eucharist. One of the more distinctive characteristics of the Lumko model is the strong relationship that is built among the BECs in a given cluster. They are often organized together by way of a parish pastoral council comprised of BEC representatives.

The 1994 African synod gave BECs a particular prominence. Of the over two hundred interventions made by bishops at the synod, twenty-nine concerned the pastoral significance of BECs.[71] Many bishops noted the relationship between small Christian communities and the African sense of the church as the family of God as unique ways in which the African church was receiving and implementing Vatican II's ecclesiology of communion. Along with the close association with parish life evident in the Lumko model, another distinctive feature of African BECs is that their membership often comprises individuals who share a blood relationship, an occupation, or some other significant class connection as reflective of their tribal cultures and the emphasis on family. As a general rule, African BECs have also been somewhat less inclined toward social analysis than was the case with small Christian communities in Latin America.

There are several possible reasons for this. Some have noted that, unlike the situation in Latin America, BECs emerged in Africa not out of concrete pastoral practice but as the result of programmatic episcopal initiatives. In other

---

[69] The Lumko Institute publishes a series of leadership training guides that develop this pastoral theology in some detail.

[70] Anselm Prior, *Towards a Community Church: The Way Ahead for Today's Parish*, Training for Community Ministers 28 (Delmenville, South Africa: Lumko Institute, 1997).

[71] Joseph G. Healey, "The Church-as-Family and SCCs: Themes from the African Synod," *AFER* 37 (February 1995): 44-48.

words, the call for BECs came from above rather than below. A second possible reason is that the BECs in Africa may have followed the lead of the already influential sodalities, such as the St. Anne's Society and the Sacred Heart Society, which were brought from Europe to Africa by the missionaries and long played an important role in local church life in many parts of Africa. When I visited South Africa, any time I walked down the roads of a small South African village I would see the women proudly wearing the colors of their particular sodality. These sodalities gathered in order to encourage traditional devotional life but also to meet basic human needs of local community members. The members made a point of visiting the sick, ministering in prisons, and meeting for prayer and faith-sharing several times a month. However, there was virtually no place in these sodality meetings for a critique of the members' larger social situation. Elochukwu Uzukwu confirms the tendency of African BECs to stress "the caritative dimension" over social analysis:

> This may not only be explained by the cultural preferences of Africa but also by the type of Christianity which was received into Africa—a Christianity which did not connect action in the socioeconomic and political domains with the love of God and neighbor.[72]

In any event, in their final message at the African synod, the African bishops recognized the need for further development of these BECs, insisting that these communities comprise members from different ethnic groups and classes. Only in this way could the church be saved from the tribalism and ethnocentric tendencies of African cultures.[73]

Finally, BECs have also played a vital role in the maturation of the Asian church. In the many documents of the Federation of Asian Bishops' Conferences it is evident that the Asian bishops also viewed BECs as part of the "new way of being church" that they saw emerging in Asia. At the FABC-sponsored 1977 Hong Kong meeting of the Asian Colloquium on Ministries in the Church, the bishops and other Asian church leaders acknowledged the importance of BECs for the development of an authentically Asian church. They highlighted the grassroots character of these communities.

> *Such Christian communities emerge "from the bottom."* They spring up from the grassroots *inspired and raised by the Spirit Who blows* where He wills. We

---

[72] Elochukwu E. Uzukwu, *A Listening Church: Autonomy and Communion in African Churches* (Maryknoll, N.Y.: Orbis Books, 1996), 118.

[73] See the synod's, "Final Message," in *The African Synod: Documents, Reflections, Perspectives,* ed. Maura Browne and the Africa Faith & Justice Network (Maryknoll, N.Y.: Orbis Books, 1996), 78 (#28).

cannot create them nor organize them "from above." We can only facilitate their emergence, and animate and guide their growth. When they do emerge, we should recognize and encourage them.[74]

Of particular significance is the Asian bishops' recognition that the emergence of these grassroots communities called for new models of church leadership.

These Basic Christian Communities are raising questions about leadership styles in the Church. Bishops and priests must learn to listen to the voice of their people. The local Christian community leaders have also to develop a style of leadership that fits the culture, attitudes and values of their local situation. We believe that shared participative leadership can be promoted as a style for our Basic Christian Communities where there is consultation, dialogue and sharing. Thus the people will feel responsible for and part of the decision-making process in matters that affect the whole community.[75]

The emphasis on grassroots participation in the life of the church is a particularly prominent feature in Asian articulations of the place of BECs.

The Asian bishops also shared with their African counterparts a concern that these communities not become insular but remain in visible communion with the larger church. This may explain the popularity and influence of training materials from the African Lumko Institute in the Asian church in general and in the Philippines in particular.

What explains the growing ecclesial significance of BECs not only in Latin America, Africa, and Asia but also in North America? First, there is a felt need, in light of the renewal of the Second Vatican Council, for laypeople to have a more intense and personal participation in the life and mission of the church. Second, there is a growing recognition that the gospel must speak to the ordinary lives of believers if the church is to continue to have any relevance in the world today. Basic ecclesial communities provide unique opportunities for believers to engage their daily lives—the overlapping spheres of work, politics, family, and leisure—with the values and teachings of the Christian gospel.

An African Ecclesiology of Communion: Church as Family of God

The church of Africa has made its own contributions to the rebirth of the local church and the subsequent reconsideration of the universal church as a com-

---

[74] *For All the Peoples of Asia,* 1:149 (emphasis original).
[75] "Asian Colloquium on Ministries in the Church: Conclusions," in *For All the Peoples of Asia,* 1:77 (# 46).

munion of churches. Central to this development is the church of Africa's critical appropriation of African notions of the extended family as a way of reconceiving the church as communion.[76]

In the 1960s the African president of the then newly established country of Tanzania, Julius Nyerere, put the Swahili term *ujamaa*—a word that has a rich and broad semantic field of meaning suggesting the notion of extended family—to the service of his program of African socialism.[77] In the last several decades, African theologians have appropriated the term, shorn of its political/ideological overtones, and applied it to the church. These theologians have brought into relief the ways in which *ujamaa* connotes a broad network of reciprocal relations of care and concern. The meaning, purpose, and value of the individual are inseparable from the African sense of familial and tribal obligation. Nigerian theologian Oliver Alozie Onwubiko explains that "the concept of *ujamaa*, properly understood as 'togetherness', 'familyhood', does not depend on consanguinity. It depicts a 'community spirit' of togetherness which considers all peoples 'brothers.'"[78] This community spirit in turn shapes distinctive African understandings of personhood. In most African societies there is little sense of an autonomous individual. Uzukwu writes of this African anthropological perspective: "One is human because of others, with others, and for others (*motho ke motho ka batho ka bang*—a Sotho, South African, proverb): 'I am because we are, and since we are therefore I am.' 'I belong, therefore I am.'"[79] Michael Kpakala Francis writes that for the traditional African

> the social aspect in this regard predominates over the individualistic aspect. A man exists as a person, naturally and necessarily enmeshed in a web of relationships. His very existence, his reality is bound up in those relationships. These relationships provide the most prolific, the most profound, the most intense sources of motivation for living and for action.[80]

In the minds of these theologians, the term *ujamaa* is highly suggestive as a way of describing the church as the "family of God."

---

[76] For in-depth analyses of both the strengths and weaknesses of the African image of the church as family, see Joseph Healey and Donald Sybertz, *Towards an African Narrative Theology* (Maryknoll, N.Y.: Orbis Books, 1996), 104-67; Aidan G. Msafiri, "The Church as Family Model: Strengths and Weaknesses," in *African Theology Today,* ed. Emmanuel Katongole (Scranton, Pa.: University of Scranton Press, 2002), 85-98.

[77] Julius Nyerere, *Ujamaa: Essays on Socialism* (Dar-es-Salaam: Oxford University Press, 1968).

[78] Oliver Alozie Onwubiko, "The Church as the Family of God," in idem, *The Church in Mission in the Light of Ecclesia in Africa* (Nairobi, Kenya: Paulines Publications Africa, 2001), 26-169, at 36.

[79] Uzukwu, 37.

[80] Michael Kpakala Francis, "The Church in Africa Today," in *The African Synod,* ed. Browne et al., 121.

It is not surprising, then, that this metaphor played a prominent role in the African synod. The church-as-family represents a natural development of Vatican II's vision of the church as the people of God, with roots as well in the conciliar theology of the church as communion. In the synod's final message the bishops write: "The Church-Family has its origin in the Blessed Trinity at the depths of which the Holy Spirit is the bond of communion."[81] Imagining the church as family offers a helpful path for relating the relationality of familial life to the trinitarian foundations of the church. Africans who see the church as a distinctive form of family readily grasp the sense of reciprocal responsibilities and overarching interdependence that must exist among all church members. Given the traditional African emphasis on the extended family as a place of belonging and the context for a deep experience of solidarity and care for others, the church as family provided an apt starting point for African ecclesial reflection. The aptness of this image is further evident when one recognizes that in traditional African cultures, no account of the family is complete without appeal to one's ancestors. Ancestors are acknowledged not only as a source of wisdom and example for righteous conduct but as spiritual presences capable of providing guidance and support in one's daily life. African ancestral veneration, not unlike its Asian counterpart, provides the opportunity for a uniquely African appropriation of traditional Catholic understandings of the communion of saints. This in turn leads to a fresh exploration of the christological foundations of the church. Bénézet Bujo, for example, has sketched out an African understanding of Christ as the proto-ancestor.[82] Just as many African clans assemble in memory of some founding ancestor, so too Africans can see the church as a community founded by Christ the proto-ancestor. Similarly, the strong emphasis on the communal meals of the clan easily lends itself to an African form of eucharistic ecclesiology. Bujo sees the eucharist as a "proto-ancestral meal" that strengthens the bonds of the community.[83]

Nevertheless, the church/family model has some real limits. Although the network of familial relationships provides an indispensable foundation for African society, Kpakala Francis also notes of Africans that

> our view of man's social nature and consequent commitments is limited to biological relationships and maybe a little beyond. Where the biological basis for relationship is not palpably obvious, we tend to ignore the possi-

---

[81] "Message of the Synod," in *The African Synod*, ed. Browne et al., 76 (#20).

[82] Bénézet Bujo, "On the Road toward an African Ecclesiology," in *African Synod*, Browne et al., 139-51, at 140-42.

[83] Bénézet Bujo, *African Christian Morality at the Age of Inculturation*, Christian Leadership in Africa (Nairobi: St. Paul Publications, 1990), 83.

bility or even deny any relationship. We are somewhat blind to the unity of the whole human race.[84]

Finally, even the African practice of ancestor veneration has been subject to critique. Recently, the Southern African Bishops' Conference has criticized, with perhaps an excessive harshness, abuses in ancestral veneration that treat ancestors as quasi-deities who exercise an independent supernatural influence, affecting not only healing but curses.[85]

In this chapter we have briefly traced the history of Christian conceptions of the church's unity. We have focused, in particular, on the changing relationship between the local and universal church. The trinitarian and eucharistic foundations of most of the ecclesiologies of the first millennium allowed for considerable practical diversity in ecclesial life while still affirming a unity rooted in the spiritual *koinōnia* of the churches. At least in the West, the theological and sacramental foundations for church unity were gradually displaced by juridical foundations over the course of the second millennium. The local church lost much of its theological integrity and was increasingly seen as a mere subset of the universal church. Vatican II recovered an ancient theology of the local church and with it, a nascent vision of the church as a communion of churches.

The council's ecclesiology of communion also allowed it to achieve a more positive evaluation of the real if imperfect bond shared with Christian communities not in full communion with the church of Rome. The global ecumenical movement received new life from the dramatic shift in Catholicism's attitude toward the work of ecumenism.

Since the council, a new and more global appreciation for a theology of the local church has sprung up in the global South. These churches understood that the theological integrity of the local church was a precondition for the processes of authentic inculturation of the gospel. These churches also recognized the ecclesial significance of basic ecclesial communities as a means of enhancing the solidarity of local believers and facilitating local Christians' engagement with the pressing issues of their time and place.

Although the language of *koinōnia*-communion cannot serve as a panacea for resolving all contemporary ecclesiological issues, it has proven itself to be extraordinarily helpful for encouraging a more relational view of the church, one that celebrates local churches not as autonomous congregations but as local incarnations, if you will, of the one Christian faith. This relational framework

---

[84] Kpakala Francis, 125.

[85] Southern African Bishops' Conference, "Christian Faith and Indigenous Religion: Ancestors and Healing," *Origins* 36 (September 7, 2006): 196-201.

has also proved helpful for reconsidering a number of thorny questions related to ministry in the church, the topic of our next chapter.

QUESTIONS FOR REFLECTION

1. We saw how important controversies surrounding the eucharist in the ninth through thirteenth centuries had profound consequences for ecclesiology. What are some ways in which contemporary controversies regarding liturgy and the eucharist (e.g., liturgical translations, the placement of tabernacles, the role of eucharistic adoration) are having an analogous impact on our experience and understanding of church today?
2. In the minds of many, four decades after the close of Vatican II, the ecumenical movement has stalled. Do you agree with that assessment and, if so, what are the principal factors that have led to this situation? How might the movement be reinvigorated?
3. Reflect on any personal experience you may have had with basic ecclesial communities. Why do you think they have proven to be such a vital engine for church renewal in so many parts of the world?
4. We saw how influential the image of "family" is in African ecclesiology. Do you think the image is equally helpful in a first world context, or does the increasing breakdown of traditional family structures make the image problematic?

SUGGESTIONS FOR FURTHER READING AND STUDY

Azevedo, Marcello de Carvalho. *Basic Ecclesial Communities in Brazil: The Challenge of a New Way of Being Church*. Washington, D.C.: Georgetown University Press, 1987.

Bellitto, Christopher M. *Renewing Christianity: A History of Church Reform from Day One to Vatican II*. New York: Paulist Press, 2001.

Boff, Leonardo. *Ecclesiogenesis: The Base Communities Reinvent the Church*. Maryknoll, N.Y.: Orbis Books, 1977.

Browne, Maura, and the Africa Faith & Justice Network, eds. *The African Synod: Documents, Reflections, Perspectives*. Maryknoll, N.Y.: Orbis Books, 1996.

Dunn, James D. G. *Unity and Diversity in the New Testament: An Inquiry into the Character of Earliest Christianity*. 3rd ed. London: SCM, 2006.

Gros, Jeffrey, Eamon McManus, and Ann Riggs. *Introduction to Ecumenism*. New York: Paulist Press, 1998.

Kroeger, James H. *Becoming Local Church: Historical, Theological, and Missiological Essays*. Quezon City, Philippines: Claretian Publications, 2003.

Kroeger, James H., and Peter C. Phan, eds. *The Future of the Asian Churches: The Asian Synod & Ecclesia in Asia*. Quezon City, Philippines: Claretian Publications, 2002.

Pieris, Aloysius. *An Asian Theology of Liberation.* Faith Meets Faith. Maryknoll, N.Y.: Orbis Books, 1988.

Roberson, Ronald. *The Eastern Christian Churches.* 6th ed. Rome: Edizioni Orientalia Christiana, 1999.

Sullivan, Francis A. *The Church We Believe In: One, Holy, Catholic and Apostolic.* Mahwah, N.J.: Paulist Press, 1988.

Uzukwu, Elochukwu E. *A Listening Church: Autonomy and Communion in African Churches.* Maryknoll, N.Y.: Orbis Books, 1996.

4

A People Called to Ministry

In Roman Catholicism, the decades after Vatican II witnessed an unprecedented interest in theologies of ministry. Major contributions were made by such eminent theologians as Edward Schillebeeckx, Bernard Cooke, Thomas O'Meara, George Tavard, Kenan Osborne, and others. It is a bit surprising in one sense, because the Second Vatican Council did not really explore any theology of ministry per se. Its treatment of ordained ministry focused much more on the episcopate than on either the presbyterate or the diaconate, and there was virtually no explicit treatment of lay ministry.

So why the renewed interest in a theology of ministry? Although it is true that the council offered no systematic treatise on ministry, a careful reading of conciliar teaching demonstrates that what the council did propose had significant implications for our understanding of ministry. The church's positive orientation toward the world, its affirmation of the dignity of baptism, and its renewal of the liturgy all represented insights that encouraged fresh reflection on ministry in the church. Moreover, where the council did talk about ministry, as in its treatment of the episcopate, provocative new perspectives were scattered amidst more standard accounts of ministry.

In this chapter we will begin with a consideration of some of these new perspectives on ministry offered at Vatican II, then briefly consider perspectives on ministry that owe much to contemporary ecumenical dialogue. That will lead us to a description of the *status quaestionis* of ministry in today's postmodern church. Finally, we will conclude with a brief sketch of a theology of ministry appropriate to a global church.

TEACHING OF VATICAN II AND IMPLICATIONS FOR THEOLOGY OF MINISTRY

Where questions regarding the council's teaching on the church are concerned, attention is predictably drawn to the council's two constitutions on the church, *Lumen Gentium* and *Gaudium et Spes*. Yet, as we have already seen, some of the most important ecclesiological themes to emerge in conciliar teaching actually first made their appearance in the council's Constitution on the Sacred Liturgy.

Liturgical Ecclesiology of Vatican II and Implications for Theology of Ministry

In the first chapter of the liturgy constitution, under "The Reform of the Liturgy," we find a subsection entitled, "Norms Drawn from the Hierarchic and Communal Nature of the Liturgy." Though it does not appear in the body of the text, this title introduces a formulation that will appear in later conciliar documents,[1] namely, demand for being in *communio hierarchica*, "hierarchical communion," with the pope and bishops.

In the last chapter we encountered the origins of the word "hierarchy" in the Neoplatonic vision of Pseudo-Dionysius. As appropriated by several medieval theologians, the term came to connote a thoroughly hierocratic vision of the church as a pyramidal structure in which the fullness of power (*plenitudo potestatis*) and truth was given to the pope and shared in diminishing degrees with the lower levels of church life. One might think of this as a spiritualized, medieval precursor to "Reagonomics" or "trickle-down theory"!

Feminist theologians have rightly challenged this pyramidal understanding of "hierarchy" as one of the many concepts employed in the church to subordinate the laity in general and women in particular.[2] Yet perhaps the term "hierarchical" can be retained if we purge it of those pyramidal and patriarchal conceptions.[3] I contend that when the Constitution on the Sacred Liturgy refers to the "hierarchic and communal nature of the liturgy" it does not have in mind a return to a pyramidal ecclesiology. The liturgy can be said to be hierarchical, not in the sense of a chain of command or a pyramidal structure, but in the sense that the liturgy manifests the church as an *ordered* communion with a great diversity of ministries and Christian activities that together build up the life of the church.[4] The church of Jesus Christ, animated by the Spirit,

---

[1] LG 21, 22; CD 4, 5; PO 7. It appears a sixth time in par. 2 of the *Nota Praevia Explicativa* attached at the eleventh hour to *Lumen Gentium*, without conciliar approval, "by higher authority."

[2] Rosemary Radford Ruether, *Women-Church—Theology and Practice of Feminist Liturgical Communities* (San Francisco: Harper & Row, 1985); Elisabeth Schüssler Fiorenza, *Discipleship of Equals: A Critical Feminist Ekklesia-logy of Liberation* (New York: Crossroad, 1993).

[3] For an attempt to retrieve the notion of "hierarchy" by distinguishing between "command hierarchy" and "participatory hierarchy," see Terence L. Nichols, *That All May Be One: Hierarchy and Participation in the Church* (Collegeville, Minn.: Liturgical Press, 1997).

[4] This view of the church as an ordered communion parallels in some ways Ghislain Lafont's presentation of the postconciliar church as a "structured communion." See his *Imagining the Catholic Church: Structured Communion in the Spirit* (Collegeville, Minn.: Liturgical Press, 2000).

is now and has always been subject to church ordering as it receives its life from the God who, in Christian faith, is ordered in eternal self-giving as a triune communion of persons.

Sacrosanctum Concilium reminded us, not only in its call for the reform of the rites of initiation but in its focus on the whole worshiping assembly, that our primary identity as Christians is not as lay or cleric but as a member of the baptized called to active participation in Christian worship and the mission of the church. Article 14 of the constitution speaks of full participation of the baptized in the liturgy as both a right and an obligation. Baptism is an ecclesial event that lays claim on our identity as Christians and demands much of us. As the early-twentieth-century French theologian and historian Yves de Montcheuil put it, "It is not Christians who, in coming together, constitute the Church; it is the Church that makes Christians."[5]

If baptism constitutes the most fundamental ordering of the people of God, Catholics believe that some among the baptized are further ordered or reconfigured for leadership in the sacrament of holy orders. And according to the council, the fullness of orders is conferred on the bishop. One of the most overlooked contributions of the constitution on the liturgy is its placement of the bishop at the center of the liturgical life of the diocese. The council asserted, moreover, that the most profound manifestation of the local church was encountered at diocesan liturgies presided over by the bishop (SC 41).

Regrettably, the council did not explore the full implications of defining the ministry of the bishop in terms of his eucharistic presidency. A more extended exploration might have noted that as liturgical presider, the bishop is placed in a relationship of reciprocity with the gathered assembly.[6] As presider, the bishop gathers the people of God together for corporate worship, proclaims the Scriptures, receives the gifts of bread and wine from the people, offers them up to God for and with the people and then returns these gifts to the people, now transformed into the bread of life and cup of salvation. At no point in the liturgy does the eucharist ever become the bishop's own private work; even as he engages in his unique presidential ministry, the bishop remains in communion with his people. Moreover, we might note that in his eucharistic presidency the mutual exchange of gifts includes not only bread and wine, but also the very faith of the church. In other words, along with bread and wine the community's faith itself is offered by the people to the bishop by way of their

---

[5] Yves de Montcheuil, *Aspects de l'Eglise* (Paris: Cerf, 1949), 51.

[6] For a development of this liturgical view of the bishop, see the Joint International Commission for Theological Dialogue between the Orthodox Church and the Roman Catholic Church's document "The Mystery of the Church and of the Eucharist in the Light of the Mystery of the Holy Trinity," in *The Quest for Unity: Orthodox and Catholics in Dialogue* (Washington, D.C.: United States Catholic Conference, 1996), 59.

life witness and communal reflections, and that same faith is returned by the bishop to the people in his teaching and preaching. This gift exchange reminds us that the faith which the bishop is ordained to safeguard is nothing other than the faith he has received from the people.

According to Vatican II, the priest shares and collaborates in the bishop's ministry of apostolic oversight, or *episkopē*. This is why the presbyter presides over any eucharist in which the bishop is not present. The presbyter collaborates and extends the ministry of apostolic oversight entrusted to the bishop. Consequently, a basic theology of the presbyterate ought to begin with an understanding of the presbyter's sharing in the ministry of pastoral oversight, which is liturgically enacted whenever the presbyter presides over the community's eucharist.[7] The deacon's ministry is also liturgically enacted. He does not ordinarily exercise the ministry of *episkopē*, or apostolic oversight, either liturgically or in his pastoral ministry, but rather stands at the service of the exercise of oversight. This is reflected in the ordination ritual for deacons found in Hippolytus's *Apostolic Tradition*, in which the deacon is ordained not into the priesthood but into "service of the bishop" (*in ministerio episcopi*).[8] The deacon is the one who is "sent forth" by the bishop (and at times, indirectly by the local pastor) in service of the needs of the church as seen by the one charged with oversight of the local church. It is true that all ministries, lay and ordained, are in some sense subject to the ordering of the bishop or pastor, but the ministry of the deacon is not only *ordered by* the one responsible for apostolic oversight, but his ministry is explicitly *placed at the service of* that ministry of oversight.

In a passage from the liturgy constitution that now seems rather tame and obvious, the council wrote that "servers, readers, commentators, and members of the choir also *exercise a genuine liturgical ministry*" (SC 29; emphasis mine). What the constitution says of liturgical ministries is true for all ministries in the church. There is no competition in the life of public service on behalf of the church. Lectors, special ministers of communion, ministers of hospitality, deacons, priests, and bishops—these ministries do not compete with one another

---

[7] I realize that this raises questions regarding those priests who are professed religious and for diocesan priests who are not engaged in parish ministry. This is a complicated issue that cannot be fully addressed here. Let me simply say that I think these developments in the theology of the priesthood emerged as historical accommodations to pressing pastoral needs and therefore constitute legitimate exceptions. But one does not, generally speaking, theologize from the exception but rather from the norm.

[8] Bernard Botte, ed., *La Tradition Apostolique*, Sources Chretiennes 11 (Paris: Cerf, 1984), chapter 8. It is certainly noteworthy that while *Lumen Gentium* 29 draws on this formula, *non ad sacerdotium, sed ad ministerium*, it does not make any explicit reference to the clause found in the *Apostolic Tradition* regarding service to the bishop. This point was made by the International Theological Commission in their document as well, *From the Diakonia of Christ to the Diakonia of the Apostles* (Mundelein, Ill.: Hillenbrand Books, 2004), 85.

in the liturgy but cooperate in a wonderful way to build up the body of Christ at worship. This sense of liturgical cooperation must extend as well to our understanding of all ecclesial ministries. What distinguishes the bishop from the priest from the deacon from the lector is not, as it used to be thought, the question of power. A careful reading of the conciliar documents reveals that the council avoided the preconciliar emphasis on matters of power and juris-diction where ministry was concerned. The consistent theme in the council documents, rather, is that of pastoral care and service.

The council's nascent liturgical ecclesiology does not begin with what unique powers the bishop has but the priest does not, or what power the priest has that the deacon does not. Its liturgical ecclesiology begins with the unique ministerial relationship of the bishop that cannot be replaced by the deacon or lector but is not for that reason intrinsically superior to the deacon or lector. The eucharistic gathering of the church is ritually enacted as an ordered com-munion. The liturgy reveals an ecclesial structuration of ministries according to a diversity of ministerial relations, not according to a descending hierarchy of ministerial powers.

The Rediscovery of "Charism" as a Ministerial Concept

As we saw in chapter 1, over the last few centuries Christianity has struggled with an ongoing polemic between Protestant and Catholic scholars over whether the early church was founded primarily on stable church offices (the hierarchical structure of the church) or on charisms given to all believers. The Second Vatican Council took decisive steps toward overcoming this impasse. During the first session of the council, Cardinal Léon-Joseph Suenens gave an impassioned speech in favor of making greater use of the biblical category of "charism" as a way of speaking of the gifts given by the Spirit to all the faith-ful. In his address he posed the following question to the bishops:

> Does not each one of us know lay people both men and women, in his own diocese who are truly called by God? These people have received various different charisms from the Spirit, for catechesis, evangelization, apostolic action of various types, social work, and charitable activity. . . . Without these charisms, the ministry of the Church would be impoverished and sterile.[9]

---

[9] As quoted in Albert Vanhoye, "The Biblical Question of 'Charisms' after Vatican II," in *Vatican II: Assessments and Perspectives,* vol. 1, ed. René Latourelle (New York: Paulist Press, 1988), 439-68, at 442-43.

Suenens's view was a direct challenge to the dominant Catholic position that charisms were extraordinary gifts that were not essential to the ordinary life of the church. His position won the day as the council explicitly mentioned the role of charisms in a number of key passages. In *Lumen Gentium* the bishops wrote:

> The Spirit dwells in the church and in the hearts of the faithful, as in a temple, prays and bears witness in them that they are his adopted children. He guides the church in the way of all truth and, uniting it in fellowship and ministry, bestows upon it different hierarchic and charismatic gifts, and in this way directs it and adorns it with his fruits. (LG 4)

In this text, "hierarchic gifts" refers to stable church office, and "charismatic gifts" refers to those many charisms that the Spirit distributes among all the faithful. Charism and office cannot be opposed to one another, since both have the Spirit as their origin. Implicitly, the council was teaching that church office could not exist unless it was animated by the Holy Spirit and charisms could not survive unless they submitted to an ordering that sought the good of the whole church.

By appealing to the biblical concept of charism, the council was able to affirm the role of all the faithful in building up the church and assisting in the fulfillment of the church's mission in the world:

> It is not only through the sacraments and the ministries that the holy Spirit makes the people holy, leads them and enriches them with his virtues. Allotting his gifts "at will to each individual," he also distributes special graces among the faithful of every rank. By these gifts, he makes them fit and ready to undertake various tasks and offices for the renewal and building up of the church. (LG 12)

Although few if any at the council could have anticipated the flourishing of lay ministries that would occur in the decades after the council, it is this pneumatological theme that provided a helpful theological framework for interpreting that later postconciliar development.

A Basic Reorientation of Ordained Ministry

From the eleventh century onward, it had become common to see the priesthood as the summit of ordained ministry; bishops were often viewed as priests who were granted greater jurisdictional authority. Vatican II returned to the vision of the first millennium in which the primary locus of ordained ministry was not the ministry of the priest but that of the bishop. The council taught that the episcopate constituted the fullness of the sacrament of holy orders (LG 21). Given the longstanding tendency to think of the bishop as a priest with greater administrative authority, the council instead stressed the bishops' preeminent responsibilities for the ministry of preaching and teaching (CD 12). The bishops were to be much more than administrators.

> They should therefore see to it that the faithful know and live the paschal mystery more deeply through the Eucharist, forming one closely-knit body, united by the charity of Christ; devoting themselves to prayer and the ministry of the word. They should aim to make of one mind in prayer all who are entrusted to their care, and to ensure their advancement in grace through the reception of the sacraments, and that they become faithful witnesses to the Lord. (CD 15)

The bishops should not be aloof or distant from their people; rather they should "be with their people as those who serve," seeking to know the particular conditions and concerns that define the lives of their flock (CD 16). The full import of the council's teaching on the office of the bishop will be considered in chapter 7.

Although the council dedicated most of its energies to a reconsideration of the episcopate, it also offered much toward a renewed ministry of the priest-presbyter. The council asserted that the priest's ministry must be understood in relation to the bishop:

> All priests, whether diocesan or religious, share and exercise with the bishop the one priesthood of Christ. They are thus constituted providential cooperators of the episcopal order. The diocesan clergy have, however, a primary role in the care of souls because, being incardinated in or appointed to a particular church, they are wholly dedicated in its service to the care of a particular section of the Lord's flock, and accordingly form one priestly body and one family of which the bishop is the father. (CD 28)

The bishops taught that by reason of his ordination the priest was uniquely configured to the one priesthood of Christ (LG 28), yet the council assiduously avoided the *alter Christus* theology of the priesthood associated with the seventeenth-century French school.

That mode of thought had built an entire theology of the priesthood on one essential moment, when the priest pronounces the words of institution (i.e., "This is my body") in the eucharist. The priest represented Christ not in his action or service on behalf of the kingdom, but in his very being. This spirituality spread worldwide at the hands of religious orders like the Oratorians, the Vincentians, and the Sulpicians, who staffed numerous seminaries throughout the world. Indeed, for much of the first half of the twentieth century, priests were nourished on a classic expression of this spirituality in Dom Marmion's *Christ—The Ideal of the Priest.*[10] This theology was responsible for the rather elevated view of priests that could be found in early-twentieth-century Catholicism.

The council distanced itself from this earlier theology. The christological view of the priesthood presented in the council documents is much broader and richer. The priest's acting "in the person of Christ" referred not only or even primarily to the priest's power to "confect the eucharist" and absolve sins but to his entire pastoral ministry as a proclaimer of the gospel and a shepherd of the people of God (in collaboration with his bishop). This much more pastoral consideration of the office of the priest was reflected in the council's decision in *Presbyterorum Ordinis* to use the Latin term *presbyter* rather than the more cultic term *sacerdos.* This terminological choice is lost, unfortunately, in most English translations of the council's documents, which translate *presbyter* as "priest."

Alongside this more christological view of the priesthood we can find in the council documents another, more pneumatological framework. We saw earlier the important acknowledgment of those charisms which the Spirit bestows on all the Christian faithful. In several passages the council also suggested a possible theology of ordained pastoral leadership within a community animated by many charisms. It asserted that the pastoral leadership of the ordained need not compete with the exercise of the many gifts and charisms of the faithful. Each required the other. The council bishops taught that those ordained to pastoral leadership were not to absorb into their own ministry the entire task of building up the church on their own. Indeed, it was an essential aspect of their ministry that they recognize, empower, and affirm the gifts of all God's people. In the Decree on the Apostolate of the Laity the council held that pastors should recognize the charisms given to all the faithful:

> It is for the pastors to pass judgment on the authenticity and good use of these gifts, not certainly with a view to quenching the Spirit but to testing everything and keeping what is good. (AA 3)

In the Decree on Priestly Ministry and Life the council insisted that the priest affirm and nurture the gifts of the faithful:

---

[10] Abbot Columba Marmion, *Christ—The Ideal of the Priest* (St. Louis: Herder, 1952).

While testing the spirits to discover if they be of God, they must discover with faith, recognize with joy, and foster diligently the many and varied charismatic gifts of the laity, whether these be of a humble or more exalted kind. (PO 9)

These passages situated presbyteral ministry not above but within the Christian community. The ordained minister who exercises *episkopē* is responsible for the discernment and coordination of the charisms and ministries of all the baptized.

The council's treatment of the diaconate was considerably briefer than its consideration of both the episcopate and the presbyterate. There was no separate document dedicated to the ministry of the deacon. This was doubtless because for centuries the diaconate existed mostly in name only. However brief its treatment, what the council did offer regarding the diaconate was momentous. It called for the restoration of the diaconate "as a proper and permanent rank of the hierarchy" (LG 29). The deacon was ordained to a ministry of service, and the council offered a broad range of ministries proper to the deacon. More importantly, the restoration of the diaconate as a permanent and stable office represented an initial step toward the dismantling of the *cursus honorum*.

By the end of the second century the ministries of bishop, presbyter, and deacon had developed as stable, distinctive "orders" in the church subject to sacramental ordination. In the Middle Ages, as the basic distinction between the clergy and the laity became more pronounced, these sacramental "orders" were hierarchically configured, along with a number of other "minor orders," into what came to be known as the *cursus honorum*. Not all ordained ministers ascended this hierarchical ladder; we know of deacons such as St. Francis of Assisi who remained deacons throughout their life. Nevertheless, the dominant ministerial path, particularly for diocesan clergy, was one in which the minister was expected to ascend the ministerial ranks, culminating in ordination to the priesthood. In the church of Rome this *cursus honorum* took the following form: porter, lector, exorcist, acolyte (the minor orders), followed by sub-deacon, deacon, presbyter, and bishop (the major orders).[11] Over time the diaconate gradually lost its status as a stable, integral ministry of the church and was reduced to a stepping stone on the way to presbyteral ordination.

The restoration of the diaconate as a permanent ministry recalls a much more ancient tradition, a time when each of these ministries was valued for its

---

[11] David Power, "Church Order," in *The New Dictionary of Sacramental Worship* (Collegeville, Minn.: Liturgical Press, 1990), 216. For further studies on the history and contemporary significance of the "minor orders," see Winfried Haunerland, "The Heirs of the Clergy? The New Pastoral Ministries and the Reform of the Minor Orders," *Worship* 75 (July 2001): 305-20.

own sake. "Promotion" was then a matter of the church recognizing that the gifts an individual exercised in a given ministry might justify being called to a new ministry of ecclesial leadership.

The council's restoration of the diaconate made a second contribution to a renewed theology of ministry by way of its recognition that celibacy need not be a condition for ordained ministry. By allowing married deacons—not as a dispensation from the law but as part of the permanent ordering of the community—the council was, in effect, saying that it was possible to respond to an ecclesial call to ordained ministry while fulfilling the universal call to holiness through the vowed life of marriage.

The Contributions and Limits of the Council's Theology of Ministry

In many ways it is misleading even to refer to a "theology of ministry" associated with the council, since nowhere in the sixteen documents do we find anything approaching a systematic theology of ministry. Nevertheless, as our brief survey indicates, important elements of the council's teaching would have a substantial impact on the reform of ministry in the postconciliar church. Nothing was more significant than the council's recovering of a theology of baptism. That theology undercut the preconciliar tendency to ground ecclesiology in the lay/clergy distinction. This emphasis on baptism, in turn, situated the necessary role of the ministerial priesthood within the more comprehensive framework of the priesthood of the baptized. This insight was picked up by the *Catechism of the Catholic Church,* which teaches:

> While the common priesthood of the faithful is exercised by the unfolding of baptismal grace—a life of faith, hope, and charity, a life according to the Spirit—the ministerial priesthood is at the service of the common priesthood. It is directed at the unfolding of the baptismal grace of all Christians. (CCC 1547)

Indeed, it is no exaggeration to say that the council's teaching on ordained ministry instigated a shift from a theology of ministry preoccupied with power and its appropriate exercise to a theology of ministry oriented toward Christian service and pastoral care.

The full sacramentality of the episcopate was affirmed and, with it, the primacy of episcopal pastoral care over administration. Bishops were presented as genuine pastors of local churches and not papal surrogates. Bishops and priests were encouraged to honor the vital role of the laity in the life of the church, to empower the gifts of all God's people, and to order them in service of the church's mission. Little was said of the diaconate, but its restoration as a permanent ministry did much to undermine a centuries-long practice of viewing the various ordained ministries as an ecclesiastical career ladder.

Although the council had little to say regarding lay ministry, it certainly opened the door to that momentous postconciliar development with its articulation of a theology of charism. A long-standing dichotomy between charism and office was overcome as the council recognized that church office is, in a sense, a stable charism, and charisms can become anarchic without the ordering ministry of church office.

Finally, the council's recovery of a theology of the local church and its conception of the universal church as a communion of local churches created an opening for a greater diversity in specific ministerial forms in accord with the needs of the local church. We shall have more to say on this later.

ECUMENICAL DEVELOPMENTS TOWARD A COMMON THEOLOGY OF MINISTRY

What Vatican II accomplished did not go without notice in the larger Christian world. The council adopted a much more positive assessment of the worldwide ecumenical movement, and many of its documents reflected the contributions both of non-Catholic Christian observers who attended the council and larger currents in contemporary Protestant scholarship. This openness was reciprocated by leaders and scholars in many Protestant churches who sought to overcome long-standing church divisions on the question of ministry. The fruit of this new spirit of ecumenical dialogue was manifested most dramatically in the groundbreaking document of the World Council of Churches' Faith and Order Commission published in 1982 as *Baptism, Eucharist and Ministry*, also known as the Lima document, since it was approved during the commission's meeting in Lima, Peru. Although that document has much to say about apostolicity and apostolic office, I will defer discussion of those issues until the final chapter.

The Lima document highlighted an emerging consensus on key issues while also mapping out real convergences that still fell short of complete consensus. In the section on ministry, one of the most noteworthy features was the foregrounding of the threefold order of ministry (bishop, presbyter, deacon), the historical provenance of which justified its serious consideration by all churches. The document hews close to biblical conceptions of church and ministry wherever possible. Charisms that can be exercised by any believer are emphasized yet at the same time the document acknowledges that from the very beginning "the church has never been without persons holding specific authority and responsibility."[12] These ministers must see their ministry as rooted in service of the community. It recognizes that ordained ministers

> are representatives of Jesus Christ to the community and proclaim his message of reconciliation. As leaders and teachers they call the community to submit to the authority of Jesus Christ, the teacher and prophet, in whom law and prophets were fulfilled. As pastors, under Jesus Christ the chief shepherd, they assemble and guide the dispersed people of God, in anticipation of the coming Kingdom.[13]

On the tricky question of an ordained priesthood, the document affirms, without much elaboration, the unique priesthood of Christ, the priesthood of all believers and, finally the appropriateness of referring to certain ordained ministers as priests "because they fulfill a particular priestly service by strengthening and building up the royal and prophetic priesthood of the faithful."[14] The entire section on ministry was obviously written in view of the desired goal of a mutual recognition of ministries among the distinct Christian communions.

The Lima document has been generally well received among the various churches. A number of Protestant churches have achieved sufficient consensus to formalize the mutual recognition of ministries (e.g., between the Evangelical Lutheran Church of America and the U.S. Episcopalian Church). Official leadership of the Roman Catholic Church, however, while welcoming the document as an important step forward, still see crucial issues remaining. The official position of Roman Catholicism has continued to be that the historical episcopate is essential to the life of the church and is required for a valid ordained ministry, which, in turn, is necessary for a valid celebration of the eucharist. Some Catholic theologians, however, take a more positive view of contemporary developments, wondering whether the recognition of ministries and sacraments must be an "all-or-nothing" approach. Even Cardinal Ratzinger appeared to renounce the "all-or-nothing" view of sacramental validity when he wrote to a German Lutheran bishop the following:

> I reckon as one of the important results of ecumenical conversations particularly the realization that the question of the Eucharist cannot be restricted to the problem of "validity." Even a theology along the lines of

---

[12] *Baptism, Eucharist and Ministry*, Faith and Order Paper No. 111 (Geneva: WCC, 1982), 21.
[13] Ibid.
[14] Ibid., 23.

the concept of succession, as is in force in the Catholic and in the Orthodox Church, should in no way deny the saving presence of the Lord in the
Evangelical Lord's Supper.[15]

In a recent address to the Catholic Theological Society of America, Lutheran
ecumenist Michael Root suggested that a "scaler" approach to ministry, one
that admitted degrees of fullness, was preferable to what I have called the
binary, validity-invalidity view.[16] The avoidance of binary formulations concerning the recognition of ministries seems crucial to any further progress on
these questions.

MINISTRY IN A POSTMODERN CHURCH

One feature shared by many of the most important postconciliar studies in ministry is a heightened historical consciousness sensitive to the extent to which
the structures of ministry have changed significantly over the past two millennia. This is fully in keeping with the tendency of many postmodern thinkers to
challenge naïve and historically ill-informed claims to historical continuity
where church structures are concerned. In their reading, too often these claims
to historical continuity regarding such structures as the papacy or the liturgy,
mask significant differences in doctrine, theology, and practice over time.

In the second century, *presbyters* functioned primarily as pastoral advisers to
bishops and appeared to exercise little if any sacramental ministry. Their ministry was eclipsed in pastoral importance by the deacon, who from the second
to the fourth century was in many ways the most significant pastoral minister
in the church. Most bishops were chosen from the ranks of deacons, not presbyters. By the twelfth century, however, the ministry of the deacon had become
insignificant, whereas the priesthood had come to represent the culmination of
ordained ministry.

Modern scholarship has helped us to recognize that many contemporary
features of church ministerial structure are not the result of the unfolding of
some preordained script. A careful study of the history of ministerial structures
such as the priesthood makes it evident that changes and developments in these
structures were significantly influenced by cultural forces and social institutions. Given different historical and cultural contexts, church ministry might

---

[15] The text is found in Joseph Cardinal Ratzinger, *Pilgrim Fellowship of Faith* (San Francisco:
Ignatius Press, 2005), 248.

[16] Michael Root, "Bishops, Ministry, and the Unity of the Church in Ecumenical Dialogue: Dead-
lock, Breakthrough or Both?" *CTSA Proceedings* 62 (2007): 19-35, at 32-34.

have developed in quite different ways. That does not mean that we cannot stand at the present moment and look back on history, seeking to identify the movements of the Spirit.[17] But our present perspective is always partial and to a considerable extent, it undergoes revision over time. What today strikes us as an obviously providential development of a given structure might conceivably, one hundred years from now, be viewed as a dead-end street.

New Features in the Structure and Practice of Ministry

We cannot consider church ministries as a set of Platonic forms. We must maintain a healthy respect for the tradition of the church and a confidence that the influence of the Spirit has played a role in the many twists and turns that have occurred in the history of ministry, but it is undeniable that the specific shape of Christian ministry has often been influenced by cultural context and the particular demands of a given historical epoch. This is no less the situation today; the effective structuring of ministry must take into account a number of features characteristic of our global church.

Priest Shortage—Communities' Right to the Eucharist

Many dioceses in the United States are now experiencing the pastoral pressures created by an aging priesthood with fewer numbers of newly ordained priests to replace those approaching retirement. In the United States it is now quite common to see priests pastoring multiple parishes. In 2000 there were twenty-five hundred parishes in the United States without a resident pastor.[18] The invocation of canon 517.2 allowing for deacons and lay persons to function as parish administrators in the absence of a parish priest is becoming a common practice. A number of North American dioceses, anticipating the increasingly dire shortage of priests, are making parish administration an integral part of their lay and diaconal formation programs. Yet the situation in the United States is nowhere near as desperate as the church in other parts of the world. In many parts of Latin America and Oceania the priest shortage is far more acute, in some cases with a 1:50,000 ratio of priests to Catholics.

The consequences of this widespread shortage, continued for an extended period of time, are only beginning to make themselves felt. The most obvious effect concerns the growing number of Catholics who are losing contact with

---

[17] John Thiel, *Senses of Tradition: Continuity and Development in Catholic Faith* (New York: Oxford University Press, 2000), 84-95.

[18] Bryan T. Froehle and Mary L. Gautier, eds., *Catholicism USA: A Portrait of the Catholic Church in the United States* (Maryknoll, N.Y.: Orbis Books, 2000), 121.

the eucharist as central to the life of the Catholic Christian community. Over the church's two-thousand-year history, no ecclesial practice has been as decisive in shaping Catholic Christian identity as the regular celebration of the eucharist. It is now increasingly common, in many parts of the world, for vast numbers of Catholics to celebrate the eucharist only a few times a year. Creative pastoral initiatives, using both lay ministers and deacons, have enabled the proliferation of communion services in many countries where the priest shortage is most severe. The resiliency of such communities and their ability to retain something of a eucharistic consciousness are a testimony to their strength and vitality. Yet, as any sacramental theologian will remind us, a communion service is not the eucharist. Communion services by their nature do not draw the believing community into the eucharistic dynamism of Christ offering himself as gift for the world. The extended practice of exposure to the eucharist by way of communion services alone, risks the possibility that the eucharist will become for many Catholics nothing more than an object to be consumed or adored rather than an ecclesial event in which Christ acts on our behalf to make the people of God into Christ's body on earth.[19]

What we are contending with here is at best a pastoral oddity and at worst an ecclesial scandal. Thousands of Christian communities are being deprived of the most central practice of Christian worship because of a lack of ordained ministers. The scandal exists because this shortage of ordained ministers appears to so many as unnecessary.

Some church leaders cite the shortage of candidates for the priesthood as a symptom of the pervasive secularization of the modern world and a cultural narcissism that makes the self-sacrificial life of the priest unappealing to many. There are a number of difficulties with this analysis. First, it does not explain the often severe shortage of priests evident in regions of the world far removed from the so-called secularizing forces of the West. Second, even in the West, there does not seem to be a true shortage of ministerial vocations. In the United States alone there are almost thirty thousand lay ecclesial ministers and over thirteen thousand permanent deacons. Since one can presume that few if any of these people are pursuing their ministries out of a desire for selfish monetary gain, it would appear that there is no shortage of Catholics open to ministerial service in the church. Although many church leaders insist that reconsidering the Western discipline of priestly celibacy is not a "silver bullet" for solving the priest shortage, many others see it as an obvious and logical first step toward a resolution of this crisis.

---

[19] For a reflection on the dangers of the commodification of the eucharist, see Richard R. Gaillardetz, *Transforming Our Days: Finding God Amid the Noise of Modern Life,* rev. ed. (Liguori, Mo.: Liguori, 2007), esp. chap. 4.

We must remember that calls for a reconsideration of priestly celibacy do not constitute an attack on the charism of celibacy itself. Since the earliest centuries of the church, Christians have chosen both individually and communally to witness to fundamental gospel values by way of committed celibacy. They found biblical warrant in Jesus' teaching in the Gospel of Matthew regarding those who chose celibacy "for the sake of the kingdom" along with the exhortation of St. Paul for believers to remain celibate if possible. They did so as a response to a divine call to live the gospel with a particular public intensity that has continued to be a great gift to the church. For centuries, this unique form of Christian living was considered a gift, a charism if you will.[20] It was not until the eleventh century that celibacy became mandatory for Western clergy.

The second millennium of Western Christianity witnessed the gradual emergence of a clerical culture in which priestly celibacy played a central role. When Western Christianity undertook its many ambitious missionary endeavors beginning in the fifteenth century, this clerical celibate culture was often imposed on indigenous cultures for which committed celibacy held very little value. With many indigenous peoples in Latin America and Africa, for example, marriage and family are seen as crucial indicators of adult maturity and leadership potential. In some instances this has made it difficult for the church to foster indigenous vocations to the priesthood. In other instances it has led to a *de facto* nonobservance of priestly celibacy, a situation ripe for scandal and the real potential for the abuse of women often taken by priests as tacit concubines.

Whatever legitimate arguments for the Western discipline of priestly celibacy may be raised, it is difficult to sustain the defense of an ecclesiastical tradition without doctrinal authority in the face of the undeniable crisis in church life created by many Catholics' lack of access to the eucharist. Kenan Osborne puts the matter quite plainly: "How, then, can a 'law,' a 'tradition,' or a 'discipline' become a matter of higher priority than a community's need to have Sunday Mass?"[21]

Lay Ecclesial Ministries and Their Implications for a Theology of Ministry

A second contemporary feature of church ministry that demands further reflection is the emergence of lay ministry. Although the Second Vatican Council broke new ground in its positive reevaluation of the laity in the church, few at

---

[20] Heinz-J. Vogels, *Celibacy—Gift or Law?* (Kansas City: Sheed & Ward, 1993; originally published in German in 1978 and then in a revised edition in 1992).

[21] Kenan B. Osborne, *Orders and Ministry: Leadership in the World Church*, Theology in Global Perspective (Maryknoll, N.Y.: Orbis Books, 2006), 142.

the council could have anticipated the tremendous flourishing of lay ministries over the past four decades, particularly in North America. A 1999 study reported that in the United States alone there were over twenty-nine thousand lay ecclesial ministers, twenty thousand of whom worked full time.[22]

There is a story of a prominent American cardinal who, during his *ad limina* audience with Pope John Paul II, asked the pope why he was so vigorous in his support of the many new lay movements (e.g., Opus Dei, Focolare, Communion and Liberation, the Neocatechumenal Way). The pope responded that only in North America did the renewal of parish life envisioned by Vatican II ever really take place. In the many other parts of the world where parish life continued to atrophy, the lay movements offered the best hope for the revitalization of the church. Whether the story is true or not, it does make the point that, for all the faults of the North American church, it has been blessed with a widespread parish revitalization that is the envy of many church leaders in Western Europe. It is also undeniable that the flourishing of lay ministries in the United States has had a significant role in that revitalization.

The North American church has struggled, however, to find a theology of ministry capable of doing justice to this new ministerial situation. Many American clergy have felt threatened by the growing number of ministries now undertaken by the laity. Some critics see lay ecclesial ministry as a distraction from the council's teaching that the proper sphere of lay activity is in the world. A significant number of lay ministers have themselves complained about being treated as ministerial auxiliaries by the clergy. Important issues regarding adequate lay formation and just remuneration continue to be raised. An important step in addressing these issues, however, came in a resource document published by the United States Conference of Catholic Bishops, "Co-Workers in the Vineyard of the Lord."[23] This document sketched out a truly integrated theology of ministry, ordained and nonordained, that presented lay ministry as an authentic form of ministry that was not to be reduced to the status of a clerical auxiliary.

The Permanent Diaconate

By the sixth century, the diaconate, once the central ordained ministry in the pastoral life of the church, had been reduced to a mere stepping stone in ecclesiastical advancement, what we have already referred to as the *cursus honorum*.

---

[22] Philip J. Murnion and David DeLambo, *Parishes and Parish Ministers: A Study of Parish Lay Ministry* (New York: National Pastoral Life Center, 1999), 45-46. For an informative study of this new ministerial phenomenon, see Zeni Fox, *New Ecclesial Ministry: Lay Professionals Serving the Church,* rev. and expanded ed. (Franklin, Wis.: Sheed & Ward, 2002).

[23] USCCB, "Co-Workers in the Vineyard of the Lord," *Origins* 35 (December 1, 2005): 404-27.

Calls for the restoration of the diaconate as a stable ministry in the church were being made with increasing vigor in the decades before the council. Although the Second Vatican Council wrote very little about the diaconate, the council's call for its restoration opened the door to one of the most dramatic new developments in the ministerial life of the church over the last four decades.[24]

The permanent diaconate was officially restored by Pope Paul VI in 1967 and has since become one of the fastest-growing ministries in the North American church. Not only has the number of deacons mushroomed (there are over thirteen thousand permanent deacons in the United States alone); so has their outreach. Some deacons work as chaplains in jails and hospitals; others engage in catechetical ministry. Many preach and preside at baptisms, weddings, and funerals. Most assist liturgically at the celebration of the Sunday eucharist. A growing number are serving as administrators for parishes without a resident priest-pastor in accord with canon 517.2.

In many churches in the United States the permanent diaconate has been very well received. Priests have found deacons to offer indispensable assistance in the exercise of their sacramental ministry. Early problems regarding inadequate diaconal formation have begun to be addressed both at the level of the universal church and here in the United States. An important turning point was the 1993 pastoral letter of Cardinal Joseph Bernardin on the permanent diaconate.[25] This document offered a developed and balanced exposition of the diaconate in terms of the threefold *munera:* the deacon is to exercise a ministry of service in the proclamation of the word (teaching), in the assistance at the liturgy and fulfillment of other liturgical functions (sanctification), and in the work of charity (governance). In 1998 the Congregation for Catholic Education and the Congregation for the Clergy issued two documents, *Basic Norms for the Formation of Permanent Deacons* and *Directory for the Ministry and Life of Permanent Deacons,* that were intended to expand and standardize diaconal formation.[26]

At least in the United States, the status of the diaconate today is remarkably like that of lay ecclesial ministry: both are largely postconciliar realities with ancient church roots. Both, in their contemporary forms, have grown at a rate that has outpaced theological reflection. I am not sure that we can adequately

---

[24] Material in this section is drawn from Richard R. Gaillardetz, "Toward a Contemporary Theology of the Diaconate," *Worship* 79 (September 2005): 419-38.

[25] Cardinal Joseph Bernardin, *The Call to Service: Pastoral Statement on the Permanent Diaconate* (Chicago: Archdiocese of Chicago, 1993).

[26] Congregation for Catholic Education and the Congregation for the Clergy, *Basic Norms for the Formation of Permanent Deacons* and *Directory for the Ministry and Life of Permanent Deacons* (Washington, D.C.: USCCB, 1998).

understand one without the other. In a recent review of literature on the diaconate, William Ditewig described the current pastoral theological context for the diaconate as a "confluence of three realities": (1) the growth of lay ecclesial ministry in the decades since the council, (2) the restoration of the diaconate as a permanent and stable ministry, and (3) the decline in the numbers of presbyters.[27]

Finally, we must acknowledge that the restoration of the diaconate has not been received with equal enthusiasm throughout the church. There are many churches, such as the church of Africa, that have made little use of this ancient ministry, fearing a further clericalization of ministry that would impede the empowerment of the laity. It remains to be seen whether this becomes a ministry of global significance in the church of the twenty-first century.

Women and Ministry

Women have constituted the majority of church membership for much of the church's history. At the same time, opportunities for women to participate in the public ministries of the church have been carefully circumscribed. Although recent studies have been quite suggestive regarding the participation of women in a variety of ministries in the early church, it was not long before the participation of women in public ministries was discouraged when not simply prohibited by church leadership.

In spite of these obstacles, many committed Christian women continued to use their gifts in the church, often surreptitiously and in general anonymity. The Middle Ages offers courageous examples of women like Sts. Hildegard of Bingen and Catherine of Siena, who exerted an enormous influence in the life of the church, but their public presence was, lamentably, the exception rather than the rule. The Beguines represented perhaps the first organized women's movement in the history of Christianity.[28] They comprised communities of laywomen who generally did not take vows, although many were committed to celibacy. They were committed to an evangelical life structured around common prayer and a commitment to charitable works. There were also other women's religious communities that were often closely aligned with male religious orders. They almost always lived in a strictly enclosed community with limited contact with the outside world.

An important turning point occurred in the sixteenth century. The Company of St. Ursula was founded by St. Angela Merici in 1535. Her community

---

[27] William Ditewig, "The Once and Future Diaconate: Notes from the Past, Possibilities for the Future," *Church* 20 (Summer 2004): 51-54.

[28] Caroline Walker Bynum, "Religious Women in the Later Middle Ages," in *Christian Spirituality: High Middle Ages and Reformation*, ed. Jill Raitt, World Spirituality 17 (New York: Crossroad, 1987), 121.

of women was committed to the education of orphans and ministry to the sick. In a significant departure from earlier religious women's communities, her community was not associated with a male order and there was no commitment to be an "enclosed community." So novel was Merici's vision of her community that, after the Council of Trent, renewed strictures were put in place that pressed the need for women's communities to be strictly enclosed. In the seventeenth century the Ursulines became a community under strict enclosure. Nevertheless, Angela Merici's pioneering vision opened the door for later women's religious communities committed to apostolic work rather than an enclosed contemplative life. Soon women's religious communities grew in great numbers with their members working in health care, education, and outreach to the least fortunate in society.[29] From the sixteenth century to the twentieth these women religious communities would be the primary vehicle of opportunity for Catholic women to engage in church ministry.

In North America, the development of lay ministry provided a new opportunity for women interested in public ministry in the church. A recent study reports that 82 percent of lay parish ministers in the United States are women. It would be difficult to exaggerate the impact of the predominance of women lay ministers on the American Catholic church. At the least it has guaranteed a distinct female presence in the life of the church. Whole generations of Catholics no longer accept once traditional views about the unsuitability of women for public ministry because they grew up in parishes where they were catechized and nurtured in their faith by women. Although greater percentages of laypeople working at the diocesan level are men as compared to parish ministry, we still see in the U.S. church a growing presence of women in diocesan offices, with some even serving in such traditionally clerical positions as that of chancellor.

The highly visible presence of women in positions of public ministry in the American church has brought significant tensions to the surface as well. As many Catholics experience firsthand the obvious gifts and competence of women for ministry and leadership, doctrinal and canonical barriers to certain ministries become less defensible. In spite of the many new opportunities for women to serve publicly in the church, the ordained ministries are still closed to them, as are the instituted ministries of lector and acolyte.

Some American Protestant traditions such as Methodism began ordaining women as early as the late nineteenth century, although women were given full clergy rights in American Methodism only in 1956. The 1970s and '80s saw other Anglican and Protestant churches beginning to ordain women to public

---

[29] R. Kevin Seasoltz, "Institutes of Consecrated Life: Identity, Integrity and Ministry," in *Ordering the Baptismal Priesthood,* ed. Susan K. Wood (Collegeville, Minn.: Liturgical Press, 2003), 228-55, at 243.

ministry. Although this had been universally condemned in Roman Catholicism, in the decades after the council we find a renewed debate regarding the possibility of ordaining women to the ministerial priesthood. In 1976, the Congregation for the Doctrine of the Faith issued its statement *Inter Insigniores*.[30] This statement concluded that both Scripture and tradition supported the traditional prohibition of the ordination of women. It also produced a third argument made from "the analogy of faith" that was based on the priest's iconic representation of Christ as head of the church, a form of representation that demanded that the priest be male. This statement, far from quelling debate on the topic, only served to spur numerous studies that addressed the historical and biblical arguments.[31] Some theologians rallied to support magisterial teaching, with a particular emphasis on developing the third, so-called iconic argument.[32] In the face of growing challenges to the church's official position, in 1994, Pope John Paul II issued his apostolic letter *Ordinatio Sacerdotalis*, in which he stated that the church did not have the authority to ordain women since it was counter to the will of Christ. In spite of the elevated authoritative status that the pope's letter granted to this teaching, controversy has continued as many theologians have struggled to accept the arguments that have been offered in support of this teaching.[33]

Recently the possibility of ordaining women to the diaconate has received renewed attention. A report of the International Theological Commission offered a negative judgment on the question of whether ordaining women to the diaconate could be justified in the light of the existence of deaconesses in the early church. In their view these deaconesses did not perform the same ministries as male deacons and therefore may not have shared in holy orders.[34] However, their report does not represent a formal judgment by the magisterium, and significant studies have argued in favor of the restoration of women deacons.[35]

---

[30] *Inter Insigniores, Origins* 6 (February 3, 1977): 517-24.

[31] As but two examples of the many collected studies challenging the historical and biblical arguments of the CDF, see Ute E. Eisen, *Women Officeholders in Early Christianity* (Collegeville, Minn.: Liturgical Press, 2000); Carroll Stuhlmueller, ed., *Women and Priesthood: Future Directions* (Collegeville, Minn.: Liturgical Press, 1978). An important historical study defending the official church position but published prior to the CDF statement is Haye van der Meer, *Women Priests in the Catholic Church: A Theological Historical Investigation* (Philadelphia: Temple University Press, 1973).

[32] See Donald J. Keefe, "Sacramental Sexuality and the Ordination of Women," *Communio* 5 (Fall 1978): 228-51.

[33] For a documentary history of this issue in Catholic church teaching, see Deborah Halter, *The Papal "No": A Comprehensive Guide to the Vatican's Rejection of Women's Ordination* (New York: Crossroad, 2004).

[34] International Theological Commission, *From the Diakonia of Christ to the Diakonia of the Apostles*.

[35] Ad Hoc Committee of the Canon Law Society of America, *The Canonical Implications of Ordaining Women to the Permanent Diaconate* (Washington, D.C.: CLSA, 1995).

The question of women's role in ministry has not received significant attention in the church outside of North America and Western Europe. In large part this is because in North America and Western Europe there are commonly accepted views regarding the full equality of women and men. Consequently, in these regional churches official explanations of the Catholic Church's teaching strive to demonstrate how this teaching does not undermine the dignity of women and is not, therefore, an instance of church sexism. In other parts of the world, however, the issue is framed quite differently. Kenan Osborne writes:

> If European and American progressives take it as a universal truth that women's social position must change to reflect the equality of men and women and that gender roles mandated by patriarchal cultures must be ended, there are opposing voices who see this as the worst kind of globalization where Western cultural norms are being forced on the rest of the world.[36]

This suggests that this issue must be considered not only from a biblical, doctrinal, and theological perspective but also from a cultural perspective. If progressive Western scholars make a solid case that this teaching rests on biblical, historical, and theological assumptions that are no longer tenable, and both feminist and liberationist theologians highlight what seems to them the fundamental incompatibility of this teaching with belief in a just God who created all humanity in the divine image, a more global consideration of the issue suggests the need to be careful about moving forward with reform in ways that are insensitive to quite different cultural sensibilities. Moreover, it is possible to accept the authority of the Catholic Church's official position on this question while suggesting that important scholarly developments and a changing global context make fresh considerations of the issue more and more pressing. The rigorous suppression of responsible debate on this topic must be challenged not only on ethical and ecclesial grounds but on pragmatic ones. In the modern age, artificial suppression of debate on controverted topics not only fails in its intention to squelch debate but undermines the integrity of the teaching office, which is seen as motivated by fear of challenge rather than by fidelity to a received tradition.

In this section we have briefly considered four factors that have had an impact on questions of ministry in the decades since Vatican II. However, there is yet another factor that requires a more extended consideration—the global character of the church itself.

---

[36] Osborne, 145-46.

New Ministries in a Global Context

The global nature of the church was not an explicit theme of the council, but it was implicit in the council's recognition of the plurality of cultures and the need for all missionary endeavors to honor the particularity and integrity of these cultures. The council wrote:

> The church is faithful to its traditions and is at the same time conscious of its universal mission; it can, then, enter into communion with different forms of culture, thereby enriching both itself and the cultures themselves. (GS 58)

This passage has not always been honored in the decades since the council. Too much reflection on Christian mission has focused on how the gospel can enrich the various cultures that it encounters. If we are to take seriously the possibility that diverse cultures might themselves enrich the church, then it is worth considering how the engagement between the church and local cultures might be contributing to our understanding of Christian ministry.

Ministry in an African Context

Christianity is growing on the continent of Africa at a staggering rate. During the last fifty years, the total population of Africa grew 313 percent while the Catholic population in Africa grew an incredible 708 percent.[37] Between 1978 and 2004 alone, the number of Catholics in Africa tripled.[38] There are now over 130 million Catholics in Africa, and the growth of other Christian traditions equals or exceeds the Catholic growth rate. As African Christianity has begun to shed European vestiges from centuries of missionary endeavors, new forms of church and ministry have emerged.

The engagement between church and culture in Africa is particularly fascinating because it illustrates well the multidirectional nature of such engagement. Ancient ministerial forms have been reshaped in sometimes subtle and other times quite decisive ways. An obvious contact point for an African theology of ministry is indigenous African societies' openness to the spiritual dimension of both the cosmos and the human person. Traditional African cultures generally presume a sacral cosmos and believe that all persons are in touch with a spiritual realm of existence. This explains why more Pentecostal forms of Christianity have equaled and, in places, outpaced Catholicism in church growth. These forms of Christianity have historically been much more open to

---

[37] Bryan T. Froehle and Mary L. Gautier, eds., *Global Catholicism: Portrait of a World Church* (Maryknoll, N.Y.: Orbis Books, 2003).

[38] *Statistical Yearbook of the Church (2004)* (Vatican City: Libreria Editrice Vaticana, 2006).

the possibility that each believer might have direct access to the realm of the Spirit. Elochukwu Uzukwu sees this openness to the spiritual realm as an obvious opportunity to develop a Christian theology of ministry grounded in the biblical notion of charism.

> While the missionary churches (especially the Roman Catholic church) hold such charisms suspect, the independent churches delight in and even exaggerate such manifestations of the Spirit. The creativity which is embodied in the charisms both builds the community and heals the individual Christian. Aside from their exaggerations, the charisms experienced in the independent or "spiritualist" churches are in tune with the African universe and with the early experience of the Christian church-community. The services that the Spirit of God causes to be rendered to the community and the world are multiple, and they are communicated through these gifts.[39]

Uzukwu is suggesting that Africa provides a unique opportunity to put into effect the council's teaching on the vital place of charism in the life of the church. As we shall see, some African pastoral initiatives have already begun to explore a vision of local communities animated by the many charisms of the people.

An important new pastoral initiative that has emerged in Africa over the last two decades has wedded the success of BECs in Africa with an African cultural openness to a theology of charism. We spoke in the last chapter about the Lumko Institute and its pastoral training initiatives. Out of that initiative has emerged a proposed model for ordained ministry championed by Lumko's founder, Bishop Fritz Lobinger.[40] At the heart of Lobinger's ecclesial vision is the proposal to ordain *viri probati*, mature married men, to the ministerial priesthood. The ordination of *viri probati* has been widely debated in the church for some time now. What is distinctive about Lobinger's proposal is his conviction that no change in church practice be undertaken until the local communities requesting the ordination of *viri probati* have undergone a fundamental community transformation.

As we saw in the last chapter, Lobinger's argument is that most parishes today, in Africa and in much of the developed world as well, are still built on the "provided for church" model in which the majority of Catholics see

---

[39] Elochukwu E. Uzukwu, *A Listening Church: Autonomy and Communion in African Churches* (Maryknoll, N.Y.: Orbis Books, 1996), 110.

[40] Bishop Lobinger has articulated this pastoral theology of the local church and church ministry in two volumes, *Like His Brothers and Sisters: Ordaining Community Leaders* (New York: Crossroad, 1998); *Priests for Tomorrow* (Quezon City, Philippines: Claretian Publications, 2004).

themselves as recipients of the ministerial initiatives of the ordained. The "provided-for church" is itself built on a model of the priesthood that Lobinger refers to as "the provider-priest." This presupposes a largely post-Tridentine theology of the priest as sacred person who shepherds his flock, preaches the gospel, and administers the sacraments in a way that places the rest of the community in radical dependence on his ministrations. Until that ecclesial mentality is changed, Lobinger contends that the ordination of *viri probati* would be welcomed in much the same way that permanent deacons and lay ecclesial ministers have been welcomed in other parts of the world, namely, as substitutes for the provider-priest that leave the community equally dependent on the ministry of some elite few. Something like this, he contends, has happened in parts of Africa that have created the position of lay administrator of a community where no priest is present. One example of this would be the *bakambi* ministry as it is conducted in Zaire.

Lobinger proposes that in communities that have succeeded in the process of transition from "provided-for churches" to a "communion of communities" model a new vision of presbyteral ministry might be implemented. This vision is predicated on these communities having internalized the teachings of Vatican II regarding the active participation of the whole people of God in the life of the church, a theology of charism, and a vision of ordained ministry as a ministry of service. Once parishes have undergone the requisite transformation, the church could then move forward with the establishment of two distinct forms of the priesthood. Here Lobinger finds guidance in a distinction between the ministry of St. Paul and that of local community leaders. While Paul exercised a unique ministry of leadership and support over multiple communities, traveling from one to another as a kind of itinerant minister, most of the communities with whom Paul related had their own residential ministers. Following this distinction Lobinger speaks of either Paul-priests and Corinth-priests or animator-priests and community-priests.[41] Each communion of communities would be "pastored" by either an individual or a team of animator-priests. These priests would be prepared in ways not unlike our current diocesan priests. They would have extensive seminary formation; they would devote themselves to full-time public ministry; and they would ordinarily be celibate. Each basic ecclesial community would, in turn, be led by a team of community priests or "ordained community leaders." This leadership would always be undertaken collegially (that is, there would never be a single community priest presiding over a BEC), the leadership would be drawn from the BEC membership, and

---

[41] In more recent presentations of his vision he has begun to use the pairing "animator priests" and "ordained community leaders."

their presbyteral ministry would generally be limited to their own BEC. These leaders would be free to marry and have families, and normally would have other forms of employment.

Lobinger is adamant that his proposal not be seen as a stopgap solution to the priest shortage problem. Rather, his proposal follows from his sense that our current model of priesthood not only perpetuates a certain kind of clericalism but also stifles the kind of community transformation envisioned by the council. In fact, a frank assessment of ministry in Africa must honestly acknowledge a persistent clericalism among many of the African clergy.

We have already considered the African church's employment of the "family of God" as an image of the church. It is a conception of the church that helpfully promotes the communitarian character of Christian community. However, a number of African theologians have warned of the dangers of the church-family model drawing too directly from African familial structures, which are often very patriarchal in character.[42] The Kenyan priest and theologian Benjamin Kiriswa admits that some traditional African families are reluctant to grant full equality to wives and at times are inclined to treat wives and children as property, excluding them from significant decision making. He explains that in most African cultures "[t]he father is not only perceived as the protector and head of the family but he is also the sole authority whose commands and expectations have to be followed by every member of the family."[43] In patrilineal African societies, fathers and sons are generally given preferential status in the community, as regards, for example, access to education. Without care, the assimilation of such cultural values into Christian understandings of ministry can encourage a distinctive form of African clericalism and sexism in the church.

This clericalism is also due, in part, to the assimilation of the role of the traditional African healer into Christian ministerial forms, leading to the "priest-healer."[44] Christianity, of course, has its own understanding of Christian healing grounded in God's loving embrace of humanity and an understanding of God's salvific purposes as oriented toward the healing of the whole person. This understanding of healing stands at odds with certain African conceptions of healing based on a dualistic cosmology that sets spiritual forces of good and evil in conflict in the sphere of human history and experience. The priest-healer

---

[42] John Mary Waliggo, "The Synod of Hope at a Time of Crisis in Africa," in *The African Synod: Documents, Reflections, Perspectives*, ed. Maura Browne and the Africa Faith & Justice Network (Maryknoll, N.Y.: Orbis Books, 1996), 208.

[43] Benjamin Kiriswa, "African Model of Church as Family: Implications on Ministry & Leadership," *African Ecclesial Review (AFER)* 43 (June 2001): 99-108, at 102.

[44] Uzukwu, 122-24.

is then seen as a spiritual figure with unique power over the spiritual world that is unavailable to others. The result is an attribution of enormous sacral power to the priest-healer. When these traditional African understandings of the healer are wedded to certain Roman Catholic conceptions of the priest as alone possessing sacred power over the sacraments, the result can be a dangerous form of African clericalism.

Some creative responses to the dangers of African clericalism have recently surfaced. A new generation of African feminist theologians has been particularly sensitive to this issue.[45] A group known as the Circle of Concerned African Women Theologians has been studying and speaking out against violence and discrimination against women in African society. They are convinced that many of these cultural biases are perpetuated in the life of the church. Women do provide vital ministries in many African churches, either as catechists or, frequently, as leaders of BECs.[46] However, the abject poverty found in so many African countries falls particularly hard on African women, making it difficult for them to participate in formal church ministries. There are also numerous testimonies of African priests that are threatened by women in ministry. Many African scholars agree that there is much work to be done in the advancement of African women in ministry. African biblical scholar Teresa Okure has offered the positive value of African maternal images, suggesting that they may provide a helpful cultural resource for reinterpreting Jesus as the model for Christian ministry. She does so by connecting the responsibility of the African mother to feed her young with Christ's ministry to feed his flock.[47]

Ministry in a Latin American Context
The African church's employment of basic ecclesial communities was influenced by the success of these communities in Latin America. The development of BECs in Latin America generated new ministerial forms. Preeminent among these are nonordained ministers known variously as catechists or ministers of the Word. Some of these worked in individual communities; others shared catechetical responsibilities for multiple BECs. Although these catechetical ministries have taken many different forms, common among them is the facilitation of ongoing Bible study in each basic ecclesial community. More

---

[45] See Mercy Amba Oduyoye and Musumbi R. A. Kanyoro, eds., *The Will to Arise: Women, Tradition, and the Church in Africa* (Maryknoll, N.Y.: Orbis Books, 1992); Mercy Amba Oduyoye, *Beads and Strands: Reflections of an African Woman on Christianity in Africa* (Maryknoll, N.Y.: Orbis Books, 2004).

[46] Bernadette Mbuy-Beya, "Women in the Churches in Africa: Possibilities for Presence and Promises," in *The African Synod*, ed. Browne et al., 175-87.

[47] Teresa Okure, "Leadership in the New Testament," *Nigerian Journal of Theology* 1/5 (1990): 71-93.

frequently than in the African form of catechetical ministry, many Latin American catechists would also help these BECs to engage in critical reflection on their social situation, sensitive to the ways in which the systemic injustice that they experience stands at odds with God's salvific will.

In several Latin American contexts creative pastoral initiatives have appeared that explicitly draw inspiration from indigenous cultural resources. One example of this is the creative initiative to implement the permanent diaconate in the Diocese of San Cristóbal de las Casas. Bishop Samuel Ruiz, who led his diocese for almost four full decades, from 1960 to 2000, pioneered a quite distinctive form of the permanent diaconate, one that sought to integrate fundamental values and practices of the Mayan culture dominant in the southernmost Mexican state of Chiapas.

When the Mexican bishops' conference first decided to pursue the permanent diaconate, Ruiz dutifully began the process in his own diocese, initially leaving the leadership of the formation process to his priests. However, it soon became clear to him that, as he put it, the priests charged with overseeing the formations of deacons "were forming altar boys rather than deacons."[48]

The action that Bishop Ruiz took in response to this situation came from his conviction that one of the most important teachings of the council was that each local church must be "autochthonous," that is, an authentic local church drawing from the resources of the local culture. He informed diocesan catechists of his intention to initiate the diaconate in the diocese. For one year he asked the catechists and their local tribal communities to study and pray over a set of biblical texts dealing with the ministry of deacons. After that year of study, each community proposed its own candidates for the diaconal formation process. Frequently, the deacon candidates were chosen because they had already proven themselves as catechists within the community. These deacon candidates, or pre-deacons, were already acknowledged as spiritual leaders and frequently performed many of the same ministries as those already ordained to the diaconate. The discernment process drew heavily on Mayan customs. For example, during my visit there, I interviewed a number of deacons and deacon candidates who reported the decisive role that dream interpretation played in their discernment. They would recount how God appeared to them in dreams to encourage them to pursue their ministerial formation.

As the deacons would often be the principal ministers of many indigenous communities, their ability to lead the community in prayer was of paramount importance. This is no small thing, as the Mayan peoples take communal prayer quite seriously; when they gather together they can pray together for hours on

---

[48] From an interview with the author, January 9, 2005.

end. The deacon candidate is often one in the community known to be able to pray with passion from his "heart." Also in accord with local custom, these ministerial candidates were generally accompanied in their formation process by an elder in the community, male or female.

The unique ministry of the deacon and the deacon candidate in Chiapas was exhibited at a diaconate formation weekend that I was privileged to attend. The formation weekend took place in a small hamlet named Tekiucum. The chapel in which we met was located on top of a mountain. We traveled part way in the back of a pickup truck and the rest of the way on foot up a very steep, muddy, and, when wet, quite treacherous path. The chapel was little more than a long hut pieced together with wooden boards and corrugated metal roofing. It had a dirt floor covered with pine needles.

Elders, deacon candidates, and spouses gradually began to arrive between nine o'clock and eleven in the morning. They came with packs and bedrolls on their backs, often having hiked for hours to attend. The meeting began with hymns and the recitation of formal prayers, generally in Spanish, followed by extended spontaneous prayer in Tzotzil, one of several indigenous Mayan languages found in the region. Following the prayer, the community began to deliberate regarding how they would structure the weekend. This communal decision-making process was deeply rooted in their Mayan heritage, and it is one of the most characteristic features of these communities. All decisions were made communally, and each person had the right to "speak their word." Once they decided on the plan for the day, the community participated in a traditional dance to "seal the decision" and to "animate our spirits" for the rest of the process. The community learned that one of the members in our visiting delegation was a biblical scholar, Sr. Barbara Reid, and so she was asked to provide the catechetical content for the day. After her presentation on the role of women in the Bible, the community participated in an animated discussion of the lesson. At the end of the day, after a simple meal, we all slept in bedrolls on the pine-scented chapel floor. The next morning we began the day with communal prayer that again lasted for several hours.

During the day, the community received word that a much-loved elderly woman in the community was on her deathbed. This woman had been a catechist and a respected figure in the community. Upon hearing the news, the participants decided to suspend their formation process in order to visit her. We then hiked down the mountain, drove part of the way in the pickup, and then hiked the rest of the way on foot, climbing down yet another slippery, clay path to the dying woman's home. The poverty of her surroundings was overwhelming. The shack was made of loose boards and corrugated metal. It was dark and filled with smoke from a fire, as there were no windows or chimney in the hut. Many family and friends were already gathered for the death watch, but our delegation was enthusiastically greeted. It was clear that these deacon candidates were already respected spiritual leaders in the local community. We all crammed inside the hut and the candidates gathered around the woman's bed. The elder deacon candidate led everyone in communal prayer that lasted for almost an hour. Then one leader spoke to the community in Tzotzil of the dying woman's importance to the community. The candidates each went to the bed and marked her forehead with the sign of the cross, after which we all processed outside where the family had lined up about twenty cups of coffee on a long plank, a gesture of gratitude extended to their guests. We hiked back up the mud path and returned to the chapel. The woman would die later that evening.

I must recount one final event from my weekend in Tekiucum. The weekend process was interrupted a second time by the arrival of a deacon candidate named Daniel, who had decided to drop out of the formation process. He addressed the community, explaining that he had decided not to continue because of an extended dispute he and his wife had had with the parish priest, the precise nature of which was never made clear. His wife was quite adamant about not continuing, and he was inclined to agree with her. This admission was received with a certain awkwardness, since the priest involved in the dispute was sitting there among us. In any event, Daniel went on to say that he had come to the meeting only because the night before he was instructed to do so by God in a dream. After his explanation he sat down. Members of the community were invited to offer their word. A number of them did so and one of the most respected elders continued on, addressing Daniel for approximately fifteen minutes. The candidate was both admonished for not consulting the community before making such a decision and encouraged to persevere in the process. Then the elders turned to address the priest with whom the candidate had had a dispute. They admonished him for his failure to fulfill his role as spiritual leader of the community. At the end of the discussion, the priest rose and gave a very moving speech in which he asked for forgiveness from the offended deacon candidate, his wife, and the community for his role in this dispute. This long communal process of reconciliation was then "sealed" by another communal dance.

As I left that small community I took with me a moving experience of ministry. The ministerial leadership was devoid of clericalism and was characterized by a mutual accountability. The deacon candidates were chosen for this formation process because they were already acknowledged spiritual leaders. Their theological formation, by North American standards, was quite basic. Yet the sphere of their ministry was equally basic: they visited the sick and dying; they baptized and presided over both communion services and funerals. What they needed for formation, they found in communal Scripture study and the devotional life of their community. There was no concern about minimum "contact hours" with a professor, no concern about a set curriculum, no concern about testing knowledge of the tradition. These candidates were being formed for a ministry of accompaniment with their people that had been modeled for them by their bishop and the roots of which went deep within their own cultural heritage. It is no surprise that deacons were referred to by the Mayan term, *tuhuneles* or servants.

A regrettable postscript to my experience in Chiapas came in the spring of 2006. Cardinal Arinze (prefect of the Congregation of Worship and the Discipline of the Sacraments) issued a notification that prohibited Bishop Ruiz's successor, Bishop Felipe Arizmendi, from ordaining any more permanent deacons. Those deacons who were already ordained were immediately to submit themselves for renewed catechetical formation based on the *Catechism of the Catholic Church*. The official notification denounced the notion of an "autochthonous" church, which it erroneously interpreted as meaning "autonomous." It also objected that the large numbers of permanent deacons there unjustly fueled hopes for a married priesthood that could not be realized.

TOWARD A CONSTRUCTIVE THEOLOGY OF MINISTRY FOR A GLOBAL CHURCH

Church ministry has always existed in service of the church's mission. The task of serving the church's mission in diverse historical epochs and diverse cultural contexts has produced a wonderful miscellany of ministerial forms and theologies. Every theology of ministry will perforce be both historically and culturally situated. Nevertheless, there may be a value in sketching out the broad outlines of a theology of ministry that is capable, in principle, of embracing diverse ministerial forms while at the same time linking these forms to some of our deepest Christian convictions about the nature of the church and its mission.

All Ministry Is Relational

The biblical concept of *koinōnia*, or *communio*, has proven very fertile for contemporary ecclesiology. It is a concept that is rooted in basic Christian convictions regarding the triune God. Renewed interest in the doctrine of the Trinity in the last four decades has helped to recover the fundamentally relational being of God.[49] The trinitarian missions of Word and Spirit draw humankind and

---

[49] See Anne Hunt, *Trinity: Nexus of the Mysteries of the Christian Faith*, Theology in Global Perspective (Maryknoll, N.Y.: Orbis Books, 2005).

indeed all of creation into the divine life of communion. This trinitarian starting point in turn leads to a theological anthropology. If God is perfect "being
as communion," we are created as beings made for communion.[50] What God
is in God's very being, we can become by grace. Humans are made for communion with God and one another and our relationships are to be governed by
the essential characteristics of trinitarian communion.

From theological anthropology we turn to the church, that privileged communal context in which humankind is invited into the life of communion. The
Second Vatican Council echoed this, seeing the church "as a kind of sacrament,
that is, a sign and instrument of communion with God and the unity of the
whole human race" (LG 1). Baptism sacramentally initiates believers into the life
of communion; it calls us into a new mode of living, a new relationship. The
church, as a communion, is a relational reality. The church is not an aggregate
of individual members; it is a community of relationships. This church is ordered
in particular ways. Beyond the fundamental relationship of discipleship established in our baptism, the church is ordered by other ministerial relationships
that build up the church for mission.

Admittedly, this vision of the church as a relational reality is articulated in
an abstract and formal language. However, our encounter with different cultural
contexts suggests that it is a formal view of the church that can be given substance in diverse cultural contexts. It corresponds particularly well to the thoroughly communitarian sensibilities of many indigenous cultures of Asia, Africa,
and Latin America that have not been subject to the individualistic ethos of
Western cultures influenced by the Enlightenment.

One of the principal theological merits of developing a relational theology
of ministry is that it allows us to sidestep a problematic approach to ministry
that defines ministry in terms of the conferral of sacramental power and consequently sees ordained ministry as the only true form of ecclesial ministry. In
a relational theology of ministry both the ordained and those called to exercise
the gifts given to them at baptism play vital and complementary roles in the life
of the church. When a person enters into public ministry, whether by ordination or some other liturgical rite, they enter into a new way of participating in
the church's mission and a new relationship to other believers.

---

[50] For an example of a theology of ministry that moves from God's being as communion to theo
logical anthropology and finally to ecclesiology, see John Zizioulas, *Being as Communion: Studies in Personhood and the Church* (Crestwood, N.Y.: St. Vladimir's Seminary Press, 1985). Roman Catholic
theologies of ministry influenced by this more relational perspective include Edward Hahnenberg,
Ministries: A Relational Approach (New York: Crossroad, 2003); Susan K. Wood, *Sacramental Orders,*
Lex Orandi (Collegeville, Minn.: Liturgical Press, 2000); Paul Bernier, *Ministry in the Church: A Historical and Pastoral Approach* (Mystic, Conn.: Twenty-third Publications, 1992).

A traditional Catholic theology of ministry based on powers—the bishop defined by his power to ordain and confirm, the priest by his power to celebrate the eucharist and administer the sacraments of penance and anointing, the deacon by his status as an ordinary minister of the eucharist and his authorization to preach during the eucharist—inevitably puts various ministers in a competitive relationship with one another. Each is defined by what one group can do that others cannot. It encourages a view of hierarchy conceived as a top-down command structure, a "spiritual trickle-down" theory.

Within a relational theology of ministry power is not something that one possesses but a reality that one participates in to the extent that one is open to the work of the Spirit. Power is not hoarded; it flows through authentic ecclesial relationships. Vatican II had already taught that the hierarchy does not compete with the rest of the faithful. The Spirit bequeaths to the church gifts both "hierarchic and charismatic" (LG 4). A relational theology of ministry builds on this insight and therefore is able to affirm the complementary relations of both ordained and lay ecclesial ministries. It acknowledges the hierarchical nature of the church but presents hierarchy not as a vertical command structure but as a right ordering of the church.

Ministry and Mission

A theology of ministry adequate to today's global church must be grounded in mission and discipleship. The American bishops' document on lay ecclesial ministry, "Co-Workers in the Vineyard of the Lord," offers a subtle advance in our understanding of ministry. Early in the first section "Co-Workers" affirms the teaching of both the Second Vatican Council and Pope John Paul II on the "secular character" of the lay vocation. It is a claim that has dominated the theology of the laity, at least in magisterial documents, since the time of the council. This long-standing emphasis is unfortunate since, as numerous commentators have pointed out, the council was hardly offering an *ontological* definition of the laity but merely a *typological* one, that is, a practical definition that captures the "typical" situation of the vast majority of the laity.[51] Yet since the council, the secular character of the laity has been given a quasi-ontological status. Now it is doubtless true that the majority of lay Catholics are immersed in "the ordinary circumstances of social and family life that, as it were, form

---

[51] This distinction was famously made by Cardinal John Wright in his *relatio* presenting to the council bishops the draft of this text, *Acta Synodalia Sacrosancti Concilii Oecumenici Vaticani II* (Vatican City: Typis Vaticanis, 1970–), 3/1:282. This also appeared in the *relatio* introducing chap. 4 of the *De Ecclesia* schema (see *Acta Synodalia*, 3/3:62).

the context of their existence" (LG 31). However, if pushed too far, this view of the secular character of the laity creates more problems than it solves.[52] There is a risk of turning the distinction between the sacred and the secular into a separation, by presenting the laity as the church's "foot soldiers" sent out into the world by the clergy who remain safely ensconced in the privileged realm of the sacred.[53]

"Co-Workers" deftly avoids this danger in a single sentence that is lifted almost verbatim from an earlier document of the USCCB subcommittee on lay ministry, *Lay Ecclesial Ministry: The State of the Questions*. In that 1999 document we find the following statement:

> All of the *laity* are called to work toward the transformation of the secular world. *Some* do this by working in the secular realm; others do this by working in the Church and focusing on the building of ecclesial communion, which has as *its ultimate purpose* the transformation of the world.[54]

This passage was inserted almost entirely into "Co-Workers" with, however, some important emendations:

> All of the *baptized* are called to work toward the transformation of the world. *Most* do this by working in the secular realm; some do this by working in the church and focusing on the building of ecclesial communion, which has *among its purposes* the transformation of the world.[55]

A single word change suggests a major theological development. "Co-Workers" asserts that not just the laity, as the previous text had it, but "*all of the baptized* are called to work toward the transformation of the world." This reflects the insight of the council's most mature document, *Gaudium et Spes*, which attributed the image of leaven not to the laity alone, as other conciliar passages had, but to the church itself, which "is to be a leaven and, as it were, the soul of human society in its renewal by Christ and transformation into the family of God" (GS 40).

One of the difficulties that some North American bishops and conservative commentators like Russell Shaw have had with a theology of lay ministry

---

[52] Edward Hahnenberg, "Ordained and Lay Ministry: Restarting the Conversation," *Origins* 35 (June 23, 2005): 94-99, at 96.

[53] Richard R. Gaillardetz, "Shifting Meanings in the Lay-Clergy Distinction," *Irish Theological Quarterly* 64 (1999): 115-39.

[54] USCCB Sub-Committee on Lay Ministry, *Lay Ecclesial Ministry: The State of the Questions* (Washington, D.C.: USCCB, 1999) (emphasis mine).

[55] USCCB, "Co-Workers," 407 (emphasis mine).

has been the concern that it might distract from the laity's primary orientation toward the world.[56] This concern is both legitimate and misconceived. It is legitimate in the sense that one of the perennial temptations for the church has been to ignore its orientation in mission toward the world. This was the concern of Cardinal Suenens and Archbishop Dom Helder Camara at Vatican II when they insisted that the document on the nature of the church be augmented by a document on the church oriented toward the world. In fact, today ecclesiologists tend to reject the view that Jesus first instituted a church and then gave it a mission. It is biblically and theologically more accurate to say that Jesus established a mission in the world, a mission in service of God's reign, and then called forth a community of disciples for the fulfillment of that mission. Thus, although the concern about a kind of ecclesial "navel-gazing" is legitimate, this concern is misconceived to the extent that it sees the avoidance of mission as a problem that applies to the laity only. It is our *whole* church that must embrace the demands of mission to the world. This is why the decisive change in the text of "Co-Workers" is so significant; it recognizes that no baptized Christian is exempted from the obligations of church mission and the responsibility toward the transformation of the world. In one of his earlier works, Italian theologian Bruno Forte wrote of the need to speak not so much of individual members of the laity but of the fundamental *laicity* of the whole church. Forte insisted that as regards the church's orientation toward the world

> the relationship with temporal realities is proper to all the baptized, though in a variety of forms, joined more to personal charisms than to static contrasts between laity, hierarchy and religious state. . . . No one is neutral toward the historical circumstances in which he or she is living, and an alleged neutrality can easily become a voluntary or involuntary mask for ideologies and special interests. . . . It is the entire community that has to confront the secular world, being marked by that world in its being and in its action. The entire People of God must be characterized by a positive relationship with the secular dimension.[57]

The chief problem with the hardening of the secular/sacred distinction is not, in the end, the "foot soldier" theology of the laity; it is the failure of the clergy to see how *their* ministry as leaders, sacramental ministers, and preachers must also be oriented toward the transformation of the world.

---

[56] Russell B. Shaw, *Ministry or Apostolate? What Should the Catholic Laity Be Doing?* (Huntington, Ind.: Our Sunday Visitor, 2002).

[57] Bruno Forte, *The Church: Icon of the Trinity* (Boston: St. Paul Books & Media, 1991), 54-55.

Complete Dismantling of the Cursus Honorum

We mentioned earlier the implications of the council's calling for the restoration of the permanent diaconate. Preeminent among them was that it represented a first step toward the dismantling of the *cursus honorum,* a conception of ordained ministry as a series of ascending ecclesiastical ranks. Yet in several ways, this sense of ordained ministry as a series of ascending ranks still remains. Even after Pope Paul VI suppressed the minor orders, established the installed ministries of lector and acolyte and restored the diaconate as a permanent and stable ministry, the problem remained. In part this is due to the regrettable decision to continue to require that candidates to the diaconate and priesthood first be installed to the ministries of lector and acolyte. Moreover, the diaconate has continued to function as a pastoral internship to be undertaken by a seminarian for between six and eighteen months as a preparation for presbyteral ministry. This situation has required, at least from a canonical perspective, two different diaconates, one permanent and one transitional, with two different sets of canonical rights and obligations.[58] It is a situation that has served only to perpetuate a confused theology of the diaconate. Consequently, I am in sympathy with the proposal of Susan Wood that the church consider abandoning a transitional diaconate as a sacramental prerequisite to presbyteral ordination.[59] The reasons for this are many.

First, the ancient tradition in no way presupposed that one must advance from one ordained ministry to the next. In the earliest centuries, bishops were chosen both from the ranks of the baptized and from the diaconate without having to be first ordained presbyter. The most recent scholarship now suggests that a fixed sequence of ordination—deacon, presbyter, bishop—was not firmly in place before the Middle Ages.[60] Second, the existence of a "transitional diaconate" risks denigrating diaconal ministry by reducing it to a kind of pastoral internship or field education assignment. Third, although seminarians

---

[58] John Huels, "Special Questions on the Diaconate," *Liturgical Ministry* 13 (Winter 2004): 1-9, at 7-8.

[59] Wood, *Sacramental Orders,* 166-71. Huels believes that such a move could be justified as a means of removing canonical discrepancies. See Huels, 8.

[60] See Wood's discussion in *Sacramental Orders,* 167. For recent research on the topic, see John St. H. Gibaut, *The Cursus Honorum: A Study of the Origins and Evolution of Sequential Ordination* (New York: P. Lang, 2000); Louis Weil, "Aspects of the Issue of *Per Saltum* Ordination: An Anglican Perspective," in *Rule of Prayer, Rule of Faith: Essays in Honor of Aidan Kavanagh, O.S.B.,* ed. Nathan Mitchell and John F. Baldovin (Collegeville, Minn.: Liturgical Press, 1996), 200-217; Balthasar Fischer, "Hat Ambrosius von Mailand in der Woche zwischen seiner Taufe und seiner Bischofskonsekration andere Weihe empfangen?" in *Kyriakon: Festschrift Johannes Quasten,* ed. Patrick Granfield and Josef A. Jungmann, 2 vols. (Münster/Westfalen: Aschendorff, 1970), 2:527-31; Ormonde Plater, "Direct Ordination: The Historical Evidence," *Open* 37 (1992): 1-3.

clearly benefit from a pastoral internship that includes preaching and limited sacramental/liturgical ministry, there is no reason that these ministries could not be delegated to seminarians by their bishop without diaconal ordination.[61]

A further step in this regard flows out of ecumenical debates, particularly between Catholics and Lutherans, regarding Vatican II's teaching that the episcopate represents the fullness of the sacrament of holy orders. The council advanced that teaching as a way of affirming the full sacramental significance of episcopal ministry. However, by doing so, it also created difficulties for those traditions without a historical episcopate who believe that the ministry of *episkopē* has been preserved in the pastorate. An alternative approach might affirm the full sacramentality of the episcopate as a distinct ordained ministry without recourse to the problematic "fullness" language. Instead, the episcopal order would be understood as a unique ministerial relation in the church that exercised oversight of a local church (in cooperation with the local presbyterate) but which, unlike the presbyterate, at least in the Roman Catholic Church, also facilitates the communion between the local church and the communion of churches in virtue of his participation in the college of bishops. Within this framework, the diaconate, the presbyterate, and the episcopate would each share full sacramental status without any sense of one being superior to the others or possessing a fullness of the sacrament not accessible to the others. Each ministry would be seen as a unique and vital ministerial relation in its own right.

Ministerial Accountability

One of the insights to emerge from a study of new ministerial forms and structures in the church is the need for a heightened ministerial accountability.[62] In the United States, this has been precipitated by the tragic clerical abuse scandal and the ecclesiastical cover-up that it inspired. Discussion of accountability in the church is handicapped, however, by the fact that it is a term borrowed from the political and business sectors without strong ecclesiological links. This has led many Catholic Church leaders to be wary of such language. Then bishop of Pittsburgh, Donald Wuerl, related accountability to questions of church governance and warned that "when we address accountability in the church, we must be careful not to use a political model for a reality that tran-

---

[61] However, it should be noted that *Redemptionis Sacramentum*, recently published by the Congregation for Divine Worship and the Sacraments, has prohibited even seminarians from preaching in the context of the eucharist. *Origins* 33 (May 6, 2004): 801-22, see #66.

[62] What follows is adapted from Richard R. Gaillardetz, "Accountability in the Church: Report from Chiapas," *New Theology Review* 19 (2006): 33-45.

scends human political institutions."[63] According to him, accountability in the church differs from its political analogue because the church is subject to certain God-given constraints:

> There are a number of "givens" or facts in our discussion because we are dealing with a divinely established reality. At the same time, there is a need to integrate these "givens" into the circumstances of our day. To understand governance in the Catholic Church, we have to go back to its origin and its divine institution. The Catholic church was established by Christ and its structure is articulated in two sacraments: baptism and holy orders. The hierarchy and the apostolic tradition are intrinsic to the church. Both have the God-given function of guaranteeing that the saving revelation of Jesus Christ continues to be passed on, made available, and lived in every successive generation.[64]

Wuerl defined ecclesial accountability in terms of openness and transparency sufficient to allow one to assess whether church leaders are acting in fidelity to their divine mandate. I cite Wuerl because his views reflect a common perspective held by many church leaders. They share a concern for past mistakes made by many bishops and are eager to change public perception regarding the exercise of episcopal leadership. Nevertheless, for many church leaders, the unique status of the church demands that true ecclesial accountability remain primarily vertical. Church leaders must be accountable to God and faithful to the divinely instituted elements of the church. Church teaching and church structures, to the extent that they are divinely mandated, are not open for debate. Ministerial accountability to God and accountability to the people are placed in opposition, with the latter reflecting at best an unacceptable Protestantizing, and at worst a capitulation to the secular world.

In both North America and Western Europe the rise of democratic aspirations in the modern world has often been accompanied by a repudiation of church authority. Conversely, a commitment to religious authority often meant rejecting liberal democracy, as was evident in Pope Pius IX's *Syllabus of Errors*. Although at the Second Vatican Council the Catholic Church left behind its rabid antimodern stance, one still finds a great deal of hand-wringing about the dangers of importing liberal democratic values into the church. Again I quote Bishop Wuerl:

---

[63] Bishop Donald W. Wuerl, "Reflections on Governance and Accountability in the Church," in *Governance, Accountability, and the Future of the Catholic Church*, ed. Francis Oakley and Bruce Russett (New York: Continuum, 2004), 13-24, at 18.

[64] Ibid., 13.

There is a temptation to make the church into an American democratic organization as if we, the members, had supreme authority over the body. Thus, we come to the point where we would vote on articles of the Creed, determine not only how faithful we are to the Gospel but also what the message ought to be to satisfy the circumstances of our day.[65]

Wuerl articulated a concern shared not only by other members of the North American hierarchy but by key figures in the Vatican as well. This conviction that accountability to God and accountability to the people are opposed to each other has forestalled a vital and much-needed ecclesial conversation about the character and limits of church accountability. It suggests another way in which a theology of ministry can be enriched by non-Western churches that have not been haunted by the Enlightenment and have benefited from indigenous cultures that have maintained an ethos of accountability within tribal networks.

What I encountered in Chiapas was a local church attuned to the work of the Holy Spirit. Their understanding of the church creatively integrated a Mayan commitment to communal decision making and celebration with a Christian expectation of the presence and guidance of the Spirit in the life of the church. Everyone's "word" had to be heard and honored, and all decisions were "sealed by the Spirit" through communal dance. This conviction regarding the presence of the Spirit was not, for them, opposed to legitimate church authority.

Finally, it is impossible to ignore the ecclesial implications of the moving spectacle of mutual accountability displayed in the Mayan Christian community gathered at Tekiucum. As I watched the community's confrontation of both the deacon candidate and the priest, I could not help transposing that conflict to my own church in North America. I have seen countless conflicts of this sort, but their resolution went along very different lines. First, when an individual decides to drop out of a formation process, the first inclination of others would be to support that individual's decision. This is a consequence of our default belief that vocational discernment is ultimately a private matter between the individual and God. This default belief has also contributed to the uneven quality of our ministers. We think it inappropriate for the community to test a ministerial vocation. The community gathered at Tekiucum saw things differently. They did not hesitate to admonish the candidate for making such an important decision without consulting the community and seeking its corporate wisdom in the matter.

---

[65] Ibid., 17.

We must also try to learn from the willingness of that community to challenge the conduct of their pastor. In many North American churches with which I am familiar, dissatisfaction with a pastor might lead parishioners to complain, gossip, or gripe to others in the community or even to refuse to contribute to the collection. We might write a letter to our bishop or even Rome. Yet, in spite of the firm biblical foundation for such communal action, few of our communities would feel sufficiently empowered and confident that they *are* the church as to confront a leader for acting in ways counter to the gospel. And if such a community were to feel so empowered and act on that empowerment, in most instances the communal confrontation of an ordained leader's misconduct would be greeted with shock, anger, and appeals to the prerogatives of office.

At Tekiucum I encountered a community that embodied the council's teaching that we are a pilgrim church, a people on a journey. They understood that all were called to holiness, and that holiness could best be deepened through immersion in the life of the community. Perhaps the most important thing to be learned from the church in Chiapas is that one's understanding of ecclesial accountability depends on one's vision of the church. It is not enough, from the side of church leadership, to limit accountability to greater transparency in decision making, as important as this is. For those offended by the misuse of authority, it is not enough to call for an ecclesial set of checks and balances, as helpful as those might be. What is demanded is an ecclesial vision that recognizes, first, the priority of baptism over holy orders. This priority allows for the distinctive leadership of the ordained but reminds church leaders that their fundamental identity comes from their baptism. Consequently their ministry is always subject to the scrutiny of the community of the baptized. Second, we must develop a vision of the church as subject to Christ and animated by the Spirit. Faithful obedience to Christ will be incarnated in practices of communal discernment that look for not the majority of individual opinions but the gentle voice of the Spirit of Christ speaking through a faith-filled people. When all in the church come to discover the dignity and demands of their baptism and the concrete shape of discipleship in service of the Spirit's promptings, accountability becomes simply another word for *koinōnia*, our shared communion in Christ.

QUESTIONS FOR REFLECTION

1. Do you think the term "hierarchy" can be still be useful for describing the ordered life of the community? What are the advantages/disadvantages of continuing to use this term in reference to the church?

2. What insight do you draw from Yves de Montcheuil's statement "It is not Christians who, in coming together, constitute the Church; it is the Church that makes Christians"?
3. Given our more historical understanding of the often dramatic ways in which ministry has changed and developed over the past two millennia, do you think it is still helpful to try to distinguish between divinely willed ministerial structures that are permanent and essential to the church's life (e.g., the historical episcopate for Catholics) and those that may be subject to change (e.g., priestly celibacy)?
4. What, if any, personal experience do you have of what Bishop Fritz Lobinger calls a "provided-for church"? Do you agree with his concern that the professionalization of ministry can often unintentionally perpetuate this model of church?

SUGGESTIONS FOR FURTHER READING AND STUDY

Bernier, Paul. *Ministry in the Church: A Historical and Pastoral Approach.* Mystic, Conn.: Twenty-third Publications, 1992.

Fox, Zeni. *New Ecclesial Ministry: Lay Professionals Serving the Church.* Rev. and expanded ed. Franklin, Wis.: Sheed & Ward, 2002.

Hahnenberg, Edward. *Ministries: A Relational Approach.* New York: Crossroad, 2003.

Lafont, Ghislain. *Imagining the Catholic Church: Structured Communion in the Spirit.* Collegeville, Minn.: Liturgical Press, 2000.

Lobinger, Fritz. *Like His Brothers and Sisters: Ordaining Community Leaders.* New York: Crossroad, 1998.

Nichols, Terence L. *That All May Be One: Hierarchy and Participation in the Church.* Collegeville, Minn.: Liturgical Press, 1997.

O'Meara, Thomas F. *Theology of Ministry.* Rev. ed. New York: Paulist Press, 1999.

Osborne, Kenan B. *Orders and Ministry: Leadership in the World Church.* Theology in Global Perspective. Maryknoll, N.Y.: Orbis Books, 2006.

Schüssler Fiorenza, Elisabeth. *Discipleship of Equals: A Critical Feminist Ekklesia-logy of Liberation.* New York: Crossroad, 1993.

Uzukwu, Elochukwu E. *A Listening Church: Autonomy and Communion in African Churches.* Maryknoll, N.Y.: Orbis Books, 1996.

Vogels, Heinz-J. *Celibacy—Gift or Law?* Kansas City: Sheed & Ward, 1993.

Wood, Susan K. *Sacramental Orders.* Collegeville, Minn.: Liturgical Press, 2000.

———, ed. *Ordering the Baptismal Priesthood.* Collegeville, Minn.: Liturgical Press, 2003.

World Council of Churches. *Baptism, Eucharist and Ministry.* Faith and Order Paper No. 111. Geneva: WCC, 1982.

5

A People Called to Discipleship

For ancient Israel, holiness was not an achievement; holiness was the state of being in covenantal relationship with God. Holiness was a matter of grateful fidelity to the demands of the covenant. This holiness was a response of the whole people of Israel more than that of any individual. So it was for the early Christian movement. The first Christian communities believed that holiness might be predicated of the church as a whole on the basis not of merit but of divine election. This holiness was to be realized concretely in the life of discipleship. Only gradually would Christianity come to embrace a set of distinctions within the membership of the church that could be placed in a kind of hierarchical gradation based on presumptions regarding the greater or lesser holiness of certain groups of believers.

In this chapter we will briefly review how these distinctions in the call to holiness emerged over the course of two thousand years. This will lead to the twentieth-century rediscovery of the priority of Christian baptism and faithful discipleship for an understanding of the holiness of the church. Granting this priority, we will be in a position to ask whether, embracing the universal call to holiness that is incumbent on all the baptized, it is possible to imagine distinct forms of discipleship within the one church. Finally we will explore the ways in which the church's holiness is conditioned by its pilgrim status as a people always in need of reform and renewal.

THE FOUNDATIONS OF CHRISTIAN IDENTITY
IN THE EARLY CHURCH

How did the first generation of Christians come to identify themselves? Initially, those Jews who came to follow Jesus did not see themselves as anything other than what they were, faithful Jews. Eventually Jewish Christians found it politically if not religiously difficult to maintain a kind of "dual membership," and the Jewish Christian communities died out, a historical accident that would have sad consequences for subsequent Jewish–Christian relations. Christianity would continue as the fruit of the great missionary endeavors of

St. Paul and others who recognized the universal import of the Risen One and brought the gospel to the Gentiles.

Acts of the Apostles reports that it was in Antioch that the first followers of Jesus came to be called "Christians." The first self-appellations used by early Christians included such terms as "disciples" (Acts 6:1; 9:1) or simply "the saints" (Rom. 1:7; 1 Cor. 1:2).[1] Such terms referred not to a specific subset within the Christian community but to all believers. Some form of the word "disciple" appears in the New Testament over two hundred times. Jesus' teaching subverted accepted understandings of community membership in Judaism, understandings that privileged kinship relations. Jesus taught that under God's rule, kinship relations were to be subordinated to the spiritual bonds of discipleship. This is reflected in the story in Mark's Gospel in which Jesus is approached by his family. When told of their arrival Jesus responds: "'Who are my mother and my brothers?' And looking around at those seated in the circle he said, 'Here are my mother and my brothers. For whoever does the will of God is my brother and sister and mother'" (Mark 3:31-35). Jesus' vision of the reign of God imagined, it would seem, the creation of a new family, a new household—the household of believers. He taught his followers that their truest identity lay in the recognition that they were children of God. All other relations were subordinated to this one.

Class distinctions among the first generation of believers had no formal place in the life of the church in the first century, although Paul's admonitions to the Christian community at Corinth suggested that they were already becoming socially stratified. For Paul, however, this social stratification was a departure from the will of God and an offense against the eucharist. The New Testament knew no formal distinction between church leadership and the rest of the community; there was no distinction, in other words, between clergy and laity. *Klēros* and terms that build on its root (e.g., *klēronomia, klēronomai*), referred to the instrument for casting lots, and as applied in the New Testament suggested the "lot" or "inheritance" that all believers received as God's people. Moreover, the Greek word for priest, *hiereus,* was never applied to a set of ministers within the whole community; it was applied either to Christ himself (Heb. 2:17; 3:1; 4:14-15), or to the whole people of God, as in 1 Peter:

> you are a chosen race, a royal priesthood, a holy nation, God's own people, in order that you may proclaim the mighty acts of him who called you out of darkness and into his marvelous light. Once you were not a people, but

---

[1] Alexandre Faivre, *The Emergence of the Laity in the Early Church* (New York: Paulist Press, 1990), 5. This treatment of the emergence of the lay/clergy distinction draws primarily from this study.

now you are God's people; once you had not received mercy but now you have received mercy. (1 Pet. 2:9-10)

This passage was in keeping with the insight of Paul that all Christians were to make of their entire lives "a living sacrifice, holy and acceptable to God" (Rom. 12:1).

Whereas neither *klēros* nor *hiereus* is ever used in the New Testament to refer to ministers, the Greek term for the laity, *laikos,* does not appear in the New Testament at all. Prior to 180 C.E. there is but one recorded use of the term *laikos* in a way that may differentiate between the ordained and the nonordained. The term appears once in *1 Clement* (likely authored near the end of the first century) in which Clement, a prominent presbyter from Rome, exhorted the Corinthians to respect their presbyters and to submit to right order in the church. He appealed to ancient Israelite worship, in which there was a differentiation of tasks. Not everyone functioned as a priest, but even the layperson (*anthrōpos laikos*) had a responsibility in the offering of gifts (*1 Clem.* 40:5). Scholars are not certain of the precise meaning Clement was giving to this term, but it is highly unlikely that he was identifying some *ontological* distinction between the ordained and nonordained. It is more likely that Clement was highlighting the necessary differentiation of ministries within the community and the need for harmony and order. After this isolated usage it would be another eighty years or so before we find another appearance of *laikos* in Christian literature, and only in the third century is it employed to indicate a hard distinction between the clergy and the rest of the church.

We do find reference to a great diversity of ministries exercised in the life of early Christian communities from the very beginning. St. Paul offers several lists of such ministries in Romans 12:6-8 and 1 Corinthians 12:28. The Pastoral Letters, probably written one to two generations after Paul, offer the first traces of a consciousness of intraecclesial distinctions as these texts discuss the criteria for choosing leaders within the community, but there is no sense that there are two distinct groups of believers, public ministers and the rest of the faithful. In the mid-second century St. Justin Martyr will describe Christian worship and make reference to deacons, those who liturgically proclaim the Scriptures as well as those who preside over the worship. But here again, there is no sense that these belong to a distinct subset of persons within the larger community (*1 Apology* 67). Justin assumes a fundamental equality among believers grounded in their shared call to discipleship established at their baptism. Tertullian will distinguish between the whole people (*plebs*) and those called to particular, more formal ministries (*ordo*), but, once more, nothing suggests that those who exercised a more formal public ministry were thought to belong to a distinct class of believers set apart from others.

The relativization of intraecclesial distinctions common in the early church may have extended to gender identity as well. As we saw in the first chapter, Jesus' treatment of women constituted a striking departure from rabbinic custom, both in his seeking out disciples and in the inclusion of women among his company. Jesus' acceptance of women as disciples and the radical inclusivity of his teaching on the reign of God may have opened the door to a form of gender equality in some early Christian communities reflected in Paul's bracing proclamation:

> There is no longer Jew or Greek, there is no longer slave or free, there is no longer male and female; for all of you are one in Christ Jesus. And if you belong to Christ, then you are Abraham's offspring, heirs according to the promise. (Gal. 3:26-29)

It is difficult to know for sure the extent to which this vision of gender equality was actually lived out in early Christian communities.[2] The ecclesiastical marginalization of women began early, however. Tertullian, for example, who was quick to affirm the priestly status of the laity, apparently did not believe that women belonged to the laity![3] He was not the last to hold this view.

In general we can say that early Christian reflection during the first two centuries of the church was less preoccupied with distinctions *within* the community than between the Christian community as a whole and the world in which Christians lived. Consequently, differences between lay and cleric were eclipsed by a concern for the common demands of discipleship.[4] One of the first qualifying theological characteristics to be applied to the church in early creedal statements was that of "holiness." Christians professed their belief in a *sancta ecclesia*, a "holy church."[5] This description of the church proceeded from ancient reflection on biblical assertions that the people of Israel and the early Christian community were consecrated by God and not by their own merit. The holiness of God's people followed from the presence of the Holy One in their midst. According to Alexandre Faivre,

> [i]n the first two centuries of its life, the church had this remarkable characteristic: its unity was too theocentric—or rather too Christocentric—to

---

[2] See Elisabeth Schüssler Fiorenza's suggestive reconstruction in, *In Memory of Her: A Feminist Theological Reconstruction of Christian Origins* (New York: Crossroad, 1983), 160-250.

[3] Faivre, 51.

[4] Kenan B. Osborne, *Ministry: Lay Ministry in the Roman Catholic Church* (New York: Paulist Press, 1993), 115.

[5] Paul O'Callaghan, "The Holiness of the Church in Early Christian Creeds," *Irish Theological Quarterly* 54 (1988): 59-65.

accommodate itself to a theology emphasizing a human centralism. Because they are gratuitous gifts of God, the charisms of the church do not belong to any man in particular, but are destined always to be shared and distributed among all those who may be called and illuminated in their turn. . . . For this reason, it is impossible to find a dependence in the early church of lay people on a clergy. There were only Christians and disciples claiming Christ as their master.[6]

In other words, the governing division in early Christian life was not that between lay and clergy, it was between the church and a world that so often appeared hostile to it.

THE ORIGINS AND DEVELOPMENT
OF THE LAY/CLERGY DISTINCTION

In the third and fourth centuries Christianity would begin a gradual shift from a community that defined itself by its common vocation to discipleship and a corporate life of holiness to a church in which the particular demands of discipleship and holiness would be distinguished by one's status as cleric or layperson. This shift transpired on multiple fronts.

The Rise of Two Kinds of Christians

First, as Christianity grew, the ministry of teaching or catechesis also grew in importance. Although there were lay teachers of great repute such as Origen of Alexandria (he would be ordained to the priesthood only after establishing his reputation as a teacher), the growing importance of this ministry led to the view that teaching, once viewed as an obligation incumbent on all followers of Christ, ought to be the exclusive responsibility of the clergy.

On a second front, Christianity, which had initially sought to distance itself from Jewish concepts of law, sacrifice, and priesthood, began to return to these categories as a means of understanding Christian worship and ministry. The eucharist was reconceived in sacrificial terms, with important Christian modifications to be sure, and the ministry of those who presided over the eucharist was described in language drawn from the Levitical priesthood. St. Cyprian of Carthage saw the eucharist as a continuation of Jewish ritual sacrifice, albeit

---

[6] Faivre, 40.

with an entirely new theological understanding. It followed, then, that the Christian priesthood ought to be governed by the purity rules that were binding for the Levitical priesthood. A new rationale emerges for clerical abstinence from sexual relations (married clergy were initially the norm) in keeping with Levitical conceptions of ritual purity, which precluded the priest from having sexual relations immediately prior to "offering the sacrifice." The inability to enforce such sexual abstinence would eventually elicit calls for clerical celibacy.

Of course a tradition of adhering to celibacy as a spiritual discipline can be traced back to Paul's own recommendation of celibacy (1 Cor. 7:1-9) and the Matthean logion in which Jesus suggests that some are to be "eunuchs for the kingdom" (Matt. 19:12). Yet consecrated celibacy does not appear to have been a significant practice in the first two centuries of Christianity. We do have evidence of clerical celibacy practiced by Tertullian and, in the third century, by Origen, but this is alongside ample testimony to married clergy, including bishops and popes. Legislation proposing clerical abstinence is found in the canons promulgated by the Spanish Council of Elvira (ca. 306), but it is difficult to determine the extent to which such legislation was ever implemented. Again, at least part of the motivation for sexual abstinence by clergy stemmed from Levitical conceptions demanding ritual purity on the part of the one offering the eucharistic sacrifice.

On a third front, Christianity's minority and persecuted status changed at the beginning of the fourth century when the emperor Constantine legalized Christianity in an attempt to use this growing religion as a unifying force in the empire. As Christianity was drawn into a more public engagement with the Roman world, it encountered a Roman society divided into different *ordines*, or orders (e.g., *ordo senatorius, ordo equester*). Eventually the diversity of principal ministries in the early church was reconfigured along the analogy of these civic orders. Although ordination rituals appeared by the end of the second century, a fully developed theology of ministerial ordination was almost certainly influenced by Greco-Roman class structure. Even so, it is only in the fifth century that priests begin to wear distinctive garb. Pope Celestine I in 428 chastises Honoratus, the abbot of Lerins, for the introduction of such garb: "We should be distinguished from others, not by our dress, but by our knowledge, our conversation, not by our manner of life" (*Epist.* 4.1.2).[7]

Finally, the emergence of monasticism also played a role in hardening the lay/clergy distinction. Monasticism arose in the fourth and fifth centuries, in

---

[7] *Epist.* 4. 1, 2 [PL 50:431] as quoted in Yves Congar, *Power and Poverty in the Church* (London: Chapman, 1964), 57n.1.

part as a reaction to the increasing "worldliness" of Christianity after Constantine. Thomas Merton's summary reflection on desert monasticism captures it well:

> Society . . . was regarded by them as a shipwreck from which each single individual man had to swim for his life. . . . These were men who believed that to let oneself drift along, passively accepting the tenets and values of what they knew as society was purely and simply a disaster. The fact that the Emperor was now Christian and that the "world" was coming to know the Cross as a sign of temporal power only strengthened them in their resolve.[8]

In its origins, monasticism was largely a lay affair with no distinctive privileges given to clerics in monastic communities. Yet many bishops in the West viewed monastic spirituality as a healthy antidote to the worldliness of diocesan clergy. Such episcopal luminaries as St. Augustine of Hippo, St. Martin of Tours, and St. Paulinus of Nola all recommended a monastic lifestyle for their clergy.[9] The Eastern church would soon develop the tradition, one that has continued to the present, of drawing candidates for the episcopate from monastic communities.

The wedding of ordained ministry and a monastic lifestyle further accentuated the distinction between the laity and the clergy. In the fourth and fifth centuries we also encounter the gradual transfer and reduction of ministerial responsibility, once undertaken by many different Christians, some formally ordained and many not, to the clergy alone. By the end of the fifth century the decisive ecclesiological division between lay and clergy was fully established.

This distinction, now more of a rigid ecclesiastical division, is fortified during the Carolingian period (eighth-ninth centuries). It is during this period that the liturgy becomes almost exclusively a clerical affair. The laity are reduced to spectators and frequently do not bother to receive communion at all. As the church inherited the Roman legal tradition, a tradition built on subtle legal distinctions regarding class, rights, and obligations, the division between lay and cleric was further strengthened and codified by Gratian in the eleventh century: "There are two kinds of Christians, clerics and lay people."[10] The exclusion of the laity from active participation in the liturgy is also evident in key shifts in church architecture during the medieval period. A chancel or screen would come to separate the choir and altar from the nave of the church, further isolating the clergy from the laity.

---

[8] Thomas Merton, *The Wisdom of the Desert* (New York: New Directions, 1960), 3.

[9] Thomas F. O'Meara, *Theology of Ministry*, rev. ed. (New York: Paulist Press, 1999), 98.

[10] *Concordia discordantium canonum*, causa 12, q.1 c.7.

Late Medieval and Reformation Developments

In the Middle Ages the laity were never completely reduced to passive objects in the life of the church. In liturgy, their exclusion from active participation in the eucharist led to flourishing popular devotions, some of which were enacted *during* the Mass itself. Lay movements like the twelfth-century Beguines were often creative in finding ways to bring the laity into active participation in the life of the church. A vigorous medieval piety would emerge in the twelfth through fifteenth centuries culminating in the *devotio moderna,* a somewhat anti-institutional form of piety based on the cultivation of the interior life and the imitation of Christ.

The Reformation, which was initially less a unified ecclesial force for change than a set of converging reform movements, broadly challenged much of the hierarchical structure of Western Christianity at the time. For Martin Luther at least, the thoroughly gratuitous character of God's saving action on behalf of humanity, leading to an unmerited justification that came by faith alone, undermined any claim to ontological divisions among Christians. Luther stressed the priority of the biblical category of the priesthood of all believers and wished to liberate the Scriptures from the control of the clergy, making them accessible for ordinary believers. This was encouraged most dramatically in his pivotal production of a vernacular translation of the Bible. Luther also dismissed monasticism as an unacceptable escape from the demands of authentic Christian discipleship and encouraged monks to leave their communities and marry. Luther's ecclesiological vision was dominated by his view of the church as a holy community, the communion of saints. This biblical understanding of the church, as Luther saw it, represented a frontal assault on the entire clerical system as it had developed in the late medieval church.[11] At the same time, it must be noted that Luther did not wish to repudiate entirely a distinction between the laity and the clergy, and in his later thought there was much less emphasis on the priesthood of believers.[12] Luther was an exegete, a preacher, and a genius in discerning the psychology of religious experience, but he was not a systematic thinker. An unresolved tension remained in his thought regarding his commitment to a spiritual vision of the church and the pragmatic need for public office.

In the work of that other great reformer, John Calvin, we find an acceptance of the Lutheran doctrine of the priesthood of all believers, but it did not play as dominant a role in Calvin's thought, in part because Calvin had a more

---

[11] Roger Haight, *Christian Community in History,* 2 vols. (New York: Continuum, 2005), 2:45.
[12] Martin Brecht, *Martin Luther* (Philadelphia: Fortress, 1985-93), 2:447.

positive evaluation of church office and the need for authoritative church structures.[13] Calvin possessed a strong sense of the holiness of the entire church. This holiness possessed both objective characteristics preserved in church office and the celebration of the sacraments, and subjective dimensions preserved in the demand for an existential righteousness among believers.[14] In the end, however, it is hard to disagree with the conclusion of Kenan Osborne that "for Calvin, the true church remained a church with clerics and lay people."[15]

Both Luther and Calvin recognized the need for a pastorate distinct from the laity. Later, however, the so-called Radical Reformation gave rise to certain reformist groups (e.g., the Anabaptists) who were convinced that Christians should have nothing to do with governments, or any part of the "world," for that matter. These diverse Christian groups laid a striking emphasis on the common demands of discipleship, demands that issued forth from adult baptism and created communities starkly distinguished from the fallen and broken world around them. The call to discipleship and the demand for holiness could not be realized through institutional structures but through the voluntary association of committed believers animated by the Word of God and the Holy Spirit. The task of the Christian community was to give radical witness to the gospel as faithful disciples. They did not recognize any ordinations and were reluctant to grant any special authority to a pastor beyond that which he merited by his spiritual maturity.

Roman Catholicism responded to the various reform movements with a predictable defense of the hierarchical structure of the church. It implicitly acknowledged, however, the existing patterns of clerical abuse and called for a series of stringent clerical reforms, including the beginning of a more developed program for clerical formation and the requirement that bishops reside in the dioceses to which they were assigned. The council called for the creation of a new catechism.[16] That text, authored largely by St. Charles Borromeo and published under the authority of Pope Pius V in 1566, offered a relatively balanced ecclesiology that tried to affirm the dignity of all the baptized and to avoid any overly passive understanding of the laity. It described the church as "the faithful dispersed throughout the world."[17] Nevertheless, baroque Catholic polemics bent on defending the institutional structure of the church led to the further marginalization of the laity within Catholic ecclesiology.

---

[13] Haight, 2:108-12, 132.

[14] Ibid., 2:145-46.

[15] Osborne, 417.

[16] T. Howland Sanks, *Salt, Leaven and Light: The Community Called Church* (New York: Crossroad, 1992), 88-91.

[17] *The Catechism of the Council of Trent* (London: George Routledge, 1852), 93.

Status of the Laity in Eastern Christianity

Alongside the developments of Western Christianity, divisions in the Christian community followed a somewhat different line of development in the East. Eastern Christianity flourished in Byzantium under the strong authority of the emperor long after the fall of the Roman empire in the West forced civic responsibilities upon Western church leadership. Eastern clergy, consequently, never became significant participants in the preservation of the secular society, as did the clergy of the West. The Eastern conception of church and ministry remained firmly rooted in the liturgy; the distinct orders in the church were understood to be primarily liturgical in character. Indeed, there is some thought that Pseudo-Dionysius, the sixth-century Neoplatonic Christian who first coined the term *hierarchia,* may have had in mind the ministerial differentiations encountered in the celebration of the liturgy.[18] The Eastern church saw baptism as initiating believers into the eucharistic *synaxis,* drawing them into the preeminent Christian act of worship. Presbyteral and episcopal ordination constituted an ecclesial reconfiguration of the *ordinand,* introducing him into a new ecclesial relation as presider over the eucharistic assembly. In the late Middle Ages, Orthodoxy would come under the influence of Western scholasticism, and the distinctly liturgical foundations of its ecclesiology would recede into the background, only to be recovered again in the nineteenth and twentieth centuries.

In nineteenth-century Russia, Metropolitan Filaret taught that every believer was fundamentally ecclesial because he or she shared in the relationality of the triune God.[19] Filaret taught that the relationship between God and humankind was to be a relationship grounded in love. As the basis for all ecclesial relationships is love, he maintained that juridical criteria for ecclesial unity were insufficient. Within this ecclesiology there was simply no room for a passive laity and an active clergy. Another nineteenth-century luminary in Russian Orthodoxy, Alexei Khomiakov, also explored an understanding of the church as a living organism animated by the Holy Spirit. For Khomiakov, the apostolic faith resided in the whole church, laity and clergy.

In the twentieth century, the explicit eucharistic foundations of Eastern ecclesiology would be recovered in the work of Nicolas Afanassieff and, later, John Zizioulas.[20] Zizioulas would suggest not a theology of the layperson but

---

[18] See John Meyendorff, *Christ in Eastern Christian Thought* (Crestwood, N.Y.: St. Vladimir's Seminary Press, 1997; originally published 1969).

[19] Paul Evdokimov, "The Principal Currents of Orthodox Ecclesiology in the Nineteenth Century," *Eastern Churches Review* 10 (1978): 30.

[20] Nicolas Afanassieff, "*Una Sancta,*" *Irénikon* 36 (1963): 436-75; idem, *The Church of the Holy Spirit*

a theology of the baptized, called by baptism into the life of the church, which was enacted most profoundly in the eucharist. Consequently, Zizioulas would insist that what was distinctive to the Orthodox tradition was its insistence on a relational understanding of the layperson as a member of the community of the baptized.

Catholic Views of Laity on the Eve of Vatican II

In Roman Catholicism, attempts at a more organic description of the church, one that granted a more active role for the laity, could be found in the nineteenth-century Tübingen's school's renewed interest in the ecclesial patterns and theology of early Christianity. In England, John Henry Newman made important contributions toward a more positive theological evaluation of the layperson, insisting that, because of their active participation in the life of the church, the bishops ought to consider consulting the faithful, "even in matters of doctrine."[21] In spite of these promising Catholic theological developments, official articulations of Catholic ecclesiology gave relatively little attention to the laity. In the early twentieth century, Pope Pius X would make the following statement as if it were a self-evident fact of the church:

> It follows that the Church is essentially an unequal society, that is, a society comprising two categories of persons, the Pastors and the flock, those who occupy a rank in the different degrees of the hierarchy and the multitude of the faithful. So distinct are these categories that with the pastoral body only rests the necessary right and authority for promoting the end of the society and directing all its members towards that end; the one duty of the multitude is to allow themselves to be led, and, like a docile flock, to follow the Pastors.[22]

Although in the decades immediately prior to the Second Vatican Council new movements like Catholic Action helped promote more lay involvement in the church's mission, this was still conceived as a way for the laity to participate or assist in the apostolate of the clergy. Still, theologians like Yves Congar, Marie-

---

(Notre Dame, Ind.: University of Notre Dame Press, 2007); John D. Zizioulas, *Being as Communion* (Crestwood, N.Y.: St. Vladimir's Seminary Press, 1985).

[21] John Henry Newman, *On Consulting the Faithful in Matters of Doctrine* (reprint, 1859; Kansas City, Mo.: Sheed & Ward, 1961).

[22] Pope Pius X, *Vehementer nos* # 8; English translation from *The Papal Encyclicals*, ed. Claudia Carlen (New York: McGrath, 1981), 3:47-48.

Dominique Chenu, and Karl Rahner explored more positive theologies of the laity,[23] and many of their insights were incorporated into the council's teaching. Yet few were ready to challenge the theological adequacy of the lay/clergy distinction itself. This would change in the decades after the council.

RECOVERY OF THE PRIORITY OF BAPTISM, DISCIPLESHIP, AND MISSION AT VATICAN II

In Roman Catholicism, the Second Vatican Council continued to embrace the distinction between the clergy and the laity while at the same time correcting the second-class status that had long since been attached to the laity. It did so by articulating a positive theology of the laity, granting to them a distinctive apostolate that was open to a realization in some forms of church ministry but which was primarily to be realized through the transformation of the world in their families, the workplace, and political/civic life (LG 31).

This more positive theology of the laity was also reflected in conciliar developments regarding a theological account of the holiness of the church. In the preparatory schema on the church given to the bishops during the first session, the fifth chapter was entitled "The States of Evangelical Perfection." The chapter presupposed that perfection in holiness was achieved preeminently by those who pursued the evangelical counsels of poverty, chastity, and obedience. There was virtually no consideration of the other 99+ percent of the church who were not called to ordination or to professed religious life. In the second schema, the tenor of this chapter changed dramatically.

Reimagining a Holy Church

The chapter on the states of evangelical perfection found in the preparatory draft on the church was reshaped to focus on the universal call to holiness and the conception of a gradation of "states of perfection" was quietly abandoned. The council taught

> that all Christians in whatever state or walk of life are called to the fullness of Christian life and to the perfection of charity, and this holiness is conducive to a more human way of living even in society here on earth. (LG 40)

---

[23] Yves Congar, *Lay People in the Church* (first published in French, 1954; Westminster: Newman Press, 1965); Marie-Dominique Chenu, "Consecratio Mundi," *Nouvelle revue théologique* 86 (1964): 608-16; Karl Rahner, "Consecration of the Layman to the Care of Souls," in *Theological Investigations* (Baltimore: Helicon, 1967), 3:263-76; first published in German, 1967.

Other conciliar texts suggest the new considerations the council gave to its understanding of the holiness of the church.

Francis Sullivan recognizes three elements in the council's understanding of the church's holiness.[24] First, the church is holy by virtue of certain formal elements, namely, the charisms, offices, sacraments, and popular devotional practices that, in the Catholic tradition, mediate grace. The emphasis on these formal elements is important because they reflect the Catholic inclination toward what might be called a sacramental imagination, a conviction that God's presence is mediated through human persons, symbols, rituals, and other more visible elements. *Lumen Gentium* teaches that the Holy Spirit offers to the church gifts "both hierarchic and charismatic" (LG 4). God's holiness was mediated to the church through both institutional structures and the gifts given to each believer. Indeed, the council considered the church itself to be a sacrament of salvation. Second, the council retrieved the biblical insight that the church is holy in virtue of its consecration by God. Recovering a biblical tradition neglected in modern Catholicism, LG 10 affirms that the entire community of the baptized are consecrated into a royal priesthood:

> Christ the Lord, high priest taken from the midst of humanity, made the new people "a kingdom of priests to his God and Father." The baptized, by regeneration and the anointing of the holy Spirit, are consecrated as a spiritual house and a holy priesthood, that through all their Christian activities they may offer spiritual sacrifices and proclaim the marvels of him who has called them out of darkness into his wonderful light. Therefore all the disciples of Christ, persevering in prayer and praising God, should present themselves as a sacrifice, living, holy and pleasing to God. They should everywhere on earth bear witness to Christ and give an answer to everyone who asks a reason for their hope of eternal life.

Finally, the church is holy because among its number are those who respond to God's grace with lives of virtue, sometimes heroic, sometimes in more ordinary ways. Again, the council writes:

> The Lord Jesus, divine teacher and model of all perfection, preached holiness of life, which he both initiates and brings to perfection, to each and every one of his disciples no matter what their condition of life: "You, therefore, must be perfect, as your heavenly Father is perfect." For he sent the

---

[24] Francis A. Sullivan, *The Church We Believe In: One, Holy, Catholic and Apostolic* (Mahwah, N.J.: Paulist Press, 1988), 69-78.

holy Spirit to all to move them interiorly to love God with their whole heart, with their whole soul, with their whole understanding and with their whole strength, and to love one another as Christ loved them. The followers of Christ, called by God not for what they had done but by his design and grace, and justified in the Lord Jesus, have been made sons and daughters of God by the Baptism of faith and partakers of the divine nature, and so are truly sanctified. They must therefore hold on to and perfect in their lives that holiness which they have received from God. (LG 40)

The consistent theme of the council was that any adequate reflection on the universal call to holiness must begin with Christian baptism.

Baptismal Ordering of the Community of Disciples

When the Second Vatican Council faced the serious inadequacies of church distinctions based on either ordination or religious profession, its response was to return to an ecclesiology grounded in a theology of baptism. This new orientation emerged in the first document debated and promulgated by the council, *Sacrosanctum Concilium*, the Constitution on the Sacred Liturgy. It is possible to tease out of this early conciliar text the beginnings of a liturgical ecclesiology that begins with baptism.

The council's document on the liturgy suggests that the most fundamental sacramental ordering of the church occurs not through ministerial ordination but by way of Christian initiation. This conviction is reflected in the council's call for a fundamental reform of its initiatory rites, including the restoration of the catechumenate for adults, the revision of the baptismal rite for infants and the reconsideration of the rites of confirmation. These calls for ritual reform were in keeping with the larger agenda of the council often captured in the French term *ressourcement,* a "return to the sources." In this case the council was reaching back to a more ancient vision of Christian initiation.

From a biblical perspective, Christian initiation "orders"—or, if you prefer, "configures"—the believer to Christ *within* the community of faith, Christ's body. Christian initiation does not just make one a different kind of individual; it draws the believer into a profound ecclesial relationship, one's ecclesial *ordo* within the life of the church. The distinctive character of this baptismally ordered relationship unfolds in three dimensions. Vertically, we are baptized into communion with God, in Christ, by the power of the Spirit. Yet this relation is inseparable from our horizontal relationship with all our brothers and sisters in baptism who constitute together a communion of believers. These two dimensions of the baptismal ordering must, in turn, be conjoined to a third dimension, the movement outward toward the world in mission. Baptism is a matter of being both called *and* sent. This three-dimensional ecclesial relation established by Christian initiation offers us our primal identity as Christian believers and it can never be abandoned. It constitutes the very essence of Christian discipleship.

Sacrosanctum Concilium furthered this liturgical ecclesiology by way of its focus on the whole worshiping assembly. It is the whole community of the baptized, Christ's body, that is the subject of the eucharistic celebration. Consequently, the participation of all the baptized is required "by the very nature of the liturgy" (SC 14). If the liturgy is a ritual enactment of what the church truly is, then we can say that all God's people are subjects in the life of the church and not merely passive recipients of clerical directives. The Constitution on the Sacred Liturgy offered a new framework for situating any and all distinctions in the church. That new framework was further explored in the Dogmatic Constitution on the Church, *Lumen Gentium*.

The second draft of the constitution on the church that would eventually become *Lumen Gentium* had four chapters, the first on the church as mystery, the second on the hierarchy, the third on the people of God and the laity, and the fourth on the universal call to holiness. In between the first and second sessions of the council the decision was made to divide the chapter on the people of God and the laity into two, and place the chapter on the church as people of God prior to the chapter on the hierarchy. The message could not be clearer: our reflection on the church must begin with what we share in common, faith and baptism, not with what distinguishes us (ordination or religious profession).

> Although by Christ's will some are appointed teachers, dispensers of the mysteries and pastors for the others, yet all the faithful enjoy a true equality with regard to the dignity and the activity which they share in the building up of the body of Christ. (LG 32)

In baptism we are initiated into Christ's body the church and, in a sense, discover ourselves fully, our truest identity, in the life of the church. At the same time, by baptism into Christ's body the church we are drawn by the power of the Holy Spirit into participation in the triune life of God. All Christians, by baptism, are called in discipleship to follow the way of Jesus of Nazareth, to grow in holiness and to help further the reign of God. This commitment, far from being one among many human commitments that one might undertake, is in itself more than a religion. As the early Christians understood it, this commitment brought one into a new form of existence, a new understanding of the human vocation.

The Priesthood of the Faithful

This baptismal matrix is further reinforced by the council's appeal to the common priesthood of all believers, a biblical concept prominent in Luther's thought and consequently avoided in modern Catholicism prior to the council.[25] Here again, the precedent was set by the constitution on the liturgy, which taught that the whole community, in its celebration of the liturgy, participates in the one priesthood of Christ (SC 7). Christ's priestly action in the liturgy is realized not only by the ordained presbyter or bishop but by the entire community. The council would write: "Offering the immaculate victim, not only through the hands of the priest but also together with him, they should learn to offer themselves" (SC 48). According to the council, the priesthood of the baptized consisted in the offering of their very lives as a living sacrifice to God. The eucharist is not the privileged arena for the exercise of the ministerial priesthood; it is the ritual celebration of the work of God's priestly people. For if in the liturgy the eucharistic gifts of bread and wine are offered to God at the hands of the ordained priest, this offering is at the same time the offering of the whole people who, in that bread and wine, place their own lives on the altar. This is reflected in the prayer over the gifts:

> Blessed are you, Lord, God of all creation. Through your goodness we have this bread to offer, which earth has given and human hands have made. It will become for us the bread of life. Blessed are you, Lord, God of all creation. Through your goodness we have this wine to offer, fruit of the vine and work of human hands. It will become our spiritual drink.

Thus, the priestly work of the entire assembly gathered at prayer is at the same time always oriented toward the priestly work of all God's people in the midst of their daily lives. If in the eucharist God's priestly people unite themselves with the self-gift of Christ, who offers himself to us in a pattern of self-emptying love, then they become sharers in the dynamism of divine giving and are sent in mission to make their very lives a gift to God and to participate in the priestly work of transforming the world itself as humanity's gift to God. The recovery of the priesthood of the faithful is in a real sense a recovery of the ancient biblical insight so often articulated by the prophets, who called not for cultic practices bent on appeasing an angry God but on the offering of one's whole life, a life given over to covenantal love and the work of justice, as the only offering that God desires.

---

[25] For an extended meditation on the significance of the priesthood of the faithful, see Paul J. Philibert, *The Priesthood of the Faithful: Key to a Living Church* (Collegeville, Minn.: Liturgical Press, 2005).

> I hate, I despise your festivals,
>> and I take no delight in your solemn assemblies.
> Even though you offer me your burnt offerings and grain
>> offerings,
>> I will not accept them . . .
> But let justice roll down like water,
>> and righteousness like an ever-flowing stream.
>>> (Amos 5: 21, 24)

The substance of this common priesthood is the life of discipleship, following Christ in such a way that one's entire life becomes an offering to God. This suggests that ordinary believers engage in priestly ministry whenever they seek to cooperate with God's grace in transforming their lives and the world around them in accord with the ethos of God's reign revealed in the teaching and ministry of Jesus. Participation in the liturgy is essential to the life of the community in part because it sends believers forth into the world, empowered for the fulfillment of their own priestly ministry, in order that they might serve the coming reign of God.

Baptism and Mission

The implications of the council's theology of baptism and discipleship can be properly grasped only in the context of its theology of mission, a theology articulated not only in the Pastoral Constitution on the Church in the Modern World, *Gaudium et Spes,* but also in the Decree on the Church's Missionary Activity, *Ad Gentes.* In that document the council famously asserted that "the church on earth is by its very nature missionary since, according to the plan of the Father, it has its origin in the mission of the Son and the holy Spirit" (AG 2). The church's whole reason for being is to be in mission in the world, preaching the good news of Christ and serving the coming of God's reign. *Gaudium et Spes* insisted that the church could not afford to be aloof from the concerns of the world.

> Thus the church, at once a visible organization and a spiritual community, travels the same journey as all of humanity and shares the same earthly lot with the world: it is to be a leaven and, as it were, the soul of human society in its renewal by Christ and transformation into the family of God. (GS 40)

Of particular significance was the attribution of the metaphor of "leaven" not only to the laity but to the whole church. There is no place in this vision for church leadership to be disengaged from the problems of the world. The priority of mission in the council's teaching reflected a shift in Catholic reflection on the church. The central preoccupation of the church was no longer to be the simple maintenance of the inner life of the church. Rather, the focus was to be on God's saving intention for the whole world. The council came to this insight somewhat tentatively in its teaching on the church's relationship to the kingdom of God, a connection, however, that Pope John Paul II and numerous theologians would develop in the decades after the council.

The Church Is the New People of God

None of these themes—discipleship, mission, the priesthood of the faithful—can be adequately appreciated apart from the larger framework of the council's teaching on the church as the new people of God. The first chapter of *Lumen Gentium*, "The Mystery of the Church," highlights the trinitarian and incarnational foundations of the church. The second chapter, "The People of God," shifts the focus to the church as it lives in history united by faith and baptism and responding to the impulse of the Spirit.

> Christ instituted this new covenant, the new covenant in blood; he called a people together made up of Jews and Gentiles which would be one, not according to the flesh, but in the Spirit, and it would be the new people of God. (LG 9)

By beginning reflection on the divine initiative in electing a people to be God's own, the council's use of the metaphor of the people of God allowed for a renewed emphasis on the equality of all God's people. Yves Congar, a *peritus* at the council who was heavily involved in the authorship of this text, saw the theme of the people of God as one of the central orienting principles in the council's teaching, and, for him, it was this theme more than anything else that enabled the shift away from a hierarchical conception of the church to the priority of baptism, discipleship, and mission.[26] As we shall see, it was a theme that particularly fired the imagination of the church in Latin America.

DISCIPLESHIP IN A GLOBAL CHURCH

In the wake of Vatican II, the church of Latin America was drawn in particular to *Gaudium et Spes* as the focal point of its theological reflections. Latin

---

[26] Yves Congar, "The Church: The People of God," in *The Church and Mankind, Concilium* vol. 1 (Mahway, N.J.: Paulist Press, 1965), 12-13.

American church leaders and theologians found in that document a theology of the church called to engage the world by a critical reading of the "signs of the times." For many, the council's teaching demanded a response to the abject poverty that so dominated the Latin American region. Precisely as followers of Jesus, Christians were compelled to proclaim the liberative message of the reign of God and the promise of salvation from all that oppresses humankind and impedes authentic human flourishing.

It was the inspiration of *Gaudium et Spes* that led the bishops of Latin America to gather first at Medellín (1968), then at Puebla (1979) and Santo Domingo (1992), and most recently in Aparecida (2007) to condemn the "inhuman misery" perpetuated in their region by unjust socioeconomic structures and oppressive political regimes. It was the bishops of Latin America who have articulated God's preferential option for the poor, not as an article of class struggle, as if God loved some and not others, but as a statement of God's, and therefore the church's, radical solidarity with all the oppressed and marginalized of the world. The church of Latin America took to heart the contention of *Gaudium et Spes* that "one of the gravest errors of our time is the dichotomy between the faith which many profess and their day-to-day conduct" (GS 43). God's saving offer must have some purchase on the daily plight of believers.

Liberation theology as an academic endeavor may be identified with certain prominent theologians, but all of them would insist that the real theology of liberation emerged in Latin America out of the faith reflection of the people who were invited to consider the circumstances in which they lived, announcing God's liberating presence and denouncing all the forces that would destroy the dignity of the human person.

The priority of Christian discipleship over any and all other ecclesial distinctions was forged in liberationist perspectives on the church that insisted that the true church must be a church *of* the poor. This does not mean merely that the church must have a place for the poor in its midst, nor that it must be a church *for* the poor by way of its charitable ministries and services. The church is a church *of* the poor to the extent that it stands in solidarity with the powerlessness of the poor in this world and looks to the crucified Christ, who embraced powerlessness on the cross and effected its transformation in the resurrection. The church of the poor is a church in which faithful discipleship will demand conversion from preoccupation with power and privilege. This need not mean abandoning ecclesial distinctions in the church, including those established by way of ordination or religious profession, but it will place such distinctions at the service of the fundamental vocation of all Christians to be disciples of Jesus. It will demand the priority of discipleship and service over power. An ecclesiology that begins with the rights and responsibilities incumbent on the baptized and the demands of discipleship is bound to look critically at the historical forms of the church that have been inordinately concerned with the distribution and exercise of power.

The ecclesiological preoccupation with the dynamics of power began, in many ways, with the Gregorian reforms of the eleventh century. These reforms were begun by Pope Gregory VII as a means of securing the proper autonomy of the church and its mission in the face of the unacceptable influence of the feudal nobility. However historically defensible these reforms may have been, the end result was a fundamental reconstruction of ecclesiology based not on the themes of grace, trinity, and the sacramental life of the church, but rather on the legal categories of power and jurisdiction. This essentially juridical framework would receive further development and limited theological embellishment over the course of the second millennium, but was only occasionally subject to critique.

The noted Brazilian theologian Leonardo Boff advanced such a critique in his book *Church: Charism and Power*. There he criticized the continued dominance of this hierarchical paradigm of the church: "this Church understands itself primarily as the community invested with power (the hierarchy) together with the community deprived of power (the People of God, laity)."[27] Boff offers a scathing account of the pathologies of power still operative in the church today. According to Boff, this is reflected in the hegemonic exercise of teaching authority by the magisterium in ways that imagine truth as a "deposit" that is mastered and controlled by an ecclesiastical elite and apostolic office as an instrument for apodictic teaching without any effort at listening to the wisdom of the larger church. It is reflected in a sacramental economy that divides the church into producers of grace (the clergy) and passive consumers (the laity). The solution lies in an ecclesial conversion that must penetrate to the institutional level of church. It is not power itself that is at issue but the diabolical forms that power can take.

Jon Sobrino contends that to see the church as truly a church of the poor does not mean simply a sociopolitical revolution that would transfer power and control from one group (the ecclesiastical elite) to another (the poor). Rather, for the church to become truly a church of the poor it must be willing to undergo a conversion in its very conception of power:

> The church of the poor does not involve a transfer of power from the hierarchy to the poor as a sociological group without the idea of power undergoing change in the process. The process entails a radical change in the

---

[27] Leonardo Boff, *Church: Charism and Power: Liberation Theology and the Institutional Church* (New York: Crossroad, 1985), 51.

notion of power as a mediation of God. The "Church of the poor" concept proposes, first and foremost, that the entire church should migrate to the periphery and share the powerlessness of the poor, at the feet of a crucified God, so that it might there cultivate Christian hope and develop effective (and, in this sense, powerful) activity. Here, at this level, the most necessary radical change in the Church takes place.[28]

One can balk at the often harsh tone of the liberationist critique of ecclesiastical power and still recognize much truth in its analysis. Boff and Sobrino are calling for an ecclesial renunciation of power as dominance in favor of a more biblical conception of power (*exousia*) as a kenotic service to the demands of God's reign. Within the church, this power has its origin not in the sacrament of holy orders but in baptism and the call to discipleship.

The council itself consistently framed issues of power within the framework of service. This is reflected in its avoidance of "kingly" language in favor of the language of "shepherd/pastor" when treating the threefold office of priest, prophet, and king. From a theological point of view, when exercised in the life of the church, power is not something that one possesses but a reality that one participates in, to the extent that one is open to the work of the Spirit.

For liberation theology, this renunciation of worldly power lies at the heart of any claims to the church's holiness. The church is holy when in faithful discipleship it follows Christ, who renounced the way of worldly power in the act of *kenōsis*. As Sobrino writes:

> The church thus recovers the deepest dimension of the holiness of Jesus, namely, his kenosis or self-emptying. If the Church of the poor succeeds in doing this—and to see that it does we need only recall the thousands of Latin American Christians who have been threatened, persecuted, slandered, imprisoned, tortured and murdered—it is because the poor compel it to do so. The holiness of the Church and the kenotic dimension of this holiness are not in the intention of stooping in to save the world but in the objective structural exigency that the poor represent. To opt for the poor is automatically to opt for the form of holiness proper to the Servant.[29]

The church is holy to the extent that it is participating in the kenotic love of God and committing itself to the integral liberation of all humankind.

In Latin America one of the decisive contexts for living out the call to faithful discipleship is forged in small gatherings of believers, in what came to be

---

[28] Jon Sobrino, *The True Church and the Poor* (Maryknoll, N.Y.: Orbis Books, 1985), 98.
[29] Ibid., 109.

referred to as basic ecclesial communities (*communidades de base*) or BECs, which we have already discussed in chapter 3.[30] In these communities, particularly as they flourished in Latin America, faithful Christians learn how to engage in social analysis, seeking a greater understanding of the many structures and forces that perpetuate their impoverished and marginalized condition. At the same time they fulfill the most basic of the demands of discipleship—they submit themselves to the Scriptures and the stories of God's love for all humankind incarnate in Jesus of Nazareth. Over time, millions of Christians would reject the prior reduction of their Christian identity to that of passive recipients of the sacraments administered by a small group of clerics. Within these base communities Christians are formed in the life of discipleship. As Gustavo Gutiérrez has observed, "poor peoples have begun to stand up for their right to life and dignity; through their adversity and uncertainty they seek to take the reins of their destiny into their own hands."[31] Christians in Latin America began to live out the council's call to active discipleship, to a faithful following of Christ:

> the church, urged on by the Spirit of Christ, must walk the road Christ himself walked, a way of poverty and obedience, of service and self-sacrifice even to death, a death from which he merged victorious by his resurrection. (AG 5)

In so doing these base communities, precisely as communities grounded in a shared discipleship, offer a new vision of the holiness of the church. It is not the holiness of the austere mystic but that holiness reflected in the courageous work for justice and that peace which is so much more than the absence of conflict. It is a holiness that emanates from a people committed to making a space for the *shalom* of God in human history. It is the holiness that shines forth from any and all human initiatives that are responding to God's graced invitation to put their lives at the service of God's reign.

What is perhaps most striking is that, in the midst of this rediscovery of the priority of discipleship in Latin America, members of these base communities did not find it necessary to abandon the central tenets of their Christian faith, the sacraments of the church and the legitimacy of the church's sacramental ministers. What occurred was not a repudiation of the structural ele-

---

[30] Marcello de Carvalho Azevedo, *Basic Ecclesial Communities in Brazil: The Challenge of a New Way of Being Church* (Washington, D.C.: Georgetown University Press, 1987).

[31] Gustavo Gutiérrez, "The Meaning and Scope of Medellín," in *The Density of the Present: Selected Writings: Gustavo Gutiérrez* (Maryknoll, N.Y.: Orbis Books, 1999), 77.

ments of their Christian faith but rather a dramatic reconfiguration of those elements from the perspective of the demands of faithful discipleship.[32]

The important contributions of liberation theologians to a recovery of the priority of discipleship in the church has been enriched and broadened by work in feminist, black, latino/a, and womanist theologies.[33] These theological approaches criticized early expressions of liberationist thought that focused on a definition of the poor in terms of material deprivation. They called for the preferential option for the poor to be expanded to include all who are pushed to the margins of church and society and rendered mute: women, ethnic minorities, gays and lesbians. This has had the merit of relocating "liberation theology" from a kind of geopolitical ghetto (the problems unique to "third world" or "underdeveloped" countries) to one's own neighborhood. Where in the world are we *not* faced with social forces that render some among us invisible and mute?

These theological voices offer a new imperative for the church to acknowledge and extend the full rights and obligations of discipleship to *all* in the church. And what might these rights and obligations include? (1) The right and obligation to serve the coming reign of God by pursuing the work of justice and peace in the world; (2) the right and obligation to exercise the charisms the baptized have received from the Spirit for "the good of humanity and the development of the church" (AA 3); (3) the right and obligation to exercise the supernatural instinct of faith (*sensus fidei*) given at baptism (LG 12) by participating in the church's corporate discernment of the will of God and an appropriate participation in the decision-making processes of church leadership; (4) the right and obligation to pursue the call to ministry and to have that call tested by the wisdom, insight, and experience of the whole church; (5) the right and obligation to call the church itself to a reform that must always consist in "an increase in fidelity to its own calling" (UR 6); and (6) the right and obligation to seek out the revelation of God's saving and liberating love for all creation through (a) a faithful, critical study of Scripture, (b) a faithful, critical study of the living tradition of the church, (c) a faithful, critical study of the church's doctrinal heritage as one expression of that living tradition, (d) the

---

[32] Leonardo Boff, *Ecclesiogenesis: The Base Communities Reinvent the Church* (Maryknoll, N.Y.: Orbis Books, 1986), 6-9.

[33] As but a few examples of a burgeoning literature, see James Cone, *A Black Theology of Liberation* (Philadelphia: Lippincott, 1970); Roberto Goizueta, *Caminemos con Jesús: Toward a Hispanic/Latino Theology of Accompaniment* (Maryknoll, N.Y.: Orbis Books, 1995); Ada María Isasi-Díaz, *Mujerista Theology* (Maryknoll, N.Y.: Orbis Books, 1996); Diana L. Hayes, *Hagar's Daughters: Womanist Ways of Being in the World* (New York: Paulist Press, 1995).

celebration of the liturgy of the church, (e) a humble attentiveness to the witness of contemporary believers, (f) a humble attentiveness to the wisdom of theologians and spiritual masters, and (g) a humble attentiveness to the manifestations of divine grace and wisdom in other religious traditions as well as any and all human movements working for justice and peace.

ONE VOCATION OR MANY?

Theologies of Christian vocation first came to the fore in the wake of the Protestant Reformation. Most of these theologies presupposed that one could identify the impulse of God at work within one's soul, directing one's life in a concrete direction. These theologies coincided with a modern emphasis on religious experience and interior discernment. In Roman Catholicism these theologies of vocation gradually identified three distinct vocations in the church: (1) ordained ministry, (2) professed religious life and (3) marriage, although the third was seen as clearly subordinate to the first two vocations.

As with so many aspects of early-twentieth-century Catholicism, this view of Christian vocation came under scrutiny during the Second Vatican Council. At a conference held at the University of Notre Dame soon after the close of Vatican II Canon Charles Moeller, a professor at Louvain, commented on the significance of the structure of the middle four chapters of *Lumen Gentium*: chapter 3 on the hierarchy, chapter 4 on the laity, chapter 5 on the universal call to holiness, and chapter 6 on consecrated religious life. Moeller pointed out that the structure of these chapters suggested an important shift in a Catholic theology of vocation. The council, he contended, had rejected the traditional threefold distinction between clergy, religious and laity, in favor of a twofold consideration of church life. Chapters 3 and 4 deal with church structure: mission and ministry; chapters 5 and 6 attend to the call to holiness.[34]

We have already discussed the distinctions related to mission and ministry in earlier chapters. Now let us consider the second pairing. Chapter 5 of *Lumen Gentium* considers the call to holiness directed toward all the baptized. I think it is possible to see a deeper logic in the council's deliberations, a logic of which the council members may have themselves been only dimly aware. The chapter on the universal call to holiness suggests that at the most basic level of Christian life there is only one primordial vocation for all Christians, the vocation to be a baptized disciple of Jesus. All other ways of Christian living become simply particular embodiments of this one vocation.

---

[34] *Vatican II: An Interfaith Appraisal,* ed. John H. Miller (Notre Dame, Ind.: University of Notre Dame Press, 1966), 269.

Consequently, it is only after establishing the common call to discipleship in chapter 5 that the council addresses the situation of professed religious men and women. The council's treatment of the call to holiness suggests that it is not a question of professed life offering a way of holiness that takes one *beyond* the demands of one's baptism, but rather of living those baptismal demands in a particularly public way.

In this regard, I have long felt that the council missed an important opportunity. If chapter 6 was to be about religious profession as constituting a way of life that gives public witness to the demands of discipleship in a particularly dramatic way, then the council should have also considered the vocation to marriage in the same chapter. Marriage and religious profession share a public form of Christian living constituted by vows that shape one's entire life. Sandra Schneiders, in the second volume of her projected three-volume study of professed religious life, recognizes this connection between religious profession and marriage:

> Religious Life is a *state of life*, like marriage. Profession establishes a stable set of permanent and distinctive relationships to God, one's congregation/ community, and the Church. Although rooted in the baptismal commitment common to all Christians, Religious profession shapes that commitment in a particular way that is distinctive within the Christian community. ... Essentially, Religious Life (again, like marriage) is a way of definitively shaping one's relational capacity in a particular way.[35]

Of course, the differences in the two states of life are many and obvious.

Schneiders locates the heart of professed religious life in consecrated celibacy and the "single-heartedness" that it offers.[36] Marriage is distinguished by the covenantal commitment between two people to a life of fruitful, lifelong companionship. Statistically, professed religious life has been chosen by only a very few among the people of God, whereas marriage remains a far more common way in which Christians have lived out their baptismal call. Marriage is now numbered among the sacraments of the church, whereas religious profession is not. Both marriage and professed religious life, however, as they are understood within the Catholic Christian tradition today, are states of life constituted by a public profession before the people of God that is customarily expressed in a set of perpetual vows or promises. These vows, whether through marriage or religious profession, implicate those who make them in a distinc-

---

[35] Sandra Schneiders, *Selling All: Commitment, Consecrated Celibacy, and Community in Catholic Religious Life* (New York: Paulist Press, 2001), 9-10.
[36] Ibid., xxii.

tive way of life constituted by the free and public embrace of a set of tangible relational constraints for the sake of a life of loving service. For those who embrace them, these vows, both marital and professed, constitute the existential context for the working out of their salvation. These same vows, both marital and professed, are also undertaken as a witness to the larger Christian community of the paschal shape of Christian discipleship. In other words, one may understand the distinctive lifestyles of those who take public vows as simply one way of illuminating the most decisive vows made by any Christian, those associated with one's baptism.

Theological reflections on both professed religious life and marriage that have emerged outside of North America and Western Europe share the tendency to ground both in the common call to discipleship. Jon Sobrino has written about professed religious life in his book *The True Church and the Poor*. For him, religious life constitutes a particular way of *becoming* Christian:

> Religious life is one way of becoming Christian by living in accordance with basic Christian values. But the religious, unlike the layperson does this through the mediation of the three traditional vows of poverty, chastity and obedience.[37]

The vows must not be unduly sacralized, in Sobrino's view. They are but a particular set of channels by which the way of following Jesus is to be concretized. Sobrino considers a number of theories of religious life, judging each to be ultimately insufficient: (1) *ascetical theories* locate the meaning of the vows in what is being renounced; (2) *imitational theories* see the vows as ways of making one's own certain essential attitudes and virtues associated with Jesus; (3) *personalist theories* understand the vows as means to personal fulfillment; (4) *communitarian theories* presume that the vows function as a means of building solidarity in community; (5) *eschatological theories* see the vows as a historical anticipation of the life proper to the eschaton. Although he finds values in each of these approaches, Sobrino believes that the most adequate starting point for a theology of religious life is an *apostolic theory* that identifies the vows and other structures of religious life as having an intelligibility ultimately rooted in their capacity to facilitate an authentic way of following Jesus.[38] The following of Jesus is, of course, a claim made on all the baptized. Although varying historical circumstances will require distinct forms, Sobrino describes the substance of the way of Jesus as follows:

---

[37] Sobrino, 317.
[38] Ibid., 317-21.

It is a way to the Father who is love and who has shown his partiality for the poor and oppressed; the Father who is, moreover, effective love, that is, who wants to establish his reign on this earth. And since the world is ruled by sin, which reduces the lowly and the poor to a state of subjection, this love finds its privileged form in justice. God not only wants to love human beings; he also wants to re-create them when they have been dehumanized by oppressive power or by the results of the exercise of this power.[39]

This way of Jesus is a way demanded by all who would take the name "disciple." For those in professed religious life, this radical living of the way of Jesus will be mediated through historical structures like the professed vows that possess a distinct *abnormality*. "Yet this very abnormality brings out what is characteristic of the following of Christ."[40] The visible and obvious abnormality of living committed celibacy, voluntary poverty, and obedience brings into sharp relief the origins and distinctiveness of the fundamental life of discipleship demanded of all believers: a life of ongoing conversion and embrace of the distinctive Christian shape of paschal living.

Theologians from the third world have also challenged many accepted understandings of Christian marriage and have placed a renewed emphasis on marriage understood in light of the common vocation to discipleship. The lay Filipino theologian José de Mesa has placed discipleship at the heart of Christian marriage.[41] Mesa contends that for too long, at least in the Catholic tradition, marriage has been viewed as a second-class vocation, either because of its carnal character or because one's responsibilities toward one's spouse and/or children made it impossible to give an "undivided heart" to God. He insists that the true theological significance of marriage is found in its relationship to the one primordial call to all Christians to be disciples of Jesus in service to God's reign. Christian discipleship, in all of its forms, is a "thankful response to God's act toward us in Jesus Christ, in a life of serving and caring patterned after the life of Christ." For Mesa, Christian married couples give particular shape to Jesus' claim that "by this will all people know that you are my disciples, if you have love for one another."[42]

The placement of marriage within the framework of the common call to discipleship is demanded by Jesus' teaching on the reign of God. As we saw earlier, one of the most radical dimensions of Jesus' teaching was his claim that to

---

[39] Ibid., 322.
[40] Ibid., 323.
[41] José de Mesa, *Marriage Is Discipleship* (Quezon City, Philippines: East Asian Pastoral Institute, 1995).
[42] Ibid., 80, quoting John 13:34-35.

be one of his disciples meant being drawn into a new family, one established not by blood and kinship relations but in faith and common service of God's reign. Does this not challenge any theology of marriage and family? Feminist theologians have often drawn on this aspect of Jesus' teaching to challenge oppressive understandings of marriage that subject women to servitude in the household. Elisabeth Schüssler Fiorenza sees Jesus' teaching as an unambiguous assertion that "faithful discipleship, not biological motherhood, is the eschatological calling of women."[43] Jesus' anti-family sayings ought to be read in this light—they are a repudiation of patriarchal conceptions of family as opposed to the life of discipleship and the values of God's reign. When marriage is viewed within the framework of the call to Christian discipleship, there is no room, Mesa contends, for hierarchical conceptions of marriage with the husband being "head" of the spouse. He sees this as a particularly important point to make in a Filipino culture that often exempts husbands from equal responsibility for the success of the marriage relationship.[44] When one's marital commitment is grounded in one's baptismal commitment to the reign of God, there is no room for marital inequality.

According to Mesa, to consider marriage from the perspective of discipleship is to understand marriage as a concrete way of serving God's coming reign and contributing to the transformation of society. Marriage constitutes, Mesa insists, a particular form of "covenant community"; it creates a "domestic church." Here he draws on a theme that has received considerable theological attention since it was first treated at Vatican II.[45] The council reflected on the domestic church in several texts. The expression was used in *Lumen Gentium* 11 to emphasize parents' role as "the first preachers of the faith." But of particular significance is the council's treatment of marriage and family in its Decree on the Apostolate of the Laity, *Apostolicam Actuositatem*, where it specifically describes marriage and family from the perspective of the church's mission in the world to serve God's coming reign:

> The mission of being the primary vital cell of society has been given to the family by God. This mission will be accomplished if the family, by the mutual affection of its members and by family prayer, presents itself as a domestic sanctuary of the church; if the whole family takes its part in the church's liturgical worship; if, finally, it offers active hospitality, and practices justice and other good works for the benefit of all its sisters and broth-

---

[43] Schüssler Fiorenza, 146.

[44] Mesa, 108.

[45] Florence Caffrey Bourg, *Where Two or Three Are Gathered: Christian Families as Domestic Churches* (Notre Dame, Ind.: University of Notre Dame Press, 2004).

ers who suffer from want. Among the various works of the family apostolate the following may be listed: adopting abandoned children, showing a
loving welcome to strangers, helping with the running of schools, supporting adolescents with advice and help. (AA 11)

Pope John Paul II would often return to the theme of the domestic church,
and in his apostolic exhortation *Familiaris Consortio* he describes the family as
a "school of deeper humanity" (FC 21). In that document the pope explicitly
relates the family to discipleship and service of God's reign:

Among the fundamental tasks of the Christian family is its ecclesial task: the
family is placed at the service of the building up of the Kingdom of God in
history by participating in the life and mission of the Church. (FC 49)

This view of marriage is far removed from that which would see marriage and
family as a self-contained refuge from a hostile world. A Christian theology of
marriage and family must never be presented as some inward-looking reality
that does little more than ward off the evil "secular" influences of our broader
society. To be a member of a family is always at the same time to be engaged
in the concerns of the broader society.

Mesa sees the exercise of the ancient practice of hospitality as a particularly
apt expression of the fulfillment of the call to discipleship within marriage and
family.[46] We live in a world ravaged by the mentality of exclusivity: women,
minorities, gays and lesbians, and above all the poor all experience exclusion in
our society. This pattern of exclusivity must be met head on by the practice of
Christian hospitality.

Hospitality is too often associated with having friends and family over for
a meal or with an attitude of friendliness toward those we do not know. The
ancient practice of hospitality has long since been transferred to institutions like
hospitals, nursing homes, and welfare agencies. Yet a perusal of our tradition
reveals hospitality as a constitutive feature of Christian community.[47] For St.
Benedict, offering hospitality to the stranger was as vital to the life of the
monastery as were prayer and common labor. Early Christians took to heart the
injunction in the Letter to the Hebrews: "Let mutual love continue. Do not
neglect hospitality for through it some have unknowingly entertained angels"
(Heb. 13:1-2). Hospitality pares the concern for justice down to the basics.

---

[46] Mesa, 128-33.
[47] Christine Pohl, *Making Room: Recovering Hospitality as a Christian Tradition* (Grand Rapids: Eerdmans, 1999).

Those on the periphery of society, those who live on the margins, suffer not only material impoverishment but the effacement of the human spirit. It is all too easy for these people to internalize the second-class status that society too often accords to them. Hospitality does not merely provide shelter, food, and other material comforts (state agencies can and do offer these things without offering what Christians mean by "hospitality"); it offers recognition of one's dignity as a person. "When a person who is not valued by a society is received by a socially respected person or group as a human being with dignity and worth, small transformations occur."[48] Mesa believes that "to make room, to give space to the unwelcomed in our lives also implies working and struggling for their becoming welcome in society as a whole."[49]

I have suggested in this section that traditional Catholic treatments of the vocation of marriage and religious life need to be thoroughly reconceived from the perspective of the primary vocation of discipleship. Any consideration of marriage and religious life must also be attentive to one very real danger. For centuries within the Roman Catholic tradition, marriage was seen as a second-class vocation when compared with either priesthood or professed religious life. In the view I am proposing, it is single people who risk being considered second-class Christians. I hope this danger can be avoided by noting that there is no sense in which married couples or professed religious men and women are in any way more holy or more faithful followers of Jesus. Those who live out their baptismal call as single people are called to the same holiness as married and professed religious. If their Christian commitment is not defined by the kind of distinctive public profession that characterizes marriage and religious life, nevertheless, its demands on them are no less radical. They too will discover that their vocation to discipleship will be mediated by the kinds of commitments they make to friends, movements, communities, and so on. These commitments, great and small, will draw them into the paschal dynamism of Christian life whereby all are called to die in order to rise, to abandon the preoccupation with individual fulfillment in favor of lives of generous service, to see justice as the very shape of God's liberating love at work in the world.

THE COMMUNITY OF DISCIPLES AS A PILGRIM CHURCH

The language of discipleship opens out into a closely related theme articulated by the council, that of pilgrimage. In the seventh chapter of *Lumen Gentium*, the church is considered not merely a community of pilgrims but as itself pil-

---

[48] Ibid., 62.
[49] Mesa, 133.

grim. As pilgrim, the church is firmly situated in history as a community of disciples walking a common path, confident that by the grace of the Spirit they are traveling in the right direction, but humble enough to realize that they have not yet arrived. It is an image of the church that demands an eschatological humility, a sense of modesty in the face of the realization that, as the council put it,

> The Church, to which we are all called in Christ Jesus, and in which by the grace of God we attain holiness, will receive its perfection only in the glory of heaven, when the time for the renewal of all things will have come. (LG 48)

This eschatological humility is also the fruit of the honest recognition that, as a pilgrim people, the church will always be in need of reform and renewal:

> Christ summons the church, as she goes her pilgrim way, to that continual reformation of which she always has need, insofar as she is a human institution here on earth. Consequently, if, in various times and circumstances, there have been deficiencies in moral conduct or in church discipline, or even in the way that church teaching has been formulated—to be carefully distinguished from the deposit of faith itself—these should be set right at the opportune moment and in the proper way. (UR 6)

In the decades since Vatican II, the council's moving reflections on the pilgrim status of the church have led some to question whether any assertions of the church's holiness must also be accompanied by a frank admission of the church's sinfulness.

The pontificate of Pope John Paul II indirectly invited such reflection, as one of the most prominent features of his pontificate was the request for forgiveness for sins perpetrated in the name of Christianity. Luigi Accattoli documents over ninety instances in which John Paul II asked forgiveness for the failings of Christians.[50] Over the course of his remarkable pontificate John Paul II offered apologies for the Galileo affair, crimes of anti-Semitism, abuse of women, and crimes against non-Catholic Christians, among others. He often referred to this process as the church's necessary "purification of memory."[51] So novel was this papal endeavor that the International Theological Commission felt compelled to undertake a study of the theological appropriateness of attributing sinfulness to the church. The result was a report titled

---

[50] Luigi Accattoli, *When a Pope Asks Forgiveness: The Mea Culpa's of John Paul II* (Boston: Pauline Books, 1998).

[51] See *Novo Millennio Ineunte* 6 (Apostolic Letter of John Paul II, January 6, 2001).

Memory and Reconciliation: The Church and the Faults of the Past.[52] The document rejected any claim that the church was itself sinful in virtue of the sin of its members. Unfortunately, the document relied very little on the conciliar image of the church as pilgrim, preferring instead to speak of the relationship between "Holy Mother Church" and "her sinful children." The ITC presumed a distinction between the church, *qua* church, and the members that comprise the church. Bernard Prusak complains that "by constantly distinguishing the sinfulness of the members of the church from the holiness of the church, the document sets apart the church from its members."[53]

Now properly speaking, it is certainly true that sin is the act of an individual, yet we often use the term analogously in other senses, as when we speak of original sin as a reality qualifying the entire human condition, or when we speak of structural sin as the perpetuation of sinful attitudes in various institutional structures. Certainly to speak of the church as sinful cannot mean that the church *qua* church, actually sins, but rather that the sinfulness of its members participates in the ecclesiality of the community and to some extent compromises the church's mission. More importantly, we must recognize that sinners do not act within the church simply as individual believers. Many of their actions are overtly ecclesial, that is, they are actions that are enacted in and through church laws, policies, structures, and even doctrines. If we are bound to assert and condemn the presence of structural sin in the world, we must also acknowledge a kind of structural sin in the church. The sinfulness of individual members is both extended and prolonged by way of church laws, policies, structures, and doctrines, and these sinful structures deface the church's face to the world, compromising its ability to be a sacrament of God's saving love. In a famous essay on this topic, Karl Rahner wrote:

> There exists no dogma according to which the assistance of the Holy Spirit which always remains with the Church would limit the effect of the sinfulness of the men who administer the Church to their purely private lives and not permit it to have any influence on those events which must be characterised as unmistakably acts of the Church, if the concept of the Church is not to evaporate into the abstract ideal of an invisible Church.[54]

---

[52] International Theological Commission, *Memory and Reconciliation: The Church and the Faults of the Past* (Boston: Pauline Books, 2000).

[53] Bernard Prusak, "Theological Considerations—Hermeneutical, Ecclesiological, Eschatological Regarding *Memory and Reconciliation: The Church and the Faults of the Past,*" *Horizons* 32 (Spring 2005): 136-52, at 142.

[54] Karl Rahner, "The Church of Sinners," in *Theological Investigations* (New York: Crossroad, 1982), 6:261.

A pilgrim church, a church on the way, a community of disciples, will always be composed of saints and sinners, all of whom will, in some way, leave their mark on the church.

CONCLUSION

In 1985 Pope John Paul II convened an extraordinary synod of bishops in order to assess the church's progress in assimilating the teaching of Vatican II. Although the synod offered, for the most part, a ringing endorsement of conciliar teaching, various episcopal interventions and even the final report voiced uneasiness over the emphasis on the metaphor of the people of God in postconciliar ecclesiology. Some worried about a kind of horizontalism that so emphasized the church's place in history and the equality of believers that it ignored the transcendent dimension of the church, its dependence on God, and its hierarchical ordering. Many were in sympathy with the views of Cardinal Ratzinger, then prefect of the Congregation for the Doctrine of the Faith, who that same year published a frank interview with an Italian journalist in which he suggested that the image of the people of God was more sociological in character and therefore could not have the same theological significance as that of the church as the body of Christ.[55] What emerged out of that synod was a cautious diminishment of the theological import of the metaphor of the people of God in favor of the theological concept of communion which the synod asserted had been central at the council. Many commentators objected that both Cardinal Ratzinger and the extraordinary synod were setting up a false alternative between the church as people of God and the church as communion. It is true that a "people of God" ecclesiology highlights the historical dimensions of the church but, as José Comblin points out, "Vatican II never understood 'people of God' as a sociological concept—its analysis is essentially biblical and theological, referring to something revealed by God and founded by Jesus."[56]

The Second Vatican Council's return to an ecclesiology grounded in baptism, discipleship, and mission was an attempt to correct ecclesiological tendencies that began with what distinguished groups of Christians from one another and articulated the holiness of the church in an ahistorical fashion. Giving prominence to discipleship in mission as the primal identity of Christians has the merit of linking the church today with the self-understanding of early Christians.

---

[55] Vitorio Messori, ed., *The Ratzinger Report* (San Francisco: Ignatius Press, 1985).
[56] José Comblin, *People of God* (Maryknoll, N.Y.: Orbis Books, 2004), 55.

The most basic meaning of the term "disciple" is a "follower." This suggests several distinctive dimensions of Christian life. To follow another is to admit, at a deep level, one's own insufficiency. I lack something within that I believe the one I "follow" can offer me. And so it was for the first followers of Jesus: "Lord to whom shall we go? You have the words of everlasting life" (John 6:67-68). The journey of Christian discipleship leads one to follow and emulate "the master." And yet discipleship is about more than an admission of personal inadequacy; it is also a vocation characterized by trust and hope. I trust that the one I follow knows the way and has something to teach me and I find hope in the promise of a more fulfilling existence. Finally, to be a disciple is to be oriented toward community. I am not a solitary follower but join company with others who look in confidence to the Risen One as "the way, the truth, and the life." As a community of disciples, the church is not its own lord; to be a member of the church is to be in the company of disciples who, by definition, are dependent on their master, Christ.

QUESTIONS FOR REFLECTION

1. Do you believe it is worthwhile for the church to retain the language of "lay" and "clergy"? Why or why not? What are some essential elements embedded in this terminology that need to be retained even if the terms themselves are abandoned?
2. What do you think is intended by the distinction between a church *for* the poor and a church *of* the poor?
3. In this chapter we considered a new theology of vocation for marriage and professed religious life. Do you believe there is an analogous vocation to single life? If so, what ought to be the principal characteristics of a spirituality for the single vocation?
4. What is your response to liberation theology's call for a conception of holiness oriented toward the cause of peace and justice, or what some have called "social holiness"?

SUGGESTIONS FOR FURTHER READING AND STUDY

Boff, Leonardo. *Church: Charism and Power: Liberation Theology and the Institutional Church.* New York: Crossroad, 1985.

Bourg, Florence Caffrey. *Where Two or Three Are Gathered: Christian Families as Domestic Churches.* Notre Dame, Ind.: University of Notre Dame Press, 2004.

Comblin, José. *People of God.* Maryknoll, N.Y.: Orbis Books, 2004.

Faivre, Alexandre. *The Emergence of the Laity in the Early Church.* New York: Paulist Press, 1990.

Lakeland, Paul. *The Liberation of The Laity: In Search of an Accountable Church.* New York: Continuum, 2003.

Mesa, José de. *Marriage Is Discipleship.* Quezon City, Philippines: East Asian Pastoral Institute, 1995.

Pohl, Christine. *Making Room: Recovering Hospitality as a Christian Tradition.* Grand Rapids: Eerdmans, 1999.

Schneiders, Sandra. *Selling All: Commitment, Consecrated Celibacy, and Community in Catholic Religious Life.* New York: Paulist Press, 2001.

Schüssler Fiorenza, Elisabeth. *In Memory of Her: A Feminist Theological Reconstruction of Christian Origins.* New York: Crossroad, 1983.

Sobrino, Jon. *The True Church and the Poor.* Maryknoll, N.Y.: Orbis Books, 1985.

6

A People Sustained by Memory

Of the four so-called marks of the church, *apostolicity* was the last to be asserted in an ancient creed.[1] This is also the mark of the church that has been, over the last few decades, the most controversial in contemporary ecumenical dialogue. As a theologian, Pope Benedict XVI once referred to this issue as "the key question in the Catholic/Protestant debate."[2] In this chapter we will consider this traditional affirmation of the church from multiple perspectives, but our focus will be on the notion of communal memory as an interpretive lens for comprehending the church's claim to apostolicity. It may be helpful, however, if we place the topic in context by considering briefly some standard approaches.

In a helpful new study on apostolicity, Franciscan theologian John Burkhard has proposed that, within the Christian tradition, apostolicity has been understood in at least four different ways: (1) apostolicity of origin, (2) apostolicity of doctrine, (3) apostolicity of life, and (4) apostolic succession.[3]

Apostolicity of origin articulates the ancient belief that in the early years of Christianity, certain local churches had been, at least by reputation, established by one or more of the apostles (e.g., Rome, Antioch, Alexandria). This relationship to an apostle gave these churches particular authority. Eamon Duffy explains why a church's apostolic relationship was so important:

> For the earliest Christians apostolic authority was no antiquarian curiosity, a mere fact about the origins of a particular community. The Apostles were living presences, precious guarantors of truth. The apostolic churches possessed more than a pedigree, they spoke with the voices of their founders, and provided living access to their teaching.[4]

---

[1] See Jared Wicks, "Ecclesial Apostolicity Confessed in the Creed," *Pro Ecclesia* 9 (2000): 150-64.

[2] Joseph Ratzinger, *Principles of Catholic Theology: Building Stones for a Fundamental Theology* (San Francisco: Ignatius Press, 1987), 239.

[3] John J. Burkhard, *Apostolicity Then and Now: An Ecumenical Church in a Postmodern World* (Collegeville, Minn.: Liturgical Press, 2004), 26-41.

[4] Eamon Duffy, *Saints and Sinners: A History of the Popes* (New Haven: Yale University Press, 1997), 13.

This helps us understand the unique prestige of the church of Rome in the early centuries. Rome's prestige had little to do with the belief that its bishop was the successor to Peter (that claim appears not to have been made until the mid-third century). Rome's preeminence was due, rather, to its unique claim to have witnessed the martyrdom of not one but two apostles, Peter *and* Paul. The apostolicity of the church was attributed to the faith of the whole community, since it was the whole community that had received the apostle's teaching or at least the unique witness to the faith manifested in an apostle's martyrdom. It is worth recalling that the Greek word *martyrion*, means "witness" or "testimony." The deaths of believers on account of their faith was considered a profound testimony to the Christian message itself; their martyrdom was, if you will, an evangelical and catechetical act. Apostolicity described the faith of the church itself, a faith that it had, one way or another, received from the apostles. This apostolicity could be extended, however, when these apostolic churches in turn established other churches.[5] A church could also be viewed as apostolic if its own faith was considered in harmony with the faith professed by one of the principal apostolic churches.

Apostolicity could also be understood in relation to the teaching or doctrine held by a given church. In the face of rival Christian sects that offered strikingly different accounts of Christian belief, attention was naturally drawn to the content of a community's belief. For a church to be considered apostolic it had to affirm the Christian *kerygma* that had been taught by the apostles themselves. This apostolic doctrine was found, preeminently, in the community's sacred texts. The meaning of these texts, however, was at times ambiguous, and so it was held that this apostolic doctrine was also preserved in summary statements that captured the core of the apostolic faith. These summary assertions were referred to by key second- and third-century figures like St. Irenaeus of Lyons and Tertullian as the *regula fidei* or the *regula veritatis*, the "rule of faith" or the "rule of truth." "They were not meant to replace or supersede the Scriptures," Burkhard writes, "but to assist the believer in understanding the Scriptures, which always remained the point of reference."[6]

A third perspective on the church's apostolicity considered the life of the church itself, including such ecclesial practices as communal worship and the ministerial outreach to the poor and marginalized. But the apostolic life of the church could also include the daily witness of its ordinary believers, the community's artistic expressions, its laws, customs, and so on. To assert a

---

[5] J. F. McCure, "Apostles and Apostolic Succession in the Patristic Era," in *Eucharist and Ministry*, ed. Paul C. Empie and T. Austin Murphy, Lutherans and Catholics in Dialogue 4 (Washington, D.C.: USCC, 1970), 138-77.

[6] Burkhard, 53.

church's apostolicity in this sense was to claim that in and through the church's life a vital connection and fidelity to that apostolic message and mission could be discerned. Burkhard refers to this often-overlooked aspect as "substantive apostolicity."[7]

The final perspective on apostolicity is captured by the term "apostolic succession." The historical origins of this perspective are complex and cannot be considered in detail here. It emerged out of a gradual recognition that a stable ministry or office was necessary to ensure the continued apostolicity of the church. By the end of the second century this apostolic office had been identified with the emergence of the monoepiscopate, that is, the practice of each church being led by a single overseer (*episkopos*) or bishop. As the monoepiscopal leadership structure became universal, these bishops were thought to have succeeded to the authority of the apostles.

Unfortunately, although all four perspectives can be found in the ecclesial consciousness of the early church, the polemics of the Protestant Reformation led to an often bitter opposition between the apostolicity of doctrine emphasized in the various churches of the Reformation and the Roman Catholic emphasis on apostolic succession. In the context of its anti-Protestant polemics, baroque Catholicism reduced apostolic succession to an unbroken historical chain of valid episcopal ordinations that could be traced back to the apostles. This apostolic succession, preserved in the historical episcopate, was considered, at least within Roman Catholicism, as the sole guarantee of the church's fidelity to the apostolic faith. Roman Catholicism, Eastern Orthodoxy, and, to some extent, the churches in the Anglican Communion, have shared a commitment to the essential place of apostolic succession as it has been manifested in the historical episcopate. The issue of apostolic succession has continued to be a stumbling block in ecumenical dialogue. In the next chapter we will consider the question of apostolic succession and the value of a stable apostolic office in the life of the church, but in this chapter we shall try to shed new light on how the apostolicity of the church can be better understood today.

APOSTOLICITY AND A THEOLOGY OF TRADITION

At the heart of the affirmation of the church's apostolicity lies a conviction regarding communal identity. Christians have long recognized that the church is not its own lord. Put simply, Christians do not believe they can "make things up as they go." The church is bound to its origins in the life and ministry of

---

[7] Ibid., 34.

Jesus as proclaimed by the apostolic community. It believes that in Jesus Christ it has received a revelation that comes from God by the power of the Holy Spirit, was testified to by the apostolic community, and continues to be pre- served in the life of the church. That revelation, and the faith that it elicits, constitutes the core of the church's identity.

An incipient theology of tradition developed out of the need for early Chris- tian communities to affirm their identity as one in continuity with the faith of the apostles. This need to demonstrate a continuity in faith came in response to the emergence of new sects, particularly those associated with Gnosticism, that were believed to have broken with that faith and claimed a salvation avail- able only to those in possession of an immediate and private revelation. St. Ire- naeus of Lyons wrote of a *paradosis* (*traditio* in Latin), by which he meant the faithful "handing on" of the apostolic *kērygma* received from the apostolic com- munity. This apostolic tradition was not something distinct from Scripture, as it would be for some Catholic theologians after the Reformation. For Irenaeus, this tradition referred to the whole substance of the apostolic faith, the gospel message in its entirety as it was handed on in the churches. Consequently, tra- dition included the sacred texts that were already being collected by local churches (although at the time of Irenaeus there was as yet no fixed Christian canon).

We must credit the great Dominican theologian Yves Congar for calling attention to early Christianity's more organic understanding of tradition as including the whole living gospel in all of its various historical embodiments.[8] Congar pointed out the many patristic images that portrayed tradition as a river flowing from its gospel source. He insisted that for most of the first thou- sand years of church history, tradition referred to both the process by which the faith was handed on and the content of that faith as testified to in Scripture and preserved through the example of martyrs, the witness of ordinary believers, the celebration of the liturgy and sacraments, theological reflection and Christian art. Only in the late Middle Ages did one begin to speak of traditions (at that time "tradition" was only rarely employed in the singular) as a collection both of church teachings and customs distinct from Scripture.

This apparent separation between Scripture and tradition gave rise to the Reformation doctrine *sola scriptura*. The Reformers objected to the haze of accumulated customs, practices, and speculative propositions that had prolif- erated in late medieval Catholicism, all of which, in their view, clouded over and even distorted the evangelical message of the Bible. The first formal Catholic

---

[8] Yves Congar, *Tradition and Traditions: An Historical and Theological Essay* (New York: Macmillan, 1966).

explanation of its own understanding of the relationship between Scripture and tradition came at the Council of Trent, largely in response to the Reformers. In one of its decrees the council tried to articulate the proper relationship between these two terms. An early draft proposed that divine truths were contained "partly" in the "written books" and "partly" in unwritten traditions. The final text, however, was changed to read that truth was found "both in the written books and in unwritten traditions."[9] The first formulation suggested that these were two distinct sources of divine truth, yet the final formulation was at least open to the interpretation that there were not different *sources* of truth at all but only different *modes of expression*. Unfortunately, many theologians would, after the Reformation, maintain the view more reflective of the first formulation. The tendency to separate Scripture and tradition, accompanied by a gradual process whereby tradition was identified with the "organs of tradition," chief among which was the papal teaching office, continued well into the twentieth century. However, a more organic understanding of tradition as inclusive of the whole apostolic faith and life was never entirely lost. In the nineteenth century, theologians like Johann Adam Möhler and John Henry Newman continued to keep this more ancient view of tradition alive.

There is a story, perhaps apocryphal, that during the First Vatican Council, Pope Pius IX learned of the desire of some bishops to have the council affirm that the papal teaching must be in accord with the great tradition of the church. The pope is said to have retorted in exasperation, "Tradition? *I am* tradition!" The story certainly reflects a then common view of the papacy as the principal "organ of tradition." This tendency to identify the magisterium in general, and the papacy in particular, with tradition strengthened the sense that tradition was a source of divine truth entirely separate from Scripture. It was a theological assumption that would be challenged at Vatican II.

Vatican II on Tradition

It would be only with the teaching of the Second Vatican Council that Catholicism would get beyond its anti-Protestant polemics and recover the more ancient understanding of tradition that Congar had emphasized. This theology of tradition was developed in the council's Dogmatic Constitution on Divine Revelation, *Dei Verbum*, a document that owes a great debt, not coincidentally, to Congar himself.

---

[9] "Decree on the Acceptance of the Sacred Books and Apostolic Traditions," in *Decrees of the Ecumenical Councils*, ed. Norman P. Tanner (Washington, D.C.: Georgetown University Press, 1990), 2:663-64.

That document moved away from a neoscholastic theology of divine revelation, which we might characterize as "propositional." This neoscholastic perspective saw revelation as a set of propositional truths collected in one *depositum fidei,* "deposit of faith," which was in the possession of the magisterium. These were viewed as eternal truths immune to the vicissitudes of human history. Without ever denying that revelation disclosed eternal truth, the council moved away from this propositional approach and presented revelation in the context of a relationship between God and humankind.

> By this revelation, then, the invisible God, from the fullness of his love, addresses men and women as his friends, and lives among them, in order to invite and receive them into his own company. (DV 2)

This revelation found its fullest expression in Christ, "who is himself both the mediator and the sum total of all revelation" (DV 2). As such, God's revelation was communicated in "works" and "words."

According to the council, this one revelation in Christ is faithfully communicated in Scripture. Tradition then relates to Scripture as the ongoing growth of the Christian community's apprehension of revelation. But how does the development of tradition take place? For centuries, the answer to that question in Catholic theology would have been fairly straightforward: it occurs primarily through the teaching of the magisterium in history. In this view tradition and the teaching of the magisterium were one and the same.

The council offered, however, a quite different understanding of Christian tradition. First, the council noted that the apostolic tradition includes "everything that serves to make the people of God live their lives in holiness and increase their faith" (DV 8). According to the council, tradition develops

> through the contemplation and study of believers who ponder these things in their hearts. It comes from the intimate sense of spiritual realities which they experience. And it comes from the preaching of those who, on succeeding to the office of bishop, have received the sure charism of truth. Thus, as the centuries go by, the church is always advancing towards the plenitude of divine truth, until eventually the words of God are fulfilled in it. (DV 8)

This passage is foundational to the council's teaching on apostolicity and the place of tradition in the life of the church. It recovers the ancient insight that tradition includes more than doctrine; it embraces the whole life of the church. Moreover, the council taught that this apostolic faith resides not exclusively with those who hold apostolic office but with all believers "who ponder these things in their hearts" and actively participate in the dynamic unfolding of tradition. The passage affirms the essential role of the bishops, but its primary emphasis is on the community of faith itself as the bearer of the church's apostolicity. Finally, the passage reminds us that divine truth is not something that the church ever really possesses. As befits a "pilgrim church," the council modestly acknowledged only that the church was advancing "towards the plenitude of divine truth." There is a kind of eschatological humility in evidence here. It is one thing to say that the church abides in the truth as it abides in God. It is altogether something different to say that the church possesses the plenitude of truth. According to the council, truth is never fully in the church's possession.

We must also note, however, what this influential passage failed to say. Missing is the important distinction between *tradition* as the ongoing life of the church testifying to the gospel of Jesus Christ and *traditions* as constituent distinctive elements of the church's life that vary significantly in the degree to which they transmit in a permanent and enduring manner the one gospel of Jesus Christ. It was a distinction that Congar had worked hard to recover in his own work on a theology of tradition. During the council, Cardinal Albert Gregory Meyer of Chicago complained about this very omission. He insisted that the language of this text did not sufficiently encourage a critical stance toward various church traditions. The church must freely admit that among the many legitimate components in the church's tradition there were also serious deficiencies and distortions that must be forthrightly addressed.[10]

Implicit in Cardinal Meyer's concern is the much larger question of whether the language of "development," "evolution," or "progress" is even helpful when applied to tradition when viewed over time. Can one not speak as well of occasional periods of regression and impoverishment in church tradition? John Thiel has made this point well when he includes among four "senses of tradition" one that (dramatic development) embraces a reversal of past beliefs and practices.[11] Tradition is not always the story of enduring or developing beliefs and practices; sometimes it is the story of beliefs and practices that have been abandoned or rejected over time. Tradition involves not only the recognition of continuities with the past, but sometimes the recognition of dramatic discontinuity and even the reversal of positions. Some beliefs and practices simply lose their authority over time. We are tempted to imagine contemporary church

---

[10] *Acta Synodalia Sacrosancti Concilii Oecumenici Vaticani II* (Vatican City: Typis Vaticanis, 1970–), 3/3:150-1.

[11] Following the medieval practice of distinguishing between four "senses of Scripture," Thiel identifies four senses of tradition: (1) the literal, (2) development-in-continuity, (3) dramatic development, and (4) incipient development. John Thiel, *Senses of Tradition: Continuity and Development in Catholic Faith* (New York: Oxford University Press, 2000), 31-160.

teachings as having been invisibly and inexorably directed toward their present formulation. We stand at the present moment and look back on history, trying to recognize the movements of the Spirit. But our present perspective is always partial and to a considerable extent, it undergoes revision over time. What today strikes us as an obviously providential development of a given insight might conceivably, one hundred years from now, be viewed as a dead-end street. Up to the nineteenth century, many Christians saw slavery as part of God's divine plan. Today, Christians recognize this position for what it is: a tragic misreading of divine providence. The grudging rejection of this viewpoint in the consciousness of the church represented a communal recognition of dramatic *discontinuity* with its past. In a similar way the church has found it necessary to repudiate long-standing beliefs about the immorality of charging interest when lending money, the inherent inferiority of women in the natural order, and the denial of religious liberty to nonbelievers.

Vatican II on the Sensus Fidei

An important and often neglected feature of the council's teaching was its incipient pneumatology. For much of the history of Western ecclesiology, the role of the Holy Spirit had been eclipsed by what some theologians have referred to as a Christomonism, that is, a tendency to focus exclusively on the saving work of Christ.[12] The work of the Holy Spirit was reduced to functioning as a guarantor of the efficacy of those church sacraments and church offices thought to be instituted by Christ. This failure is still evident in certain conciliar texts; one of the most striking lacunae in the council's treatment of the hierarchy in chapter 3 of *Lumen Gentium* is any developed integration of pneumatology. Other passages, however, reveal a tentative move to integrate a more pneumatological perspective into the council's consideration of the church. This was evident in the council's consideration of the proper participation of all the baptized in the prophetic office of the church:

> The holy people of God shares also in Christ's prophetic office; it spreads abroad a living witness to him, especially by a life of faith and love and by offering to God a sacrifice of praise, the fruit of lips confessing his name. The whole body of the faithful who have received an anointing which comes from the holy one cannot be mistaken in belief. It shows this characteristic

---

[12] Yves Congar, "Pneumatologie ou 'Christomonisme' dans la traditione latine," in *Ecclesia a Spiritu Sancto edocta: Mélanges théologiques, hommages à Mgr Gérard Philips,* Bibliotheca ephemeridum theologicarum Lovaniensium 27 (Gembloux: Duculot, 1970), 41-63.

through the entire peoples' supernatural sense of faith, when, "from the bishops to the last of the faithful" it manifests a universal consensus in matters
of faith and morals. By this sense of the faith, aroused and sustained by the
Spirit of truth, the people of God, guided by the sacred magisterium which
it faithfully obeys, receives not the word of human beings, but truly the word
of God, "the faith once for all delivered to the saints." The people unfailingly
adheres to this faith, penetrates it more deeply through right judgment, and
applies it more fully in daily life. (LG 12)

According to the passage, one of the gifts with which the faithful are equipped
by the Spirit is the *sensus fidei,* the "sense of faith." This instinct or spiritual
capacity for discernment is "aroused and sustained" by the Spirit. It allows the
faithful to recognize God's Word, but not simply in a passive sense. For this
recognition also involves a deeper penetration of the gospel and an ability to
apply it more fully. This passage builds on *Dei Verbum's* declaration that all the
faithful contribute to the development of tradition through "the intimate sense
of spiritual realities which they experience." Neither *Dei Verbum* nor *Lumen
Gentium* neglects the indispensable role of the bishops, but neither do they
suggest that the apostolic faith resides in the bishops alone. Rather, these documents presuppose what Cardinal Newman once referred to as the *conspiratio
fidelium et pastorum,* "the breathing together of the faithful and the pastors."[13]

The council's teaching on tradition and the Spirit-assisted participation of
the faithful in the contemporary discernment, penetration, and application of
the gospel lends new insight into our understanding of apostolicity. It firmly
roots apostolicity in the life and belief of the whole church and insists that
apostolicity not be understood strictly as a static possession or property of the
church but rather as a dynamic dimension of a church seeking to be faithful to
the gospel in the present moment.

An important advance in the ecumenical movement took place in 1963 in the
city of Montreal, where a conference of the WCC Faith and Order Commis-
sion chose to consider the topic of Scripture and tradition at the same time that
Vatican II was debating the topic. In their statement, *Scripture, Tradition and
Traditions,* there was a remarkable convergence of thought with that of Vatican
II.[14] This was doubtless due to the fact that some of the participants in the
Montreal conference were also invited observers at Vatican II and vice versa.
The Montreal statement acknowledged that Scripture itself came into existence
through a "traditioning" process (*paradosis*). The ecumenical report states:

---

[13] John Henry Newman, *On Consulting the Faithful in Matters of Doctrine* (1859; reprint, Kansas City,
Mo.: Sheed & Ward, 1961), 71-72.

[14] Michael Kinnamon and Brian E. Cope, eds., *The Ecumenical Movement: An Anthology of Key Texts
and Voices* (Grand Rapids: Eerdmans, 1997), 139-44.

> What is transmitted in the process of tradition is the Christian faith, not only as a sum of tenets, but as a living reality transmitted through the operation of the Holy Spirit. We can speak of the Christian Tradition (with a capital T), whose content is God's revelation and self-giving in Christ, present in the life of the Church. (# 46)

The document goes on to distinguish (as Vatican II did not) between Tradition and traditions. It acknowledges that both Scripture and tradition are subject to the ongoing interpretation of the church. Echoing themes considered at the council, the Montreal statement also insisted that "the Tradition of the Church is not an object which we possess, but a reality in which we are possessed" (#56). Finally the document honestly recognizes areas where there is not yet complete ecumenical consensus, including questions related to the normative criteria for interpreting Scripture and tradition and the breadth of diversity that is permissible among various traditions. In spite of these questions, we should not minimize the progress made on an issue that was once a bone of contention in Christianity.

For all its many contributions, Vatican II was by no means the final word for our contemporary understanding of the apostolicity of the church. The limits of the council's approach stem from the fact that the council marked the Catholic Church's first real engagement with modernity precisely at the moment in which modernity itself was beginning to give way to what has come to be called postmodernity. The council's confident view of tradition as organic development, for example, gave scant attention to the possibility that tradition might be manifested not only as development but as reversal. For all of the advances in the council's theology of revelation, it still was ill-equipped to address the challenge to contemporary understandings of religious truth raised by critical theory, feminist interpretation, and liberationist thought, all of which, in one way or another, have insisted that the "hermeneutics of trust" still presupposed by the council documents must be augmented by a "hermeneutics of suspicion." This new hermeneutical perspective asserts that much of what one appeals to authoritatively as "tradition" may be ideologically distorted. So, for example, some feminist scholars want to challenge the way in which the received tradition that one brings to the interpretation of a text may be ideologically distorted by patriarchal and sexist assumptions about men and women.[15]

Postmodern thought has not abandoned any appeal to truth, as many of its critics assert, but it does highlight the way in which truth is always perspectival and embedded in particular accounts such that the apprehension of "truth"

---

[15] See Sandra M. Schneiders, *The Revelatory Text: Interpreting the New Testament as Sacred Scripture* (New York: HarperCollins, 1991), esp. chaps. 6 and 7.

cannot be gained save through a serious engagement with contemporary cultural and religious pluralism. One concept that has shown some promise for guiding reflection on apostolicity in a postmodern key is the category of memory.

APOSTOLICITY AND COMMUNAL MEMORY

One of the most powerful features of human memory is the way in which it is capable of sustaining the identity of a community. Liturgical scholar Mary Collins has offered insight into the power of memory as reflected in the Greek word for memory, *anamnēsis,* a term that, as we shall see, plays a significant role in the biblical tradition. To understand the biblical sense of *anamnēsis,* she suggests that we focus on its opposite, *amnesia.* "The amnesiac is not the person who has misplaced her glasses one time too many. She is the person who has forgotten who she is. She has lost her conscious awareness of the basic relationships that give her her identity."[16] It is, Collins would add, a malady almost endemic to modern Western society.

> The biblical and liturgical use of the word "anamnesis" rises from a perception that there is a disorder analogous to clinical amnesia that plagues the human community. To be human is to be threatened with spiritual amnesia. At the level of our spiritual identity we do not remember for long who we really are. Those ultimate relationships that give us our spiritual identity slip from consciousness all too easily, and we lapse into noncomprehension about our deepest identity.[17]

We find ourselves in the stories, symbols, and rituals that mediate our community's memory.

Considering apostolicity and tradition in relation to the notion of memory requires, however, that we avoid an overly romantic view of memory. As important as memory is to the life of a community, we must acknowledge the hard truth that memory is capable of distortion. We know of communities that are capable of keeping alive stories of hate and bigotry. We also know well the ways in which certain communal memories can become a social poison preventing any possibility of communal healing and reconciliation. One need only consider long-standing conflicts in Northern Ireland or the Balkans or the disputes

---

[16] Mary Collins, *Contemplative Participation: Sacrosanctum Concilium, Twenty-five Years Later* (Collegeville, Minn.: Liturgical Press, 1990), 55.

[17] Ibid.

between Israelis and Palestinians to know the danger of communal memory functioning as an obstacle to healing. Protestant theologian Miroslav Volf has even suggested that there are times when healing and reconciliation may require a selective and conscious choosing to forget wrongs inflicted upon one self or one's people.[18]

We considered earlier the need to incorporate a "hermeneutics of suspicion" into a consideration of the Christian tradition. This becomes a corrective to a hermeneutic of trust, which is grounded in a faith-inspired confidence that the memory of the church found in Scripture is in some sense "God-breathed." The hermeneutic of suspicion does not reject the received memory of the church, but it acknowledges the fact that memories are never free of ideology. By ideology I mean the distinct set of "interests" at stake in those who are the purveyors and interpreters of a community's memory. These interests, often in ways unknown to those involved, shape how the memories are passed on. This insight is captured in the saying "history is always told by the winners." That is, memory is often mediated by those who have the power to transmit memories. Disadvantaged groups often find their own memories suppressed by those who hold power or wealth in a particular community.

This awareness of the role of ideology in the maintenance of communal memory does not require the rejection of memory but a constant need for a *critical* appropriation of the community's memory. This critical appropriation is, in particular, the work of biblical scholars, historians, and theologians, who are called to assist the community in the ongoing task of interpreting the memory of the church. For, even with its dangers, memory has, in the Judeo-Christian tradition, always played a vital role in sustaining communal identity and compelling communal action. This is particularly evident in the biblical foundations of Christianity.

Biblical Conceptions of Memory

The communal function of memory ran deep in the ancient Judeo-Christian tradition. It was evident in the Tanakh, where the Hebrew verb for remembering, *zkr*, connected memory with communal action.[19] Integral to the Hebrew conception of memory was its ethical imperative. The recollection of God's saving deeds was intended to transform behaviors and actions for the subjects of the act of memory. Xavier Léon-Dufour writes that for ancient Israel

---

[18] Miroslav Volf, *The End of Memory: Remembering Rightly in a Violent World* (Grand Rapids: Eerdmans, 2006).

[19] Xavier Léon-Dufour, *Sharing the Eucharistic Bread* (New York: Paulist Press, 1987), 102.

Memory and action are thus the two sides—the internal and the external—of the relationship between God and human beings. God saves human beings—which is certainly a "memorable" action; when they remember this action, they renew their fidelity to the covenant.[20]

For the Hebrew people, what was to be "remembered" above all was the covenant made between God and the people of Israel. To "remember" this covenant was to allow the covenant to lay claim on their present reality. Remembrance meant becoming aware of present obligations to remain faithful to God. The Hebrew communal memory would be sustained in the various rabbinic schools but also in its ritual life.[21] In the complex system of ritual sacrifices and the developing calendar of liturgical feasts, the unifying principle was an active remembering which constituted the unique identity of the Jewish people. Liturgical feasts ritually enacted this process of remembering. This ritual memory is at the heart of the Passover ritual with its narrative of God's past deeds recalled specifically to invoke and celebrate God's present liberating and salvific activity in the life of Israel.

This understanding of memory would be taken up by the early Christian community. As Nils Dahl observes in his study of memory in early Christianity, St. Paul's writings to various communities are filled with exhortations to them to "remember" what he had taught. "The first obligation of an apostle vis-à-vis the community is to make the faithful remember what they have received and already know—or should know."[22] Early Christians also placed memory in the context of their ritual life. Christ's mandate at the Last Supper, "Do this in memory of me" (Luke 22:19; 1 Cor. 11:23-26), involved remembering in the celebration of the eucharist the past event of Christ's own passing over from death into new life in such a way that the celebrating community was ritually drawn up into this spiritual movement. What is distinctive about this Christian ritual of memory, particularly in comparison with that of the Jewish Passover, is that what is remembered in the Christian eucharist is not only an event (the exodus) but a person, Jesus.[23]

Transmission and Reception of Memory in the Life of the Church

Memory resides in the hearts and minds of individuals and communities. These memories are sustained through the medium of rituals, symbols, and narra-

---

[20] Ibid., 105.

[21] Bruce T. Morrill, *Anamnesis as Dangerous Memory: Political and Liturgical Theology in Dialogue* (Collegeville, Minn.: Liturgical Press, 2000), 149.

[22] Nils Alstrup Dahl, *Jesus in the Memory of the Early Church* (Minneapolis: Augsburg, 1976), 15.

[23] Léon-Dufour, 112.

tives. These rituals, symbols, and narratives are, in turn, appropriated and passed on within distinct cultural matrices. Christianity's communal memory has always been mediated by the distinct memories of local Christian communities. Recalling this helps maintain for us the historical structure of tradition as inseparable from the dynamic process of handing on and receiving the Christian faith in distinct sociocultural contexts.[24] It will also be helpful to consider how, historically, the church has formed and preserved its corporate memory. These memories have been preserved through (1) the liturgical life of Christian communities, (2) the biblical canon, (3) the dynamic testimonies of believing communities, and (4) apostolic office. The last of these will be considered in the following chapter.

Ritual Memory

One of most common assumptions regarding the place of religious ritual in the life of the community is that rituals encode belief. In this view it is generally assumed that a religious community first possesses a set of beliefs and then encodes those beliefs in ritual worship. The primary responsibility of those who would study community rituals would then be to decode them so that the originating beliefs could be recovered. When applied to Christianity this approach to ritual assumes that Christians first held some beliefs regarding, for example, the nature of the triune God and the salvific character of Christ's life, death, and resurrection. These beliefs were then encoded in Christian rituals such as baptism and the eucharist. In short, belief holds primacy over ritual.

This view of ritual has largely been debunked by contemporary ritual theorists. For example, in a very influential essay, Theodore W. Jennings contends that, although it is true that beliefs may be mediated through ritual, this does not occur through a process of ritual encoding and decoding. Rather, ritual involves a unique form of symbolic expression that is rooted in our experience of ourselves as embodied. Jennings writes that "ritual knowledge is gained through a bodily action which alters the world or the place of the ritual participant in the world."[25] What Jennings is saying is that there is a unique form of knowledge that is not primarily cerebral but corporeal. Certain practices, when undertaken, give us a "body knowledge" that disposes us to encounter our world in new ways. This reverses the way in which we tend to view such things. We conventionally believe that we first "think" something and then "perform" it. But, in fact, it is often the reverse. We engage in some bodily

---

[24] Nicholas Lash, *Change in Focus: A Study of Doctrinal Change and Continuity* (London: Sheed & Ward, 1973), 71-72, 168-82.

[25] Theodore W. Jennings, "On Ritual Knowledge," in *Readings in Ritual Studies,* ed. Ronald L. Grimes (Upper Saddle River, N.J.: Prentice-Hall, 1996), 327.

activity that affects us in profound ways and then we try to "cerebrally 're-cognize'" the action. A key claim of Jennings is that ritual knowledge is not that knowledge that comes by observing a ritual: "Ritual knowledge is gained not through detachment but through engagement—an engagement which does not leave things as they are but which alters and transforms them."[26] The existence of not only cognitive but ritual knowledge suggests as well that we possess a kind of ritual memory. Although we often think of our memory as residing in our brain, this is true only in a very limited way. Our most profound memories are visceral; they are filled with affect and emotion that elude rational analysis.

For example, I was once trapped by some friends in a small tunnel as a child. Since then I have suffered from claustrophobia. Now, rationally, I know I have nothing to fear from a small elevator, for example. But at the bodily level, there is a memory of what occurred decades ago that continues to affect me. It is often these memories that are the strongest and most influential.

This does not mean that rituals cannot be interpreted in either an analytical or narrative form, it simply means that rituals cannot be reduced to a particular meaning or meanings. Narrative accounts of the "meaning" of a ritual must never be confused with the ritual itself and the knowledge or memory embedded in it.

David Power contends that the embodied character of ritual can be understood in two senses.[27] We have already spoken of a ritual's impact on an individual body. But in an analogous way the church is itself a social "body," so reflection on the ways in which ritual is embodied leads us to consider the impact of ritual not only on the individual but on the whole Christian community. Within the community, ritual action produces a corporate body memory. The vital liturgical life of the Christian community preserves a communal memory more powerful than any mere transmission of propositional beliefs. As the liturgy of the church is celebrated from generation to generation, the ritual knowledge gained by the corporate performance of the ritual funds the community's memory.

This reflection on ritual knowledge and ritual memory helps us flesh out the meaning of what Burkhard referred to as substantive apostolicity, or an apostolicity of life. It suggests that if the church's apostolicity is preserved in its communal memory, then the liturgical life of the church plays as vital a role in sustaining the substantive apostolicity of the church as in the transmission of apostolic doctrine.

---

[26] Ibid.
[27] David N. Power, *Sacrament: The Language of God's Giving* (New York: Herder & Herder, 1999), 124-31.

Two of the most essential Christian rituals, baptism and eucharist, have played a particularly influential role in the sustenance of Christian memory because these communal ritual actions have, over the centuries, in their diverse ecclesial forms, transmitted vital elements of the Christian memory in the very actions of bathing and feasting. We can, of course, speak of doctrinal insights reflected in these rituals, insights regarding the nature of salvation, initiation into Christian community, spiritual nourishment, sacramental presence, etc. But these doctrinal articulations cannot replace the more primal communal memory embedded in the actual performance of these rituals. The apostolicity of the church is not found only in second-order statements about these rituals, the belief of which can be traced back to the early church. The apostolicity of the church is embedded and preserved in the communal performance of these actions as a unique and untranslatable form of ritual memory. The distinctive identity of the early Christian community was sustained in large part by shared ritual "practices" that linked them with the apostolic source of the Christian *kērygma*, not because any given ritual could be traced back to the apostles, but because these rituals engaged the believer and the believing community in a process of transformation that united them with the very life and mission of Jesus proclaimed by the apostles.

We should not overlook one final feature of the place of ritual in sustaining the apostolic memory of the church. For the first two to three centuries of the church these central rituals were celebrated from community to community without ever following a standard form. Each ritual was shaped by the community that practiced it. Some churches baptized by submersion, in which the candidate was completely submerged in a font, others by immersion in which they knelt in a shallow pool and had water poured over them.[28] Baptism in the churches of Syria was quite different from baptism in Rome or North Africa. The shape of the Christian eucharist in Milan was quite distinct from that being practiced in Alexandria. The particularities of language, local aesthetic sensibilities, philosophical and theological frameworks, distinct liturgical traditions— all shaped the practice of these rituals. Contemporary liturgical scholarship now demonstrates clearly the significant diversity in liturgical practice that existed in the first centuries of Christianity.[29] And yet Christians who traveled from their home church to visit a community in another region were generally able to affirm, often amid significant ritual diversity, a common memory, a shared identity. In doing so, they were implicitly affirming the "apostolicity" of their churches.

---

[28] For a consideration of the diversity of ritual practices in the early church, see S. Anita Stauffer, *On Baptismal Fonts: Ancient and Modern* (Nottingham: Grove Books, 1994), 9-10.

[29] Paul F. Bradshaw, *The Search for the Origins of Ancient Christian Worship: Sources and Methods for the Study of Early Liturgy*, 2nd ed. (New York: Oxford University Press, 2002).

Communal Memory and the Formation of the Biblical Canon

Christian memory was sustained by the early Christian communities not only through their ritual life but also through their sacred texts. The role of memory in early Christian communities helps explain why tensions between the unity of the churches and their real diversity have always been present. As culturally mediated, these memories were always particular to the specific cultural context in which the gospel was proclaimed. Differences between Eastern Syriac Christianity and that of North Africa were due to the distinctive cultural contexts in which the transformative memories of the Risen One were nourished. Yet as memories that had their spiritual origins in a saving encounter with the Risen One, these unique communal memories shared a common core. Recognizing the commonality in the midst of a dizzying diversity of memories of Jesus happened only gradually, in fits and starts, and not without a high degree of political intrigue. This is evident in the messy historical process by which the biblical canon emerged.

The term "canon" is derived from the Greek word referring to a "reed" or instrument of measure. In its early church usage "canon" referred not to the Bible but to the apostolic memory, a "canon or rule of faith," as it was proclaimed in a living oral tradition. This was the first "measure" of the Christian faith. The development of a written canon developed only later.

Early Jewish Christians embraced the Hebrew Scriptures as their own. But at the time of Jesus, there was as yet no fixed Jewish canon of any kind. Judaism certainly believed in a set of inspired writings, but the idea that these writings needed to be definitively set apart from other literature had not yet developed.[30] The Jewish belief that a sacred biblical canon had long existed and had closed with Ezra emerged only *after* the rise of Christianity. At the time of Jesus, some Jews accepted as sacred those writings authored during the "Second Temple" period (from the fifth century B.C.E. to the first century C.E.) between Ezra and Jesus, and others did not. Christian communities seem to have come to their own judgment based largely on more pragmatic considerations, with the criterion of liturgical usage playing a significant role.

Between 50 and 110 C.E. Paul's letters soon found wide circulation and later generations would emulate his pastoral approach, even to the point of writing under his name, as with the pastoral letters. The four Gospels were likely authored between 65 and 90 C.E. Later citations from early church writers suggest that the four Gospels and many of Paul's letters were used widely among many Christian churches by the end of the second century. A number of com-

---

[30] Albert Sundberg, "The Bible Canon and the Christian Doctrine of Inspiration," *Interpretation* 29 (1975): 352-71.

plex factors came into play in the gradual process of discerning a text's canonicity. Paramount was a concern for apostolicity, that is, the identification of some link between a particular text and an early Christian apostle. In fact, the apostolicity of a text may have been more a matter of legend, but *the claim* to apostolicity remained a significant factor in determining the canonical status of a text.

What is noteworthy, from our point of view, is the way in which the apostolicity of these texts was gradually accepted among the various Christian communities. Initially, many early Christian communities would have treasured their community's particular memory of God's saving work in Christ, perhaps associated with their putative founder and enshrined in a set of oral traditions or written texts that preserved their own communal memory. Some early communities would have had their own set of "canonical" texts, which they would have read during their worship. In the first half of the second century for some communities this might have included perhaps one Gospel, say the Gospel of Luke, and a few epistles by Paul. Perhaps they held in their possession an ancient Gospel text other than one of the four that would be eventually received as canonical (e.g., the *Gospel of Peter*).

The rocky history of the formation of an official biblical canon is the history of both Jewish and early Christian communities discerning the authentic revelation of God within not only the authentic texts of their own community but also within those they received from other communities. Particular Jewish and Christian communities engaged in a process of receiving or not receiving the formative texts of other communities. When a Christian community in Rome received and accepted a text that came from Ephesus, it was because the Roman community was able to identify a commonality underlying the distinctive memory of the Ephesians. This is equally evident in the Old Testament. Quite diverse communal traditions or memories were held together, even when the holding of the two memories revealed a startling dissonance. This is evident when one considers, for example, the very different understandings of divine providence and evil in the Deuteronomistic History, which assumed that all evil that befell individuals reflected God's judgment, and the Book of Job, which boldly asserted the possibility of innocent suffering. The preservation of both traditions in the one canon indicated the remarkable capacity of both the ancient Jewish and Christian communities to hold together two quite distinct memories as each being authentic while remaining in a certain tension with one another.

Thus, the emergence of a shared Christian canon, a process that took virtually four centuries, demonstrates an elemental ecclesial process whereby distinct Christian memories are enshrined in the sacred texts of particular communities. As those communities established relationships with one another, they shared with other communities their own communal memories by way of their own sacred texts. When one community embraced the texts of another they were in effect saying that they could recognize in the communal recollection being offered to them a vital connection with their own memories of the apostolic message.

The messy historical process by which the biblical canon emerged in early Christianity negates any appeals to the origin of a universal, transcultural Christian memory as normative. What the Bible enshrines is the cross-pollination of sets of communal memories, each incarnated in distinct cultural contexts and theological frameworks in which it is only in the dynamic process of handing on and receiving these memories that a common apostolic heritage or tradition emerged.

If our understanding of the apostolicity of the church is to follow the example of the early church's struggles to produce a canon of sacred texts, it must continue to wrestle with the likelihood that even today local churches will preserve quite distinct ecclesial memories that may each be both authentic and irreducible. This respect for the diversity within the church's apostolic memory requires the assertion, discussed earlier, regarding the simultaneity of the local churches and universal church as interpenetrating realities.

The Role of Reception and the Sense of the Faithful in the Transmission of the Apostolic Memory of the Church

As we noted earlier, one of the most important developments in the ecclesiology of Vatican II was its affirmation of the sense of the faith (*sensus fidei*) given by the Spirit to all believers at baptism. This teaching explicitly acknowledged the participation of the whole Christian community in the recognition, preservation, and handing on of the apostolic faith. Since the council, more attention has been given to a related concept, ecclesial reception.[31] The central insight is that the handing on of the faith from community to community and generation to generation presupposes an active reception of that faith. In every act of ecclesial reception, the receiver contributes something to that which is being received. The ongoing process of both handing on and receiving the faith is, in fact, how ecclesial memory is sustained. Indeed, there is a sense in which the process of both "handing on" and "receiving" the faith is constitutive of the church itself. Thomas Rausch remarks that "what resulted from the reception of the apostolic preaching by those who became the converts of the apostles and

---

[31] For a survey of these developments, see Richard R. Gaillardetz, "The Reception of Doctrine: New Perspectives," in *Authority in the Roman Catholic Church*, ed. Bernard Hoose (London: Ashgate, 2002), 95–114. The treatment of ecclesial reception that follows is drawn substantially from this essay.

other early Christian missionaries was the Church itself." [32] We quoted earlier the Venerable Bede's observation that "every day the church gives birth to the church."[33] Commenting on Bede's statement, Joseph Komonchak writes:

> The apostolic Gospel comes with the power of the Spirit and is received by faith, and where this event of communication takes place, the Church is born again. Where this event does not take place, where the Gospel is preached in vain, no Church arises. Where the Gospel ceases to be believed, the Church ceases to exist. The whole ontology of the Church—the real "objective" existence of the Church—consists in the reception by faith of the Gospel. Reception is constitutive of the Church.[34]

This is the nature of human memory, personal and communal. It is both handed on and received in such a way that it becomes a living reality.

When a local church receives a custom or theological tradition from another community, the process of reception guarantees that this custom or tradition will in some meaningful sense be changed in the process. Something of the receiving community now contributes to the dynamic memory of the church. Reception means not mere acceptance but transformation, both of the receiving community and that which is received. Consequently, while reception is always receiving something that has been recognized as familiar, at the same time, it "produces something new."[35] There is an undeniably creative element, an element that involves the unexpected or unforeseen, which makes the event of reception so necessary to the continued vitality of ecclesial memory.

This understanding has been enhanced by recent work being done in the study of popular religion. A number of theologians have challenged academia's tendency to dismiss popular religion as primitive, a product of syncretism and rife with superstition.[36] Rather, they would see popular religion as a "privileged

---

[32] Thomas Rausch, "Reception Past and Present," *Theological Studies* 47 (1986): 498-99.

[33] PL 93:166d.

[34] Joseph Komonchak, "The Epistemology of Reception," *Jurist* 57 (1997): 193.

[35] Bernard Sesboüé, "Reception of Councils from Nicea to Constantinople II: Conceptual Divergences and Unity in the Faith, Yesterday and Today," *Jurist* 57 (1997): 116.

[36] Most of these contributions have been made by Latino theologians. For some indicative texts, see Orlando O. Espín, *The Faith of the People: Theological Reflections on Popular Catholicism* (Maryknoll, N.Y.: Orbis Books, 1997); Roberto Goizueta, *Caminemos con Jesús: Toward a Hispanic/Latino Theology of Accompaniment* (Maryknoll, N.Y.: Orbis Books, 1995); Alex García-Rivera, *St. Martin de Porres: The "Little Stories" and the Semiotics of Culture* (Maryknoll, N.Y.: Orbis Books, 1995); Alan Figueroa Deck, ed., *Frontiers of Hispanic Theology in the United States* (Maryknoll, N.Y.: Orbis Books, 1992). One of the first works by a Latino theologian to offer a positive theological assessment of popular Catholicism was Virgilio Elizondo, *Galilean Journey: The Mexico-American Promise* (Maryknoll, N.Y.: Orbis Books, 1983).

locus of divine revelation."[37] Orlando Espín has emphasized the culturally mediated character of all religious perception, learning, and understanding.[38] Each distinctive culture provides a particular lens for making sense of religious experience. Popular religion offers a privileged perspective on this interpretive process because its constellation of myths, rituals, and devotions are often found much closer to the people's religious experience than are the more sanitized articulations of religious experience found either in formal church doctrine or academic theology. Too often, Espín contends, we have thought of tradition, or what we have been calling the apostolic memory of the church, as sustained exclusively by way of the decrees of ecumenical councils and papal statements. While this view cannot be ignored, it must be augmented by an appreciation for the way in which the church's ecclesial memory is sustained and nurtured in "the living witness and faith of the Christian people."[39] For this to happen, that memory will inevitably be incarnated in quite particular narratives, rituals, and symbols. So conceived, the narratives, rituals, and symbols of popular religion can be seen as bearers of the dynamic memory of the church just as much as a conciliar decree.

Let us consider one example from Espín's own work. In his book *The Faith of the People,* he considers the popularity of graphic, bloody portraits of the crucified Jesus in Latino spirituality. Although these representations are often dismissed as one-sided, pious christological distortions, Espín makes a persuasive case that these artistic portraits in fact offer us a rich theology of the vanquished Christ perceived by a people who have themselves experienced vanquishment.[40]

> The Christ of Latino passion symbolism is a tortured, suffering human being. The images leave no room for doubt. This dying Jesus, however, is so special because he is not just one more human who suffers unfairly at the hands of evil men. He is the divine Christ, and that makes his innocent suffering all the more dramatic. . . . In his passion and death he has come to be in solidarity with all those throughout history who have also innocently suffered at the hands of evildoers. In other words, it seems that Latino faith intuitively sensed the true humanness of Jesus, like ours in all things except sinful guilt.[41]

---

[37] Roberto Goizueta, "Foreword," in Espín, *Faith of the People,* xi.

[38] Espín, *Faith of the People,* 17. Espín, in turn, has been influenced by theories concerning the social construction of reality developed, in quite different ways, by Peter Berger and Antonio Gramsci. For further developments in Espín's thought on this topic, see "Traditioning: Culture, Daily Life and Popular Religion, and Their Impact on Christian Tradition," in *Futuring Our Past: Explorations in the Theology of Tradition,* ed. Orlando O. Espín and Gary Macy (Maryknoll, N.Y.: Orbis Books, 2006), 1-22.

[39] Espín, *Faith of the People,* 65.

[40] Ibid., 23.

[41] Ibid., 72.

These artistic portraits are examples of a creative cultural manifestation and reception of the apostolic memory of the church in a particular cultural context that seeks to render that memory meaningful to a vanquished people.

Espín's approach to popular religion is particularly helpful because it foregrounds the way in which the living and always inculturated memory of the church both precedes and follows doctrinal expression. Popular images of the crucified Christ are obviously examples of a cultural reception of christological doctrine at a particular historical juncture for a particular people. On the other hand, we might just as easily consider Marian devotion in popular religion to be a historical instance where the popular religious practices in fact preceded the articulation of doctrine (e.g., the Marian dogmas of the Immaculate Conception and Assumption of Mary). This constitutes a challenge to the unidirectional view that it is the faithful who receive from the official teachers of the church. Often it is also the case that the official teachers, in the process of formally articulating church doctrine, have first received that which they teach from the living and inculturated memory of the people.

Apostolicity as Eschatological Memory

In the Western church, both Catholic and Protestant, apostolicity has been concerned primarily with a form of historical memory, both a normative continuity with the past and a recalling into the present the power of the past. This historical view of apostolicity privileges the conviction that the church stands in historical continuity with its apostolic origins. The apostles represent the first authoritative witnesses to the Christian gospel. Yet in the Eastern Christian tradition, apostolicity combines this historical dimension, the affirmation of the origins of the church in the apostolic mission, with an eschatological perspective.

John Zizioulas, one of Eastern Orthodoxy's most distinguished theologians, contends that the historical view of the church's apostolicity looks to the apostles as individuals sent in mission by Christ to spread the gospel. "In an approach inspired by the idea of mission, the apostles represent a *link* between Christ and the Church and form part of a historical process with a decisive and perhaps *normative* role to play." [42] Yet the East also looks to the apostles as eschatological symbol. Here they are not viewed as individuals sent in mission but as a college. "The difference," Zizioulas writes, "is considerable and corresponds to that between mission and eschatology. Mission requires *send-*

---

[42] John Zizioulas, *Being as Communion: Studies in Personhood and the Church* (Crestwood, N.Y.: St. Vladimir's Seminary Press, 1985), 173 (emphasis in original).

ing to the ends of the earth, whereas the eschata imply the convocation of the dispersed people of God from the ends of the earth to one place."[43] When viewed as a college, as "the Twelve," the apostles no longer serve as a link between Christ and the church; rather they surround Christ in the eschaton. Much as the Twelve functioned in the Gospel of Luke and Acts as symbols of the reconstitution of the twelve tribes of Israel, so the Twelve serve as the realization of God's kingdom in the eschaton, the full gathering or convocation of God's people. Apostolicity thereby affirms the church's future manifested in the present. Here too there is an exercise of memory, but an eschatological one, the church remembers its future. The church, as apostolic, becomes a sign of the eschatological future of humanity.

How are these two perspectives on apostolicity to be brought together? Zizioulas writes: "There is, indeed, no other experience in the Church's life in which the synthesis of the historical and the eschatological can be realized more fully than in the eucharist."[44] There Christians remember their apostolic origins and there they experience the sacramental manifestation of their future. Yet this does not represent a spiritual escape from the world and human history. Russian Orthodox theologian Alexander Schmemann has insisted that the liturgy "is not an escape from the world, rather it is the arrival at a vantage point from which we can see more deeply into the reality of the world."[45] The result is a holding together of history and eschatology through the eucharist, which functions as a kind of sacramental hinge.

One limitation of this otherwise fruitful eschatological perspective is that the eschatology presupposed here is a sacramentally realized eschatology, that is, an eschatology that sees the eucharist manifesting our eschatological future in the present celebration of the eucharist. But this configuration of history to eschatology overlooks the insights of a more apocalyptic eschatology, one that sees eschatology serving as a challenge to history, a caesura that interrupts the customary way of viewing history and demands nothing less than historical transformation. Such a perspective would share a commitment to an eschatological view of apostolic memory but in a quite different key.

The Dangerous Memories of Jesus

If the Eastern tradition has highlighted the eschatological dimensions of apostolicity, the church's graced "remembering" of its eschatological future, politi-

---

[43] Ibid., 174.

[44] Ibid., 187.

[45] Alexander Schmemann, *For the Life of the World: Sacraments and Orthodoxy* (Crestwood, N.Y.: St. Vladimir's Seminary Press, 1973), 27.

cal theologians like Johann Baptist Metz have developed in a powerful way the political implications of this eschatological memory.[46] For Metz the substance of the gospel lies in the dangerous memories of Jesus, the *memoria passionis, mortis, et resurrectionis Jesu Christi.* This memory of Jesus is "dangerous" because it means remembering what Jesus preached about the kingdom of God; it means remembering Jesus' radical solidarity with the dispossessed, which led him to the cross. It means remembering God's vindication of Jesus in the resurrection. But it also means remembering a future consummation of the kingdom, which promises liberation to the oppressed of this world.[47] To remember this liberating future is to experience an interruption of the status quo, which, according to Metz, is the sense for many middle-class Christians of time simply moving on without any culmination. In this sense, Metz wishes to recover not so much a realized eschatology that simply speaks of God's presence in the world today, but an apocalyptic eschatology that sees the future as "interruption,"[48] shocking Christians into political action:

> What is meant here is . . . not the memory that sees the past in a transfiguring light, nor the memory that sets a seal on the past by being reconciled with all that is dangerous and challenging in that past. It is also not the memory in which past happiness and salvation are applied merely individually. What is meant in this context is that dangerous memory that threatens the present and calls it into question because it remembers a future that is still outstanding.[49]

Metz will speak of an anticipatory memory that makes demands on us and calls forth "a new moral imagination."[50] The dangerous memories of Christ make possible a new vision of our world; they allow us to imagine the promise of God's coming reign and to live into that promise through lives of discipleship intent on the radical imitation of Christ.

Striking in Metz's early writing is his failure to connect the power of the dangerous memories of Christ with the celebration of the liturgy.[51] He corrects this somewhat later, in an essay entitled "The Church after Auschwitz," in

---

[46] For an insightful study of the ways in which Schmemann and Metz can be brought into theological conversation through their respective uses of the category of memory, see Morrill.

[47] Johann Baptist Metz, *Faith in History and Society: Towards a Practical Fundamental Theology* (New York: Crossroad, 1980), 88-93.

[48] See Lieven Boeve, *Interrupting Tradition: An Essay on Christian Faith in a Postmodern Context* (Leuven: Peeters, 2004).

[49] Metz, *Faith in History and Society,* 200.

[50] Ibid., 117.

[51] Morrill, 67-68.

which he notes the tragic consequences of European Christianity having lost contact with its Jewish origins and the distinctively Jewish commitment to the power of memory. It is in this context that he notes the ritual origins of a biblical sense of memory:

> Yet it is true also for the faith of Christians that it not only *has* a remembrance, but *is* a remembrance: the memory of the suffering, the death and resurrection of Jesus Christ. We Christians have certainly preserved this remembrance-structure of our faith in our cult ("Do this in remembrance of me."). But have we cultivated it enough also in the public sphere?[52]

Here, then, Metz challenges the disconnect between a ritual memory and a public memory capable of calling a community to transformation.

Metz's exploration of the connection between memory and eschatology has also been employed in liberation theologies born out of awareness of the systemic socioeconomic injustice that has been so widespread in Latin America. In these contexts of socioeconomic and political oppression, the people have directly borne the dangerous memories of Christ. These memories were sustained and cultivated through their careful reading of Scripture and lives of communal prayer in basic Christian communities in which they learned to apply their communal memory to the social context in which they live. The result has been a process referred to as *conscientization,* the raising of the consciousness of Christians regarding their concrete human situation, a situation characterized by oppression and, more importantly, a situation opposed by God. Consequently, liberation theology in its many forms is committed to the conviction that the dangerous memories of the Christian faith demanded, as Gustavo Gutiérrez put it, both *denunciation* and *annunciation.* The liberative memory of Christ, the core of the church's apostolic heritage, is a memory that must *denounce* "every dehumanizing situation, which is contrary to brotherhood, justice and liberty."[53] This denunciation can never be separated, however, from the Christian work of *announcing* "the love of the Father which calls all [people] in Christ and through the action of the Spirit to union among themselves and communion with him."[54]

Although critics of political and liberation theologies legitimately warn of a *reduction* of God's saving Word to the realm of socioeconomic and political realities, we cannot ignore the concrete political implications of the communal memory of the life and deeds of Jesus. To immerse oneself in the life of the

---

[52] Johann Baptist Metz, "The Church after Auschwitz," in idem, *A Passion for God: The Mystical-Political Dimension of Christianity* (New York: Paulist Press, 1998), 131.

[53] Gustavo Gutierrez, *A Theology of Liberation* (Maryknoll, N.Y.: Orbis Books, 1973), 267.

[54] Ibid., 268.

church is to allow oneself to be shaped by this ecclesial memory. The identity a Christian assumes as a follower of Jesus will always have a countercultural element, a sense of worldly disorientation. In some ways it is this experience of disorientation in the world, a realization that all is not as it should be, that confirms that an ecclesial memory does preserve an authentic, alternative way of existence. This alternative way, remembered within the community, places demands on our present; it challenges the various projects that occupy our time and asks us to evaluate them in the light of the gospel.

DOGMA AND DOCTRINE IN A NEW KEY

In addition to Metz's frequent appeal to the dangerous memories of Jesus found in the Scriptures, and his later allusion to ritual memory, he also finds a place for dogma in the mediation of the church's memory. In a provocative, if underdeveloped, excursus entitled "Dogma as a Dangerous Memory," Metz does indeed write of the necessity of ecclesial memory being mediated through dogmatic statements. Dogmatic statements possess the potential to function as interruption, as a way of jolting us out of our bourgeois existence. Metz writes that "dogmas prevent me from letting my own religious experience operate simply as the function of a prevailing consciousness."[55] Doctrine's danger, however, lies in the tendency of its normative formulations to become domesticated, purged of all that might trouble us and call us to a new mode of Christian existence.

Liberation theologians have privileged the role of transformative memory over dogma in their reflections on the church's apostolicity. They have been led to do so largely because of the past (and present?) tendency of many to reduce the church's dangerous memories to what Juan Luis Segundo has described as a "digital genre." Early Christian thought presented revelation as a divine pedagogy aimed at the transformation of humankind. A "digital" presentation, however, purges dogma of its imaginative and transformative character and renders it strictly informational.[56] Segundo contends that

> revelation presupposes . . . the constitution of a people that will *hand on* a wisdom from generation to generation. Through things ever imperfect and transitory, handed down by the very existence of the community, that "people" becomes "tradition." This means that memory and collective pedagogy have a decisive function in the very process of revelation: thanks to these,

---

[55] Metz, *Faith in History and Society*, 202.

[56] Juan Luis Segundo, *The Liberation of Dogma: Faith, Revelation and Dogmatic Teaching Authority* (Maryknoll, N.Y.: Orbis Books, 1992), 108.

each new generation is exempt from starting its . . . learning "from scratch." Through a process of remembering and readopting, in a vital fashion peculiar to its own identity, the past experiences of another process in which the search, solutions, and challenges of history converge, each generation is thrust toward a more perfect maturity, and toward a new, deeper, and richer truth.[57]

Segundo and Metz offer a provocative opening for a fresh consideration of dogma and doctrine in the Christian tradition.

Segundo's concerns about dogma interpreted within a "digital genre" fits well with what has been said earlier regarding the propositional model of revelation. In this digital mode, there is a danger of identifying divine revelation with propositional statements or doctrines, and thereby reducing God to some body of knowledge available for our cognitive mastery.[58] The German theologian Magnus Löhrer identifies a basic tension between divine revelation in its primary mediation as *kērygma,* the proclamation of the saving gospel of Jesus Christ, and its secondary mediation as *dogma.* Löhrer contends that *dogma* exists solely to mediate *kērygma.*[59] When the dogmatic obscures the kerygmatic, the result is a dogmatism that tracks along the same path as evangelical Christian fundamentalism; it traffics in easy certitudes and a preoccupation with determining who is inside the circle of orthodoxy and who is not. However, when the kerygmatic dimension of revelation is kept in the foreground, the richness of the church's pluriform communal memory is preserved. The priority of the kerygmatic dimension of divine revelation helps us situate church dogma as symbolic mediations of a divine promise and reality that it can communicate but never exhaust. The kerygmatic priority of divine revelation also reminds us that at the heart of revelation is the central Christian mystery—God's offer of salvation. According to the patristic and medieval tradition, only those doctrinal teachings which directly mediated God's saving offer, regardless of the formal authority by which they had been proposed, could truly qualify as articles of faith, what we now call dogma.[60] Indeed, the church's earliest creedal statements functioned in quite different ways.

---

[57] Ibid., 246.

[58] A point made by then theologian Joseph Ratzinger, in his commentary on *Dei Verbum,* "The Dogmatic Constitution on Divine Revelation," in *Commentary on the Documents of Vatican II,* ed. Herbert Vorgrimler (New York: Crossroad, 1989), 3:190-91.

[59] Magnus Löhrer, "Träger der Vermittlung," in *Mysterium Salutis,* ed. Johannes Feiner and Magnus Löhrer (Einsiedeln: Benziger, 1965), 1:545-87, esp. 545-55. See also Walter Kasper, "The Relationship between Gospel and Dogma: An Historical Approach," *Man as Man & Believer,* ed. Edward Schillebeeckx and Boniface Willems, *Concilium* 21 (New York: Paulist Press, 1967), 153-67.

[60] See Richard R. Gaillardetz, *Teaching with Authority: A Theology of the Magisterium in the Church* (Collegeville, Minn.: Liturgical Press, 1997), esp. chap. 3.

The Functions of Creedal Statements in Early Christianity

The earliest creedal statements were brief confessional formulas like that referred to in 1 Corinthians 12:3, "Jesus is lord!" or that of the Ethiopian eunuch in Acts: "I believe that Jesus Christ is the Son of God" (Acts 8:37).[61] In the early postbiblical period these brief creedal statements developed further, often taking on an interrogatory form that reflected their predominantly confessional character.[62] This early interrogatory form suggests that these were formulations intended to elicit a response of faith. Consequently, the language of these creedal statements was more "performative" in nature. That is, the utterance of such an "I believe" was not primarily an affirmation of some objective state of affairs. Rather, the profession itself brought the one making the profession into a particular relationship with God.

Early creedal statements also functioned doxologically. The trinitarian structure that dominated virtually all of the early creeds suggests that this profession of faith was also an act of worship, an offering of praise and thanksgiving to the one who has brought about our salvation in Christ by the power of the Spirit. The profession of the creed served to give both narrative and propositional "shape" to the offering of praise by recapitulating the substance of baptismal faith.

One important transition in the history of creeds involved the gradual shift from the interrogatory form to the declarative form. By the fourth century the latter form had become dominant. This shift reflected the growing use of creeds as catechetical tools, concise summaries of the Christian faith. The role of creeds in the actual celebration of the sacrament of initiation led to their use in the catechetical preparation for this sacrament. This catechetical usage is reflected in one of the names given to early Christian creeds, *symbolum,* the "symbol" or summary of the Christian faith. To study the creed was to study the meaning of Christian discipleship, the nature of the identity one would assume through initiation into the church. The catechetical use of creeds drew on the narrative structure that was particularly evident in the earlier creeds.

As we have already seen, early in the history of Christianity, certainly by the mid-second century, there was a widespread recognition of the need to "regulate" the faith. This "regulation" of the faith entailed the practice of marking off

---

[61] This confession, however, is not found in the earliest manuscripts of Acts. For a consideration of creedal formulas in the New Testament, see James D. G. Dunn, *Unity and Diversity in the New Testament: An Inquiry into the Character of Earliest Christianity,* 2nd ed. (Philadelphia: Trinity Press International, 1990), 33-59.

[62] The classic study is that of the Lutheran ecumenical theologian Edmund Schlink, "Die Struktur der dogmatischen Aussage als ökumenisches Problem," *Kerygma und Dogma* 3 (1957): 251-306.

authentic articulations of the received apostolic faith from those viewed as coun-
terfeit. By the fourth century, in the midst of serious christological and trinitarian controversies, creedal statements came to "norm" Christian faith in a
particular way by marking off authentic or "orthodox" belief from those articulations of the apostolic faith that were viewed by the Christian communities,
for various reasons, as distortions. Walter Kasper has remarked on the significance of this development:

> The development from confession to doctrinal formulation started at an
> early date. Unlike the Nicene-Constantinopolitan Creed, that of Chalcedon
> was not incorporated in the liturgy. The dogma then became the correct
> interpretation of the confession which was taken for granted. It is no longer
> a matter of opposing faith to unbelief but rather of orthodoxy to hetero-
> doxy, and it now sought to build up the confession of faith. Thus the dogma
> became the rule of faith (*regula fidei, regula veritatis, canon veritatis*).[63]

Consequently, the focus of later dogmas or creedal statements was less on their
confessional, liturgical, or catechetical appropriateness than on the kind of conceptual clarity essential for a statement to serve as a norm for all present and
future expressions of the apostolic faith. Only this kind of clarity could help in
the determination of "orthodoxy," or "right belief." The wording of the creeds
themselves drew less on biblical and liturgical sources in favor of a growing
lexicon of abstract and speculative terminology employed so as to differentiate
the orthodox understanding of the faith from the often subtle shades of
heterodoxy.

The need for formal regulation in church belief is difficult to dispute. At
the same time, one can lament the way in which this regulative function came
to eclipse other uses of church dogma. The ascendancy of this digital, or propositional approach to revelation obscured the ways in which doctrinal statements
were originally understood as symbolic expressions of both God's saving offer
and the altogether demanding claims of Christian discipleship.

Finding Our Way between "Consumer Catholicism" and "Creeping Infallibility"

Today we are seeing a resurgence of this propositional or digital view of revelation. This is in large part the consequence of the church's attempt to respond
to one of the most characteristic features of the postmodern moment, namely,

---

[63] Kasper, 158.

the experience of the fragmentation of religious identity. Suffice it to say that for many cultural commentators, one of the decisive characteristics of post-modernity is the struggle that many experience trying to maintain a coherent identity in the face of a disorienting pluralism encountered at the level of ideology, religion, and culture. Identity is no longer experienced as something that is largely inherited; rather identity is experienced as something to be constructed. This situation is exacerbated by a consumer culture in which the modern person is schooled from the earliest age to view all significant choices as consumer choices. Not surprisingly, in the area of religion, a consumer culture disposes persons to pick and choose from various cultural and religious artifacts, customs, and beliefs, cobbling them together in an attempt to construct a personal religious identity. The result, too often, is a rather superficial and relatively rootless sense of religious belonging.

It is a commonplace, and not only in the church of the North, for church leaders to complain about a form of "consumer Catholicism" popular with many young people. At the same time, we have witnessed in North America not the secularization of society so long predicted by sociologists but rather the continued flourishing of religion in a uniquely "deregulated" form.[64] Deregulated religion is religion in which the resources of the religious tradition remain, but they are drawn upon ad hoc, according to one's needs and independent of the demands of church authorities. In this context, it is understandable that many church leaders would wish to reassert the authority of church doctrine as a response to this consumerist and deregulated approach to religious identity.[65] This vigorous reassertion of church doctrine, unfortunately, often leads to the opposite extreme, a form of "creeping infallibility" that succumbs to a naïve, ahistorical, and—as both Metz and Segundo warned—dangerously domesticated view of dogma and doctrine. The avoidance of these two extremes requires that we keep the following principles in mind:

1. *Church dogma symbolically mediates divine revelation but does not exhaust it.* In its contemporary usage in Roman Catholicism, the term *dogma* refers to any propositional formulation that is (a) divinely revealed and (b) proposed as such by the magisterium, either through a solemn definition of a pope or council, or by the teaching of the college of bishops in their ordinary and universal magisterium.[66] It is because Catholics believe dogma to be divinely revealed that we

---

[64] David Lyon, *Jesus in Disneyland: Religion in Postmodern Times* (Malden, Mass.: Blackwell, 2000), 34.

[65] For a probing analysis of the relationship between consumerism and religion, see Vincent J. Miller, *Consuming Religion: Christian Faith and Practice in a Consumer Culture* (New York: Continuum, 2003).

[66] See Gaillardetz, *By What Authority? A Primer on Scripture, the Magisterium and the Sense of the Faithful* (Collegeville, Minn.: Liturgical Press, 2003), chap. 6.

speak of it as taught infallibly and believe it to be essentially irreversible teaching. However, as we noted above, the danger with dogma lies in the assumption that it communicates divine information. The best antidote to this view is to consider divine revelation from the perspective of symbolic mediation.[67]

Revelation is not just a subjective experience; revelation does possess some genuine objective content, as the propositional approach rightly affirms. But here lies the difficulty. God is infinite, incomprehensible mystery, and we are finite creatures. Consequently, God's communication of God's self to us cannot be like my communicating a bus schedule to a friend. Surely as limited creatures we cannot receive God as God is. God cannot be known and mastered the way a beginning chemistry student might strive to master the periodic table. If God really wishes to communicate with us, God must communicate God's self to us in a manner appropriate to our status as finite, embodied creatures. This is reflected in a medieval dictum, "that which is received is received according to the mode of the receiver" (*quidquid recipitur, recipitur ad modum recipientis*). God comes to us in a manner appropriate to our natures as finite, embodied creatures. And as embodied creatures, the primary way in which we come to know our world is through symbols. We learn through language, concepts, images, and metaphors.

Sometimes these revelatory symbols are linguistic, as with historical narratives, parables, hymns, and dogmatic statements. Sometimes they take the form of distinctive Christian practices, as with the liturgical life of the church. One might also regard art and architecture as revelatory symbols. The Christian community returns time and again to these symbols because it realizes that these symbols continue to have the power to draw us into relationship *with* God even as they offer us new insight, new meanings *about* God. Dogma stands within the larger category of revelatory symbols. Dogmatic statements do communicate, however imperfectly, something of God's saving promise to us. To say that such dogmatic statements are truthful cannot mean, however, that they exhaust the holy mystery of God nor even that they are themselves immune to reformulation. The claim that dogmas have been taught infallibly means, fundamentally that we can trust that such pronouncements will not lead us away from the path of salvation; it does not preclude our finding better ways to communicate their abiding truth.

2. *All dogmatic statements are historically conditioned and have to be interpreted as such.* Dogmatic statements must not be abused by treating them as independent and self-evident statements of divine truth. They emerged in quite

---

[67] For a fuller development of this understanding of revelation, see Avery Dulles, *Models of Revelation* (Garden City, N.Y.: Doubleday, 1983), 131-54.

distinct historical circumstances to respond to specific issues facing the church. The intelligibility of any dogmatic statement is inseparable from an understanding of the context in which it emerged. Nicholas Lash writes:

> In other words, any creedal formula is "particular," not only in the sense that it was produced in one cultural and linguistic context rather than in another, but also in the sense that it always more or less deliberately represented a *reaction* by the church against theological tendencies which were felt to threaten the apostolic faith. There is an element of reactive interpretation in any creed.[68]

The implications of the historical particularity of dogmatic statements was affirmed in the CDF's 1973 declaration "In Defense of Catholic Doctrine," a response to some of the positions of the Swiss theologian Hans Küng.

> [W]hen the Church makes new pronouncements she intends to confirm or clarify what is in some way contained in Sacred Scripture or in previous expressions of Tradition; but at the same time she usually has the intention of solving certain questions or removing certain errors. All these things have to be taken into account in order that these pronouncements may be properly interpreted.[69]

The history of Christian dogma tells us that the origin of most dogmatic statements can be found in controversies that demanded a formal and normative articulation in order to resolve the dispute. This means that if these doctrinal formulations are to continue to have value and fulfill their regulative function, they must be interpreted in the context of the historical crises and issues of the time. This kind of interpretive analysis may also involve a frank recognition of the many contemporary issues that a dogmatic statement was never intended to address.

Even when functioning regulatively, a dogmatic formulation does not offer the *only* legitimate interpretation or understanding of the communal memory of the church. Indeed, the philosophical precision with which most dogmatic statements are formulated suggests that these formulations will generally not employ the language that would be more common to everyday Christian catechesis. Again we must recall that dogma is not the primary mode in which we

---

[68] Lash, 50.

[69] CDF, "In Defense of Catholic Doctrine" [*Mysterium Ecclesiae*], *Origins* 3 (July 19, 1973) 110-11. This point is affirmed in a more sophisticated fashion in the International Theological Commission's "On the Interpretation of Dogmas."

encounter divine revelation and preserve the church's apostolic memory. Dogmas are propositional statements that must always be interpreted within the framework of a much richer and more diverse Christian memory.

It is certainly true that if the orthodoxy of some alternative theological formulation is called into question, the burden of proof lies with the proponents of the alternative formulation to demonstrate the congruity of their formulation with that expressed in the dogmatic statement. In this sense a dogmatic statement can serve as a kind of normative benchmark or reference point for further theological interpretation. The recognition of this congruity is no easy task, and it would be a mistake to assume that this determination falls upon the magisterium alone. The magisterium of the church, that is, the bishops in communion with the bishop of Rome, is certainly empowered to make binding judgments on these matters. However, the recognition that a new theological formulation is congruent with a formal doctrinal statement will generally also require protracted study by the theological community and discernment of the ways such an alternative formulation "cashes out" in the life of worship and the Christian behaviors that it engenders.

3. *Among church dogmas there exists a "hierarchy of truths."* The Second Vatican Council recognized a certain ordering of church dogma in its teaching on the "hierarchy of truths." In its Decree on Ecumenism, *Unitatis Redintegratio,* the council offered guidelines for how Catholic theologians ought to conduct themselves in formal ecumenical dialogue with other non-Catholic Christians. It then offered this counsel:

> When comparing doctrines with one another, they should remember that in catholic doctrine there exists an order or "hierarchy" of truths, since they vary in their relation to the foundation of the christian faith. (UR 11)

The conciliar text insists that church dogmas must be understood and interpreted in the light of their relationship to the foundation of Christian faith. This "foundation" refers to the entire economy of salvation—what God has done for us in Christ by the power of the Spirit. The council taught that church dogmas have differing relations or links to this foundation. This interpretation is confirmed by the 1973 CDF declaration "In Defense of Catholic Doctrine," article 4, which affirms that some dogmas or "truths" lean on more principal "truths" and are illumined by them. It is also true that some dogmatic pronouncements addressed questions that were quite important during one period of church history, but have diminished in their importance today. This insight can be helpful for catechists who are sometimes tempted to treat every dogmatic teaching as equally weighty. Any catechist who begins an introductory presentation on the Catholic faith with a consideration of church teaching on purgatory or the immaculate conception of Mary rather than with God's saving promise offered to us in Christ by the power of the Spirit has fundamentally misunderstood the council's teaching on the hierarchy of truths!

4. *There is a gradation in the authority of church teaching.* Up to now we have been considering the role of church dogma, those central creedal statements that symbolically mediate God's saving offer. Examples of church dogma would include the belief in the divinity of Christ, the law of love, the resurrection of the body, and the affirmation of the real presence of Christ in the eucharist. It is possible for faithful Catholics to fail to attend to certain dogmas, particularly those that emerged out of relatively technical historical disputes with little to offer believers today. However, in general the church's central dogmatic pronouncements, particularly those professed in the creed at Mass each Sunday, are considered central to the faith of the church and the obstinate and sustained repudiation of any of these teachings risks placing the person outside the community of faith (though not necessarily outside the sphere of God's saving action!).

Over time the church has developed a set of basic distinctions regarding the authority of church teaching. In addition to *dogmatic statements*, we might speak of *definitive doctrine, authoritative doctrine,* and *concrete moral applications and church discipline.*

Definitive doctrine, at least in its explicit formulation, is a relatively recent category of church teaching. Definitive doctrine includes teachings that are not divinely revealed but are necessary to safeguard and expound revelation (e.g., the Council of Trent's declaration of the books to be included in the canon of the Bible). It is commonly thought (though it has never been formally defined as such) that because of the vital role these teachings play in protecting divine revelation, they, along with church dogma, are also taught infallibly. Serious questions remain regarding the scope of this category of church teaching. I have defined it restrictively as those teachings *necessary* to safeguard and expound divine revelation. Magisterial documents are inconsistent on this score, in some places accepting this more restrictive interpretation and in others offering a more expansive one that would include all teachings related to divine revelation "by historical or logical necessity."[70] Finally, we must be concerned about the danger of such an ill-defined category being used as a way of artificially elevating the authoritative status of a church teaching as a means of suppressing theological dissent.

---

[70] For a more in-depth consideration of this issue, see Richard R. Gaillardetz, *"Ad tuendam fidem:* An Emerging Pattern in Current Papal Teaching," *New Theology Review* 12 (February 1999): 43-51; idem, "The Ordinary Universal Magisterium: Unresolved Questions," *Theological Studies* 63 (September 2002): 447-71.

I find no evidence in tradition that the denial of definitive doctrine has ever been viewed as heresy in the modern sense of the word (the obstinate repudiation of dogmatic teaching). Consequently, disagreement with a definitive doctrine would not seem to demand the same consequences as the denial of a dogma of the church. Provided that one's disagreement with a definitive doctrine is well informed and in keeping with a firm desire to be united with the faith of the church, the withholding of an internal assent from such a teaching, although potentially a serious error, would not place one outside the Roman Catholic communion.

The third category of church teaching is often referred to as *authoritative doctrine*. This category includes teachings that the magisterium proposes authoritatively, but not infallibly, to guide the faith of believers. This third category of church teaching is drawn from communal reflection on Scripture and tradition. Included among authoritative doctrine are many specific moral teachings such as the church's teaching on the conditions that must be met for a war to be considered "just" or the prohibition of artificial birth control. Yet even as these teachings are proposed authoritatively, the church's teaching office is not ready to commit itself irrevocably to them as divinely revealed. Practically speaking, this means that, however remote, there is a possibility of error with respect to such teachings.

What is the appropriate response of believers to these teachings? Put simply, one must make a genuine effort to incorporate the given teaching into one's personal religious convictions. In so doing, the believer is attempting to give an "internal assent" to the teaching. Generally, we do this readily and without difficulty. Most Catholic Christians assent to the teachings of the church, even where infallibility is not invoked. But occasionally, well-meaning Catholics find that they cannot give assent to an authoritative doctrine of the church. In those instances it seems only appropriate that one give a good-faith effort to come to a fuller understanding of the official teaching and assess honestly one's motives in struggling with the teaching (is it a genuine inability to see this teaching as consonant with one's experience of God's love or is it a fear of the demand for conversion?). After having done so and having still not arrived at a place where one can internally assent to that teaching, one would remain in full communion with the church and may indeed be an instrument of the Spirit in calling for further discernment of the church on the matter in question.

Finally, we might mention a fourth category of church teaching, *concrete moral applications and church discipline*. This includes specific applications of church doctrine that church leadership might make to a particular situation. For example, if the church's position on the criteria for engaging in a just war is authoritative doctrine, an individual bishop's judgment (including the bishop of Rome) that those criteria have or have not been fulfilled is a concrete application of church teaching that requires a prudential judgment and is not binding on ordinary believers. Similarly, we might include church law (e.g., the laws of fasting and abstinence or liturgical law) in this fourth category. It is worth remembering that church law exists to maintain church order, assist individual members in the call to discipleship, and further the mission of the church. When the application of the law in a given instance does not demonstrably further these goals, it may yield to alternative actions that do further these goals.

These gradations in the authority of church doctrine play an important role in the life of the church. They remind us of the church's pilgrim status. As a pilgrim community on a journey we are confident that we are not wandering blindly; we cling to the most central dogmatic affirmations of our faith, believing that they have emerged in the life of the church through the assistance of the Holy Spirit. At the same time, although we find guidance in the authoritative doctrine, concrete moral applications, and church discipline offered by church leaders, we recognize that these do not possess the same level of authority and require the careful discernment of the people of God.

Above all, we must remember the admonition of Segundo against reducing our doctrinal tradition to a digital mode that robs it of its vital relationship to transformative memories calling the people of God to conversion and discipleship. Dogma and doctrine play an important role in the church when they remain rooted in the transformative memory of the church and call us back to fidelity to the demands of Christian discipleship. When they are used as weapons at the hands of "orthodoxy police" eager to stamp out any and all legitimate diversity and constructive disagreement, they become not instruments but obstacles to the life and mission of the church.

CONCLUSION: LAS ABEJAS AND THE WITNESS TO THE POWER OF CHRISTIAN MEMORY

To illustrate much of what we have considered in this chapter regarding apostolicity and memory, I would like to consider the story of a remarkable Christian community I encountered during my visit to Chiapas, Mexico. As I noted earlier, in January of 2005 I was part of a small delegation of scholars and students visiting the Diocese of San Cristóbal de Las Casas. Almost 80 percent of the diocese is comprised of indigenous Mayan peoples. The indigenous belong to the lowest rung of the social ladder in Mexico and have been the victims of well over a century of economic and political repression and human rights violations. The social unrest in the region and the controversial approval of NAFTA (North American Free Trade Agreement) helped give birth to the

Zapatista movement associated with the Zapatista Army of National Liberation (the Spanish acronym is EZLN—Ejército Zapatista de Liberación Nacional). For nine days in January of 1994, the EZLN engaged in an armed occupation of five towns in the state of Chiapas as a protest to the ratification of NAFTA. The bishop of San Cristóbal, Don Samuel Ruiz, wishing to quell the violence, agreed to act as arbiter, and succeeded in brokering a truce with the Zapatistas while securing a set of agreements granting the Zapatistas limited autonomy in the region under what came to be known as the San Andreas Accords (accords that the government later refused to ratify). Since at the heart of the Zapatista agenda was substantive land reform aimed at returning ancestral lands to the control of the indigenous peoples, the Zapatista movement continued to be opposed in the region by those who supported the influential political party PRI (Partido Revolucionario Institucional) and who sponsored paramilitary groups, often trained by the federal army, to harass the Zapatistas and any peasant sympathizers. These supporters were often referred to as "Priistas."

Within this hotbed of social unrest, the Catholic Church, under the leadership of Bishop Ruiz, sought to align itself with the concerns of the indigenous peoples. The pastoral programs undertaken under Ruiz were intended to empower the people to reflect on their plight and the needs of their community from the perspective of their Catholic Christian faith.

Two years earlier, in 1992, an internecine family dispute had led to the unjust arrest of a local community leader. In response to the man's arrest, a large number of the community marched to San Cristóbal to protest and eventually secured his release. Having seen the power of such nonviolent resistance, these people decided to organize together, determined to continue in acts of nonviolent resistance. Most but not all were active members in local Catholic communities where Scripture study, under the encouragement of Bishop Ruiz, had led to their determination to respond to the injustice around them in distinctively Christian ways. When the Zapatista movement began several years later, members of this group were generally quite sympathetic to the Zapatistas' call for land reform, autonomous self-governance for the indigenous peoples, and a recovery of indigenous traditions, but they did not agree with the Zapatistas' threat of violence. They also were explicitly Christian in their focus, determined to follow what they saw as Christ's consistent teaching on nonviolence. They called themselves *Las Abejas*, "the bees," since, like bees, they worked together as a community for a common purpose. Their "queen" was variously described as the community itself, the reign of God (there is a Spanish wordplay here, as the word for queen is *La Reina*, and the word for reign as *El Reino*) or La Virgen de Guadalupe.

Late 1996 and 1997 saw an increase of violence in the region, mostly between the Zapatistas and the Priistas. Las Abejas sought dialogue as a way of resolving the conflict, but their refusal to side with one side or the other led them to be held in suspicion by both. The Priistas, with apparent military support and training, recruited disenfranchised indigenous people to form paramilitary groups to harass both the Zapatistas and the members of Las Abejas. On December 22, 1997, a number of members of Las Abejas were in a small wooden chapel in Acteal and were beginning a third day of fasting and prayer for peace in the area when approximately sixty armed paramilitary members, driven to Acteal in police vehicles, surrounded the compound where the chapel was located and at about 10:30 in the morning began shooting anyone they saw. They moved into the chapel and shot at members who were still praying. In the end, forty-five members were slaughtered, including nine men, fifteen children, and twenty-one women, four of whom were pregnant. There were a few survivors, who later reported what happened.

Our study group had the opportunity to visit Acteal, the site of the massacre. We visited the crypt where all forty-five martyrs were buried and were encouraged to pray above their graves asking for their support and strength in living the Christian faith. After our prayer in the crypt, we moved to the small chapel, the site of the massacre, for Mass.

The chapel was a modest shack, with bullet holes still visible in the walls and roof. Inside there were about six small benches and a shrine with the blessed sacrament, a crucifix, and several images of Mary. However, another small statue of Mary, bent over and wrapped in the distinctively patterned shawls of the women of this community, was enclosed in a glass case. This was "La Virgen de la Massacre." She was "wounded" by a bullet during the massacre but the community decided not to have the statue repaired, seeing it as a symbol of Mary's solidarity with the wounds of the community.

After the Mass we were invited up to another building in the Acteal compound to meet with the *Mesa Directiva*, the board of directors of Las Abejas. There we sat in a semicircle facing five men wearing the dark woolen shawls that were the emblem of moral authority in the community. The president was a surprisingly young man wearing the red bandana denoting an elder especially honored for his wisdom. After we introduced ourselves, Sebastian, the president, offered a brief history of Las Abejas and outlined their continued work in nonviolent resistance to injustice and their commitment to dialogue and reconciliation. When I asked him if it was difficult to remain committed to nonviolence after the massacre, he responded honestly, saying that in fact some members had left the community since the massacre because they did not feel they could continue in the path of nonviolence. He insisted, however, that most remained and that what sustained them in this was the memory, kept alive in the life of the community, of the teaching of Jesus that they must love their enemies.

After our meeting we were invited to join the leaders for a simple meal in their meeting room. There we were served by two adult members of the community, one of whom had survived the massacre by pulling the dead body of his brother on top of himself and pretending to be dead. He had witnessed the execution of all nine members of his family.

My experience in Acteal provides an opportunity to reflect concretely on all that we have considered concerning the power of Christian memory to sustain the authentic apostolicity of the church. This community had found a way to keep alive the dangerous memories of Christ. This they accomplished in many different ways. First, they were a community that had sustained the vital ecclesial practice of communal and prayerful study of Scripture. Moreover, they were willing to consider what Scripture might have to say to their contemporary situation. Second, they were a people who sustained their distinctive memory through locally realized customs and symbols. The statue of the *la virgen de la massacre*, around which they prayed and before which they would often march in festive procession, became a tangible local and thoroughly inculturated symbol of Mary's, and by extension God's, solidarity and compassion for them. Third, a traditional dogma of the church had been given a distinctive local shape that allowed it to maintain its transformative power. I have in mind the traditional Catholic belief in the communion of saints. This belief was enacted in the community's shrine erected to remember its martyrs. Not content to wait for official Roman approbation, the Christian community of Acteal had simply and intuitively created a crypt and shrine, a few yards away from the chapel in which they had been martyred, before which they would stand in prayer as an act of cosmic ecclesial solidarity. This too was an act of memory. For in remembering the courage of those who died praying for peace, the living believed they were lifted up by the strength and prayer of the martyrs to do the same.

Finally, the celebration of the eucharist, though a relatively rare event for this community (due to the acute shortage of priests), was celebrated with reverence, careful planning, and the full participation of the community gathered. A concern for liturgical rubrics (many of which were obviously ignored in this celebration) gave way to a simple confidence in the transformative power of this ritual action, which united them with Christ, who gave himself for the suffering of the world.

These extended reflections on the relationship between apostolicity and memory have had as their goal a certain reorientation of traditional ecclesiological reflections on apostolicity as a note or mark of the church. For much of the history of Christianity, the apostolicity of the church has been considered from the perspective of apostolic office and apostolic doctrine. This one-sided emphasis on the propositional and institutional manifestations of fidelity to the church's apostolic origins has led to numerous difficulties. Fidelity to the church's origins was too often understood in an ahistorical mode that saw both office and doctrine as frozen in normative forms immune to historical change. Dogma and doctrine were presented in a "digital genre" that undermined their symbolic power and reduced divine revelation to the status of divine information about God. Apostolic office would over time become inculturated in the forms of empire, nobility, and monarchy, only to be set above the church as a transhistorical arbiter of belief and practice.

The consideration of apostolicity through the category of memory helped us recover the ancient conviction that the apostolic faith resides in the community itself. Normative expressions of that faith (doctrine), and the authoritative preservation of that faith (apostolic office) did not precede but rather followed upon the ancient conviction that the apostolic faith resided first and foremost in the life of the community. It was the Christian community itself that was the subject of the church's memory. Ordinary believers exercised their supernatural instinct for the faith (*sensus fidei*) to recognize, penetrate, and apply the gospel within their distinct communities of faith. They thereby contributed, in a substantive way, to the handing on of the faith.

Our brief consideration of the formation of the biblical canon reminded us that our canonical Scriptures are themselves testimony to the pluriform character of the church's apostolic memory. Scripture offers no single master memory, but rather a set of communal memories of what God had done for people, sustained by quite diverse communities who were able, in the midst of their real differences, to recognize in the stories each community told a commonality that allowed them to declare themselves in *koinōnia* with one another.

In the final analysis, the claim to the church's apostolicity is a claim to fidelity, fidelity to a past that provides us with our core identity as followers of Jesus, and fidelity to a future that is still outstanding and that demands our action and cooperation with God's grace in the bringing forth of the reign of God.

QUESTIONS FOR REFLECTION

1. Theologian John Thiel contends that our understanding of tradition must include not only a sense of continuity and development but also a sense of novelty and even reversal. Some find it hard to reconcile the possibility of genuine reversal in tradition with a belief that tradition develops under the guidance of the Spirit. What is your view?
2. What are some concrete ways in which the church could give more attention to the role of the "sense of the faithful"?

3. Consider some aspects of the memory of Jesus that would be most "dangerous" for the world in which we live today.
4. In this chapter we discussed four distinct functions of creeds: the performative, doxological, catechetical, and regulative. Which of these functions do you think most needs to be recovered in the church today and why?

SUGGESTIONS FOR FURTHER READING AND STUDY

Boeve, Lieven. *Interrupting Tradition: An Essay on Christian Faith in a Postmodern Context.* Leuven: Peeters, 2004.

Burkhard, John J. *Apostolicity Then and Now: An Ecumenical Church in a Postmodern World.* Collegeville, Minn.: Liturgical Press, 2004.

Congar, Yves. *Tradition and Traditions: An Historical and Theological Essay.* New York: Macmillan, 1966.

Dahl, Nils Alstrup. *Jesus in the Memory of the Early Church.* Minneapolis: Augsburg, 1976.

Espín, Orlando. *The Faith of the People: Theological Reflections on Popular Catholicism.* Maryknoll, N.Y.: Orbis Books, 1997.

Espín, Orlando, and Gary Macy, eds. *Futuring Our Past: Explorations in the Theology of Tradition.* Maryknoll, N.Y.: Orbis Books, 2006.

Metz, Johann Baptist. *Faith in History and Society: Towards a Practical Fundamental Theology.* New York: Crossroad, 1980.

Segundo, Juan Luis. *The Liberation of Dogma: Faith, Revelation and Dogmatic Teaching Authority.* Maryknoll, N.Y.: Orbis Books, 1992.

Thiel, John. *Senses of Tradition: Continuity and Development in Catholic Faith.* New York: Oxford University Press, 2000.

7

A People Led by a Ministry of Memory

The sacred memory that bound Christians together had its origins in the testimony of those who had either known Jesus of Nazareth in his historical ministry or, like Paul, had encountered him as risen. These witnesses were called "apostles," those who were sent to give testimony. The testimony these apostles gave, testimony that constituted the decisive core of the Christian churches' communal memory, was then qualified as "apostolic." This apostolic memory was deemed authentic and reliable by virtue of its origins in the testimony of those who had directly encountered Christ. When we speak of the "faith" of the early Christians, the substance of that faith was preserved in the communal memory of God's saving purposes accomplished in Jesus Christ by the power of the Spirit. This memory was a communal reality, and although it had its origins in the preaching of the apostles, all who had been baptized into Christ claimed it for themselves. It was preserved in the many ways in which Christians shared the story of their faith: the witness of daily life, religious art, hymnody, storytelling, preaching, catechetical instruction, and ritual action.

Assertions regarding the apostolicity of the Christian faith/memory were, in effect, assertions about that faith/memory's authenticity and reliability. The issue of the reliability of communal memories of Christ had come to the forefront quickly in the early centuries. Christianity spread rapidly, predominantly in urban centers, during the first two centuries, in spite of sporadic persecutions by the Romans. Early proponents of competing accounts or "memories" of Christ and his mission often vied with one another for new adherents. A crisis gradually emerged regarding how one was to recognize the authenticity or apostolicity of these competing memories. One response to this crisis of communal identity was the gradual development of the biblical canon, which we discussed in the last chapter. A second means of ensuring the apostolicity of the corporate memory of the Christian communities was the emergence of an apostolic office.

THE EMERGENCE OF AN APOSTOLIC OFFICE

It is difficult to make any definitive claims for normative institutional church structures in the New Testament. The texts of the New Testament were all

249

written between 50 and 120 c.e. when the ecclesial life of most Christian communities was at its earliest stage of development and was characterized by structural diversity and fluidity. Nevertheless, fairly early on we find in the biblical texts provocative hints regarding the role of the apostle in the church.

Apostles in the New Testament

The present consensus of biblical scholarship does not see the term *apostolos* itself going back to Jesus' historical ministry; it appears to be a postresurrection development. The Greek word *apostolos* (from *apostellein,* "to send") appears in the New Testament eighty times. One can identify, in general, three distinct usages of the term.[1]

First, we find the term used in the Synoptic Gospels and the Acts of the Apostles in connection with "the Twelve." There are more than twenty-five New Testament references to either "the twelve apostles" or simply "the Twelve." The biblical tradition presents these as special figures called forth specifically by Jesus from among a larger group of disciples. Some, like Peter, James, and John, will play a prominent role in the Gospels. The others are little more than names. A noted biblical scholar, John Meier, holds that the selection of twelve figures may indeed have its origins in Jesus' historical ministry. Meier contends that this act would have functioned symbolically, representing the reconstitution of the twelve tribes of Israel.[2] This symbolic act can be understood only in the context of the central motif of Jesus' own teaching, namely, the in-breaking of the reign of God inaugurated in his own life and ministry. There is little justification for seeing Jesus' action as a commissioning for ministry. The choice of the twelve by Jesus is best interpreted as a symbolic act, not unlike those undertaken by Hebrew prophets such as Ezekiel, representing the new and final stage in the historical consummation of God's reign. John Burkhard writes:

> What is true of Jesus' proclamation of the kingdom is also true of his gesture in choosing twelve men and fashioning ("creating") them into a first order symbol for the gathering in of the people of God at the end of times.

---

[1] Christopher O'Donnell, "Apostles," in *Ecclesia: A Theological Encyclopedia of the Church* (Collegeville, Minn.: Liturgical Press, 1996), 16-18. For an excellent contemporary appraisal of the research on this topic, see Francis H. Agnew, "The Origin of the NT Apostle-Concept: A Review of Research," *Journal of Biblical Literature* 105 (1986): 75-96.

[2] John P. Meier, "The Circle of the Twelve: Did It Exist During Jesus' Public Ministry?" *Journal of Biblical Literature* 116 (1997): 635-72.

This is no demotion or denigration of the Twelve. On the contrary, from this point of view they can truly emerge for us as a prophetic deed posited by Jesus to precipitate the arrival of God's kingdom—in part here and now in time and fully at the point that sums up all of time. Understanding the Twelve as symbol of the "true Israel" gathered around Jesus also helps us understand how their role is unique. There can be no succession to the Twelve and their indispensable role in salvation history.[3]

The gospel traditions recall Jesus' symbolic selection of key followers but overlay this with their own theological interpretations. The Synoptic Gospels seem to present the Twelve as, in some sense, an extension of Jesus' own ministry and mission in the time after the resurrection. The Acts of the Apostles offers us an idealistic portrayal of the ministry of the apostles in the early church. In Luke's account, the Twelve functioned as leaders of the church in Jerusalem whose authority was acknowledged and respected (though not above challenge) among the other churches. For Luke the preaching/teaching of the apostles is central even as the symbolic significance of the number twelve diminishes; their preaching serves as an indispensable foundation for the life of the church.[4]

The two other distinct usages of the term are found in the writings of St. Paul. First, in a more specific sense, Paul applies the term to himself, and in doing so seeks to authenticate his own authority as on a par with the "pillars in Jerusalem." Consequently, he is not reluctant to challenge the authority even of someone as revered as Peter (Gal. 2:11-14). Paul contends that he too merits the title because he too has "seen the Lord."

> Am I not free? Am I not an apostle? Have I not seen Jesus our Lord? Are not you my workmanship in the Lord? If to others I am not an apostle, at least I am to you; for you are the seal of my apostleship in the Lord. (1 Cor. 9:1-2)

Paul grounds his own apostolicity not only in his encounter with the risen Christ but in the fact that he has received from Christ a mission to preach the gospel (Gal. 1:16) and in the fruitfulness of his ministry.

Paul also uses the term in a broader sense when he refers to co-workers in the work of the church, including Apollos (1 Cor. 4:6), Silvanus and Timothy (1 Thess. 1:1 read in conjunction with 1 Thess. 2:6-7). This broader usage

---

[3] John J. Burkhard, *Apostolicity Then and Now: An Ecumenical Church in a Postmodern World* (Collegeville, Minn.: Liturgical Press, 2004), 9. See also Gerhard Lohfink, *Jesus and Community: The Social Dimensions of Christian Faith* (New York: Paulist Press, 1984), 10.

[4] Burkhard, 13-14.

also includes those in local communities who seem to hold at least an incipient form of church office. These Paul acknowledges when he writes of "some people God has designated in the church to be, first, apostles; second, prophets; third teachers" (1 Cor. 12:28). These may be those Paul has in mind when he refers to the "apostles of the churches" (2 Cor. 8:23), leaders sent from one community to another either to preach the gospel or to fulfill some particular task.

Also noteworthy is the reference to Andronicus and Junia, who Paul says are "prominent among the apostles" (Rom. 16:7). The tradition generally understood "Junia" to be a male, but there is fairly compelling evidence that Junia in fact was the name of a female leader of the church. That some within the tradition viewed Junia as a woman is confirmed by the testimony of St. John Chrysostom, who wrote:

> It is certainly a great thing to be an apostle; but to be outstanding among the apostles—think what praise that is! She was outstanding in her works, in her good deeds; oh, and how great is the philosophy of this woman, that she was regarded as worthy to be counted among the apostles![5]

Although this is the only specific New Testament reference to a woman as an apostle, early church literature granted this title to St. Mary Magdalene, referred to in the East as "the apostle to the apostles" because she was commanded by the angel at the tomb of Jesus to "go tell his disciples that he is risen from the dead" (Matt. 28:7). In John's account it is the risen Christ himself who commands her: "go to my brothers and tell them" (John 20:17).

Emergence of a Stable Apostolic Office in the Postbiblical Period

What we do know is that at the beginning of the second century, church leadership began to coalesce around a single leader of each eucharistic community, known as an *episkopos,* or "overseer," rendered in modern English as "bishop." The early-second-century letters of St. Ignatius of Antioch suggest that at least some churches had developed a tripartite structure of church leadership led by a single bishop (*episkopos*) who was surrounded by a group of presbyters (*presbyteroi*) and deacons (*diakonoi*).

The move from the unique authority of those who had witnessed the risen Christ (the apostles) to those who took on formal church office as leaders of

---

[5] Quoted in Ute E. Eisen, *Women Officeholders in Early Christianity* (Collegeville, Minn.: Liturgical Press, 2000), 48.

local churches occurred only gradually. It is doubtful that most of the early "bishops" were formally installed by apostles, but it was not long before the churches attributed to these bishops a succession, not to the office of the apostle and certainly not to the unique role of the Twelve, but rather to the *authority* of the apostles. By the end of the second century, the monoepiscopate—one bishop leading each local church—was almost universally accepted. This is sometimes referred to as a monarchical episcopate, an unfortunate term, Christopher O'Donnell has observed, since "the bishop does not act alone but always with his presbyters and deacons."[6] Hermann Pottmeyer has noted the surprising speed with which this occurred, particularly since "there was no central authority demanding or guiding this development."[7] He suggests that its rapid acceptance may have been due to (1) the gradual conjoining of pastoral leadership over a local church and the presidency over the celebration of that church's worship and (2) the success of the presidential episcopate in preserving church unity in the face of growing conflicts.

In response to growing heretical groups, the late second century saw expanded assertions of the teaching authority of the bishops. Christianity held that the authentic apostolic faith could be found in the testimony of the apostolic churches, those churches thought to be founded by apostles, and in the public teaching of the bishops who led those churches. In the face of conflicting claims of various groups to possess the truth of the faith, the question was asked, "Where is the sure faith of the apostolic community to be found?" It was answered, "In the teaching of the bishops."

In the third century a number of churches, particularly those in North Africa, struggled with schismatic groups, often over the treatment of the *lapsi*, those who had abandoned the Christian faith under persecution and now sought readmission into the church. In response to the threat of schism, St. Cyprian of Carthage would advocate a strong theology of episcopal authority. In one of his many letters Cyprian wrote: "By that you ought to realize that the bishop is in the Church and the Church is in the bishop, and whoever is not with the bishop is not in the Church" (*Epistle* 66, 8). Cyprian shared the conviction of Tertullian and Irenaeus regarding the teaching authority of the bishops, but he did not view the bishop as having divine truth as his private possession. What the bishops taught was what their churches believed. Hence, there is a consistent witness to the close relationship that was to be maintained between the bishop and the church he served. Bishops were not democratically

---

[6] Christopher O'Donnell, "Bishops," in *Ecclesia: A Theological Encyclopedia of the Church*, 52-57, at 53.

[7] Hermann J. Pottmeyer, "The Episcopacy," in *The Gift of the Church*, ed. Peter C. Phan (Collegeville, Minn.: Liturgical Press, 2000), 337-53 at 343.

elected "delegates" of their local church, but acceptance by the local church was widely considered necessary for a candidate to be ordained as bishop of the local church. Just as the participation of neighboring bishops in an episcopal ordination manifested the larger church's affirmation that this candidate held the faith of the whole church, so too the acceptance of the local community reflected their affirmation that the candidate embodied the faith of the local church. One of the first documents containing an ordination ritual, the early-third-century *Apostolic Tradition*, forthrightly states:

> Let the bishop be ordained after he has been chosen by all the people; when he has been named and shall please all, let him, with the presbytery and such bishops as may be present, assemble with the people on Sunday. While all give their consent, the bishops shall lay hands upon him. (1.2.3)

Cyprian himself wrote: "Moreover, we can see that divine authority is also the source for the practice whereby bishops are chosen in the presence of the laity and before the eyes of all, and they are judged as being suitable and worthy after public scrutiny and testimony" (*Epistle* 67, 4).[8] The bishop was bound to the people because the apostolic faith taught and preserved by the bishop was, in fact, that apostolic faith that already resided in the faith of the people. It is for this reason that Cyprian believed that consulting all the faithful of his local church was essential for his teaching ministry. Addressing a letter to his clergy while away from his diocese, Cyprian wrote:

> from the beginning of my episcopate, I decided to do nothing of my own opinion privately without your advice and the consent of the people. When I come to you through the grace of God, then we shall discuss in common either what has been done or what must be done concerning these matters, as our mutual honor demands. (*Epistle* 14, 4)

Elsewhere he insisted that the effectiveness and authority of the bishop as teacher depended on his ability to be a humble learner:

> But it is unrepentant presumption and insolence that induces men to defend their own perverse errors instead of giving assent to what is right and true, but has come from another. The blessed apostle Paul foresaw this when he wrote to Timothy with the admonition that a bishop should be not wrangling or quarrelsome but gentle and teachable. Now a man is teachable if he

---

[8] For the ecclesiological presuppositions that framed Cyprian's perspective, see Paul J. Fitzgerald, "A Model for Dialogue: Cyprian of Carthage on Ecclesial Discernment," *Theological Studies* 59 (June 1998): 236-53.

is meek and gentle and patient in learning. It is thus a bishop's duty not only to teach but also to learn. For he becomes a better teacher if he makes daily progress and advancement in learning what is better. (*Epistle* 74, 10)

The bishops' ministry was to be apostolic inasmuch as they served as the authoritative guardians of the apostolic faith. They did this, however, as leaders of churches that were themselves bearers of apostolicity. This conviction informed the bold assertion of the early-fifth-century bishop St. Paulinus of Nola: "Let us listen to what all the faithful say, because in every one of them the Spirit of God breathes" (*Epistle* 23, 36).

In their teaching, the bishops did not impart a secret knowledge with which the members of their churches were unfamiliar. They proclaimed the apostolic faith with authority, but in so doing functioned as custodians of the faith given to the whole church. In apostolic service to their communities, the bishops received, verified, validated, and proclaimed the apostolic faith that was prayed and lived in their communities.

Up until the mid-third century, the bishop's apostolic teaching responsibility was inseparable from his pastoral leadership of a local eucharistic community. Deacons assisted the bishop in a number of ways (e.g., seeing to the temporal needs of the local church, visiting the sick, preaching), and presbyters served as counselors or advisers to the bishop. However, by the time of Cyprian, satellite communities had begun to develop within individual dioceses, particularly in rural areas. In some instances another bishop, known as a *chorbishop*, was assigned to these communities, always under the authority of the main bishop. In other instances presbyters were sent by the bishop to preside over the celebration of the eucharist. This shift would mark the beginning of a gradual movement of the bishop from the center to the periphery of the sacramental life of the local church. As the sacrament of holy orders would become more oriented toward presiding over eucharist, the distinctive character of the bishop with respect to the presbyter became less clear. St. Jerome's opinion on this is often cited, since he asserted the equality of priest/presbyters and bishops.[9] The anonymous author known as Ambrosiaster shared much the same view.

COLLEGIAL EXERCISE OF APOSTOLIC OFFICE

We have already discussed the role of synods and councils in preserving the communion among the churches. These church gatherings were also vital

---

[9] "Letter to Evangelus," in *Nicene and Post-Nicene Fathers, Second Series,* ed. Philip Schaff and Henry Wace, 14 vols. (Peabody, Mass.: Hendrickson, 1994), 288-89.

instruments for preserving the apostolic memory of the church. In the fourth century, an Alexandrian presbyter, Arius, offered a popular interpretation of the divine origins of Christ that soon became the source of considerable controversy. The emperor Constantine, concerned that the dispute was threatening the unity of the empire, called for a special council to address the controversy. It would be the first of many other imperial interventions. This meeting, held in Nicaea, would later be regarded as the first of a series of "ecumenical councils," so named because the teaching of these councils pertained to, and was eventually accepted by, the *oikoumenē*, the universal church.

Ecumenical Councils

The ecumenicity was ultimately conferred on these councils was derived not from some juridical feature of the councils themselves but from both the weighty doctrinal problems addressed by the councils and the fact that the solutions that these councils provided were ultimately accepted and *received* by the whole church. "Reception" here refers to the process by which the local churches took a teaching of pope or council and made it their own. One of the foremost scholars of the history and theology of ecumenical councils, Hermann Josef Sieben, has contended that the church's recognition of a council as genuinely "ecumenical" depended on whether the determinations of the council were accepted as expressions of a twofold consensus, a *consensio antiquitatis et universitatis* (a consensus with antiquity and with the universal church).[10] *Universitas* involved the "horizontal" or synchronic consensus of the whole church. When a council sought to teach a matter of doctrine authoritatively, it did so out of the conviction that it was teaching the faith of the churches. Council participants never believed themselves to be imposing something foreign to the faith of their respective communities. Although a council presumed itself to be expressing this *universitas* or horizontal consensus in its teaching, the verification of that authority demanded that the local churches receive the teaching of the council and come to profess it as their own. This could take considerable time. Often a key moment in the reception of a council's teaching would be its acceptance at a subsequent council. Yves Congar offers the example of the creed of the Council of Nicaea, which was only truly "received" fifty-six years later when it was accepted at the Council of Constantinople (381). The reception of the teaching of Constantinople, in turn, occurred only at the Council of Chalcedon (451).[11]

---

[10] Hermann Josef Sieben, *Die Konzilsidee der Alten Kirche* (Paderborn: Schöningh, 1979), 511-16.

[11] Yves Congar, "Reception as an Ecclesiological Reality," in *Election and Consensus in the Church*, ed. Giuseppe Alberigo and Anton Weiler, *Concilium* 77 (New York: Herder, 1972), 46-48.

If the *consensio universitatis* was authenticated by the council's reception by the churches, the *consensio antiquitatis,* or agreement with the apostolic tradition, had to be demonstrated by the council itself. Here we see a diachronic view of ecclesial reception. The burden was on the council to demonstrate how its teaching was faithful to that tradition.[12] In defending the Council of Nicaea, St. Athanasius felt compelled to write:

> The Fathers, in matters of faith, never said: Thus it has been decreed, but: This is what the Catholic Church believes; and they confessed what they believed directly, so as to show unmistakably that their thought was not new, but apostolic.[13]

It fell again to the local churches to determine whether a council had preserved this agreement with antiquity. By the ninth century we find claims that the teachings of these councils were taught infallibly.

It is a consistent theme in the theological reflection on teaching authority of the first millennium that authoritative proclamation of the apostolic faith could not be divorced from the authentic reception of that teaching by the Christian communities. The faith of the people and the teaching of the bishops were inextricably connected. As Congar has observed, it was the task of the ancient councils to bring to full expression the church's common memory:

> In a council it is either a question of clarifying the tradition of the Church or the *sensus ecclesiae,* or of producing a solution to a contemporary question. Both the *sensus ecclesiae* and the desired solution lie hidden in the memory or consciousness of the Church—or rather, in the memories or consciousness of the persons who compose the Church. These memories and consciousnesses must communicate in order to produce a common expression and sum total, so to speak, of the memory and consciousness of the Church. This is not a collection of personal convictions, for although it only exists personified in actual men—and, at the highest level in the consciousness of Christ and in his Spirit . . . it nonetheless transcends these men and through them belongs to the Church. The council aims at achieving a totalization of the memory of the Church, by a communication of the consciences which house this memory.[14]

---

[12] Edward Kilmartin, "Reception in History: An Ecclesiological Phenomenon and Its Significance," *Journal of Ecumenical Studies* 21 (1984): 48-50.

[13] Athanasius, *De Synodus 5,* as quoted in Yves Congar, "A Brief History of the Forms of the Magisterium and Its Relations with Scholars," in *Readings in Moral Theology No. 3: The Magisterium and Morality,* ed. Charles E. Curran and Richard A. McCormick (New York: Paulist Press, 1982), 316.

[14] Yves Congar, "The Council as an Assembly and the Church as Essentially Conciliar," in *Theologians Today: Yves Congar* (London/New York: Sheed & Ward, 1972), 110-11.

The bishops, individually and as a college, were the authoritative custodians of the faith; they were, as Congar has suggested, the keepers of the church's apostolic memory.

Emerging Papal Office

When the church of Jerusalem died out near the end of the first century, Rome gradually supplanted Jerusalem as Christianity's "mother church." The Roman church was granted a certain priority among the churches in virtue of the tradition that it had received the apostolic teaching of, not one, but two apostles, Sts. Peter and Paul. There is ancient testimony to the unique prestige held by the church of Rome. At the beginning of the second century, St. Ignatius would refer to Rome as the church "foremost in love" (*Epistle to the Romans* 4), and by the end of the same century St. Irenaeus of Lyons would refer to it as the church "of most excellent origins" (*Against the Heresies* 3.3.2). Yet the authority of Rome, by the end of the third century, differed only in degree, not in kind, from the authority of other churches with claims to apostolicity. For example, there was no sense as yet that the bishop of Rome could exercise any veto power regarding synodal decisions outside the Roman province.[15]

It was only in the fourth century that bishops of the church of Rome explicitly claimed to be the unique successors to the authority of Peter.[16] The authority of the papacy would grow dramatically in the fourth and fifth centuries with Pope Leo (440-61), for example, having a considerable influence on the Council of Chalcedon's teaching. In the face of growing feuds among various regional synods, Rome often became a court of final appeal. Nevertheless, when it came to teaching on doctrinal matters, bishops continued to see themselves as the primary teachers in their own churches while recognizing that the common teaching shared by all the bishops (including the bishop of Rome) offered a sure foundation for Christian faith. When it was felt necessary to make more formal pronouncements on doctrinal matters, this was accomplished either regionally or in ecumenical councils.

Nevertheless, the assertions of papal teaching authority over the whole church would increase after the fifth century. The formulary of Pope Hormisdas (514-23) stated that the apostolic faith has been preserved "without spot"

---

[15] Eamon Duffy, *Saints and Sinners: A History of the Popes* (New Haven: Yale University Press, 1997), 13.

[16] I say "explicitly" because we do have indirect documentary evidence of the third-century Bishop Steven claiming authority as the unique successor of Peter. This is reported in a letter of Firmilian, bishop of Caesurea, to Cyprian.

in the church of Rome.[17] A century and a half later a similar claim would be made by Pope Agatho (678-81) who insisted that just as Jesus prayed that Peter's faith would not fail, so too Rome's own faith had been preserved without blemish (Luke 22:32).[18] By the end of the first millennium claims to the inerrancy of the Roman apostolic tradition would become quite common, often relying on this text from Luke. In spite of these increasingly common claims to the trustworthiness of the Roman profession of faith, it would be historically inaccurate to speak of an explicit doctrine of papal infallibility during the first millennium. The witness of the see of Rome was quite important because of its *principalitas*, or origin as the church of Sts. Peter and Paul (although by the fourth century the significance of the Pauline connection had virtually disappeared). Rome was considered the outstanding example of fidelity to the apostolic *kerygma*. Consequently, the West generally acknowledged the right of the pope to settle matters of faith authoritatively. But it would be a mistake to imagine a formal doctrine of papal infallibility at work here. The emphasis still lay not on the formal authority of the pope alone but on the faith of the whole church of Rome and on that apostolic tradition to which the Roman church and its bishop gave witness.[19] Through most of the first thousand years of Christianity the conviction endured that the pope and bishops *together* shared responsibility for preserving the apostolic faith of the churches.

Medieval Shifts in the Nature of Apostolic Office

A discernible shift in the locus of apostolic authority begins to make itself evident in the eleventh century. Gregory VII's crackdown on the inappropriate influence of the nobility over episcopal office led to sweeping assertions of virtually unchecked papal authority. Canonical accounts of church office like those found in Gratian's *Decretals* soon replaced the sacramental foundations of the church so prominent in the first millennium.

Throughout the Middle Ages we will see repeated and largely failed attempts at church reform bent on restoring the integrity of episcopal office. The practices of awarding benefices, simony, corrupt or simply incompetent bishops who did not reside in, let alone minister in, their assigned churches— all created a climate ripe for more reform. This shift is marked by a gradual diminishment of the office of the bishop in favor of the enhanced authority of the papal office. Many of these abuses were rightly attacked by church reform-

---

[17] This formulary is treated in Trevor Jalland, *Church and Papacy* (London: SPCK, 1944), 338.

[18] PL 87.1169, 1205.

[19] Yves Congar, *L'Ecclésiologie du haut moyen-age* (Paris: Cerf, 1968), 160.

ers from Savonarola to Hus, Luther, and Calvin. Luther, in particular, focused his criticism on the ways in which church authorities had held the Bible captive. He did not deny the need for some apostolic office (Luther apparently wished to preserve the office of the bishop) but he stressed the apostolicity of the faith that resided in the church itself.

In summary one might say that the central concern of the Reformers regarding apostolic office was to stress the apostolicity of faith that resided in the Christian communities themselves and to treat church office from the biblical tradition's emphasis on service rather than power. However, their reaction to Catholic abuses of church authority led to a pronounced de-emphasis on the need for an apostolic office dedicated to preserving the integrity of the apostolic faith and the unity of the churches.

Hermann Pottmeyer has contended that much of the history of ecclesiastical authority in the second millennium was shaped in the spirit of reaction. The papacy, in particular, reacted to what it experienced as three great "traumas": conciliarism, increased incursions of the state on church affairs, and the emergence of Enlightenment-inspired liberalism.[20]

The conciliarist controversy emerged over the crisis created in the church by first two and then three claimants to the papacy in the late fourteenth and early fifteenth centuries. As leading church figures looked for a way out of this situation, they turned to the ideas of some influential political theorists, figures such as Marsilius of Padua. Marsilius had dared to hold that the state had a rightful autonomy in political matters and was not subject to the church. Applying some of these new theories to the church, some held that a council could also have a religious authority independent of the pope, since the council's religious authority was ultimately rooted in Christ. Conciliarism took various forms. Some more radical versions opposed the authority of council to pope and insisted on the former's inherent superiority. More moderate views sought simply to assert limits on the exercise of papal power. When the political tide turned at the Council of Florence (largely because proponents of more extreme positions were excluded) and papal primacy was reaffirmed, the long-term fallout was a persistent suspicion of any legitimate affirmation of conciliar or episcopal authority as a threat to the papacy.

The second trauma concerned the emergence of the state and the rise of absolute monarchies that were unwilling to bend to the demands of Rome and, indeed, increasingly inserted themselves into church affairs. The model in Europe was the state-controlled church in France. States increasingly sought control, for example, of church-sponsored systems of education.

---

[20] Hermann Pottmeyer, *Towards a Papacy in Communion* (New York: Crossroad, 1998), 36-50.

Ironically, it was the claims of absolute authority on the part of secular monarchs that led, in the nineteenth century, to a countervailing movement in Catholicism known as Ultramontanism (looking "beyond" the "mountains" in obedience to the views of Rome), which was bent on the centralization of church authority in the papacy. Catholic theorists like Joseph de Maistre asserted that the papacy itself functioned as an absolute sovereignty. This view would be very influential in Vatican I's treatment of the papacy in its constitution *Pastor Aeternus*. Nuncios, representatives of the pope assigned to engage national leaders about matters of concern to the Catholic Church, were given expanded authority, often being called upon to police church affairs internal to a country or region. The papacy revived the practice of *ad limina* visits, whereby individual bishops visited Rome every five years to pay homage at the tombs of the apostles and to give an accounting of the affairs of their diocese to Roman officials.

The third trauma was created by the Enlightenment. The Age of Reason challenged the authority of both Scripture and church office and championed instead the authority of autonomous human reason and the right to self-determination. Much Catholic thought in the nineteenth century was oriented toward a condemnation of a "liberalism" perceived as a frontal assault on the authority of the church. Pope Pius IX promulgated the *Syllabus of Errors* in 1864 as a sweeping condemnation of modern liberalism. Although Vatican I's treatment of papal authority was in fact carefully circumscribed, the council's failure to produce a comprehensive account of the church and the nature and scope of church authority gave raise to a pronounced papo-centrism that would continue until Vatican II.

RENEWAL OF APOSTOLIC OFFICE IN THE MODERN CHURCH

The broad renewal in Catholic thought that occurred at Vatican II extended as well to Catholic understandings of apostolic office.[21] When the council considered the ministry of the individual bishop, it reversed a trend that had begun in the eleventh century, a trend that saw the priesthood as the summit of ordained ministry. Vatican II returned to the vision of the first millennium when the primary locus of ordained ministry was not the ministry of the priest but that of the bishop.

---

[21] For a more in-depth analysis of the council's teaching on the episcopate, see Richard R. Gaillardetz, *The Church in the Making: Lumen Gentium, Christus Dominus, Orientalium Ecclesiarum* (Mahwah, N.J.: Paulist Press, 2006).

Vatican II on the Episcopate

Vatican II's consideration of the episcopate was central to its overall agenda. On the eve of the council, both theologians and bishops were aware of two unresolved theological issues related to the episcopate. The first concerned the relationship between the papal primacy and the authority of the college of bishops. Vatican I's *Pastor Aeternus* contained, for example, but one paragraph that attended to the relationship between papal primacy and the authority of the bishops. The council was determined to address this lacuna. The second issue was related to the theology of orders itself. A debate had continued for centuries regarding whether the episcopal office existed by divine institution and whether the bishop received both the power of orders and jurisdiction at episcopal consecration. Vatican II also set about resolving this issue. Let me very briefly summarize, then, the council's principal contributions to the development of doctrine regarding the episcopate.

The Ministry of the Bishop

The first contribution to a conciliar reassessment of episcopal office appeared in the liturgy constitution debated during the first session of the council. In *Sacrosanctum Concilium* the council placed the bishop at the center of the liturgical life of the diocese, teaching that the most profound manifestation of the local church was encountered at diocesan liturgies presided over by the bishop (SC 41). Here we see a nascent eucharistic ecclesiology beginning to emerge in this earliest of conciliar texts. This renewed emphasis on the bishop's bond to his local church was further explored, albeit inconsistently, in *Lumen Gentium.*

In its third chapter, the dogmatic constitution began with the assertion that, by the will of Christ, bishops are successors to the apostles in serving as the shepherds of the church (LG 18). In article 21 we find a clarification of the centuries-old question concerning whether episcopal consecration was truly sacramental. The council answered in the affirmative, noting as well that all three offices, or *munera*—sanctifying, teaching, and governing—were conferred at episcopal ordination and not by a subsequent papal act. The infamous *nota explicativa praevia,* attached to the constitution at the eleventh hour and without council vote, did specify that these *munera* were not "fully ready to act" without a further canonical determination by the appropriate church authority. There can be no question whether the council grasped the full ecclesiological implications of this teaching. In LG 27 the council insisted that bishops were not vicars of the pope but exercised a power that was proper to them in virtue of their office.

This restoration of the full dignity and authority of the local bishop was further strengthened in *Christus Dominus* by the council's deliberate abandonment of the centuries-old "concessions system," a system in which the pope *conceded* certain faculties (e.g., regarding marriage and penal law) to bishops for five-year terms. The canonical assumption underlying this system was that the faculties were proper to the pope but could be delegated to the individual bishops. Instead, Vatican II assumed that these faculties were proper to the bishops with only certain cases "reserved" to the pope (CD 8).

In both *Lumen Gentium* and *Christus Dominus,* the council consistently affirmed as well the *pastoral* character of the bishops' office. The Decree on the Pastoral Office of the Bishop insisted that bishops should not be aloof or distant from their people; rather they should "stand in the midst of their people as those who serve," seeking to know the particular conditions and concerns that define the lives of their flock (CD 16). Even the determination of the boundaries of particular dioceses ought to be made with the welfare of the people of God uppermost in mind (CD 22-24).

Episcopal Collegiality

The council also recalled the bond of communion shared among bishops and with the bishop of Rome, a communion attested to in the ancient tradition and reflected in the common practice of gathering bishops at synods and councils. The council taught that although the college of bishops has no authority on its own apart from communion with its head, the pope, the college nevertheless shares with the bishop of Rome, and never apart from him, "supreme and full power over the universal church" (LG 22).

The exposition of the council's teaching on episcopal collegiality marked a significant advance in church doctrine. The potential sweep of the doctrine was limited, however, by an excessive caution. In the very first article of the third chapter of *Lumen Gentium,* the council repeated the teaching of Vatican I on both papal primacy and infallibility. According to one influential *peritus,* Gérard Philips, the flow of the chapter was hobbled by a determination to forestall any construal of the teaching on collegiality as a rejection of Vatican I.[22] Throughout the text we find repeated assurances of the unfettered authority of the pope over the college of bishops, passages clearly aimed at the nervous minority concerned about illegitimate doctrinal development.

Many bishops and *periti* complained that the force of the council's teaching on episcopal collegiality was weakened also by the *nota praevia* that had been attached to *Lumen Gentium* without the approval or even debate of the coun-

---

[22] Gérard Philips, "Dogmatic Constitution on the Church: History of the Constitution," in *Commentary on the Documents of Vatican II,* ed. Herbert Vorgrimler (New York: Crossroad, 1989), 1:129.

cil on the order of "higher authority." In paragraph 3, the *nota* appeared to return to a more juridical, neoscholastic position, describing the distinction between the pope alone and the pope with the college as "two inadequately distinct subjects" of supreme authority in the church. The difficulty with the teaching of the *nota* was that it stood at odds with the theological force of the council's teaching that the pope never truly acts "alone"; as pope he is always head of the college and therefore, one might legitimately infer, remains in spiritual communion with the college.

Postconciliar Developments

Since Vatican II, various attempts have been made to implement the council's teaching on collegiality and the exercise of papal authority, with mixed success.

Institutional Expressions of Collegiality

At the council, there were several suggestions regarding the creation of a permanent synod of bishops that would work with the bishop of Rome in shared pastoral ministry of the universal church. Many had the model of standing synods in the Eastern church. Pope Paul VI responded to these requests in *Apostolica Solicitudo*. In that document he established not a standing synod with deliberative authority but an occasional gathering of representative bishops for a limited period of time with strictly consultative power. As the synod of bishops has developed over the intervening four decades, three different synodal forms have emerged: ordinary synods that meet every three or four years; extraordinary synods that are convened to address special topics, often at the behest of the pope; and special synods that address issues of concern to particular regional churches. Many critics feel that the synod of bishops, as conceived by Pope Paul VI, has fallen far short of the council's hopes. James Coriden has summarized a number of criticisms that have been raised regarding the synods as presently configured: (1) there is excessive curial control of the synodal process; (2) frustration exists regarding inaction on synodal proposals; (3) post-synodal exhortations have been written by popes, not the synods, and often have little relationship to synodal debates; (4) the synodal process itself involves participants having to listen to endless unrelated episcopal speeches; (5) real discussion of participants is limited; (6) the drafting committee often eliminates many proposals that emerge from the language groups; (7) only propositions garnering 95 percent approval of voting members are passed on to the pope.[23] More recently, Pope Benedict XVI has responded to

---

[23] James Coriden, "The Synod of Bishops: Episcopal Collegiality Still Seeks Adequate Expression," *Jurist* 64 (2004): 116-36, at 125.

some of these criticisms by shortening the length of the speeches and scheduling a daily session for open debate among the participants.

Since the council, the creation of episcopal conferences as a way to facilitate addressing common concerns by regional groups of bishops became much more common. Some conferences, such as the U.S. bishops' conference or CELAM in Latin America (Consejo Episcopal Latinoamericano), became quite influential. The controversial promulgation of Pope Paul VI's encyclical on birth control, *Humanae Vitae,* led many episcopal conferences to issue formal interpretations of that document. In the 1980s the U.S. bishops' conference began to issue several high-visibility pastoral letters. The high profile of these documents revived questions about the doctrinal teaching authority of these conferences.

At the 1985 extraordinary synod called by Pope John Paul II to assess the reception of the Second Vatican Council, the bishops requested a study of the status and authority of episcopal conferences. After over a decade of wide-ranging debate on the ecclesial status and teaching authority of episcopal conferences, in 1998 Pope John Paul II promulgated the long-awaited apostolic letter *Apostolos Suos.* In that document the pope praised the contributions of episcopal conferences in the life of the church and confirmed their limited doctrinal authority as partial expressions of collegiality. However, the pope stipulated that episcopal conferences could issue binding doctrinal statements only when (1) they issued the document in a plenary session (not by way of a committee), (2) the document was approved unanimously, or (3) the document was approved by a two thirds majority and received a *recognitio* (formal approval) from Rome. Like the postconciliar development of the synod of bishops, John Paul II's treatment of episcopal conferences as expressions of collegiality has met with some criticism. For example, some have contended that *Apostolos Suos* goes out of its way to avoid the comparison made at the council between the authority of contemporary episcopal conferences and the authority of the ancient synods of bishops that were so important to the life of the early church.[24] Others have noted that the letter ultimately grants to episcopal conferences nothing more than either the aggregate authority of the individual bishops (when the bishops unanimously approve a document) or the authority of papal teaching (when the Holy See gives a document its *recognitio*).[25] It becomes difficult, from this perspective, to see any genuine collegial authority in such documents.

---

[24] Joseph Komonchak, "On the Authority of Bishops' Conferences," *America* (September 12, 1998): 7-10.

[25] Francis A. Sullivan, "The Teaching Authority of Episcopal Conferences," *Theological Studies* 63 (September 2002): 472-93.

The Exercise of Papal Authority

Soon after the council, debates regarding the relationship between the ministry of the pope and that of the college of bishops continued. In 1968, in the midst of the controversy of Pope Paul VI's forthcoming encyclical on birth control, Cardinal Léon-Joseph Suenens, primate of Belgium and arguably the single most influential bishop at Vatican II, published a book titled *Coresponsibility in the Church*. In it the cardinal explored the notion of shared responsibility in the church at multiple levels. In particular, Suenens focused on the pope's proper relationship to the college of bishops:

> For ecumenical reasons, as well as for theological reasons, we must avoid presenting the role of the Pope in a way that would isolate him from the college of bishops, whose head he is. When it is pointed out that the Pope has the right to act and to speak "alone," this word "alone" never means "separately" or "in isolation". Even when the Pope acts without the formal collaboration of the episcopal body—as he is indeed legally entitled to do—he always acts as its head.[26]

Suenens's perspective, however, received a decidedly tepid response from the pope.

Under the pontificate of Pope John Paul II one encountered a much more centralized exercise of papal authority. In matters ranging from the appointment of bishops to the approval of vernacular translations of liturgical texts, the pontificate of John Paul II was marked by a pattern of expansive Vatican interventionism. This was further reflected, as we saw above, in Vatican reservations regarding the authority of episcopal conferences and curial control over the conduct of the synod of bishops.

This stock portrait of the pontificate of John Paul II has to be balanced, however, by his articulation of a much more collegial vision of the exercise of papal authority in his encyclical on ecumenism, *Ut Unum Sint*. In the encyclical the pope presented a compelling vision of papal primacy with a striking similarity to the views Suenens expressed decades before. The pope saw papal primacy and episcopal collegiality as inseparable dimensions of the exercise of authority over the church universal. He portrayed the ministry of the bishop of Rome as one of service to the unity of the church. As such, the pope was not above the college but within it:

> This service of unity, rooted in the action of divine mercy, is entrusted within the College of Bishops to one among those who have received from the

---

[26] Quoted in Cardinal Léon-Joseph Suenens, *Memories and Hopes* (Dublin: Veritas, 1992), 210.

Spirit the task, not of exercising power over the people—as the rulers of the Gentiles and their great men do—but of leading them towards peaceful pastures. . . . The mission of the Bishop of Rome within the College of all the Pastors consists precisely in "keeping watch" (*episkopein*), like a sentinel, so that, through the efforts of the Pastors, the true voice of Christ the Shepherd may be heard in all the particular Churches. . . . With the power and the authority without which such an office would be illusory, the Bishop of Rome must ensure the communion of all the Churches. For this reason, he is the first servant of unity. . . . All this however must always be done in communion. When the Catholic Church affirms that the office of the Bishop of Rome corresponds to the will of Christ, she does not separate this office from the mission entrusted to the whole body of Bishops, who are also "vicars and ambassadors of Christ." The Bishop of Rome is a member of the "College," and the Bishops are his brothers in the ministry. (UUS 94-95)

In an unprecedented gesture, the pope also invited leaders of other Christian churches to explore with him ways in which the Petrine ministry might become less an obstacle and more a means to church unity.

Ecumenism and Apostolic Office

The structural reforms undertaken by the Second Vatican Council in the Roman Catholic Church and the council's commitment to more active participation in the ecumenical movement led to a resurgence of interest in the question of apostolic office in ecumenical dialogue.

Is There an Ecumenical Consensus on the Need for an Apostolic Office?

Catholic teaching in the documents of Vatican II helped, to a certain extent, to alleviate Protestant concerns regarding the relationship between Scripture and tradition in Roman Catholicism. The council's affirmation that apostolicity resided not only in church office but in the faith of the whole church also received a sympathetic reception from many Protestant observers. The time seemed ripe, after the council, for Christians to enter into dialogue regarding the various traditions' understandings of apostolic office.

It may be helpful to consider very briefly some Protestant perspectives on the issue. Luther had initially hoped that some bishops would accept his proposed reforms and agree to ordain pastors for ministry in churches sympathetic to his cause. When this did not happen, he embraced the presbyterate or pastorate as an apostolic office, justifying the move by appealing to the views of Jerome and Ambrosiaster regarding the equality of the presbyterate and episcopate. Eventually Lutheranism would move in two different directions.[27] Some would start with Luther's emphasis on the priesthood of believers and invoke a "transference theory" in which the authority and power to preach and administer the sacraments were given to all the baptized but, for reasons of practicality, could be transferred to a designated ministry. Others would begin with Luther's original desire to remain within the Catholic Church, advocating an "institutional theory" that would identify as Luther's primary goal the reform rather than the abolishment of an institutional ministry such that it would serve rather than eclipse the priesthood of believers.

In practice Lutheranism would continue on both fronts. The office of the bishop would come to be viewed as *adiaphora*, that is, a matter about which the church is "indifferent." This meant that particular Lutheran communions were free to adopt an episcopal structure if they wished. So, for example, the Lutheran Church in Sweden has maintained a historical episcopate. Some other Lutheran communions have recently returned to an episcopate, but for the most part Lutheranism has held that the ministry of the bishop is adequately preserved in the role of the pastor.

Anglicanism and Eastern Orthodoxy had always maintained a commitment to a historical episcopate as an essential means of preserving the apostolicity of the church. Yet contemporary Orthodox commentators remain critical of the current theology and practice of the episcopate within contemporary Roman Catholicism. In a classic expression of the Orthodox heritage, Bishop Kallistos Ware articulates what he sees as the Orthodox understanding of the apostolic office of the bishop:

> The relation between the bishop and his flock is a mutual one. The bishop is the divinely appointed *teacher* of the faith, but the *guardian* of the faith is not the episcopate alone, but the whole people of God, bishops, clergy, and laity together. The proclamation of the truth is not the same as the possession of the truth: all the people possess the truth, but it is the bishop's particular office to proclaim it.[28]

Ware is presumably contrasting the Orthodox view with what he sees as a Roman Catholic theology of the episcopate that is prone to see the apostolic faith as the private possession of the bishop.

In ongoing ecumenical dialogues, new and important dimensions of a ministry of apostolic oversight emerge. In the 1999 Anglican-Roman Catholic

---

[27] Burkhard, 205ff. See also Brian A. Gerrish, "Priesthood and Ministry in the Theology of Luther," *Church History* 34 (1965): 404-22.

[28] Timothy Ware, *The Orthodox Church* (New York: Penguin Books, 1963), 255.

International Commission (ARCIC)'s remarkable statement "The Gift of Authority," the ministry of *episkopē* is characterized as a "ministry of memory." Here apostolic office is situated within a rich theology of tradition as communal memory that reinforces the perspectives on apostolic memory explored in the last chapter.

> Tradition makes the witness of the apostolic community present in the church today through its corporate *memory*. Through the proclamation of the word and the celebration of the sacraments, the Holy Spirit opens the hearts of believers and manifests the risen Lord to them. . . . The purpose of Tradition is fulfilled when, through the Spirit, the Word is received and lived out in faith and hope. The witness of proclamation, sacraments and life in communion is at one and the same time the content of Tradition and its result. Thus memory bears fruit in the faithful life of believers within the communion of their local church.[29]

Consequently, the statement asserts, it is the "people of God as a whole" which is "the bearer of the living Tradition."[30] This participation is described in terms of the exercise of the *sensus fidei* of all the baptized and it is within this context that the unique ministry of the bishops as teachers is described:

> Those who exercise *episcope* in the body of Christ must not be separated from the "symphony" of the whole people of God in which they have their part to play. They need to be alert to the *sensus fidelium*, in which they share, if they are to be made aware when something is needed for the well-being of the community or when some element of the Tradition needs to be received in a fresh way. The charism and function of *episcope* are specifically connected to the *ministry of memory*, which constantly renews the church in hope. Through such ministry the Holy Spirit keeps alive in the church the memory of what God did and revealed and the hope of what God will do to bring all things into unity in Christ.[31]

This statement beautifully articulates the bishop's ministry of *episkopē* as a ministry of memory always bound to the corporate memory of the church.

Even where there is less agreement regarding the need for a historical episcopate we can note some significant developments in ecumenical dialogue. This

---

[29] Anglican-Roman Catholic International Commission, "The Gift of Authority," *Origins* 29 (May 27, 1999): 17-29, at 22.

[30] Ibid.

[31] Ibid.

has particularly been the case in the national and international Lutheran–Catholic dialogues. As we saw earlier, Luther did not necessarily reject the episcopacy as an apostolic institution. The Catholic Church at the time of the Reformation had been able to articulate neither a fully coherent theology of the sacraments in general nor a theology of ordained ministry in particular.

> It was really only with Trent that the Catholic Church came into the clear possession of a more or less full exposition of the sacraments. The Reformers were not reacting to a well-reasoned, complete, and balanced theology of the sacraments, but to a series of minimal theological claims and a system of sacramental practices.[32]

This renders much more understandable the Reformers' own ambiguity regarding the role of the episcopate and the concrete shape of apostolic office. The U.S. Lutheran–Roman Catholic Dialogue, in its Agreed Statement, "The Church as Koinonia of Salvation: Its Structures and Ministries," published in 2005, stated:

> When the Lutheran churches felt compelled to ordain pastors apart from the Catholic hierarchy, they were not consciously rejecting any concept of episcopal succession, for such a concept was not current in theological discussions of the period.[33]

That statement also included the admission that the historical episcopate was *one of the ways* "in which the apostolic succession of the church is visibly expressed and personally symbolized in fidelity to the Gospel through the ages."[34] In the United States, the ELCA (Evangelical Lutheran Church of America), in its recent agreement with the U.S. Episcopal Church, expressed a commitment to "share an Episcopal succession that is both evangelical and historic."[35] From the Catholic side, the "Church as Koinonia of Salvation" statement also acknowledged that

> [w]hether a particular minister or church serves the church's apostolic mission does not depend only upon the presence of such a succession of epis-

---

[32] Burkhard, 202-3.

[33] U.S. Lutheran–Roman Catholic Dialogue, *Church as Koinonia of Salvation: Its Structures & Ministries,* ed. Randall Lee and Jeffrey Gros, Lutherans and Catholics in Dialogue 10 (Washington, D.C.: USCCB, 2005), 39.

[34] Ibid., 38.

[35] "Called to Common Mission: A Lutheran Proposal for a Revision of the Concordat of Agreement" (Chicago: ELCA, November 1998), 12.

copal consecration, as if its absence would negate the apostolicity of the church's teaching and mission.[36]

This represents a small step away from the Catholic tendency to insist that there can be no apostolicity where there is no episcopal succession.

Alongside the important developments that have transpired in the Lutheran–Roman Catholic Dialogue on the historical episcopate and apostolic office, we must also recognize the landmark character of the World Council of Churches' Lima document, *Baptism, Eucharist and Ministry* (BEM), published in 1982. At several points the Lima document affirms the importance of episcopal ministry and calls for those traditions without an episcopal ministry to reconsider their position on this ecclesiological question.[37] At the same time it invites churches with a historical episcopate to consider whether churches without an episcopate have found other legitimate ways to preserve the apostolic faith.

In the midst of these important discussions it is worth highlighting an ecclesiological distinction that has received greater attention in recent theological discussions, namely, the difference between *episkopē* as an essential ministerial relation within the life of the church given special responsibility for the work of apostolic oversight, and the *episcopate* as one of three apostolic offices (deacon, presbyter, bishop) "that have been exercised in the church from the earliest times" (LG 20). Can we acknowledge that in the first fifty to one hundred years of the church the exercise of apostolic oversight (*episkopē*), that is, a ministry concerned both with ensuring the integrity of the apostolic faith and manifesting a communion among the churches, took a multiplicity of forms, sometimes exercised collegially and at other times by one minister in the form of a monoepiscopate? If so, then the possibility might exist, in theory, for such a diversity of forms to be acknowledged today without jeopardizing the essential characteristics of the necessary ministry of apostolic oversight.[38] This was articulated in the World Council of Churches' Faith and Order Commission statement "Nature and Purpose of the Church": "The interconnectedness of the life of the Church is maintained by a ministry of *episkopé*, exercised in communal, personal and collegial ways, which sustains a life of interdependence." The commentary then offers this reflection for consideration of those committed to ecumenical dialogue:

---

[36] *The Church as Koinonia of Salvation*, 39.

[37] World Council of Churches, *Baptism, Eucharist and Ministry*, Faith and Order Paper No. 111 (Geneva: WCC, 1982), esp. ## 19-38.

[38] This point was rather provocatively made by the late ecumenist Jean-Marie R. Tillard, "Recognition of Ministries: What Is the Real Question?" *One in Christ* 21 (1985): 31-39.

Churches who exercise episkopé primarily or even uniquely in synodal form and churches for whom the office of bishop is central for the exercise of episkopé are asked to recognize that there is a ministry of episkopé in both cases. Churches which have preserved episcopal succession are challenged to recognize both the faithful continuity with the apostolic faith as well as the apostolic content of the ordained ministry which exists in churches which have not maintained such succession and also the existence in these churches of a ministry of episkopé in various forms. Churches without the episcopal succession, and living in faithful continuity with the apostolic faith and mission, are asked to consider that the continuity with the Church of the apostles can find expression in the successive laying on of hands by bishops and that such a sign can serve that continuity itself.[39]

This line of thought is likely to receive further consideration as ecumenical conversations continue regarding the question of apostolic office and apostolic succession.

Could There Be a Papacy for All Christians?

If considerable movement toward ecumenical agreement has been made toward the importance and desirability of a historical episcopate, important issues remain regarding the need for a Petrine ministry exercised by the bishop of Rome. In the Orthodox tradition, there are a number of bishops and theologians who are prepared to acknowledge a kind of universal primacy for the bishop of Rome. But this universal primacy, from the Orthodox perspective, would have to be exercised within the same constraints that are imposed on that primacy exercised at the patriarchal and metropolitan levels; that is, it could only be a "primacy of honor." This follows from the Orthodox commitment to the "principle of synodality," in which church authority ultimately resides in the bishops gathered in synod as expressive of the communion of the churches. Orthodoxy has long suspected Roman Catholicism of introducing the papacy as a fourth sacramental order, superior to the episcopate. For them papal primacy violates the principle of synodality inasmuch as the pope's universal jurisdiction, solemnly defined at Vatican I, appears to threaten the legitimate authority of the bishops.

A traditional sticking point in this dialogue has been the Orthodox insistence that the bishop of Rome could function only as *primus inter pares*, "first among equals." On the Catholic side this appears to run head-on against Vat-

---

[39] World Council of Churches, *Nature and Purpose of the Church*, Faith and Order Paper No. 181 (Geneva: WCC, 1998), commentary on #93.

ican I's teaching regarding the universal jurisdiction of the pope. However, from the Catholic perspective, most scholars of Vatican I acknowledge the limitations and even inadequacies of the overly juridical view of papal primacy offered in Vatican I's constitution *Pastor Aeternus*.

If ecclesiology, from the Roman Catholic perspective, always demands some juridical form, what Vatican I offered was an ecclesiology *reduced* to its juridical form. Careful studies of Vatican I's teaching demonstrate that in spite of its shortcomings, *Pastor Aeternus* offered a much more carefully circumscribed view of primacy than many realize.[40] Vatican I's teaching on the pope's ordinary, immediate, and universal jurisdiction implied only that proper to the bishop of Rome's office was the responsibility to ensure the welfare of the churches, intervening only because of the incapacity of the local bishop or because the good of the church required it.

Catholicism might find Orthodox insistence that the pope exercises a "primacy of honor" more acceptable if—and this is an important *if*—the Orthodox acknowledge that the "primacy of honor" so vigorously affirmed in their ancient tradition in fact included a genuine exercise of juridical authority. The patristic scholar and ecumenist Brian Daley has published a study on the understanding of a primacy of honor as articulated in the canons of the ancient Eastern councils. He has made a persuasive case that this primacy of honor was never understood in a mere ceremonial sense as an authority that was strictly moral or persuasive in character. It was assumed that the one who possessed a primacy of honor was able to make real and binding decisions.[41] Such an acknowledgment on the part of the Orthodox, coupled with reforms in the understanding and exercise of the papacy that will be outlined below, might go a long way toward overcoming the Orthodox–Roman Catholic impasse on this question.

Roman Catholic–Anglican dialogue has also made some progress on this topic. In "The Gift of Authority," the Anglicans admitted the desirability of a ministry of primacy, presuming, of course, that it was exercised not over the churches in communion with the churches and honored the faith of the whole people of God. This primacy, the statement admitted, includes "a specific ministry concerning the discernment of truth as an expression of universal primacy."[42] In this regard, this document comes closer than any other official ecumenical statement to admitting the possibility of a limited infallible teach-

---

[40] Two studies that make this point with particular force are Jean-Marie R. Tillard, *Bishop of Rome* (Wilmington, Del.: Glazier, 1983); Pottmeyer, *Towards a Papacy in Communion*.

[41] Brian Daley, "Position and Patronage in the Early Church: The Original Meaning of 'Primacy of Honor,'" *Journal of Theological Studies* 44 (1993): 529-53.

[42] "The Gift of Authority," 27.

ing authority "pronounced *within* the college of those exercising *episcope* and not outside the college." This teaching authority would need to be tied to a discernment of the received faith of the churches so that it would be "the wholly reliable teaching of the whole church that is operative in the judgment of the universal primate."[43]

In other venues for ecumenical dialogue there is a growing awareness of the value of a universal ministry in service of unity. For example, the Fifth World Assembly of the Commission on Faith and Order of the World Council of Churches, held in Santiago de Compostela, issued in one of its reports a recommendation that the commission "begin a new study concerning the question of a universal ministry of Christian unity."[44] The 1998 Faith and Order statement, "The Nature and Purpose of the Church," also spoke cautiously of the value of a universal ministry of "presidency" over the churches.[45]

Consensus on papal infallibility has, in general, been more difficult to achieve than that regarding the possibility of a universal Petrine ministry exercised in service of church unity. These reservations center on both the need for the papal teaching office to be placed at the service of the gospel and a concern that the doctrine of synodality and the coequality of the episcopate not be denied.

THE OFFICE OF THE BISHOP IN SERVICE OF THE CATHOLICITY OF THE CHURCH'S MEMORY

In the ARCIC document "Gift of Authority" we discovered a fruitful connection between the episcopal office and the communal memory of the church. Where the conventional view of apostolic office in the Catholic Church presents the bishop as the bearer of the apostolic faith to the people, the bishop as a minister of memory *receives* the memory of the church through immersion in the church's life. If the conventional view suggests that the bishop offers a *determinatio fidei,* a determination of the faith of the church, the bishop as a minister of memory offers a *testificatio fidei,* a testimony to the living memory of the community. The first model accentuates the bishop as a teacher; the second, the bishop as a learner. This new model offers real promise in ecumenical relations, as it emphasizes the apostolic office's subordination to the gospel. It reminds

---

[43] Ibid.

[44] "Report of Section II: Confessing the One Faith to God's Glory," in *On the Way to Fuller Koinonia,* ed. Thomas F. Best and Günther Gassmann, Faith and Order Paper No. 166 (Geneva: WCC, 1994), #31.2.

[45] *Nature and Purpose of the Church,* ## 103, 109.

us that the bishops do not propose new doctrine but rather elucidate, in a formal manner, what already resides in the memory of the church.

Apostolic office, as with most structural elements in the life of the church, has undergone considerable change and development over the course of almost two millennia. In spite of widespread disagreement regarding the necessity of such an office and the precise form that such an office should take, there is a considerable agreement across various Christian traditions that a stable office charged with preserving the apostolic memory of the church and the preservation of the communion of the churches is an important feature of church life.

In a book that seeks to focus on the church as a global community, it is necessary to admit honestly those criticisms leveled against the historical episcopate and the papacy that see these institutions as powerful forces suppressing the global reality of the church rather than enhancing it. Many cite examples from the church's past of an overly ambitious exercise of ecclesiastical authority (one thinks here of the "Chinese Rites" controversy) that failed properly to appreciate both the gifts and challenges of local churches. This raises an obvious question: Is the existence of a historical episcopate and a universal Petrine ministry an aid or obstacle to the flourishing of a genuinely global church?

We have already discussed an important ecclesiological debate concerning the relationship between the local and universal church. In the context of that debate we asserted the importance of giving priority to neither the local nor the universal, but following the analogy of the triune God to insist on the reciprocity and simultaneity of the local and universal dimensions of the church. This presupposes that we also accept the theological integrity of the local church as the locus where the communion among the churches is experienced. This theology of communion imagines a reciprocity in which the gifts and challenges of each local church are shared among the communion of churches by way of an ecclesial gift exchange. Vatican II said as much in LG 13:

> In virtue of this catholicity, each part contributes its own gifts to other parts and to the entire church, so that the whole and each of the parts are strengthened by the common sharing of all things and by the common effort to achieve fullness in unity. . . . For the members of the people of God are called upon to share their goods, and the words of the apostle apply also to each of the churches, "according to the gift that each has received, administer it to one another as good stewards of the manifold grace of God."

In a theology of the universal church as a global communion of churches, this "gift exchange" becomes an important dimension of the ministry of the bishop.[46] Each bishop is charged with bringing to the communion of churches the unique witness or apostolic memory of the local church, and returning to the local church the great symphony of ecclesial memories offered by other local churches. In this theology the bishop serves as facilitator of this ecclesial gift exchange within the communion of churches. This presupposes, however, a transformed vision of the episcopate.

For centuries we have understood the bishops' teaching office in relation to the church's apostolicity. We have insisted, rightly, on the responsibility of the bishop to guard the integrity of the apostolic faith as it is transmitted in his local church. However, an ecclesiology adequate to a global church requires that the bishop be not only a custodian of the church's apostolic memory but also a servant of the catholicity of that memory.

Every diocesan bishop is both pastor of a local church and a member of the college of bishops. This allows the bishop to facilitate a two-way conversation in the life of the church. The bishop proclaims the one apostolic faith to his local flock. This obligation is fulfilled in diverse ways. It is realized in episcopal preaching, in the issuance of pastoral letters, and in the bishop's oversight of the ministries of evangelization and catechesis. Yet too little attention is paid to the bishop's responsibility to preside over the creative reception of the apostolic faith in his local church. This follows from what we have already said regarding the complex processes of ecclesial reception and inculturation. Each local church, in receiving the faith, makes that faith its own. This requires, however, a more developed theology of the bishop's relationship to his local church.

Strengthening Bonds between Bishop and Local Church

In the early centuries of the church, the bishop's ministry as the agent of communion and servant of the catholicity of the church's memory was more readily apparent because the bishop's relationship to his local church was so much stronger. This was due to two factors: first, the widespread conviction that the bishop had to be chosen or at least accepted by the local church he was to serve; and, second, the prohibition of the translation or transfer of bishops from one church to another.

Today procedures in the 1983 Code of Canon Law provide for little input from the local church. In the current code, the laity's role in the selection of a bishop is reduced to selective consultation left to the discretion of the papal

---

[46] Bradford Hinze has produced an illuminating study of ecclesial practices of dialogue that embody this ecclesial gift exchange. Bradford Hinze, *Practices of Dialogue in the Roman Catholic Church: Aims and Obstacles, Lessons and Laments* (New York: Continuum, 2006).

legate (c. 377, §3); this barely acknowledges the long-standing ideal of participation by the clergy and laity in the choice of their bishop. The current pro-
cedure for appointing bishops places most of the responsibility not on the local
church but on the papal nuncio and the Congregation for Bishops. The nuncio and the Congregation for Bishops, in turn, are often influenced more by the
opinions of prominent church leaders, "bishop makers," than by the needs of
the local community and its own sense of who would be most suitable to lead.
Consequently, one obvious reform would be to develop revised procedures that
give local churches greater say in the selection of their local bishop.[47]

A second means of strengthening the relationship between bishop and the
local church would be to recall the ancient canonical prohibitions, articulated
in canon 15 of the Council of Nicaea and maintained into the ninth century,
against the "translation" of a bishop, that is, the transfer of a bishop from one
diocese to another. Occasional exceptions to this canon were made, but they
were rare. There were both theological and pastoral reasons for this prohibition.
At the theological level, the transfer of a bishop violated the nuptial symbolism of a bishop's "marriage" to his people, a symbolism reinforced in the modern ritual by the newly ordained bishop's investiture with an episcopal ring. At
a practical level, it forestalled episcopal careerism. As Michael Buckley has
observed:

> the early Church saw quite practically in this effort to move from one see
> to another an endless source of clerical ambition, rivalry, and self-promotion,
> as well as, more theologically, the violation of the union that should exist
> between the bishop and the people of his diocese.[48]

If a bishop of a relatively small diocese has aspirations for "promotion" to a
larger and more significant church, he may be more inclined to act cautiously,
concerned about how his actions might be interpreted by those with the
authority to assign him to a more influential post.

The church today is quite different in size and demographics from the
church of the early centuries. It is not uncommon today to have a few large
archdioceses with anywhere from one to ten million Catholics, a size unheard
of in the early church. Given this new situation, it is possible to imagine cases

---

[47] Joseph F. O'Callaghan, *Electing Our Bishops: How the Catholic Church Should Choose Its Leaders*
(New York: Rowman & Littlefield, 2007); Richard R. Gaillardetz and John Huels, "The Selection of
Bishops: Recovering the Enduring Values of Our Tradition," *Jurist* 59 (1999): 348-76; William W. Bas-
sett, ed., *The Choosing of Bishops* (Hartford, Conn.: Canon Law Society of America, 1971).

[48] Michael J. Buckley, "What Can We Learn from the Church in the First Millennium?" in *The
Catholic Church in the Twenty-First Century,* ed. Michael J. Himes (Liguori, Mo.: Liguori, 2004), 20.

where an exception to the prohibition of episcopal transfers might have to be made. There are some large archdioceses for which one would prefer to appoint a bishop who already possessed significant pastoral experience as a bishop. But these exceptions would, I think, be relatively few. This of course raises the question whether the church must also give serious consideration to whether such large dioceses and archdioceses are pastorally justifiable. A good case could be made that the creation of smaller dioceses would go a long way toward restoring an ancient vision of the bishop as a true pastor rather than an administrator. In any event, the central point of these reforms is that a bishop who has been welcomed by his local church, and feels himself to be "married" to his flock, however modest, is more inclined to keep the concerns of his people foremost in his mind.

Contemporary Examples of Bishops Serving the Catholicity of the Church's Memory

This account of the bishop as servant of the catholicity of the church's memory is not a mere abstraction. Though they hardly constitute the majority, there are bishops in the last few decades who have embodied this vision of episcopal ministry.

Here in the United States I recall the simple but profound witness of the late Raymond Lucker, bishop of New Ulm, Minnesota. He served as bishop of that small, rural diocese from 1976 to 2000. During that time he eschewed an episcopal residence, preferring to make his car his office while residing in various parish rectories throughout his diocese. This itinerant lifestyle allowed him to visit up to fifty parishes each year. Lucker came to know his people as few bishops have, and although his reputation during his tenure was that of an outspoken liberal bishop, Lucker always believed he was expressing positions motivated by his pastoral concern for those he served and his conviction that their own simple insights had something to offer the larger church.

As a second example I would like to draw, once again, from the Diocese of San Cristóbal de Las Casas. When Bishop Ruiz was ordained to serve the Diocese of San Cristóbal on the eve of Vatican II, his pastoral plan, such as it was, had three points: (1) teach Spanish to the indigenous peoples, (2) provide them with clothing, and (3) improve their diet.[49] Religious education was a simple matter of teaching the catechism to the people. What transpired

---

[49] Michel Andraos, "Praxis of Peace: The Pastoral Work and Theology of Bishop Samuel Ruiz and the Diocese of San Cristóbal de Las Casas, Chiapas, Mexico" (Ph.D. diss., University of St. Michael's College, Toronto, 2000), 94.

over the following decades was the transformation of both a diocese and its bishop.

By his own account, Bishop Ruiz was converted by his people.[50] As he traveled to the hundreds of small communities in the diocese to visit the people, he soon realized that his pastoral initiatives, although well intentioned, were contributing to the destruction of the indigenous cultures.[51] He began to set up local structures that allowed him to listen to the real needs of the people. He called forth catechists from the local communities and deacons who were trained to bring the Catholic faith into conversation with both the collective wisdom and the concrete concerns of the people.

A decisive turning point in the history of his diocese occurred in 1974. The First Indigenous Congress of Chiapas was conducted to commemorate both the 500th anniversary of the birth of Bartolomé de Las Casas, the first bishop of the diocese, and the 150th anniversary of Chiapas's statehood. The congress was originally convoked by the government, and the diocese was soon invited to participate in the preparations. Initial plans were for a series of talks in which the people would have an opportunity to learn more about Bartolomé de Las Casas. However, Ruiz insisted that the people themselves be given responsibility for planning the congress. Local indigenous communities set about an extended planning process. At one preparatory meeting in the Tzeltal region, four hundred local leaders were present.[52] Over two thousand people attended the congress itself. The event was dominated by wide-ranging discussion regarding the plight of the indigenous peoples, the socioeconomic and political sources of their suffering, and their need for greater solidarity. This congress is widely seen as a decisive turning point in the life of the diocese. Ruiz had helped instigate the empowerment of the local people. His subsequent pastoral initiatives would build on that sense of empowerment.

As he grew into his episcopal office, Ruiz would speak with greater frequency of his episcopal ministry as a ministry of "accompaniment" with the people. He realized that ecclesiastical structures like the presbyteral council and diocesan pastoral council were insufficient for establishing the kind of broad-based participation in the life of the diocese that he thought was necessary. These canonically mandated structures could not take into account the great regional diversity of the diocese. So he invited the various regions in his diocese to develop their own pastoral plans as a way of "incarnating" the gospel in their local communities. In so doing, the indigenous communities made use

---

[50] Bishop Samuel Ruiz (with the collaboration of Carles Torner), *Cómo me convirtieron los indígenas*, Colección Servidores y Testigos (Santander: Editorial Sal Terrae, 2002).

[51] Bishop Samuel Ruiz, "In This Hour of Grace," *Origins* 23 (February 10, 1994): 589-602, at 599.

[52] Andraos, 45.

of a traditional Mayan democratic process, the convocation of local assemblies. After over a decade of preparation, a diocesan assembly comprised of leaders from these communities met to approve a diocesan-wide pastoral plan, remarkable for its grassroots origins. A second plan would later emerge out of a diocesan synod held in 1999, just prior to Ruiz's retirement.

Throughout his episcopal ministry, Ruiz remained insistent that he was doing no more than applying Vatican II's imperative to read the signs of the times and allow the gospel to be incarnated in each culture. He never rejected the priority of the gospel and the authority of church teaching, but insisted that these needed to take root in the unique situation of each local church. He acknowledged his own episcopal authority, but felt that this did not preclude his engagement in substantive consultation with the people he served.

A third bishop who has modeled what it is to give witness to the unique contributions of a local church is Bishop Francisco Claver of Northern Luzon in the Philippines. He served as bishop of Malaybalay Diocese and later as Vicar Apostolic of the Diocese of Bontoc-Lagawe. He has often spoken quite eloquently of his experience of local non-Christian indigenous peoples "teaching" the local Christians about gospel values from the riches of their own cultural heritage. When he first became bishop in Mindanao, he began his ministry by conducting extensive interviews with the local peoples, seeking to understand their daily concerns and the ways in which the gospel spoke to their lives. He strongly supported the development of basic ecclesial communities as a way to help the people make the Christian gospel pertinent to their daily lives.

A fourth example is that of Bishop Kevin Dowling of Rustenburg, South Africa. Dowling's advocacy for his people began in the wake of apartheid and the dramatic displacement of populations that followed. Dowling encouraged the establishment of health clinics to meet the needs of the poor in his church. The resulting contact with the people and their needs exposed him to the ravages of HIV/AIDS. He never wavered in his support of Catholic Church teaching on the value of abstinence and marital fidelity. However, his willingness to be with his people allowed him to understand their plight from a different perspective. Many of the men were forced to work in mines and live in camps far from their families. These men frequently paid for sex from prostitutes, who were themselves often desperately poor women who were faced with the choice of prostitution or starvation for their children. The wives of these men could not withhold sex from their spouses. For them, Bishop Dowling believed, the use of condoms was the choice of a lesser evil, the greater evil being that of putting their own lives at risk and leaving their children parentless.

Dowling embodies the bishop as servant of the catholicity of the faith precisely because he has insisted on bringing received Catholic moral teaching into engagement with the concrete life situation of his people. Since 2001

Dowling has courageously spoken out from his pastoral experience with his people and offered their plight as an opportunity for the church universal to examine traditional moral teaching on the possible moral permissibility of the use of condoms.

Finally, I would mention the example of Cardinal Archbishop Fumio Hamao, who for many years was the bishop of Yokohama, Japan, before serving as the president of the Pontifical Council for the Pastoral Care of Migrants and Itinerant Peoples. In his role as bishop and later as one of the few Asians in the curia, he has been tireless in bringing the specific gifts of Asian Catholicism to the larger church. After his resignation as president of the pontifical council was accepted in 2006, he spoke honestly regarding his concern that the Vatican was ill-disposed truly to listen to the unique insights of the Asian churches. He also complained that many official expressions of the common faith of the church were still too Western in form and style, particularly, he contended, the catechism:

> It is all too difficult, too intellectual, too logical. We Asians are not so intellectual, but we are intelligent. We are—how can one say it—more intuitive, more aesthetic. We need something to touch our heart. The catechism does not convert people.[53]

Hamao, Dowling, Claver, Ruiz, and Lucker—all ministered as bishop on three different continents and in very different pastoral settings, yet all have embodied an episcopal ministry in which the bishop is not only a teacher but a listener and learner. They faithfully preached the gospel in their local churches, but they also brought the faith of their people to the universal church. They exhibited a neglected aspect of the bishop's office—they were servants of the catholicity of the church's communal memory.

This new vision of episcopal ministry, one that facilitates communion between the local and universal churches, is not limited to individual bishops. Since the Second Vatican Council, regional episcopal conferences have emerged throughout the world. These have also mediated the reciprocal interaction between the local and the universal church.

Regional Expressions of Episcopal Collegiality

Although some episcopal conferences had already existed before the Second Vatican Council, it was only after the council that these conferences would

---

[53] "Cardinal Hamao Calls for Change," an interview published on the Columban Missionaries Web site: http://www.columban.com/card_hamao_calls_for_change.htm.

emerge as dynamic and influential expressions of episcopal collegiality and instruments for bringing the insight of local and regional churches to the awareness of the church universal.

One of the first regional conferences to fulfill this promise was CELAM, the Spanish acronym for the Latin American Episcopal Conference. Although the conference was actually created before Vatican II (1955), its members came to see their organization as an apt vehicle for realizing the vision of the Second Vatican Council of a church dedicated to mission. They understood that mission to be one of critical engagement with the problems of the world, a mission that required church leadership to discern carefully "the signs of the times." CELAM organized a general meeting in Medellín, Colombia, that was dedicated to applying the council's renewed vision of the church to the socioeconomic situation of Latin America.

The fruit of this historic meeting was an ecclesiastical program for church renewal and a stringent critique of the unjust societal structures that were oppressing so many people in Latin America. The Medellín documents offered an unusual level of specificity to the kind of critical engagement with societal concerns that Vatican II had envisioned. According to Segundo Galilea, Medellín

[f]ormulated the specific mission of the Latin American Church at this critical moment, on the basis not only of the Christian faith but also of the historical situations in which Latin Americans live.[54]

The Medellín documents also provide a convenient marker for the emergence of a distinctive Latin American theology committed to furthering a biblically inspired critique of unjust social structures and an often stinging rebuke of the church's complicity in social injustice.

Although CELAM's application of the gospel to its own regional context at Medellín, and a little over a decade later in Puebla, Mexico, were groundbreaking, of equal importance was the way in which the pronouncements of CELAM brought the issues, concerns, and courageous faith witness of the church of Latin America into the shared consciousness of the universal church. The influence of CELAM would spread beyond Latin America. In both Asia and Africa, regional bishops' conferences were created that followed CELAM's lead by honestly engaging the unique pastoral concerns of their region and

---

[54] Segundo Galilea, "Latin America in the Medellín and Puebla Conferences: An Example of Selective and Creative Reception of Vatican II," in *The Reception of Vatican II*, ed. Giuseppe Alberigo, Jean-Pierre Jossua, and Joseph A. Komonchak (Washington D.C.: Catholic University of America Press, 1987), 59-73, at 63.

fearlessly bringing the one Christian faith into dialogue with their distinctive cultures.

In the early 1970s, the bishops of Asia, clearly influenced by CELAM but aware of the distinctiveness of their own context, created the Federation of Asian Bishops Conferences with the approval of Pope Paul VI. Most significant was FABC's commitment to the pastoral priority of the local church. Within an ecclesiology of communion, they felt it vital to allow the unique pastoral circumstances of their local churches to guide their initiatives. Though the churches of Asia manifest a significant diversity (FABC includes bishops from Bangladesh, Taiwan, India-Nepal, Indonesia, Japan, Korea, Laos-Cambodia, Malaysia-Singapore-Brunei, Myanmar, Pakistan, the Philippines, Sri Lanka, Thailand, and Vietnam),[55] they share a commitment to pastoral work grounded in a threefold dialogue with the local cultures, local religions, and local peoples.

One of the most remarkable initiatives to come forth from FABC directly relates to their distinctive vision of episcopal ministry. FABC had consistently stressed the local church as the decisive context for theological reflection and episcopal decision making. This vision called for an episcopate deeply rooted in the cares and concerns of the people they were to serve. In service of that goal, FABC adopted an episcopal social-action initiative that predated FABC and renamed it the Office for Human Development. The OHD proceeded to organize a series of immersion programs that provided opportunities for the bishops to live amid the poorest of their peoples in order to achieve a more profound understanding of the plight of the poor. These programs, lasting approximately two weeks, would also provide the bishops with opportunities to reflect and discuss with one another what they were learning. Thomas Fox has noted the impact of these programs on many of the Asian bishops:

> While many of their hearts had been in the right places, most Asian bishops had been largely shielded by years of seminary and rectory life from the harsher realities of poverty. The actual taste of poverty up close would be new for many and shocking for some.[56]

These seminars were later referred to as Bishops' Institutes for Social Action, and they played a significant role in the consciousness-raising of the Asian bishops from 1974 to 1987.

---

[55] Thomas C. Fox, *Pentecost in Asia: A New Way of Being Church* (Maryknoll, N.Y.: Orbis Books, 2002), 27.

[56] Ibid., 59.

In Africa several organizations of episcopal conferences have also followed CELAM in creating structures intended to respond to the specific challenges of the African church and to bring the witness and gifts of the African church to the church universal. These include the creation of AMECEA (Association of Member Episcopal Conferences of Eastern Africa) and SECAM (Symposium of the Episcopal Conferences of Africa and Madagascar). In the 1970s these episcopal organizations issued a number of important statements on the need for Africa to become more self-reliant and more inculturated.[57] At the same time, as with the episcopal conferences in Latin America and Asia, they brought the gifts and concerns of their people to the consciousness of the larger church. These episcopal conferences extended, in their pastoral initiatives, the ministry of the bishop as servant of the catholicity of the church's memory. They facilitated the reciprocal dialogue between local church and universal church that maintains that communal memory as a living reality.

Petrine Ministry in a Global Church

As we saw above, in spite of many advances in ecumenical relations with other Christian communions, the Petrine ministry remains a significant ecumenical stumbling block. Many ecumenical dialogue partners are willing, in principle, to accept the idea of a Petrine ministry in service of the unity of the churches, but they balk at the Petrine ministry as currently structured in Roman Catholicism. Cognizant of this fact, Pope John Paul II extended a remarkable invitation:

> I am convinced that I have a particular responsibility in this regard, above all in acknowledging the ecumenical aspirations of the majority of the Christian Communities and in heeding the request made of me to find a way of exercising the primacy which, while in no way renouncing what is essential to its mission, is nonetheless open to a new situation. . . . Could not the real but imperfect communion existing between us persuade Church leaders and their theologians to engage with me in a patient and fraternal dialogue on this subject, a dialogue in which, leaving useless controversies behind, we could listen to one another, keeping before us only the will of Christ for his Church and allowing ourselves to be deeply moved by his plea "that they may all be one . . . so that the world may believe that you have sent me." (UUS 95-96)

---

[57] Elochukwu E. Uzukwu, *A Listening Church: Autonomy and Communion in African Churches* (Maryknoll, N.Y.: Orbis Books, 1996), 146-47.

In the determination of any new form for exercising this ministry in service of unity, it will be necessary to consider the global context of such a ministry.

In 2000, two Jesuit theologians, Avery Dulles and Ladislas Orsy, debated the shape a future papacy ought to take in this global context.[58] Dulles contends that under the pontificates of Paul VI and John Paul II the papacy was successfully reconceived in a new global context. The curia was internationalized, and consultative and collegial structures such as episcopal conferences and the world synod of bishops were established or enhanced. John Paul II, in particular, refashioned the papacy through his many global travels, making the papacy a more profound symbol of church unity. Dulles contends that those who call for a decentralization of the papacy may well be the real "restorationists," since they are calling for a papacy modeled on the first five or six centuries of the church. That relatively weak papacy is ill equipped, he believes, to address the needs of today's global church. "The global character of the Catholic Church today, together with the rapidity of modern communications, makes ineluctable new demands on the papal office."[59]

Orsy offered a quite different perspective. He suggested that the needs of the global church today demanded an application of the principle of subsidiarity to the exercise of the papacy. First articulated in a church document by Pope Pius XI in his encyclical *Quadragesimo Anno*, the principle has several levels of application. First it asserts the primacy of the individual person over other associations. Second, it affirms the priority of smaller social groupings over larger, more complex groupings (e.g., the state). Finally, it asserts the obligation of larger associations to assist the smaller when necessary. Pope Pius XII extended the principle's sphere of application when he observed in 1946 that this principle, "valid for social life in all its grades" was valid "also for the life of the church without prejudice to its hierarchical structure."[60] As applied to the life of the church, the principle has two dimensions, one positive and the other negative. Positively, subsidiarity affirms the obligations of more comprehensive church entities to assist both smaller communities and individual persons

---

[58] Avery Dulles, "The Papacy for a Global Church," and Ladislas Orsy, "The Papacy for an Ecumenical Age—A Response to Avery Dulles. Both articles are found in *Readings in Church Authority: Gifts and Challenges for Contemporary Catholicism*, edited by Gerard Mannion, Richard Gaillardetz, Jan Kerkhofs, and Kenneth Wilson (London: Ashgate, 2003), 274-87.

[59] Dulles, 279.

[60] Pope Pius XII made this statement in an address to newly created cardinals, *Acta Apostolicae Sedis* 38 (1946): 144-45. He reaffirmed the ecclesial implications of the principle of subsidiarity in an address to the Second World Congress of the Lay Apostolate in 1957; see *Acta Apostolicae Sedis* 49 (1957): 926-28. For a valuable survey of the literature on this topic, see John Burkhard, "The Interpretation and Application of Subsidiarity in Ecclesiology: An Overview of the Theological and Canonical Literature," *Jurist* 58 (1998): 279-342.

in the realization of their proper goals. Negatively it precludes, under ordinary circumstances, those larger or more comprehensive church structures from interfering in the affairs of individuals or smaller communities. Orsy believes that this principle must be applied to the exercise of the papacy today. Such an application would necessarily lead to a certain de-centralization in which the papacy would intervene in the affairs of local churches only when the necessity of preserving the unity of faith and communion required it.

This concern for the papacy's exercise of subsidiarity is expressed by many church leaders throughout the world. They all readily embrace the authority of the pope, but on almost every continent stories can be told by prominent church leaders of Vatican action (or inaction) that reflected a failure of the Vatican either adequately to grasp the pastoral concerns of local churches or to trust local church leadership to make decisions appropriate to the needs of their churches. These frustrations are often directed toward the liturgical life of the church.

One bishop in the Philippines voiced to me his frustration over repeated attempts by the Filipino bishops to get approval for a Tagalog translation of the sacramentary. Carefully developed translations were produced by a committee of Filipino bishops and scholars only to be rejected by Roman officials, who often depended on Filipino graduate students studying in Rome for an analysis of the translations! These incidents are noted by non-Catholic Christian leaders and cited as instances of an overweening exercise of the papacy that could never be acceptable to their traditions.

A global and ecumenically acceptable exercise of the Petrine ministry will have to make more explicit a distinction that I believe has long been implicit in our tradition, namely, a distinction between two complementary modes of exercising papal primacy, *facilitative* and *interventionist*.[61] The most common exercise of primacy we might refer to as *facilitative*. This refers to the ordinary ministry of the bishop of Rome in which he "confirms his brothers" in the proper exercise of their ministry as pastors of local churches. This facilitative ministry might include the convocation of episcopal synods, papal visitations, and *ad limina* visits along with other means of facilitating communion among the bishops. The facilitative exercise of papal primacy would not involve any direct intervention in the affairs of local churches.

Much less frequently, there may also be a need for an *interventionist* exercise of papal primacy. This interventionist exercise of papal authority would be engaged only when the bishop of Rome, either directly or through curial offices,

---

[61] In an earlier essay I referred to these two modes as *confirmatory* and *exceptional*. See Richard R. Gaillardetz, "Reflections on the Future of Papal Primacy," *New Theology Review* 13 (November 2000): 52-66.

finds it necessary to intervene in the affairs of a local church or churches because the local structures of leadership have proven incapable of addressing a matter that threatens the unity of faith and communion. Unless the unity of faith and communion of the whole church is at risk, there seems to be little ecclesiological justification for Roman intervention. It would not be sufficient for a Roman official, or even the pope, to disagree with the actions of a local bishop or bishops. Interventionist papal authority could be justified only when the action or inaction of local leaders was inadequate or imperiled the unity of the church.

These two forms of papal primacy would not be opposed to one another. The interventionist exercise of exceptional authority is simply a more direct and authoritative means of supporting and confirming the local bishops in the fulfillment of their pastoral responsibilities, namely, the building up of the body and the preservation of unity within the body.[62]

This chapter has explored the place of apostolic office in the church from the perspective of church memory—the principal task of the church's apostolic office is to authoritatively teach and preserve the apostolic memory of the churches. For much of the second millennium, this ministry of apostolic office has focused on a theology of tradition that privileged the responsibility for authoritative teaching of the faith. The previous chapter's emphasis on the priority of communal memory in our understanding of apostolicity allows us to conceive of apostolic office as a ministry in service of the church's memory. It does not reject the need for authoritative church teaching, but situates the teaching office within a ministry in which listening and learning are equally constitutive. It also recognizes that the church's memory is peculiarly catholic; there is no one monolithic account of the gospel of Jesus Christ but a rich tradition that embraces wonderfully diverse and overlapping contextualized memories of the many Christian communities who, across the centuries, sought to keep alive the dangerous memories of Christ.

Perhaps, then, we can conclude our reflection on apostolic office by returning to the wisdom of a rapidly maturing African ecclesiology. African theology offers a provocative metaphor for this new vision of episcopal leadership. Elochukwu Uzukwu writes of an African tribe known as the Manja, which has as the totem for their chief a rabbit with "large ears." This is because the chief is to be a listener; he is to listen to God, to the ancestors, and to the community. Uzukwu writes:

---

[62] For a quite similar account of this distinction in papal primacy, see Michael J. Buckley, *Papal Primacy and the Episcopate: Toward a Relational Understanding* (New York: Crossroad, 1998), 62–74.

To tune in fully to the Manja image of leadership, we fall back on the resources of our African tradition to retrieve the dynamic personality of the chief or community leader: a person living under the gaze of God, ancestors, and spirits, a person living in attentive listening to the community in order to accomplish adequately the ministry of custodianship of that Word which belongs to the community, the Word which belongs to humanity.[63]

In African tribal culture the communities of elders are seen as custodians of the wisdom of the ancestors; they are, if you will, keepers of the tribal memory. Another African theologian, Bénézet Bujo, a priest and theologian from Zaire, has made effective use of this image in reconceiving church leadership structures.[64] In African tribal culture the communities of elders are seen as custodians of the wisdom of the ancestors. They are, if you will, keepers of the tribal memory. Bujo boldly reimagines the Petrine ministry along the lines of the role of the eldest brother in a family called, upon the death of the father, to play a custodial role in the handling of ancestral property. His ministry is characterized as twofold, first to care for the ancestral heritage, and, second, to preserve the harmony of the family.[65] Along parallel lines, Uzukwu invokes the insight of the "chief with long ears":

> The chief . . . begins by listening: he speaks only after having recorded the discussion going on in the community, so that his speech releases the healing Word of which he is the principal custodian, a Word that makes the community stand erect.[66]

This custodial understanding of leadership must be conjoined with the tradition of African *palaver*, a multilayered, open-ended form of communal conversation that seeks to arrive at consensus. This African *palaver* is not opposed to the participation of a community leader but would reject any exercise of leadership that did not flow out of this *palaver*.[67] The emerging African ecclesiology offers a compelling image of a listening church leadership humbly placing itself at the service of the conversation and inherited wisdom of the community. The testimony of Africa suggests that the renewal of apostolic office may call us to cultivate a leadership "with large ears."

---

[63] Uzukwu, 130.

[64] See Bénézet Bujo, "On the Road toward an African Ecclesiology: Reflections on the Synod," in *African Synod: Documents, Reflections, Perspectives,* ed. Maura Browne and the African Faith & Justice Network (Maryknoll, N.Y.: Orbis Books, 1996), 139-51; idem, *African Theology in Its Social Context* (Maryknoll, N.Y.: Orbis Books, 1992).

[65] Bujo, *African Theology in Its Social Context,* 25-26, 100-103.

[66] Uzukwu, 129-30.

[67] Bujo, "On the Road toward an African Ecclesiology," 148-49 and Uzukwu, 128-29.

QUESTIONS FOR REFLECTION

1. What aspects of the way the papacy was understood in the first millennium might prove useful in ecumenical dialogue regarding a possible papacy for all Christians?
2. What changes need to be made in the concrete ministry of the bishops if they are to fulfill their role as servants of the church's memory and of the church's catholicity?
3. What would be some of the concrete pastoral consequences of returning to the early church practice of (a) requiring that local churches elect their bishops, and (b) prohibiting the transfer of bishops from one diocese to another except in extraordinary circumstances?

SUGGESTIONS FOR FURTHER READING AND STUDY

Buckley, Michael J. *Papal Primacy and the Episcopate: Toward a Relational Understanding*. New York: Crossroad, 1998.

Burkhard, John J. *Apostolicity Then and Now: An Ecumenical Church in a Postmodern World*. Collegeville, Minn.: Liturgical Press, 2004.

Duffy, Eamon. *Saints and Sinners: A History of the Popes*. New Haven: Yale University Press, 1997.

Eisen, Ute E. *Women Officeholders in Early Christianity*. Collegeville, Minn.: Liturgical Press, 2000.

Fox, Thomas C. *Pentecost in Asia: A New Way of Being Church*. Maryknoll, N.Y.: Orbis Books, 2002.

Hinze, Bradford. *Practices of Dialogue in the Roman Catholic Church: Aims and Obstacles, Lessons and Laments*. New York: Continuum, 2006.

Pottmeyer, Hermann J. *Towards a Papacy in Communion*. New York: Crossroad, 1998.

Sullivan, Francis A. *From Apostles to Bishops: The Development of the Episcopacy in the Early Church*. New York: Paulist Press, 2001.

Tillard, Jean-Marie R. *Bishop of Rome*. Wilmington, Del.: Glazier, 1983.

Uzukwu, Elochukwu E. *A Listening Church: Autonomy and Communion in African Churches*. Maryknoll, N.Y.: Orbis Books, 1996.

Conclusion

As is often the case, there was a lively discussion between author and editors over the title of this volume. An early entry was straight and to the point: *A Global Ecclesiology*. This was eventually rejected as a case of theological overreaching. Quite frankly, I do not think it is possible to construct a truly global theology of the church as yet. We should find instructive the characterization of our present epoch as "postmodern." We are living in the midst of a sweeping cultural transformation, and it is difficult to describe our situation other than in terms of what it is distinct from, namely, modernity. We are a long way from fully grasping the impact of the forces of globalization, massive demographic shifts, technology, and pluralism on the shape of the church. The Catholic Church, in particular, has always been slow, perhaps rightfully so, to respond to civilizational shifts. Vatican II, for example, provided the church with an opportunity positively to engage the forces of modernity at precisely the moment in which the cultural contours of our age were being redefined as *post*-modern. The pressing issues of our time do not all yet have clear and persuasive solutions for the life of the church.

This volume has offered an initial and necessarily tentative venture toward a fully global ecclesiology. My focus has been on building an ecclesiological bridge between the church's responses to past challenges and the new issues facing the church today. On one side of that bridge has been (1) the impressive theological achievement of the generation of theologians who both paved the way for, and participated in, the Second Vatican Council; (2) the Second Vatican Council itself, including its ongoing reception in the postconciliar church; (3) the bilateral and multilateral dialogues of the ecumenical movement. On the other side has been the new theological contributions of voices from the global South: theologians, individual bishops, and regional episcopal conferences that are experiencing the global reality of the church much more acutely than those of us who still live in the shadow of the church's comfortable Euro-centrism. Also standing on that other shore have been new voices in the North who have experienced the multicultural character of dual-belonging and "life on the borders" including the work of black, latino/a, feminist, mujerista, and womanist theologians.

There is much yet to be done if the church is to be fully responsive to new global realities. It may be helpful to sketch out in these final pages some of these challenges.

1. *New questions regarding the cultural makeup and ecclesiological significance of the local church.* We have rightly attended to the important achievement of the Second Vatican Council and the postconciliar church in the recovery of the full theological significance of the local church. A communion ecclesiology that celebrates the universal church as a communion of local churches must privilege the particularity of each local church and the gifts and challenges that each church brings to the *communio ecclesiarum.* Yet the experience of local church is itself changing in complex ways.

It is simply no longer the case, if it ever was, that each local church is rooted in one distinct cultural context. One of the consequences of postmodern globalization is the cross-pollination and hybridization of cultures, in which cultures exist in a complex state of interaction. The cardinal archbishop of Los Angeles is fond of pointing out that each Sunday, Mass is celebrated in his diocese in over sixty different languages. We are only just beginning to consider the consequences of such a complex cultural phenomenon.

Yet it is not only the multicultural character of the local church that presents a challenge. The very concept of geographic locality is increasingly being called into question. With the global spread of modern communications technologies like the Internet, many commentators see a diminished sense of place. For some this is a positive reality, opening up new vistas for the creation of nonlocalized communities through Internet blogs and listservs.[1] Others wonder whether these virtual communities deprive members of a vital sense of place, rootedness, and the personal vulnerability that is so often the by-product of face-to-face communal interaction.

In yet another sense, our sense of locality has not simply dissipated but has become quite insular. It is not uncommon, particularly in North America, to encounter thriving parishes that have no sense of their connection to the larger church. This is quite in keeping with an enclave culture reflected in the thousands of gated communities one encounters throughout North American suburbia.[2] For many North American Catholics, the diocese has ceased to be a meaningful ecclesiological unit. Parishioners in these ecclesial settings encounter their bishop perhaps twice a year, once in connection with a diocesan annual appeal and once again for confirmations. This communal insularity represents a pressing challenge to the catholicity of the church.

---

[1] Howard Rheingold, *Virtual Community: Homesteading on the Electronic Frontier* (New York: Addison-Wesley, 1993).

[2] The phenomenon of an enclave culture is discussed at length in Robert Bellah et al., *Habits of the Heart: Individualism and Commitment in American Life,* updated ed. (Berkeley: University of California Press, 1996).

2. *The need for greater diversity in ministerial structures.* In this volume we have already considered the diverse ministerial models that are being developed in contexts as different as Mexico and South Africa. We have also noted the reluctance of Vatican leadership to embrace this diversity. This is a conflict that is likely only to be exacerbated in the coming decades. The tensions, I might point out, are not only between ecclesiastical center and periphery.

I recently gave a presentation to a gathering of lay ecclesial ministers in North America who were eager to learn about my experience of new developments in the churches of the global South. They were somewhat dismayed to learn that there was little use of the lay ecclesial ministry model as practiced in North America. That is not to say that the churches of the south are not making use of lay ministry; they are. It means that in those contexts lay ministry was not developing according to the North American model of ministerial professionalism.

This is not simply a matter of economic limitations, though that certainly plays a role. I have had a number of church leaders say that they did not want to adopt the North American model of lay ecclesial ministry (or the North American model of the permanent diaconate, for that matter) because it appeared to extend the already problematic clericalization of ministry by emphasizing a salaried ministerial elite who had graduate-level theological training. The model being developed in many churches in the global South, as we saw in chapter 4, focuses on small Christian communities and the calling forth of local ministers to serve only their particular faith community, but not as professional ministers. I am not suggesting that the North American model is without value—I think that, properly understood and implemented, it has much to commend it for the North American church—I wish only to remind the reader that the need for an openness to a diversity of ministerial structures is an issue not just for the Vatican but for many theologians and church leaders in North America as well.

Finally, there is no getting around the tensions that are created over (1) the canonical and doctrinal preconditions for determining the pool of candidates who can pursue ordained ministry and (2) the traditional model of ministerial formation that requires multiple years of academic work, often geographically far removed from one's local church. The global scandal created by a situation in which the majority of Catholics are deprived of the regular celebration of the eucharist simply cannot be solved by appealing to a few churches of the South where vocations to the priesthood appear to be flourishing (e.g., some parts of Africa and India) as if those churches will lead the way out of the priest shortage crisis. One can only hope that Vatican leadership will soon recognize the inevitable failure of a "one size fits all" mentality to ordained ministry and allow for regional experimentation with the kinds of new models for ministry proposed by figures like Bishop Lobinger in South Africa.

3. *The need to allow the fruit of interreligious dialogue to penetrate the church's theological self-understanding and mission.* It is perhaps misleading to compare the cause of Christian ecumenism with interreligious dialogue. The differences are significant. Yet one can only hope for a time in the church when the fruit of interreligious dialogue might exert an influence on the Catholic Church analogous to what has transpired as the result of the ecumenical movement. Admittedly, the prospects for this kind of development, at least in the short term, are dim. That being said, we must not underestimate the ample developments in Catholic Church attitudes toward non-Christian religions that occurred with the teaching of the Second Vatican Council. In *Lumen Gentium*, *Ad Gentes*, and the council's Declaration on the Relation of the Church to Non-Christian Religions (*Nostra Aetate*), the bishops denounced anti-Semitism and rejected any attribution of collective responsibility for the death of Christ to the Jewish people. The council affirmed the unique and enduring status of Judaism in the divine plan, insisted on the possibility of salvation being extended to non-Christians and acknowledged the elements of "truth and grace" that could be found in the great religions of the world. The decades following the council saw some important if tentative new openings in interreligious dialogue. Particularly significant gains have been made in Jewish–Christian relations. And one cannot exaggerate the symbolic significance of Pope John Paul II's convening in 1986 a World Day of Prayer for Peace held in Assisi, Italy. Nor can we overlook the contributions made by that same pope in his encyclical *Redemptoris Missio*, in which he boldly affirmed the presence and activity of the Holy Spirit in other religious traditions.

In spite of these gains, at present Catholic participation in interreligious dialogue struggles under the specter of the CDF document *Dominus Iesus*, promulgated in 2000. That document reasserted traditional Christian teaching regarding the unique salvific role of Jesus Christ, but at the same time suggested that other religious traditions are "objectively speaking, in a gravely deficient situation in comparison with those who, in the Church, have the fullness of the means of salvation" (DI 22). *Dominus Iesus* was soon followed by disciplinary notifications regarding the work of three Jesuit theologians, Jacques Dupuis, Roger Haight, and Jon Sobrino. All in one way or another were accused of denying or at least attenuating the unique status of Christ as the sole mediator of God's saving purposes. Taken together, these actions give ample evidence of increasing Vatican concern with the potentially negative consequences of religious pluralism. In the minds of many Vatican officials, it is impossible to embrace religious pluralism without, at the same time, embracing religious relativism.

Once again we encounter another version of the pernicious "zero-sum game" which, in this case, takes the form of the mistaken assumption that increased knowledge of other religious traditions will somehow weaken commitment to one's own tradition. This fear, coupled with an unwillingness to grant that other religious traditions might have something to teach Christians, has weakened ecclesiastical support for substantive interreligious dialogue.

The church has suffered because of it. I say "church" quite deliberately. There have been important contributions to Christian theological reflection as a consequence of contemporary interreligious dialogue. We are witnessing exciting new theological explorations of such traditional topics as God, Christ, and Mary, informed by the encounter with other religious traditions. These have begun to appear, even if, as we have seen, they have been received with suspicion by the Vatican. However, relatively little work has as yet been done in asking what other religious traditions have to teach Christians in the area of ecclesiology. One wonders what might be gained by the encounter with practitioners of other religious traditions regarding the dynamics of community, the exercise of religious leadership, the internal negotiation of differences in belief, the demands and shape of community initiation, the relationship between a community's ritual life and its ethical living, etc. Indeed, because of the paucity of such dialogue, even this list depends on *Christian* concepts and terms for assessing communal life. Obviously these topics have been investigated by scholars in comparative religions, but this is not the same as reaping the fruit of dialogue between practitioners of different religious traditions. A theology of the church that is richly informed by the conceptions of community encountered in other religious traditions remains but a hope for the future.

Throughout this volume I have been suggesting that leadership into a more global experience of the church is coming from the churches of the South. However, the dramatic influx of immigrants into Europe and North America and the considerable religious pluralism that has accompanied these immigration patterns suggests that the churches in these countries have the opportunity to take the lead in interreligous dialogue. In my own city of Toledo, Ohio, Christians are meeting regularly with members from local synagogues, the Hindu temple, and one of the Islamic mosques to learn from one another. The American culture of relative religious tolerance, religious freedom, and the high education level of many of the members of these diverse religious communities have combined to create a wonderful opportunity for a rich local dialogue. And perhaps, lacking leadership from the center, it is in these local dialogues that new insights for a theology of the church will emerge.

These are but three of the challenges that await us as we continue to work toward a genuinely global vision of the church. The difficulties before us are daunting. Indeed, we might have reason to despair were it not for the enduring Christian conviction that if the church is indeed being born anew in our time, the Holy Spirit stands ready as its midwife.

Select Bibliography

Accattoli, Luigi. *When a Pope Asks Forgiveness: The Mea Culpa's of John Paul II.* Boston: Pauline Books, 1998.

Afanassieff, Nicolas. *The Church of the Holy Spirit.* Notre Dame, Ind.: University of Notre Dame Press, 2007.

———. *"Una Sancta." Irénikon* 36 (1963): 436-75.

Agnew, Francis H. "The Origin of the NT Apostle-Concept: A Review of Research." *Journal of Biblical Literature* 105 (1986): 75-96.

Alberigo, Giuseppe, and Joseph A. Komonchak, eds. *History of Vatican II.* 5 volumes. Maryknoll, N.Y.: Orbis Books, 1995-2006.

Amaladoss, Michael. *Beyond Inculturation: Can the Many Be One?* Delhi: Indian Society for Promoting Christian Knowledge, 1998.

———. *Walking Together: The Practice of Inter-Religious Dialogue.* Anand, Gujarat, India: Gujarat Sahitya Prakash, 1992.

Andraos, Michel. "Praxis of Peace: The Pastoral Work and Theology of Bishop Samuel Ruiz and the Diocese of San Cristóbal de Las Casas, Chiapas, Mexico." Ph.D. dissertation, University of St. Michael's College, Toronto, 2000.

Archer, Margaret S. *Culture and Agency: The Place of Culture in Social Theory.* Cambridge: Cambridge University Press, 1989.

Austin, Gerard. "Restoring Equilibrium after the Struggle with Heresy." In *Source and Summit: Commemorating Josef A. Jungmann, S.J.,* edited by Joanne M. Pierce and Michael Downey, 35-47. Collegeville, Minn.: Liturgical Press, 1999.

Avis, Paul. *Beyond the Reformation? Authority, Primacy and Unity in the Conciliar Tradition.* London: T&T Clark, 2006.

Azevedo, Marcello de Carvalho. *Basic Ecclesial Communities in Brazil: The Challenge of a New Way of Being Church.* Washington, D.C.: Georgetown University Press, 1987.

Barth, Karl. *Kirchliche Dogmatik* 4/2. Zurich: Theologischer Verlag, 1953.

Bassett, William W., ed. *The Choosing of Bishops.* Hartford, Conn.: Canon Law Society of America, 1971.

Becker, Karl. "The Church and Vatican II's *Subsistit* Terminology." *Origins* 35 (January 19, 2006): 514-22.

Beinert, Wolfgang. "Catholicity as a Property of the Church." *Jurist* 52 (1992): 455-83.

Bellah, Robert, et al., *Habits of the Heart: Individualism and Commitment in American Life.* Updated edition. Berkeley: University of California Press, 1996.

Bellitto, Christopher M. *Renewing Christianity: A History of Church Reform from Day One to Vatican II.* New York: Paulist Press, 2001.

Bernier, Paul. *Ministry in the Church: A Historical and Pastoral Approach.* Mystic, Conn.: Twenty-third Publications, 1992.

Bevans, Stephen. *Models of Contextual Theology.* Revised and expanded ed. Maryknoll, N.Y.: Orbis Books, 2002.

Bevans, Stephen B., and Roger P. Schroeder. *Constants in Context: A Theology of Mission for Today.* Maryknoll, N.Y.: Orbis Books, 2004.

Boeve, Lieven. *Interrupting Tradition: An Essay on Christian Faith in a Postmodern Context.* Leuven: Peeters, 2004.

Boff, Leonardo. *Church: Charism and Power: Liberation Theology and the Institutional Church.* New York: Crossroad, 1985.

———. *Ecclesiogenesis: The Base Communities Reinvent the Church.* Maryknoll, N.Y.: Orbis Books, 1986.

Bosch, David. *Transforming Mission: Paradigm Shifts in Theology of Mission.* Maryknoll, N.Y.: Orbis Books, 1991.

Bourg, Florence Caffrey. *Where Two or Three Are Gathered: Christian Families as Domestic Churches.* Notre Dame, Ind.: University of Notre Dame Press, 2004.

Brown, Raymond E. *The Churches the Apostles Left Behind.* New York: Paulist Press, 1984.

Browne, Maura, and the Africa Faith & Justice Network, eds. *The African Synod: Documents, Reflections, Perspectives.* Maryknoll, N.Y.: Orbis Books, 1996.

Brueggemann, Walter. *The Prophetic Imagination.* 2nd edition. Minneapolis: Fortress, 2001.

Buckley, Michael J. *Papal Primacy and the Episcopate: Toward a Relational Understanding.* New York: Crossroad, 1998.

———. "What Can We Learn from the Church in the First Millennium?" In *The Catholic Church in the Twenty-First Century,* edited by Michael J. Himes, 11-28. Liguori, Mo.: Liguori, 2004.

Bujo, Bénézet. *African Christian Morality at the Age of Inculturation.* Christian Leadership in Africa. Nairobi: St. Paul Publications, 1990.

———. "On the Road toward an African Ecclesiology: Reflections on the Synod." In *African Synod: Documents, Reflections, Perspectives,* edited by Maura Browne and the Africa Faith & Justice Network, 139-51. Maryknoll, N.Y.: Orbis Books, 1996.

Burkhard, John J. *Apostolicity Then and Now: An Ecumenical Church in a Postmodern World.* Collegeville, Minn.: Liturgical Press, 2004.

Burrows, William R., ed. *Redemption and Dialogue: Reading Redemptoris Missio and Dialogue and Proclamation.* Maryknoll, N.Y.: Orbis Books, 1993.

Burtchaell, James T. *From Synagogue to Church: Public Services and Offices in the Earliest Christian Communities.* Cambridge: Cambridge University Press, 1992.

Campenhausen, Hans von. *Ecclesiastical Authority and Spiritual Power in the Church of the First Three Centuries.* Stanford, Calif.: Stanford University Press, 1969.

Canon Law Society of America, Ad Hoc Committee. *The Canonical Implications of Ordaining Women to the Permanent Diaconate.* Washington, D.C.: CLSA, 1995.

Chenu, Marie-Dominique. "Consecratio Mundi." *Nouvelle revue théologique* 86 (1964): 608-16.

Chia, Edmund. *Towards a Theology of Dialogue.* Bangkok: Edmund Chia, 2003.

Clifford, Anne. *Introducing Feminist Theology.* Maryknoll, N.Y.: Orbis Books, 2001.

Collins, John N. *Are All Christians Ministers?* Collegeville, Minn.: Liturgical Press, 1992.

———. *Deacons and the Church: Making Connections between Old and New.* Harrisburg, Pa.: Morehouse, 2002.

———. *Diakonia: Re-interpreting the Ancient Sources.* New York: Oxford University Press, 1990.

Collins, Mary. *Contemplative Participation: Sacrosanctum Concilium Twenty-five Years Later.* Collegeville, Minn.: Liturgical Press, 1990.

Comblin, José. *People of God.* Maryknoll, N.Y.: Orbis Books, 2004.

Cone, James. *A Black Theology of Liberation.* Philadelphia: Lippincott, 1970.

Congar, Yves. "The Church: The People of God." In *The Church and Mankind. Concilium* 1. New York: Paulist Press, 1965.

———. *Diversity and Communion.* Mystic, Conn.: Twenty-third Publications, 1982.

————. *Lay People in the Church*. Westminster, Md.: Newman Press, 1965.

————. *L'Église de Saint Augustin à l'époque moderne*. Paris: Cerf, 1970.

————. "Pneumatologie ou 'Christomonisme' dans la tradition latine." In *Ecclesia a Spiritu Sancto edocta: Mélanges théologiques, hommages à Mgr Gérard Philips*, 41-63. Bibliotheca ephemeridum theologicarum Lovaniensium 27. Gembloux: Duculot, 1970.

————. *Tradition and Traditions: An Historical and Theological Essay*. New York: Macmillan, 1966.

Coriden, James. "The Synod of Bishops: Episcopal Collegiality Still Seeks Adequate Expression." *Jurist* 64 (2004): 116-36.

Dahl, Nils Alstrup. *Jesus in the Memory of the Early Church*. Minneapolis: Augsburg, 1976.

Daley, Brian. "Position and Patronage in the Early Church: The Original Meaning of 'Primacy of Honor.'" *Journal of Theological Studies* 44 (1993): 529-53.

Deck, Alan Figueroa, ed. *Frontiers of Hispanic Theology in the United States*. Maryknoll, N.Y.: Orbis Books, 1992.

Ditewig, William. "The Once and Future Diaconate: Notes from the Past, Possibilities for the Future." *Church* 20 (Summer 2004): 51-54.

Donahue, John R. "The Bible and Catholic Social Teaching: Will This Engagement Lead to Marriage?" In *Modern Catholic Social Teaching: Commentaries and Interpretations*, edited by Kenneth R. Himes, 9-40. Washington, D.C.: Georgetown University Press, 2005.

Duffy, Eamon. *Saints and Sinners: A History of the Popes*. New Haven: Yale University Press, 1997.

Dujarier, Michel. *L'Église fraternité: les origines de l'expression adelphotès-fraternitas aux trois premiers siècles du christianisme*. Paris: Cerf, 1991.

Dulles, Avery. *The Catholicity of the Church*. Oxford: Clarendon, 1985.

————. *Models of Revelation*. Garden City, N.Y.: Doubleday, 1983.

Dunn, James D. G. *Acts of the Apostles*. Peterborough, U.K.: Epworth, 1996.

————. *Unity and Diversity in the New Testament: An Inquiry into the Character of Earliest Christianity*. 2nd edition. Philadelphia: Trinity, 1990.

Ehrman, Bart. *Lost Christianities: The Battles for Scripture and the Faiths We Never Knew*. New York: Oxford University Press, 2003.

Eisen, Ute E. *Women Officeholders in Early Christianity*. Collegeville, Minn.: Liturgical Press, 2000.

Elert, Werner. *Eucharist and Church Fellowship in the First Four Centuries*. Translated by N. E. Nagel. St. Louis: Concordia, 1966.

Elizondo, Virgilio. *Galilean Journey: The Mexico-American Promise*. Maryknoll, N.Y.: Orbis Books, 1983.

Espín, Orlando. *The Faith of the People: Theological Reflections on Popular Catholicism*. Maryknoll, N.Y.: Orbis Books, 1997.

Espín, Orlando, and Gary Macy, eds. *Futuring Our Past: Explorations in the Theology of Tradition*. Maryknoll, N.Y.: Orbis Books, 2006.

Faivre, Alexandre. *The Emergence of the Laity in the Early Church*. New York: Paulist Press, 1990.

Fischer, Balthasar. "Hat Ambrosius von Mailand in der Woche zwischen seiner Taufe und seiner Bischofskonsekration andere Weihe empfangen?" In *Kyriakon: Festschrift Johannes Quasten*, edited by Patrick Granfield and Josef A. Jungmann, 2:527-31. Münster/Westfalen: Aschendorff, 1970.

Fitzgerald, Paul J. "A Model for Dialogue: Cyprian of Carthage on Ecclesial Discernment." *Theological Studies* 59 (June 1998): 236-53.

Forte, Bruno. *The Church: Icon of the Trinity.* Boston: St. Paul Books & Media, 1991.

Fox, Thomas C. *Pentecost in Asia: A New Way of Being Church.* Maryknoll, N.Y.: Orbis Books, 2002.

Fox, Zeni. *New Ecclesial Ministry: Lay Professionals Serving the Church.* Revised and expanded edition. Franklin, Wis.: Sheed & Ward, 2002.

Froehle, Bryan T., and Mary L. Gautier, eds. *Catholicism USA: A Portrait of the Catholic Church in the United States.* Maryknoll, N.Y.: Orbis Books, 2000.

Gager, John C. *Kingdom and Community: The Social World of Early Christianity.* Englewood Cliffs, N.J.: Prentice-Hall, 1975.

Gaillardetz, Richard R. "Accountability in the Church: Report from Chiapas." *New Theology Review* 19 (2006): 33-45.

———. *"Ad tuendam fidem*: An Emerging Pattern in Current Papal Teaching." *New Theology Review* 12 (February 1999): 43-51.

———. "Apologetics, Evangelization and Ecumenism Today." *Origins* 35 (May 19, 2005): 9-15.

———. *By What Authority? A Primer on Scripture, the Magisterium and the Sense of the Faithful.* Collegeville, Minn.: Liturgical Press, 2003.

———. *The Church in the Making: Lumen Gentium, Christus Dominus, Orientalium Ecclesiarum.* Mahwah, N.J.: Paulist Press, 2006.

———. "Do We Need a New(-er) Apologetics?" *America* 190 (February 2, 2004): 26-33.

———. "The Ordinary Universal Magisterium: Unresolved Questions." *Theological Studies* 63 (September 2002): 447-71.

———. "The Reception of Doctrine: New Perspectives." In *Authority in the Roman Catholic Church*, edited by Bernard Hoose, 95-114. London: Ashgate, 2002.

———. "Reflections on the Future of Papal Primacy." *New Theology Review* 13 (November 2000): 52-66.

———. "Shifting Meanings in the Lay-Clergy Distinction." *Irish Theological Quarterly* 64 (1999): 115-39.

———. *Teaching with Authority: A Theology of the Magisterium in the Church.* Collegeville, Minn.: Liturgical Press, 1997.

———. *Transforming Our Days: Finding God Amid the Noise of Modern Life.* Revised edition. Liguori, Mo.: Liguori, 2007.

Gaillardetz, Richard R., and John Huels. "The Selection of Bishops: Recovering the Enduring Values of Our Tradition." *Jurist* 59 (1999): 348-76.

Galilea, Segundo. "Latin America in the Medellín and Puebla Conferences: An Example of Selective and Creative Reception of Vatican II." In *The Reception of Vatican II*, edited by Giuseppe Alberigo, Jean-Pierre Jossua, and Joseph A. Komonchak, 59-73. Washington D.C.: Catholic University of America Press, 1987.

García-Rivera, Alex. *St. Martin de Porres: The "Little Stories" and the Semiotics of Culture.* Maryknoll, N.Y.: Orbis Books, 1995.

Geertz, Clifford. *The Interpretation of Cultures.* New York: Basic Books, 1973.

Gerrish, Brian A. "Priesthood and Ministry in the Theology of Luther." *Church History* 34 (1965): 404-22.

Gibaut, John St. H. *The Cursus Honorum: A Study of the Origins and Evolution of Sequential Ordination.* New York: P. Lang, 2000.

Goizueta, Roberto. *Caminemos con Jesús: Toward a Hispanic/Latino Theology of Accompaniment.* Maryknoll, N.Y.: Orbis Books, 1995.

Gros, Jeffrey, Eamon McManus, and Ann Riggs. *Introduction to Ecumenism.* New York: Paulist Press, 1998.

Gutiérrez, Gustavo. *Las Casas: In Search of the Poor of Jesus Christ.* Maryknoll, N.Y.: Orbis Books, 1993.

———. *A Theology of Liberation.* Maryknoll, N.Y.: Orbis Books, 1973.

Hahnenberg, Edward. *Ministries: A Relational Approach.* New York: Crossroad, 2003.

———. "Ordained and Lay Ministry. Restarting the Conversation." *Origins* 35 (June 23, 2005): 94-99.

Haight, Roger. *Christian Community in History.* 2 volumes. New York: Continuum, 2004-5.

Halter, Deborah. *The Papal "No": A Comprehensive Guide to the Vatican's Rejection of Women's Ordination.* New York: Crossroad, 2004.

Hamer, Jerome. "La terminologie ecclesiologique de Vatican II et les Ministeres Protestants." *Documentation Catholique* (July 4, 1971): 625-28.

Hanson, Paul D. *The People Called: The Growth of Community in the Bible.* Louisville, Ky.: Westminster John Knox, 1986.

Harrington, Daniel J. *The Church According to the New Testament: What the Wisdom and Witness of Early Christianity Teach Us Today.* Franklin, Wis.: Sheed & Ward, 2001.

Haunerland, Winfried. "The Heirs of the Clergy? The New Pastoral Ministries and the Reform of the Minor Orders." *Worship* 75 (July 2001): 305-20.

Hayes, Diana L. *Hagar's Daughters: Womanist Ways of Being in the World.* New York: Paulist Press, 1995.

Healey, Joseph G. "The Church-as-Family and SCCs: Themes from the African Synod." *African Ecclesial Review (AFER)* 37 (February 1995): 44-48.

Healey, Joseph G., and Donald Sybertz. *Towards an African Narrative Theology.* Maryknoll, N.Y.: Orbis Books, 1996.

Hein, Kenneth. *Eucharist and Excommunication: A Study in Early Christian Doctrine and Discipline.* Frankfurt: Lang, 1975.

Henn, William. *The Honor of My Brothers: A Brief History of the Relationship between the Pope and the Bishops.* New York: Crossroad, 2000.

Hertling, Ludwig. *Communio: Church and Papacy in Early Christianity.* Chicago: Loyola University Press, 1972.

Herzog, William R., II. *Parables as Subversive Speech: Jesus as Pedagogue of the Oppressed.* Louisville, Ky.: Westminster John Knox Press, 1994.

Hinze, Bradford. *Practices of Dialogue in the Roman Catholic Church: Aims and Obstacles, Lessons and Laments.* New York: Continuum, 2006.

Hotchkin, John. "Canon Law and Ecumenism: Giving Shape to the Future." *Origins* 30 (October 19, 2000): 289-98.

Huels, John. "Special Questions on the Diaconate." *Liturgical Ministry* 13 (Winter 2004): 1-9.

Hunt, Anne. *Trinity: Nexus of the Mysteries of the Christian Faith.* Theology in Global Perspective. Maryknoll, N.Y.: Orbis Books, 2005.

International Theological Commission. *From the Diakonia of Christ to the Diakonia of the Apostles.* Mundelein, Ill.: Hillenbrand Books, 2004.

———. *Memory and Reconciliation: The Church and the Faults of the Past.* Boston: Pauline Books, 2000.

Irvin, Dale T., and Scott W. Sunquist. *History of the World Christian Movement.* Volume 1. Maryknoll, N.Y.: Orbis Books, 2001.

Isasí-Díaz, Ada María. *En la Lucha = In the Struggle: Elaborating a Mujerista Theology.* Minneapolis: Fortress, 2004.

———. *Mujerista Theology.* Maryknoll, N.Y.: Orbis Books, 1996.

Jalland, Trevor. *Church and Papacy.* London: SPCK, 1944.

Jenkins, Philip. *The Next Christendom: The Coming of Global Christianity.* New York: Oxford University Press, 2002.

Käsemann, Ernst. *Essays on New Testament Themes.* London: SCM, 1964.

Kasper, Walter. "The Relationship between Gospel and Dogma: An Historical Approach." In *Man as Man & Believer,* edited by Edward Schillebeeckx and Boniface Willems, 153-67. *Concilium* 21. New York: Paulist Press, 1967.

Keefe, Donald J. "Sacramental Sexuality and the Ordination of Women." *Communio* 5 (Fall 1978): 228-51.

Kinnamon, Michael, and Brian E. Cope, eds. *The Ecumenical Movement: An Anthology of Key Texts and Voices.* Grand Rapids: Eerdmans, 1997.

Kiriswa, Benjamin. "African Model of Church as Family: Implications on Ministry & Leadership." *African Ecclesial Review (AFER)* 43 (June 2001): 99-108.

Komonchak, Joseph. "The Epistemology of Reception." *Jurist* 57 (1997): 180-203.

———. "On the Authority of Bishops' Conferences." *America* (September 12, 1998): 7-10.

———. "Vatican II and the Encounter between Catholicism and Liberalism." In *Catholicism and Liberalism: Contributions to American Public Philosophy,* edited by Bruce Douglass and David Hollenbach, 76-99. Cambridge: Cambridge University Press, 1994.

Kroeger, James H. *Becoming Local Church: Historical, Theological, and Missiological Essays.* Quezon City, Philippines: Claretian Publications, 2003.

Kroeger, James H., and Peter C. Phan, eds. *The Future of the Asian Churches: The Asian Synod & Ecclesia in Asia.* Quezon City, Philippines: Claretian Publications, 2002.

Kumi, George Kwame. "Basic Ecclesial Communities as Communion." *African Ecclesial Review (AFER)* 37 (June 1995): 160-79.

Küng, Hans. *The Church.* New York: Sheed & Ward, 1967.

LaCugna, Catherine Mowry. *God for Us: The Trinity and Christian Life.* New York: HarperCollins, 1991.

Lafont, Ghislain. *Imagining the Catholic Church: Structured Communion in the Spirit.* Collegeville, Minn.: Liturgical Press, 2000.

Lakeland, Paul. *The Liberation of The Laity: In Search of an Accountable Church.* New York: Continuum, 2003.

———. *Postmodernity: Christian Identity in a Fragmented Age.* Minneapolis: Fortress, 1997.

Lash, Nicholas. *Change in Focus: A Study of Doctrinal Change and Continuity.* London: Sheed & Ward, 1973.

LaVerdiere, Eugene. *The Eucharist in the New Testament and the Early Church.* Collegeville, Minn.: Liturgical Press, 1996.

Legrand, Hervé. "Collégialité des évêques et communion des églises dans la réception de Vatican II." *Revue des sciences philosophiques et théologiques* 75 (1991): 545-68.

———. "*Traditio perpetuo servata?* The Non-ordination of Women: Tradition or Simply an Historical Fact?" *Worship* 65 (1991): 482-508.

Léon-Dufour, Xavier. *Sharing the Eucharistic Bread.* New York: Paulist Press, 1987.

Lobinger, Fritz. *Like His Brothers and Sisters: Ordaining Community Leaders.* New York: Crossroad, 1998.

———. *Priests for Tomorrow.* Quezon City, Philippines: Claretian Publications, 2004.

Lohfink, Gerhard. *Jesus and Community: The Social Dimension of Christian Faith.* New York: Paulist Press, 1984.

Löhrer, Magnus. "Träger der Vermittlung." In *Mysterium Salutis,* edited by Johannes Feiner and Magnus Löhrer, 1:545-87. Einsiedeln: Benziger, 1965.

Loisy, Alfred. *The Gospel and the Church.* Philadelphia: Fortress, 1976.

Louth, Andrew. *The Origins of the Christian Mystical Tradition.* Oxford: Clarendon Press, 1981.

Lubac, Henri de. *Corpus mysticum: l'eucharistie et l'Eglise au Moyen âge: Etude historique.* Paris: Aubier, 1949.

Lyon, David. *Jesus in Disneyland: Religion in Postmodern Times.* Malden, Mass.: Blackwell, 2000.

Lyotard, Jean-François. *The Postmodern Condition—A Report on Knowledge.* Manchester: Manchester University Press, 1984.

MacDonald, Margaret Y. *The Pauline Churches: A Socio-historical Study of Institutionalization in the Pauline and Deutero-Pauline Writings.* Society for New Testament Studies Monograph Series 60. Cambridge: Cambridge University Press, 1988.

Mannion, Gerard. *Ecclesiology and Postmodenrity: Questions for the Church in Our Time.* Collegeville, Minn.: Liturgical Press, 2007.

Marmion, Columba. *Christ—The Ideal of the Priest.* St. Louis: Herder, 1952.

Matsuoka, Funitaka. "A Reflection on 'Teaching Theology from an Intercultural Perspective.'" *Theological Education* 36 (1989): 35-42.

McCure, J. F. "Apostles and Apostolic Succession in the Patristic Era." In *Eucharist and Ministry,* edited by Paul C. Empie and T. Austin Murphy, 138-77. Lutherans and Catholics in Dialogue 4. 138-77. Washington, D.C.: USCC, 1970.

McDonnell, Kilian. "The Ratzinger/Kasper Debate: The Universal Church and Local Churches." *Theological Studies* 63 (2002): 227-50.

Meeks, Wayne A. *The First Urban Christians: The Social World of the Apostle Paul.* New Haven: Yale University Press, 1983.

Meer, Haye van der. *Women Priests in the Catholic Church: A Theological Historical Investigation.* Philadelphia: Temple University Press, 1973.

Meier, John P. "The Circle of the Twelve: Did It Exist During Jesus' Public Ministry?" *Journal of Biblical Literature* 116 (1997): 635-72.

Mendenhall, George E. "The Monarchy." *Interpretation* 29 (1975): 155-70.

Merton, Thomas. *The Wisdom of the Desert.* New York: New Directions, 1960.

Mesa, José de. *Marriage Is Discipleship.* Quezon City, Philippines: East Asian Pastoral Institute, 1995.

Mesters, Carlos. "The Use of the Bible in Christian Communities of the Common People." In *Liberation Theology: A Documentary History,* ed. A. T. Hennelly, 14-28. Maryknoll, N.Y.: Orbis Books, 1990.

Metz, Johann Baptist. *Faith in History and Society: Towards a Practical Fundamental Theology.* New York: Crossroad, 1980.

Meyendorff, John. *Christ in Eastern Christian Thought.* Crestwood, N.Y.: St. Vladimir's Seminary Press, 1997.

Miller, Vincent J. *Consuming Religion: Christian Faith and Practice in a Consumer Culture.* New York: Continuum, 2003.

Montcheuil, Yves de. *Aspects de l'Eglise.* Paris: Cerf, 1949.

Morrill, Bruce T. *Anamnesis as Dangerous Memory: Political and Liturgical Theology in Dialogue.* Collegeville, Minn.: Liturgical Press, 2000.

Msafiri, Aidan G. "The Church as Family Model: Strengths and Weaknesses." In *African Theology Today,* edited by Emmanuel Katongole, 85-98. Scranton, Pa.: University of Scranton Press, 2002.

Murnion, Philip J., and David DeLambo. *Parishes and Parish Ministers: A Study of Parish Lay Ministry.* New York: National Pastoral Life Center, 1999.

Nardoni, Enrique. "Charism in the Early Church since Rudolph Sohm: An Ecumenical Challenge." *Theological Studies* 53 (1992): 646-62.

Neuner, Joseph, and Jacques Dupuis, eds., *The Christian Faith in the Doctrinal Documents of the Catholic Church.* New York: Alba House, 1982.

Neusner, Jacob. *From Politics to Piety: The Emergence of Pharisaic Judaism.* Englewood Cliffs, N.J.: Prentice-Hall, 1973.

———. *The Rabbinic Traditions about the Pharisees before 70.* 3 volumes. Leiden: Brill, 1971.

Newman, John Henry. *On Consulting the Faithful in Matters of Doctrine.* 1859. Reprint, Kansas City, Mo.: Sheed & Ward, 1961.

Nichols, Terence L. *That All May Be One: Hierarchy and Participation in the Church.* Collegeville, Minn.: Liturgical Press, 1997.

Nyerere, Julius. *Ujamaa: Essays on Socialism.* Dar-es-Salaam: Oxford University Press, 1968.

Oakley, Francis. *The Conciliarist Tradition: Constitutionalism in the Catholic Church, 1300-1870.* Oxford: Oxford University Press, 2003.

———. *Council over Pope? Towards a Provisional Ecclesiology.* New York: Herder, 1969.

O'Callaghan, Joseph F. *Electing Our Bishops: How the Catholic Church Should Choose Its Leaders.* New York: Rowman & Littlefield, 2007.

O'Callaghan, Paul. "The Holiness of the Church in Early Christian Creeds." *Irish Theological Quarterly* 54 (1988): 59-65.

Oduyoye, Mercy Amba. *Beads and Strands: Reflections of an African Woman on Christianity in Africa.* Maryknoll, N.Y.: Orbis Books, 2004.

Oduyoye, Mercy Amba, and Musumbi R. A. Kanyoro, eds., *The Will to Arise: Women, Tradition, and the Church in Africa.* Maryknoll, N.Y.: Orbis Books, 1992.

Okoye, James Chukwuma. *Israel and the Nations: A Mission Theology of the Old Testament.* American Society of Missiology Series 39. Maryknoll, N.Y.: Orbis Books, 2006.

Okure, Teresa. "Leadership in the New Testament." *Nigerian Journal of Theology* 1/5 (1990): 71-93.

O'Malley, John W. "Vatican II: Did Anything Happen?" *Theological Studies* 67 (March 2006): 3-33.

O'Meara, Thomas F. *Theology of Ministry.* Rev. ed. New York: Paulist Press, 1999.

Onwubiko, Oliver Alozie. *The Church in Mission in the Light of Ecclesia in Africa.* Nairobi, Kenya: Paulines Publications Africa, 2001.

Osborne, Kenan B. *Ministry: Lay Ministry in the Roman Catholic Church.* New York: Paulist Press, 1993.

———. *Orders and Ministry: Leadership in the World Church.* Theology in Global Perspective. Maryknoll, N.Y.: Orbis Books, 2006.

Phan, Peter C. *Being Religious Interreligiously: Asian Perspectives on Interfaith Dialogue.* Maryknoll, N.Y.: Orbis Books, 2004.

———. *In Our Own Tongues: Perspectives from Asia on Mission and Inculturation.* Maryknoll, N.Y.: Orbis Books, 2003.

———. *Mission and Catechesis: Alexandre de Rhodes and Inculturation in Seventeenth Century Vietnam.* Maryknoll, N.Y.: Orbis Books, 1998.

———. "Speaking in Many Tongues: Why the Church Must Be More Catholic." *Commonweal* (January 12, 2007): 16-19.

Philibert, Paul J. *The Priesthood of the Faithful: Key to a Living Church.* Collegeville, Minn.: Liturgical Press, 2005.

Pieris, Aloysius. *An Asian Theology of Liberation.* Faith Meets Faith. Maryknoll, N.Y.: Orbis Books, 1988.

Pohl, Christine. *Making Room: Recovering Hospitality as a Christian Tradition.* Grand Rapids: Eerdmans, 1999.

Pottmeyer, Hermann J. "Dialogue as a Model for Communication in the Church." In *The Church and Communication*, edited by Patrick Granfield, 97-103. Kansas City: Sheed & Ward, 1994.

———. "The Episcopacy." In *The Gift of the Church*, edited by Peter C. Phan, 337-53. Collegeville, Minn.: Liturgical Press, 2000.

———. *Towards a Papacy in Communion.* New York: Crossroad, 1998.

Power, David N. *Sacrament: The Language of God's Giving.* New York: Herder & Herder, 1999.

Prior, Anselm. *Towards a Community Church: The Way Ahead for Today's Parish.* Training for Community Ministers 28. Delmenville, South Africa: Lumko Institute, 1997.

Prusak, Bernard. "Theological Considerations—Hermeneutical, Ecclesiological, Eschatological Regarding *Memory and Reconciliation: The Church and the Faults of the Past.*" *Horizons* 32 (Spring 2005): 136-52.

Rahner, Karl. "A Basic Theological Interpretation of the Second Vatican Council." In *Theological Investigations,* 20:77-89. New York: Crossroad, 1981.

———. *The Church and the Sacraments.* New York: Crossroad, 1963.

———. "Consecration of the Layman to the Care of Souls." In *Theological Investigations,* 3:263-76. Baltimore: Helicon, 1967.

———. *The Trinity.* New York: Herder & Herder, 1970.

Ratzinger, Joseph. "The Church and Man's Calling: Introductory Article and Chapter I." In *Commentary on the Documents of Vatican II,* edited by Herbert Vorgrimler, 5:115-63. New York: Herder, 1969.

———. *Das neue Volk Gottes: Entwürfe zur Ekklesiologie.* Düsseldorf: Patmos-Verlag, 1969.

———. "In the Encounter of Christianity and Religions, Syncretism Is Not the Goal." *L'Osservatore Romano* [English edition] (April 26, 1995): 5-8.

———. *Pilgrim Fellowship of Faith.* San Francisco: Ignatius Press, 2005.

———. *Principles of Catholic Theology: Building Stones for a Fundamental Theology.* San Francisco: Ignatius Press, 1987.

Ratzinger, Joseph, with Vittorio Messori. *The Ratzinger Report.* San Francisco: Ignatius Press, 1985.

Rausch, Thomas. "Reception Past and Present." *Theological Studies* 47 (1986): 497-508.

Reid, Barbara. *Choosing the Better Part? Women in the Gospel of Luke.* Collegeville, Minn.: Liturgical Press, 1996.

Rheingold, Howard. *Virtual Community: Homesteading on the Electronic Frontier.* New York: Addison-Wesley, 1993.

Riches, John. *Jesus and the Transformation of Judaism.* London: Darton, Longman & Todd, 1980.

Rigal, Jean. *L'ecclésiologie de communion: Son évolution historique et ses fondements.* Paris: Cerf, 1996.

Roberson, Ronald. *The Eastern Christian Churches.* 6th edition. Rome: Edizioni Orientalia Christiana, 1999.

Rosales, Gaudencio, and C. G. Arévalo, eds. *For All the Peoples of Asia, Federation of Asian Bishops' Conferences Documents from 1970 to 1991.* Volume I. Quezon City, Philippines: Claretian Publications, 1997.

Ruether, Rosemary Radford. *Women-Church—Theology and Practice of Feminist Liturgical Communities.* San Francisco: Harper & Row, 1985.

Ruiz, Bishop Samuel, with the collaboration of Carles Torner. *Cómo me convirtieron los indígenas*. Colección Servidores y Testigos. Santander: Editorial Sal Terrae, 2002.

———. "In This Hour of Grace." *Origins* 23 (February 10, 1994): 589-602.

Russell, Letty. *Feminist Interpretation of the Bible*. Philadelphia: Westminster, 1985.

Sanks, T. Howland. *Salt, Leaven and Light: The Community Called Church*. New York: Crossroad, 1992.

Sanneh, Lamin. *Translating the Message: The Missionary Impact on Culture*. Maryknoll, N.Y.: Orbis Books, 1989.

———. *Whose Religion Is Christianity? The Gospel beyond the West*. Grand Rapids: Eerdmans, 2003.

Schatz, Klaus. *Papal Primacy: From Its Origins to the Present*. Collegeville, Minn.: Liturgical Press, 1996.

Schlink, Edmund. "Die Struktur der dogmatischen Aussage als ökumenisches Problem." *Kerygma und Dogma* 3 (1957): 251-306.

Schmemann, Alexander. *For the Life of the World: Sacraments and Orthodoxy*. Crestwood, N.Y.: St. Vladimir's Seminary Press, 1973.

Schneiders, Sandra M. *The Revelatory Text: Interpreting the New Testament as Sacred Scripture*. New York: HarperCollins, 1991.

———. *Selling All: Commitment, Consecrated Celibacy, and Community in Catholic Religious Life*. New York: Paulist Press, 2001.

Schreiter, Robert J. *Constructing Local Theologies*. Maryknoll, N.Y.: Orbis Books, 1985.

———. *The New Catholicity: Theology between the Global and the Local*. Faith and Culture Series. Maryknoll, N.Y.: Orbis Books, 1997.

Schüssler Fiorenza, Elisabeth. *Bread Not Stone: The Challenge of Feminist Biblical Interpretation*. Boston: Beacon, 1984.

———. *Discipleship of Equals: A Critical Feminist Ekklesia-logy of Liberation*. New York: Crossroad, 1993.

———. *In Memory of Her: A Feminist Theological Reconstruction of Christian Origins*. New York: Crossroad, 1983.

Segundo, Juan Luis. *The Liberation of Dogma: Faith, Revelation and Dogmatic Teaching Authority*. Maryknoll, N.Y.: Orbis Books, 1992.

Semmelroth, Otto. *Church and Sacrament*. Notre Dame, Ind.: Fides, 1965.

Sesboüé, Bernard. "Reception of Councils from Nicea to Constantinople II: Conceptual Divergences and Unity in the Faith, Yesterday and Today." *Jurist* 57 (1997): 87-117.

Shaw, Russell B. *Ministry or Apostolate? What Should the Catholic Laity Be Doing?* Huntington, Ind.: Our Sunday Visitor, 2002.

Shorter, Aylward. "Faith, Culture and the Global Village." *South Pacific Journal of Mission Studies* (March 1996): 31-38.

———. *Toward a Theology of Inculturation*. Maryknoll, N.Y.: Orbis Books, 1988.

Sieben, Hermann Josef. *Die Konzilsidee der Alten Kirche*. Paderborn: Schöningh, 1979.

Sobrino, Jon. *The True Church and the Poor*. Maryknoll, N.Y.: Orbis Books, 1985.

Sohm, Rudolph. *Kirchenrecht I: Die geschichtlichen Grundlagen*. Leipzig: Duncker & Humblot, 1892.

Stauffer, S. Anita. *On Baptismal Fonts: Ancient and Modern*. Nottingham: Grove Books, 1994.

Stuhlmueller, Carroll, ed. *Women and Priesthood: Future Directions*. Collegeville, Minn.: Liturgical Press, 1978.

Suenens, Cardinal Léon-Joseph. *Memories and Hopes*. Dublin: Veritas, 1992.

Sullivan, Francis A. *From Apostles to Bishops: The Development of the Episcopacy in the Early Church.* New York: Paulist Press, 2001.

————. *The Church We Believe In: One, Holy, Catholic and Apostolic.* Mahwah, N.J.: Paulist Press, 1988.

————. "Response to Karl Becker, S.J., on the Meaning of *Subsistit In.*" *Theological Studies* 67 (June 2006): 395-409.

————. "The Teaching Authority of Episcopal Conferences." *Theological Studies* 63 (September 2002): 472-93.

Sundberg, Albert. "The Bible Canon and the Christian Doctrine of Inspiration," *Interpretation* 29 (1975): 352-71.

Tanner, Kathryn. *Theories of Culture: A New Agenda for Theology.* (Minneapolis: Fortress, 1997.

Taylor, Charles. *The Ethics of Authenticity.* Cambridge, Mass.: Harvard University Press, 1991.

Theissen, Gerd. *The Gospels in Context: Social and Political History in the Synoptic Tradition.* New York: T&T Clark, 2004.

————. *The Social Setting of Pauline Christianity: Essays on Corinth.* Philadelphia: Fortress, 1982.

Thiel, John. *Senses of Tradition: Continuity and Development in Catholic Faith.* New York: Oxford University Press, 2000.

Tierney, Brian. *Foundations of the Conciliar Theory: The Contribution of the Medieval Canonists from Gratian to the Great Schism.* Cambridge Studies in Medieval Life and Thought 4. Cambridge: Cambridge University Press, 1955.

Tillard, Jean-Marie R. *Bishop of Rome.* Wilmington, Del.: Glazier, 1983.

————. *Flesh of the Church, Flesh of Christ: At the Source of the Ecclesiology of Communion.* Collegeville, Minn.: Liturgical Press, 2001.

————. "Recognition of Ministries: What Is the Real Question?" *One in Christ* 21 (1985): 31-39.

Trible, Phyllis. *Texts of Terror: Literary Feminist Readings of Biblical Narratives.* Philadelphia: Fortress, 1984.

Uzukwu, Elochukwu E. *A Listening Church: Autonomy and Communion in African Churches.* Maryknoll, N.Y.: Orbis Books, 1996.

Vanhoye, Albert. "The Biblical Question of 'Charisms' after Vatican II." In *Vatican II: Assessments and Perspectives,* edited by René Latourelle, 1:439-68. New York: Paulist Press, 1988.

Vogels, Heinz-J. *Celibacy—Gift or Law?* Kansas City: Sheed & Ward, 1993.

Volf, Miroslav. *The End of Memory: Remembering Rightly in a Violent World.* Grand Rapids: Eerdmans, 2006.

Walls, Andrew F. *The Cross-Cultural Process in Christian History: Studies in the Transmission and Appropriation of Faith.* Maryknoll, N.Y.: Orbis Books, 2002.

————. *The Missionary Movement in Christian History.* Maryknoll, N.Y.: Orbis Books, 1996.

Walzer, Michael. *Exodus and Revolution.* New York: Basic Books, 1985.

Ware, Timothy. *The Orthodox Church.* New York: Penguin Books, 1963.

Watson, Natalie K. *Introducing Feminist Ecclesiology.* London: Sheffield Academic Press, 2002.

Weil, Louis. "Aspects of the Issue of *Per Saltum* Ordination: An Anglican Perspective." In *Rule of Prayer, Rule of Faith: Essays in Honor of Aidan Kavanagh, O.S.B.*, edited by Nathan Mitchell and John F. Baldovin, 200-217. Collegeville, Minn.: Liturgical Press, 1996.

Wicks, Jared. "Ecclesial Apostolicity Confessed in the Creed." *Pro Ecclesia* 9 (2000): 150-64.

Wood, Susan K. *Sacramental Orders.* Lex orandi. Collegeville, Minn.: Liturgical Press, 2000.

————, ed. *Ordering the Baptismal Priesthood.* Collegeville, Minn.: Liturgical Press, 2003.

World Council of Churches. *Baptism, Eucharist and Ministry.* Faith and Order Paper No. 111. Geneva: WCC, 1982.

Wostyn, Lode L. *Doing Ecclesiology: Church and Mission Today.* Quezon City: Claretian Publications, 1990.

Wuerl, Bishop Donald W. "Reflections on Governance and Accountability in the Church." In *Governance, Accountability, and the Future of the Catholic Church*, edited by Francis Oakley and Bruce Russett, 13-24. New York: Continuum, 2004.

Zizioulas, John. *Being as Communion: Studies in Personhood and the Church.* Crestwood, N.Y.: St. Vladimir's Seminary Press, 1985.

Index